D1084364

Terence and the Language of Roman Comedy

This book offers a comprehensive examination of the language of Roman comedy in general and that of Terence in particular. The study explores Terence's use of language to differentiate his characters and his language in relation to that of the comic fragments of the *palliata,* the *togata* and the *atellana.* Linguistic categories in the Terentian corpus explored include colloquialisms, archaisms, hellenisms and idiolectal features. Terence is shown to give his old men an old-fashioned and verbose tone, while low characters are represented as using colloquial diction. An examination of *Eunuchus*' language shows it to be closer to the Plautine linguistic tradition. The book also provides a thorough linguistic/stylistic commentary on all the fragments of the *palliata,* the *togata* and the *atellana.* It shows that Terence, except in the case of his *Eunuchus,* consciously distances himself from the linguistic/stylistic tradition of Plautus followed by all other comic poets.

EVANGELOS KARAKASIS is temporary Lecturer of Latin Language and Literature at the University of Ioannina, Greece, and the author of several articles on Roman comedy.

CAMBRIDGE CLASSICAL STUDIES

TERENCE AND THE LANGUAGE OF ROMAN COMEDY

EVANGELOS KARAKASIS
University of Ioannina

PUBLISHED BY THE PRESS SYNDICATE OF THE UNIVERSITY OF CAMBRIDGE
The Pitt Building, Trumpington Street, Cambridge, United Kingdom

CAMBRIDGE UNIVERSITY PRESS
The Edinburgh Building, Cambridge, CB2 2RU, UK
40 West 20th Street, New York, NY 10011–4211, USA
477 Williamstown Road, Port Melbourne, VIC 3207, Australia
Ruiz de Alarcón 13, 28014 Madrid, Spain
Dock House, The Waterfront, Cape Town 8001, South Africa

http://www.cambridge.org

First published 2005

Printed in the United Kingdom at the University Press, Cambridge

Typeface Times 11/13 pt. *System* LaTeX 2ε [TB]

A catalogue record for this book is available from the British Library

Library of Congress Cataloguing in Publication data
Karakasis, Evangelos.
Terence and the language of Roman comedy / Evangelos Karakasis.
p. cm. – (Cambridge classical studies)
Expanded and rev. version of author's thesis (Ph.D.) – Cambridge University, 2000.
Includes bibliographical references and index.
ISBN-13 978 0 521 84298 3
ISBN-10 0 521 84298 0
1. Terence – Criticism and interpretation. 2. Latin drama (Comedy) – History and criticism. 3. Latin language – Style. 4. Terence – Language. 5. Comedy.
I. Title. II. Series.
PA6768.K37 2004
872′.01 – dc22 2004045712

ISBN-13 978 0 521 84298 3 hardback
ISBN-10 0 521 84298 0 hardback

CONTENTS

ACKNOWLEDGEMENTS

This book is an expanded and revised version of my thesis, submitted for the PhD degree in 2000. During my stay in Cambridge, I received financial assistance from several sources, to which I am very much indebted. In particular, I am grateful to the Greek State Scholarship Foundation for a full three-year graduate scholarship, the Lilian Voudouri Foundation for funding the fourth year of my graduate studies, when other emoluments were fading out, and the Cambridge Faculty of Classics for awarding me the Charles Oldham Scholarship for the academic year 1999–2000.

I express my special thanks to my PhD supervisor, Professor R. L. Hunter, who read through several successive drafts of both the thesis and the book version. To his unremitting aid and valuable criticism I owe this book. His stimulating comments and thought-provoking observations have been a constant source of inspiration for me. Many thanks go to my MPhil. supervisor, Professor M. D. Reeve, for having read the manuscript and saved me from many infelicities. I also owe him much for helping me turn the thesis into a book. I am also obliged to my PhD examiners, Dr J. Clackson and P. G. McC. Brown, for their useful feedback.

Very warm thanks go to my teachers in the University of Ioannina. Especially to Professor G. P. Savantidis, D. K. Raios and to the Assistant Professor Maria Papadimitriou for letting me into the fascinating world of Roman literature. What is more, Professor D. K. Raios's inspiring lectures on Roman Comedy introduced me to the charming plays of Plautus and Terence. Special thanks are also due to Professor I. N. Perysinakis for commending me warmly to his British friends and colleagues and for giving me, as the Chairman of the Faculty Board, the opportunity to teach Latin language and literature to the students of Ioannina University.

Dr Mary Mantziou, Assistant Professor of Greek, was a great help to me throughout my graduate studies and beyond. Her constant interest both in the progress of my work and in my personal welfare, her keenness to ensure me financial help, when scholarships were petering out, her eagerness to support my application for graduate studies in Cambridge, her joy, when things were good, and her sorrow, when I was coming up against grave difficulties, make her worthy of many special thanks.

Last but not least, I want to thank my friends in Cambridge, Dr I. Manolessou, Dr P. Seranis and Mrs D. Koukouzika for their help and support. Finally, I would like to thank my mother. Without her I would never have finished.

CONSPECTUS SIGLORUM

Auctores antiqui

The references to Greek authors follow the abbreviations of Liddell, Scott and Jones, *Greek-English Lexicon*. The references to Latin texts follow the abbreviations of the *Oxford Latin Dictionary* (*OLD*). For authors/texts not contained in the *OLD*, the abbreviations of the *Thesaurus Linguae Latinae* (*ThLL*) are followed instead.

For Latin comic authors, the following abbreviations are used:

Plaut.	Plautus
Amph.	*Amphitruo*
Asin.	*Asinaria*
Aul.	*Aulularia*
Bacch.	*Bacchides*
Capt.	*Captivi*
Cas.	*Casina*
Cist.	*Cistellaria*
Curc.	*Curculio*
Epid.	*Epidicus*
Men.	*Menaechni*
Merc.	*Mercator*
Most.	*Mostellaria*
Pers.	*Persa*
Poen.	*Poenulus*
Pseud.	*Pseudolus*
Rud.	*Rudens*
Stich.	*Stichus*
Trin.	*Trinummus*

Truc.	*Truculentus*
Vid.	*Vidularia*
Ter.	Terentius
Ad.	*Adelphoe*
Andr.	*Andria*
Eun.	*Eunuchus*
Heaut.	*Heautontimoroumenos*
Hec.	*Hecyra*
Phorm.	*Phormio*
Afran.	Afranius
Aquil.	Aquilius
Caec.	Caecilius
Juvent.	Iuventius
Naev.	Naevius
Nov.	Novius
Pompon.	Pomponius
Titin.	Titinius
Turpil.	Turpilius
atel.	Reference to fragments of the *atellana*, e.g. Nov. *atel.* 12
com.	Reference to fragments of the *palliata*, e.g. Turpil. *com.* 40
tog.	Reference to fragments of the *togata*, e.g. Afran. *tog.* 32
Scriptt. R R	Scriptores Rerum Rusticarum

For Afranius, Aquilius, Atilius, Iuventius, Novius, Pomponius, Trabea the edition of Ribbeck was used; for Caecilius, Ennius (comic fragments), Livius Andronicus (comic fragments), Naevius (comic fragments), that of Warmington; for Titinius and Atta that of Guardì, and for Turpilius that of Ryschlewska. Full references to these editions are to be found in the bibliography. The readings of Ribbeck are sometimes adopted even in cases where his edition is not used; this is indicated by the abbreviation (Ribb.) after the relevant quotation.

Auctores moderni

The references to classics periodicals follow the abbreviations of the *Année Philologique*. The references to linguistics periodicals follow the abbreviations in the *Routledge Dictionary of Language and Linguistics*. Other frequent abbreviations:

Austin II	Austin, R. G. (1964) (ed.), *P. Vergili Maronis Aeneidos Liber secundus* (Oxford)
CGL	Goetz, G. (1888–1901), *Corpus Glossariorum Latinorum*, vol. V, pp. 529–39 (Leipzig)
D-K	Dziatzko, K. and Kauer, R. (1903) (eds.), *Ausgewählte Komödien des P. Terentius Afer, erklärt von K. Dz., II: Adelphoe, 2te Auflage, bearbeitet von R. K.* (Leipzig)
GLK	Keil, H. (1857–70), *Grammatici Latini* (Leipzig)
H-Sz	Hofmann, J. B. and Szantyr, A. (1965), *Lateinische Syntax und Stilistik* (Munich)
K-S	Kühner, R. and Stegmann, C. (1966), *Ausführliche Grammatik der lateinischen Sprache*, part II, vol. II (Hanover)
K-S followed by a digit	Kühner and Stegmann (1966), volume indicated by the digit
L-S	Lewis and Short (1879), *A Latin Dictionary* (Oxford)
LSJ	Liddell Scott and Jones (1940), *Greek–English Lexicon* (Oxford)
McGlynn I and II	McGlynn, P. (1963–7), *Lexicon Tetentianum*, vols I and II (London and Glasgow)

N-W	Neue, F. and Wagener, C. (1892–1905), *Formenlehre der lateinischen Sprache* (Leipzig)
OLD	*Oxford Latin Dictionary*
RD	Ruhnkenii, D. (1825), *In Terentii Comoedias dictata* (Bonn)
ThLL	*Thesaurus Linguae Latinae*

INTRODUCTION

The subject of this book is character differentiation by language in Terence and the relation of Terentian diction to the tradition of Roman comedy as a whole. It is an original study in more ways than one, since earlier studies are few in number and are often based on defective data or methodology. It is also, however, traditional, since the basic ideas at its heart are already to be found in ancient scholarship.

Ancient testimony

Ancient theorists frequently recognised the importance of selecting and using appropriate language. Aristotle, for instance, remarks on how language should differ according to age and social status (*Rh.* Γ. 1408a10–32). He implies that the diction put in the mouth of a slave should be different from the diction of a free citizen, and that the speech of a young man should be unlike that of an older person. It would be rather unbecoming, according to Aristotle, for a slave to use fine language. Similarly, the use of maxims and story-telling, appropriate to senile[1] diction, would also be inappropriate in the speech of younger people. Language should differ not only according to the age and social status of the character speaking but also according to the situation or the emotional state of the speaker; this naturally leads Aristotle to the importance of suitable language for revealing the emotional state of a speaker. Compound words, clustering of epithets and unfamiliar words are, according to him, appropriate to someone who talks with emotion.[2]

[1] 'Senile' in this book is used in the sense of 'belonging to old age'.

[2] Very similar observations are to be found in several ancient theorists of style (Demetrius, Longinus, Hermogenes), who insist on language as a means of differentiating characters according to both character speaking and situation. For a detailed discussion of such theories, cf. Katsouris (1975: 22–32).

Language may also differ according to the sex of the speaker. Several ancient testimonies from both Greek and Latin sources comment upon the linguistic differences between male and female speech. Women are characterised by linguistic conservatism (cf. Pl. *Cra.* 418-c αἵπερ μάλιστα τὴν ἀρχαίαν φωνὴν σῴζουσι, see also Cic. *de Orat.* 3.45 *mulieres incorruptam antiquitatem conservant*), as well as by a limited number of linguistic (mainly lexical) usages and stylistic options restricted to or proportionally more common in their speech. A characteristic example is constituted by oaths, e.g. in the case of Latin the exclusive use of *Castor* by women, as opposed to men's swearing upon *Hercules* (cf. Gel. pr. 11.6, the locus classicus on male and female oaths).[3]

Greek New Comedy – the case of Menander

Many scholars in recent years have observed the use of linguistic means of characterisation in New Comedy, especially in Menander.[4] Even though no systematic study of the language of Menander exists, several of the works dealing with aspects of Menandrian diction have revealed how the Greek playwright uses language for differentiating his characters. Unfortunately, most of these studies are of limited value, because the linguistic categories they distinguish are often impressionistic and imprecisely defined, devoid of secure methodological criteria. Some characteristic examples include: colourful and inflated language, easy and flexible speech, exotic compounds, flamboyant terms, etc.[5]

Menander will be discussed in more detail here, since four of Terence's comedies are modelled on Menandrian plays, and

[3] Cf. Char. GLK 1. 198. 17ff.; for a more detailed discussion of ancient testimonies, cf. Adams (1984: 43–77), Bain (1984: 24–42), Gilleland (1980: 180–3).

[4] Apart from individual comments here and there in commentaries on Menander, see also Zini (1938), Arnott (1964: 110–23), (1995: 147–64), Del Corno (1975: 13–48), Feneron (1974: 81–95), Heap (1992: 56–8), Sandbach (1970: 113–36), Katsouris (1975: 101–83), Webster (1974: 99–110), Krieter Spiro (1997: 201–53), Brenk (1987: 31–66).

[5] In this context it must be observed that there is a strong need for detailed and comprehensive study of post-classical language, based on strict methodological criteria. With particular application to literature, it would be extremely interesting to study the distribution of innovative features of the *koine* (lexical, syntactic etc.) in specific literary characters and genres. Modern linguistic theories, such as pragmatics or text linguistics, may also prove fruitful when applied to Menander and other hellenistic authors.

therefore it is plausible to suppose that the Latin comic playwright might have been influenced by his Greek prototype. Hence, the following relatively detailed description of Menandrian linguistic techniques (based for the data on the above modern works, but presented for the first time here in a global categorisation) may enable us to understand better similar patterns in Terence, and furthermore to test the hypothesis that the Latin playwright, in using linguistic characterisation, might be imitating, at least to some extent, his predecessor.

Linguistic characterisation in Menander can be discerned in the following areas:

Male vs. female speech. Menander distinguishes between male and female speakers. There are various markers of female speech that are used:

1. Exclusively by women, such as the combination (ὦ) τάλαν, in an exclamatory function, reflecting either self-pity or sympathy towards someone else (cf. *Dysc.* 438, 591), the interjection αἶ (*Epit.* 468, *Mis.* 177 etc.), individual words such as δύσμορος (*Epit.* 468, *Sam.* 69 etc.), πά(π)πα (*Mis.* 213, 248), oaths by τὼ θεώ, cf. *Georg.* 24, *Dysc.* 878, *Epit.* 543 (vs. ὦ πολυτίμητοι θεοί used by men only, cf. *Asp.* 408, *Dysc.* 202, *Mis.*165) etc.
2. Mainly by women, that is proportionally to a greater extent than by male characters, e.g. the affectionate addresses γλυκύς (*Epit.* 143, 862, 953 etc.), τέκνον (*Georg.* 25, 63) etc.

Idiolect, that is particular linguistic features restricted to or mainly used by (a) specific character types, e.g. the preponderance of oaths by Hephaest and Poseidon in the mouths of old men. On the other hand, oaths by Dionysus are used more by young men than by anyone else. (b) specific characters, e.g. Habrotonon's speech in the *Epitrepontes* exhibits several terms of endearment (cf. vv. 466, 856, 953), the slave Daos in the *Aspis* has a penchant for maxims and moralising gnomes, Chaerea in the *Dyscolus* appears to be individualised by his habit of repeating a word in consecutive sentences, cf. ἐρῶν v. 52, ἐρᾶν v. 53, ἐρῶν v. 59, whereas Onesimos in the *Epitrepontes* frequently uses nouns ending in -μος as well as adjectives and adverbs in -ικός, -ικῶς.

Binary linguistic opposition. In several instances a binary linguistic opposition between two characters belonging to the same category, i.e. two slaves, two young men, old men etc., can be detected. For example, the slaves Daos and Syros in the *Epitrepontes* are contrasted by linguistic means as well. At *Epit.* 218ff., where the two slaves confront each other on the scene, Daos' style is quite simple. He uses brief main clauses, in asyndeton or linked by a simple καί, whereas the style of the more urbane Syrus is ornate. He uses maxims and often backs up his arguments with tragic myths. Similarly, Nikeratos' speech in the *Samia* consists of short sentences composed of small units, often in asyndeton. On the other hand the sentences of the educated Demea are more carefully formed, with balancing parts, antithesis, echoing beginnings and endings.[6]

Language and contextual setting. All characters do not speak the same language in all instances. Linguistic usage does not depend only upon the character speaking, but also on the demands of the contextual setting. Sostratos' speech in *Dis Exapaton* is a clear example of such linguistic behaviour. At the beginning of the play, his agitated emotional state is reflected in his language: self-apostrophe, anacolutha etc. Later in the play, not being in any particularly animated emotional state, he does not show any syntactical irregularities, and he speaks in long sentences.

All the above clearly show that characterisation through linguistic devices is by no means absent in the comedy of Menander.[7]

Roman comedy – the case of Terence: overall review

Concerning Terence, the prevailing opinion is, broadly speaking, that of Marouzeau (1947: 47) that his 'ton est celui de la bonne compagnie . . . Le langage de ses personnages ne varie guère: hommes ou femmes, vieillards ou jeunes gens, maîtres ou esclaves, matrones ou courtisanes s'expriment dans la langue de l' auteur'. Shipp (1960: 55) also thinks that all his characters, old and young, bond and free, man and woman speak a uniform Latin. On the other hand, ancient scholiasts point out Terence's ability to manipulate the language of his characters.

This is especially the case with Donatus, who gives several references to the appropriateness of linguistic usage in Terence's

6 Cf. Arnott (1995: 157), Webster (1974: 104–5); for a similar situation between the two young men Sostratos and Gorgias in *Dyscolos*, cf. Sandbach (1970: 116).

7 For linguistic characterisation in other comic poets of the Greek New Comedy, mainly Alexis, cf. Arnott (1995: 162–4).

characters. In more detail, Donatus distinguishes the following areas of linguistic characterisation in Terence (the categorisation is mine):

Male vs. female speech. Female language, according to the ancient scholiast, has a penchant for terms of endearment (cf. ad *Hec.* 824, commenting upon Bacchis' '*mi Pamphile' inquam 'amabo'*, Donatus remarks *haec blandimenta sunt muliebria*, cf. also ad *Eun.* 656 *'mea' et 'mea tu' et 'amabo' et alia huiuscemodi mulieribus apta sunt blandimenta*) as well as expressions of despair (cf. ad *Ad.* 291).[8]

Linguistic individualisation of specific character types. Several linguistic irregularities, conceived as such by the scholiast, are found in the speech of slaves and other characters belonging to a lower social class, cf. the *vitiosa locutio* (term of the scholiast) of the slave Geta at *Phorm.* 249 *molendum esse in pistrino, vapulandum; habendae compedes*, where *habendas* should have been used instead of *habendae*. The speech of old people is often characterised by long-winded expressions due to the feebleness of old age. Cf. for example the use of the collocation *mea sententia / iudico* by the *senex* Demea at *Ad.* 959, where *mea sententia* seems to be superfluous, since the verb of the sentence (*iudico*) expresses the same idea. Donatus sees this as an instance of περισσολογία (cf. also *Ad.* 68, *Eun.* 971–3).

Linguistic individualisation of specific characters. Some characters show a penchant for a specific word, expression or construction. This is the case, for instance, with the use of the term of endearment *anime mi* by Thais in *Eunuchus*. Donatus remarks ad *Eun.* 95 *anime mi <mi> Phaedria: . . . Vide quam familiariter hoc idem repetat blandimentum; vult enim Terentius velut peculiare verbum hoc esse Thaidis.*

Linguistic usage according to the demands of the contextual setting. Linguistic usage depends not only on the character speaking but also on the situation, emotional state, contextual setting. Donatus remarks, for example, that ellipsis is a figure of speech used by Terence's characters when they are angry (cf. ad *Andr.* 496), or are in a hurry (cf. ad *Ad.* 539) or even when they speak to themselves (cf. ad *Hec.* 278). Aposiopesis is also appropriate for indignant characters. Cf. ad *Eun.* 65 *Nam amat* ἀποσιωπήσεις *nimia indignatio*.[9]

[8] For expressions of despair like *misera*, more common in female speech, cf. Salat (1967: 252–75).

[9] For ellipsis and aposiopesis in Terence, cf. Papadimitriou (1994: 77–113).

Linguistic usage and the addressee.[10] Characters in Terence's plays pay attention to their use of language depending on their interlocutors. At *Hec.* 753, when Laches says to Bacchis *lepida es*, Donatus points out the appropriateness of the term used by Laches to describe Thais. He remarks: *ut si<gnifice>t senex cum meretrice s<e> loqui, eo nomine eam laudavit, quo meretrices solent laudari quam quo mater familias*. Donatus also comments upon the way people speak to Thraso, the *miles* of the *Eunuchus*. In the presence of Thraso, the other characters tend to use military terminology. Gnatho (v. 394) uses the verb *triumphat* in order to describe Thais' pleasure over Thraso's gift. Thais is the victorious general who has Pamphila for her booty and Thraso as a victim. Donatus remarks *ut militaribus dictis tangit militem parasitus!*. In v. 417 again, Gnatho uses the verb *iugulare,* giving rise to Donatus' remark that *pulchre tangit militem 'iugularas' dicendo non 'occideras' quasi gladio, non verbo usus sit*. The slave Parmeno as well in vv. 466–7 says to Thraso *pace quod fiat tua, dare huic quae volumus, convenire et conloqui*. Donatus comments here once more upon the appropriateness of Parmeno's language *proprie, quia pax, datio, deditio, conventio, colloquium militiae verba sunt*.

Although Donatus' remarks are not always accurate, in the sense that they are often impressionistic and devoid of systematisation and secure methodological footing, all the above show that a degree of linguistic characterisation in Terence's comedies was observed in antiquity.[11]

This intriguing discrepancy between ancient and modern scholarship concerning linguistic characterisation in Terence deserves to be examined in detail, and will constitute one of the two central subjects of this book. Apart from the existence of the Menandrian model, the parallel evidence of the literature of the second century BC, where a certain degree of linguistic self-consciousness and an awareness of different linguistic registers is attested in literary texts themselves, further justifies a new examination of linguistic characterisation in Terence.

Discussions and clear references to the appropriate use of language, as well as comic representations of deviant usages, are

[10] For the importance of the addressee in modern sociolinguistic approaches, cf. also Dickey (1996: 12).

[11] For a detailed presentation and criticism of Donatus' remarks on the use of language as a differentiating factor, cf. the introductions to each chapter and also Reich (1933: 72–94).

often to be found in the literature of the second century BC. In the *Truculentus* of Plautus, for example, Astaphium censures Truculentus for employing the form *rabo* rather than the standard *arrabo*. Her rustic interlocutor takes the opportunity to display his wit by informing her that *a-* is superfluous, and if the Praenestines can say *conia* rather than *ciconia*, then he can use *rabo* instead of *arrabo* (v. 688). It is obvious here that the rustic Truculentus is used by Plautus to make fun of the way the Praenestines pronounce certain words.[12] Further instances are offered by Lucilius, who points out several times barbarisms, solecisms etc., sometimes accompanied by detailed discussions on the correct spelling of verbal and case endings and of syntactic constructions. To give an example, Lucilius (1130) mocks the rustic diction of a certain Caecilius, who tended to pronounce the diphthong [ae] as [e].[13] As can be inferred from the above brief examples, in Terence's time, and even earlier, there existed a consciousness about proper and improper usages of Latin, and sometimes deviation was used as a literary, stylistic device. With this in mind, the research into linguistic usage as a potential stylistic effect in the work of Terence is in tune with a known theoretical issue and practice of his era.

Literature review

The first steps in research into language as a differentiating factor in the Terentian corpus have already been taken:

Tschernjaew (1900), in the first comprehensive study of an aspect of Terentian diction, mainly vulgar Latin, tried to show that slaves and the rustic Demea use several vulgarisms (the author's term). His work, however, is methodologically unsafe, in that he is not consistent in his criteria for deciding upon the vulgar character of a specific feature; what is more, he often labels as vulgarisms

[12] The Praenestine dialect tended to leave out vowels, so that the word *ciconia* was reduced to *[c-conia]*, which eventually gives *conia*; cf. also Perruzzi (1976: 45–51); for techniques of linguistic characterisation in Plautine drama, see also Jocelyn (1993: 125–93), Petersmann (1995: 123–36, 1996–7: 199–211), Stockert (1982: 4–14), Arnott (1972: 54–79), Boyce (1991: 12), García and López (1995: 233–45), Hofmann (1992: 143–58); for the Punic speech in the *Poenulus*, cf. Gratwick (1971: 25–45), Branden (1984: 159–80), Krahmalkov (1988: 55–66). Cf. also Currie (1983: 85–6).

[13] Cf. also Coleman (1990: 13), Ramage (1973: 47–8).

several features that do not show any particular concentration in generally accepted sources of Vulgar Latin, especially within Early Latin. His work has already been attacked with some justification by Wahrmann (1908) and Maltby (1976). Nevertheless, Tschernjaew gives some important information on the penchant shown by specific characters and character types for specific words, expressions or stylistic choices (cf. culinary terms often occurring in the speech of parasites, Demea's penchant for a series of oaths and exclamations emphasising his anger etc.).

Arnott (1970) remarked on how imagery or figurative language is used by Terence for differentiating purposes, without however always giving a precise definition of the descriptive terms he employs (e.g. colourful language). The first scene between the two slaves, Geta and Davus, is full of figurative language. The use of figurative expressions by Geta diminishes only when Phormio enters the stage, and takes over this practice in his speech. This underplaying of Geta's language emphasises the contrast between the two. Arnott also suggests that imagery is concentrated mainly in the speech of non-freeborn characters. A similar suggestion is offered also by Fantham (1972: 74), who claims that some kind of differentiation is to be found in Terence, by means of emotive language and imagery. She, however, believes that linguistic characterisation by means of dialectal features as well as by syntactic vulgarisms is absent from Terence's comedies.

Gilleland (1979) constitutes a further important discussion of the issue. He offers a comprehensive examination of (i) Greek words, producing detailed statistics and giving full lists of occurrences, in welcome opposition to previous discussions of the subject;[14] (ii) specific interjections and oaths; (iii) diminutive formations; (iv) specific forms of address, and comes to the following conclusions:

1. Greek words are proportionally more common in male speech, especially in the diction of *servi, parasiti, milites, lenones*.
2. Some interjections and oaths (e.g. *ecastor, au*) are used only by women, whereas others (e.g. *(me) hercle, ei*) are to be found only in the speech of men.[15]

[14] Cf. also Hough (1947: 18–21), Oksala (1953: 24–35).

[15] For the distribution of oaths, see also Nicolson (1893: 99–103), Gagnér (1920).

3. Diminutives are more common in the speech of women as a whole and in the diction of *matronae, ancillae, meretrices* in particular. Among male characters, diminutives occur more frequently in the speech of *servi, milites*.
4. Women use titles (e.g. *vir, gnatus*) more often than names, and frequently accompany such addresses with the vocative *meus*, in opposition to male speech, where proper names are more common and vocative forms of *meus* are normally omitted.

The subject of female speech in Roman comedy in general and in Terence in particular has also been dealt with by Adams (1984). Following a careful statistical approach, Adams's principal conclusions can be summarised as follows:

1. Several linguistic usages in Terence are restricted to female speech, namely oaths, such as *ecastor, mecastor*; interjections like *au* (conclusions which Gilleland had already reached before); polite modifiers such as *amabo*, individual expressions like *amo* in the formulaic *merito te amo, amo te (vos)*, where *amo* expresses gratitude, whereas others occur in the language of men only, namely oaths as *hercle, mehercle*, interjections like *ei* (also pointed out by Gilleland before), polite modifiers like the parenthetic *quaeso*, imperative intensifiers like *sis, sodes, age*.[16]
2. Certain linguistic usages, although not restricted to female speech, are proportionally more common in the language of women than men, e.g. the oath *pol, obsecro*, self-pitying address forms, e.g. *misera*, intimate forms of address (*mi/mea* + vocative).
3. In Terence these linguistic differences between the two sexes are adhered to in greater degree than in the Plautine corpus.
4. The various markers of female language often occur in clusters, cf. e.g. *Eun*. 663–7 (*amabo, obsecro, mea tu, pol, miserae*).
5. Not all linguistic usages showing a particular concentration in female speech are a mere reflex of sex differentiation. The situation and the addressee, as well as the social status of both speaker and addressee, may be of particular importance. Thais, for example, in the *Eunuchus* addresses her lover Phaedria with *mi* + vocative combinations (cf. vv. 86, 95, 144, 190), but she usually addresses the *adulescentes*, Chremes and Chaerea, with a plain vocative (cf. vv. 751, 765, 880, 893).[17]

[16] For the use of *sodes* and *quaeso* in Terentian drama, cf. also Carney (1964: 57–63).

[17] For the importance of the addressee in the distribution of *sodes, quaeso* in Terentian drama, cf. also Carney (1964: n.15).

Nuñez (1995) also examines the distribution of imperative modifiers in the Terentian corpus. His main conclusions are the following:

1. Some modifiers are restricted to or found in higher ratios in female speech (*amabo*, *mi* + vocative syntagms) whereas others are associated with the speech of men (*quaeso, sis*, cf. similar remarks by Adams above).
2. Whereas politeness modifiers are more frequently used by women than by men, it is male characters who use almost exclusively the imperative intensifier *age*.
3. Not only the speaker but also the addressee is important for the distribution of a specific modifier. For example, whereas *liberae* or *libertae* women use politeness modifiers mainly when addressing a freeborn male character, women who are not free use them both when addressing freeborn citizens and slaves.

Martin (1995) offers some further insights concerning the use of language for the individualisation of a character in Terentian drama. By examining the language of Pythias in the *Eunuchus*, he points out that two features characterise Pythias' idiolect:

1. several linguistic usages, *hapax* in Terence, which appear in concentration in her speech;
2. the manner in which she uses language, wholly or predominantly used by female speakers. For example, of the total of eight examples of *amabo* (as a form of address) in the *Eunuchus* six are spoken by Pythias. Since *amabo* is used so that a closer rapport between speaker and addressee can be established, its frequent use by Pythias aims to 'define her character and to emphasize her role in the play' (142).

Martin also observes that Pythias' language differs according to both the addressee and the contextual setting. Thus, the *ancilla* has the tendency to use more 'distinctive' language (the author's term, cf. 150), full of noteworthy (the author's term again, cf. 145) linguistic usages (special forms of hyperbaton, accumulation of markers of female speech etc.) when she meets a specific character for the first time (for linguistic differences in her language between her first and second meeting with Chremes and Parmeno, cf. 145–6, 150).

Müller (1997), applying modern linguistic approaches to the language of Terentian dialogues (in the domains of pragmatics, syntax and lexicon), offers some important observations concerning the use of language as a differentiating factor in Terence, even though the main aim of the study is not to examine techniques of linguistic differentiation in Terentian drama. Müller emphasises Terence's ability to differentiate male from female speech (mainly repeating here points already made by previous scholars, Gilleland, Carney, Adams) as well as the importance of the character speaking and the social status of both the interlocutors for the distribution of a specific feature (mainly on the level of pragmatics). *Eu* + vocative combinations, for example, are used in a dialogue between two persons of equal social status or when a master addresses his slave. *Eu* + the possessive pronoun *noster*, on the other hand, are found in the speech of slaves when addressing their masters. Although important, these remarks are limited in number, dispersed throughout his work and restricted to specific levels of linguistic analysis; Muller's study falls far short of offering a comprehensive examination of Terentian techniques concerning linguistic characterisation.

Maltby's work (1976, 1979) is the only large-scale analysis of the language of Terence. By examining several archaisms and long-winded expressions, elevated features and colloquialisms, he concludes that the speech of old men has an old-fashioned as well as a verbose flavour; and low characters, especially slaves, use several colloquial features in opposition to characters belonging to a higher social rank, who, on the contrary, intersperse their language with elevated features. Additionally, he points out the following:

1. The speech of several characters in Terentian drama is individualised by their penchant for specific words and expressions that are restricted to their speech or that are proportionally more common in their language than in that of other characters.
2. Several words are associated with the speech of a specific character or character type in Terence because the meaning of these words fits some aspect of the character's behaviour (e.g. culinary terms used by parasites, military terms by soldiers etc.).
3. Language depends not only on the character speaking but also on the contextual setting.
4. Variation of language is also discernible between different plays, probably related to their dates of composition (cf. more archaisms in the *Andria*, Terence's first work etc.).

Maltby's work, however, is not free from some methodological infelicities. Even though some of his conclusions will prove to be correct, his data are often false and his approach over-simplistic. In particular:

1. His examination of data is partial.
2. A more sophisticated categorisation of his data is required.
3. He often establishes the archaic or colloquial etc. character of a specific phenomenon without taking into account the full distribution of the feature in question in the whole of Latin literature, and therefore his conclusions are inaccurate.
4. He gives limited attention to the stylistic differences between earlier and later Terentian plays.

Detailed examination and criticism of Maltby's work is to be found in the introduction of individual chapters of this book.

Compared to his partial examination of all the linguistic categories mentioned above, Maltby's later work on the distribution of Greek words in Terentian drama (1985) is complete and methodologically secure. He concludes that linguistic characterisation by means of hellenising words is absent from Terence's two first plays. From *Heautontimoroumenos* onwards Greek words characterise the speech of characters belonging to a lower social level. Several hellenising expressions are also to be found in the speech of the *senes* Chremes and Demea, in *Heautontimoroumenos* and *Adelphoe* respectively, in opposition to the language of their counterparts Menedemus and Micio.

A recent contribution to the topic of colloquialism in Terence, Papadimitriou (1998), offers a considerable amount of information, as well as a number of pertinent observations.

Aims and objectives of the present study

For all the above reasons the subject needs to be examined further and to be set on a safer methodological footing. My aim is to pursue the investigation by examining a wide range of linguistic phenomena, which were either merely touched upon by previous scholars but not exhausted, or falsely interpreted, or not examined at all.

In particular, the categories of phenomena upon which I concentrate are:

1. colloquialisms
2. archaisms
3. long-winded expressions
4. hellenisms (on the syntactic level)
5. features of elevated language
6. idiolectal elements (i.e. individual linguistic features with no particular colloquial, archaic, long-winded, hellenising, elevated character, associated with the speech of specific characters or character types).

The methodological basis for all these features will be described and discussed in detail in the methodological introduction of each chapter. Here, however, I must make clear my way of proceeding with this investigation, which is mainly heuristic: starting from standard works of reference (grammars, commentaries, investigations of the language of specific authors), I collect series of features or phenomena (phonological, morphological, syntactic, lexical, stylistic) belonging to the aforementioned broad categories, i.e. colloquialisms, archaisms etc. I then proceed to the detailed examination of the text of Terence in order to ascertain:

1. whether any of these features are present in the language of our author in significantly different quantity than in the text of other comic writers, especially Plautus;
2. what, if any, is the distribution of these features in the Terentian text, that is, if they appear in concentration in the speech of any character type or in any specific situation, or on the contrary, if they are absent from the speech of any character type;
3. whether any Terentian features of language can be considered to belong to the above broad categories although no previous research on them exists;
4. whether any chronological development from play to play can be determined.

As can be seen from the above, our starting points are the predetermined linguistic categories of colloquialism, archaism etc., which are then tested on the text. This work, however, has to deal with several considerable problems because the various cover terms colloquialism, archaism etc. do not always have a standard definition and scholars may vary in their classification of a certain feature.

Moreover, there are often no standard, clear, criteria for the characterisation of a feature as belonging to a specific category. They may be implied or understood, but they are rarely explicit (for criticism of various methodological approaches, see individual chapters).

Taking all these caveats into account, by means of a thorough linguistic analysis, the aim of this book is mainly to show that:

1. Terence's slaves, parasites, pimps and soldiers as well as people living in the country intersperse their language with colloquial features and hellenising constructions.
2. Archaic linguistic phenomena, pleonastic expressions and features having an elevated character are concentrated in the speech of old people.
3. Individual characters or character types have a particular penchant for specific linguistic features.
4. Language is often affected by the demands of the contextual setting, mainly by the emotional state of the character speaking.
5. Various characters often abandon linguistic peculiarities which characterise their speech, as proven by statistics of occurrence, in order to accommodate their diction to the speech – habits of their interlocutors. Thus, individual features which appear, as pattern exceptions, in the speech of characters or character types other than those with which the specific kind of linguistic option is usually associated (as is proven, again, by statistics of occurrence) occur only as a repartee to a character whose speech displays the linguistic peculiarity under question as an idiolectal feature, or who belongs to a character group where such a linguistic option is found in concentration. This is probably due to the psychology of the addressee who tends to mimic the speech of the speakers. In other words, the addressee is an important factor for the distribution of specific linguistic phenomena in the Terentian corpus.
6. There is an evolution in Terence's techniques of linguistic characterisation. Whereas *Andria* is still 'immature', characterisation by means of language is perfected in Terence's last drama, *Adelphoe*.

My research has also a broader aim, which is to place Terence in the overall linguistic picture of Roman comedy (*palliata, togata, atellana*), by comparing his language to that of previous (Livius Andronicus, Ennius, Naevius, Plautus), contemporary (Turpilius) and later comic dramatists (Afranius). I hope to demonstrate that:

1. the *comoedia palliata* exhibits considerable linguistic and stylistic uniformity, from which Terence largely differentiates himself, with the important exception of one play, the *Eunuchus*;

2. the *comoedia togata* and *atellana* also present a series of common features with the *palliata*, from which Terence distances himself, with the same exception.

With this in mind, a thorough linguistic commentary (the first ever), line by line, of all the comic fragments (*palliata, togata* and *atellana*) will be offered. The linguistic and stylistic entries are arranged according to generally accepted subheadings (morphology, syntax, lexicon, style), with the view to show the variety and the extent of the linguistic and stylistic rapprochement between all the authors of the *palliata*, the *togata* and the *atellana*, with the exception of Terence.

It will be shown that, with the exception of *Eunuchus*, in his other plays Terence seems to anticipate in most cases later Classical Latin usage (CL, hereafter), a development that could possibly be put down to the fact that he was educated in a mid-second-century aristocratic environment, where Greek culture was a formative influence and the Ciceronian ideal of *urbanitas*, i.e. linguistic purism, might already be important. Cicero himself praises Terence's diction (cf. *Att.* 7.3.10 *elegantiam sermonis*) in opposition to Caecilius for example, plainly characterised by Cicero as *malus auctor Latinitatis* (*Epist.* loc. cit.).[18] It will be shown indeed that several unclassical features commonly found in free use in all comic dramatists, both anterior and posterior to Terence, are avoided in Terentian drama or used for specific stylistic effect in the speech of specific characters or character types. This patterning does not hold true for *Eunuchus*, however; a likely inference is that, after the failure of *Hecyra*, Terence's most CL play from the viewpoint of language, our author needed a success, and therefore might have thought it safer to adhere to popular demand and to the old tried ways. The language of his *Eunuchus* is clearly closer to the comic linguistic tradition, as known from writers such as Naevius, Caecilius but mainly Plautus, rather than in the linguistic line of his other plays. This, along with a comparative linguistic analysis of the *palliata*, the *togata* and the *atellana*, will be the subject of the second part of this book.

[18] Cf. also Marouzeau (1926: 102–3).

What is more, it will be demonstrated that Terence opts for a more traditional language and style in some individual scenes in his other plays (apart from *Eunuchus*), where he seems to deviate from his original (last scene of the *Heautontimoroumenos*, the Sannio scene in *Adelphoe*; all such scenes are discussed thoroughly in the chapters to follow). Thus, I shall suggest that divergence from purity of diction and style can, along with other factors (e.g. the presence of four actors on stage etc.), be an indication for Terence's altering his model.

Terminological remarks

Chronology

A detailed methodological discussion of the various terms colloquial, archaic, elevated etc. will be found in the introduction to each chapter. Here some methodological remarks on the terms Early Latin (EL), Classical Latin (CL) and Post-Classical Latin (PC) as used in the present book are in order:

1. EL (Early Latin) refers to literary and epigraphic evidence from the pre-classical period, that is from the origins up to 87 BC.
2. CL is the literary Latin of prose and verse writers from Cicero to Livy (i.e. circa 87 BC–AD 17) as well as the epigraphic evidence of this period, which is characterised by an effort at rationalisation and refinement in the use of language, mainly by eliminating lexical and syntactical doublets as well as morphological uncertainties (variations of gender, declension, conjugation).
3. PC (Post-Classical Latin) refers to the Latin of literary texts and inscriptions from AD 17 till the sixth century AD, i.e. when it is believed that Romance daughter languages began to split off.[19] Within this period, two further subdivisions are made: (a) Silver period, roughly from the death of Augustus till AD 200; (b) Late Latin (known in French and German scholarship as *bas latin*, *Spätlatein*, respectively), i.e. roughly from AD 200 till the sixth century AD.

Of course, not all features found in literary or epigraphic sources of a specific period represent the linguistic practice as well as the

[19] I follow the convention adopted by the *ThLL* and examine the history of a specific linguistic feature till the end of the sixth century AD (cf. *ThLL* Praemonenda 28; see also Haverling (2000: 38)).

linguistic evolution of the period. For example, several features found in the poetic register of CL (cf. *olli* in place of *ille* in Vergil etc.) are demonstrably archaic and are used for specific stylistic and/or metrical effect. Therefore a detailed examination of the author as well as of the context in which a specific feature occurs is indispensable for deciding about its EL, CL or PC character.

Character types

Some words on the notion of character type are in order: capitalising on Maltby's (1976) methodology, two main distinctions are drawn, the first according to age and the second according to social class. The age distinction differentiates between, on the one hand, old people, that is *senes, matronae*, old slaves (Geta[20] in the *Adelphoe*, the pedagogue Geta in the *Phormio*) and nurses, and, on the other hand, younger people such as *adulescentes, virgines*, young *meretrices* etc. The distinction of social class draws a line between high and low characters. High characters are freeborn citizens of higher social status such as *senes, adulescentes, matronae, virgines*, while low characters consist of slaves, freedmen, *meretrices* or freeborn citizens of low social rank such as parasites, pimps, soldiers etc. A third dimension is provided by the differentiation, common in New Comedy, between town and country. Characters of the same social class (e.g. *senes*) can be divided into rustic people on the one hand, and their urbane counterparts on the other (e.g. in the *Adelphoe* Demea vs. Micio).

These linguistic groups present bundles of common linguistic features. This does not necessarily entail that a certain feature associated with a specific character type, as established by statistics of occurrence, cannot occasionally be found in the mouth of a character belonging to a different group. What matters in these cases is not the individual features themselves, but their relevant accumulation in the speech of a specific character or character type and their relative absence from the speech of another. In many of the divergent instances, the use of these features can be attributed

[20] For the age of the slave Geta, cf. Radice (1976: 253) 'Sostrata's elderly slave, Geta', cf. also Papadimitriou (1998: 265, 269), Sloman (1936: 88), Gratwick (1987: 241).

to the demands of the contextual setting, i.e. when a character is trying to accommodate his or her language to that of his or her interlocutor.

Although one would expect that the language of a low person for example and the language of old people would present diverse and incompatible characteristics, it is often the case that Terentian characters might belong to two character groups at the same time (e.g. the old slave Geta in *Adelphoe* or the rustic young man Chremes in *Eunuchus*). In these cases a character's speech may display features from either of the two groups to which he or she belongs.

PART I

LINGUISTIC DIFFERENTIATION IN TERENCE

CHAPTER I

COLLOQUIALISMS

Introduction

Donatus

Since the beginnings of linguistic research on Terence, colloquialisms have formed the centre of interest. Thus, the comments of ancient grammarians contain prescriptive observations on the popular or even faulty nature of certain features. Donatus remarks upon Terence's use of language to differentiate the speech of his low characters, mainly slaves. According to the grammarian, Terence has his low characters use several linguistic or stylistic irregularities that are considered appropriate to the speech of persons of a low social rank. Commenting on Parmeno's *quia enim qui eos gubernat animus eum infirmum gerunt* at *Hec.* 311, Donatus remarks that this ἀνακόλουθον is appropriate for a servant. Similarly at *Phorm.* 186 Geta says: *loquarne? incendam; taceam? instigem; purgem me? laterem lavem.* Donatus remarks on the asyndetic series of questions – answers in place of conditional clauses: *haec et perturbatae et servilis imperitaeque personae verba sine arte esse.* Censuring the reiteration of the verb *nescio* in the speech of the slave Parmeno at *Hec.* 323ff., he observes: *perturbatus Parmeno idem repetit verbum. et aptum est personae servili.*[1]

Not only slaves but other low and rustic characters are characterised by faulty diction. This is especially the case with the language of the soldier Thraso in the *Eunuchus*. Donatus points out an ἀνακόλουθον *et vitiosa responsio*, namely *vobis fretus* (v. 1063), and he adds that *nisi enim addideris 'sum' erit soloecismus conveniens loquenti, impolito homini et militi.* When Thraso says *risu omnes qui aderant emoriri* (v. 432), Donatus remarks that

[1] Cf. also Introduction, p. 5.

among the comic playwrights it is customary to attribute defective words to ridiculous and ignorant characters. The defective word that Thraso uses here, according to the grammarian, is *emoriri* in place of *emori*, used elsewhere in Terence by a high character, the *adulescens* Clitipho at *Heaut.* 971. Another linguistic mistake, according to the grammarian, is the use of the indicative in a *cum*-clause, *quom tibi do* (v. 792). He remarks *indiligenter . . . pro 'cum tibi darem', sed miles loquitur.* Chremes, the rustic young man in *Eunuchus*, is also censured for his diction. The use of the possessive pronoun at *Eun.* 803 *diminuam ego caput tuum* in place of a sympathetic dative construction *diminuam tibi caput* is considered by the grammarian as evidence of the young man's *rusticitas* (*rusticius dixit*). Of course such observations do not constitute a serious linguistic analysis of Terence, since they consist mainly in impressionistic judgements of the grammarian, devoid of systematisation or methodological criteria, as that would be conceived by modern scholarship.

Modern discussions of the subject

Such a broadly impressionistic viewpoint has also dominated the majority of modern approaches to the colloquial elements in the language of Terence, until the work of the most important and serious modern researcher of the topic, R. Maltby. It has to be emphasised at this point that previous scholarship has very little to offer in this matter, being limited to two contributions. Before Maltby, Tschernjaew had tried to show that vulgarisms (the author's term) show a particular concentration in the speech of low characters.[2] His work was criticised by Wahrmann (1908), who re-examined the issue and demanded a more systematic approach, which, by the way, led him to the conclusion that linguistic differentiation in Terence was non-existent.

'Colloquial' in studies of Latin language is a term that covers a wide range of styles, from urbane conversational style to the language of the lower classes, in the case of Rome the *plebs*, who

[2] For criticism of Tschernjaew's work, cf. Introduction, pp. 7–8.

generally lacked access to the educational system. This language is revealed either by means of non-literary texts (graffiti, inscriptions etc.) or through the medium of either literary writers (comedy, satire) attempting to imitate popular modes of speech or popular writers attempting to imitate literary modes of writing (Christian fathers, the author of the *Peregrinatio Aetheriae* etc.). These are the seismic areas whose occasional eruptions, as Palmer claims (1954: 149), reveal subterranean linguistic activity in the dead landscape of literary Latin. In other words, colloquial language is an ambiguous term, referring sometimes to the low speech of the uneducated classes and sometimes to the refined conversational language (e.g. Ciceronian dialogues, dialogue settings in Vergil, tragedy etc.). An overlapping linguistic area also exists to which belong those features found in sources of spoken Latin of both educated and less educated or uneducated people. The precise borderlines between each of these levels of linguistic differentiation are vague and often unclear.

Despite these difficulties of classification, a strict methodology, based on the comparative approach, does offer the possibility of distinguishing in many cases to which level a certain linguistic item belongs. According to the criterion set out in his methodological introduction, 'colloquial' in Maltby's thesis refers to language of a lower level, and it encompasses features which occur in the language of comedy but disappear in the classical period (except perhaps for examples in genres like satire etc.). Such features crop up again in the literature in late Vulgar Latin texts or are found as reflexes in the Romance languages. Although they lived on in the spoken register of the language (occurring occasionally in the inscriptions of less educated writers), they were avoided by the purism of the classical period. Maltby has examined the distribution of several colloquial features within Terentian drama as well as the use of Greek words and expressions often associated with colloquial speech. He concludes that slaves and rustics and characters of lower social rank use colloquialisms, as well as Greek words or expressions, more often.[3]

[3] Cf. also Introduction, p. 12.

However, even though his methodological tools are sound, most of the features discussed by him do not correspond to these actual criteria. In more detail:

1. Several of the linguistic features he discusses as colloquial are found in non-colloquial sources as well, for example the verb *beo*, found also in Horace's *Carmina* (cf. 2.3.7, 4.8.29), *porto*, found several times in Cicero, Vergil, Ovid.
2. He labels as colloquial features that are found only in EL Roman comedy and not in any other colloquial genres; cf. the syntagm *volup est*,[4] the use of *adsimulo* in place of *simulo* + 'accusativus cum infinitivo' syntagms in the sense of 'to pretend', the deponent form *opsonor* for *obsono*, the inchoative *edormiscere* in the sense of 'to sleep off'. In this case, however, we may simply have to do with EL features avoided later in the history of Latin and not with ones having a particular colloquial character.

One is justified in talking about the possibly colloquial character of a specific formation/construction/ lexical item restricted to comedy, only in cases where this item belongs to a general linguistic category that not only shows diachronically, throughout the history of Latin, a particular concentration in colloquial sources, but also is favoured within EL in comedy, satire and agricultural works and is avoided by higher poetic genres like tragedy and epic. Neither deponent formations in place of CL active equivalents, e.g. *opsonor*, or vice versa, nor inchoative verbs, e.g. *edormiscere*, show a particular colloquial flavour in EL, nor are they avoided in the higher literary genres of the era.[5] In these cases, therefore, their restriction to comedy may be simply fortuitous.

Another characteristic example of the misconceptions to which the lack of comparative research and of a strict methodological tool can lead is the work of Fantham. Although in general she denies any degree of linguistic characterisation in Terence, she once locates a vulgarism found in the speech of a slave. This is the transitive use of *ardere* at *Phorm.* 82 *hanc ardere coepit perdite.* She claims[6] that such a transitive use of the verb may be explained by analogy with *deperire*, a usage probably intended by Terence

4 The adverb *volup* in *volup facere* appears in tragic diction as well; cf. *Carm. Nelei* I (trag. p. 270).
5 For inchoative verbs, cf. also Canedo (1935–6: 257–66).
6 Cf. Fantham (1972: 8.)

to reflect vulgar language in the speech of his slave Geta. Her observation is impressionistic, however, and she does not give a methodological rationale for her classification of a specific feature as vulgar or not. The reading *ardere* is first of all textually doubtful. All the manuscripts give the reading *amare*, whereas *ardere* is restored from the grammarian Charisius. In any case such a use is found later in Vergil as well; cf. *Ecl.* 2.1 *Formosum pastor Corydon ardebat Alexin*, where the intransitive *ardere* governs a direct object, again by means of a *constructio ad sensum*. The transitive usage appears in Horace as well; cf. *Carm.* 4.9.13 *non sola comptos arsit adulter.*[7] It is difficult to be sure that a construction which appears in Vergil, and even in the *Odes* of Horace, is vulgar. What is more, no evidence from within EL as to the vulgar character of this feature is adduced.

Aims and objectives of the present study

The present chapter has as its aim the extension of Maltby's initial remarks. I shall apply to the Terentian text the strict criterion for discerning a colloquialism spelled out by Maltby at the beginning of his thesis. I shall show that:

1. Such features are used mainly by low characters (slaves, parasites, soldiers) and rustic characters (country people vs. their urbane counterparts).
2. Other characters use such features mainly when they have as their interlocutor a low or rustic character; in other words when they accommodate their diction to that of their addressee.

Methodological remarks

Before we move on to the examination of the features themselves, a few further methodological notes are in order: unlike linguists studying modern languages, scholars who endeavour to examine dead languages have to cope with a serious disadvantage. From the past we have no information from native speakers, only written

[7] For the transitive use of *ardere*, cf. also Coleman (1977: 91).

utterances; and, as Dover (1987: 16) rightly remarks, 'no written utterance can be treated as entirely spontaneous and unconsidered'. Furthermore, the linguist dealing with dead languages, especially Greek or Latin, has to examine language mainly through the medium of literary texts, composed often by skilful writers who wished to be admired for their artistry and wrote in a highly stylised, elaborate and, to some extent, artificial language. In order, therefore, to be able to characterise a linguistic element as belonging to a certain register (colloquial, archaic etc.), the linguist has to rely on strict criteria of categorisation, based on detailed examination of both texts and contexts. Even literary genres such as comedy, satire, epistolography, which, in their content or nature, are closer to everyday life, presenting everyday characters and problems, are not written in a pure everyday language, but are full of markers of literarity (such as sophisticated word play, archaisms, balanced clauses, padded style, parody of serious poetry (tragedy, epic) or official/legal/sacral language, congeries). Despite this fact, it is precisely in these genres that we find features avoided by purist classical speech and genres like epic and tragedy, which reappear in Late Latin and in so-called vulgar texts and are often censured by grammarians. In many cases, the authors of such literary genres themselves comment upon the low, inappropriate level of their diction as opposed to the more refined language of their other works belonging to a different genre. Cf. Cicero's remarks on the language of his *Epistles, Fam.* 9.21.1 *verum tamen quid tibi ego videor in epistulis? nonne plebeio sermone agere tecum?* etc.

For deciding upon the colloquial character of a specific feature I shall follow here well-established methodological techniques (cf. Väänänen (1959: 13–20), Vossler (1954: 55–76), Palmer (1954: 148–80), Grandgent (1908: 1–5), Muller and Taylor (1932: iii-x), Herman (1967: 27–35), Haadsma-Nuchelmans (1963: 13–5).[8] By

[8] For the terms 'colloquial' and 'vulgar' Latin, cf. Altheim (1932: 153–71), Baerens (1922), Battisti (1949), Coleman (1987: 37–52), Löfstedt (1982: 200–4), Marx (1909: 434–48), Meister (1909: 69–90), Nelson (1951: 220–9), Pulgram (1950: 458–66), Schmeck (1955), Sturtevant (1925: 5–25), Väänänen (1959, 1967), Wölflin (1876: 137–65); for colloquialisms or vulgarisms in individual authors: for Apuleius, Callebat (1968); for Catullus, Soles (1954), Vaccaro (1951: 33–42); for Cassiodorus and late Latin sources, Fridh

means of a distributional criterion based on the examination of linguistic variables and on the detection of linguistic affinity between different literary genres, the term colloquial in this book encompasses features which present the following distribution:

1. They are frequently found in comedy, a literary genre that may reasonably be supposed to contain elements close to the spoken, 'natural language', partly due to the fact that its subject-matter is often alien to serious literature. These colloquial features favoured in comedy are, on the other hand, avoided by the higher literary genres of the Republican time, such as the tragedies of Ennius, Naevius, Accius, Pacuvius etc, or the epic poetry of Ennius.
2. These features disappear from Classical Latin literature, with the exception of less formal genres such as satire (Horace) or epistolography (Cicero). Catullus also displays several colloquial features. Otherwise CL, i.e. the Latin of prose and verse writers from Cicero to Livy (87 BC–AD 17), is characterised by a striving for rationalisation and refinement in the use of the language, achieved mainly by eliminating lexical and syntactical doublets as well as morphological uncertainties (variations of gender, declension, conjugation).
3. Such features reappear later in non-literary texts such as inscriptions and graffiti, especially from Pompeii, as well as in *defixionum tabellae*, and they are common in PC–Late Latin or vulgar sources such as Petronius' *Cena Trimalchionis*, Apuleius' novel, the Early Latin translation of the Bible (the so-called *Itala*), the pseudo-Cyprianic *Adversus Aleatores*, the work of Lucifer Calaritanus, Victor Vitensis etc. Christian writers, at least of the first period, who self-confessedly adopt the language of the masses, are also an important source, cf. Augustine's *In psalm.* 138.20 *melius est reprehendant nos grammatici quam non intelligant populi.*[9]
4. Important information concerning linguistic level (irrespective of era) is also given (i) by technical treatises such as Vitruvius' *De architectura*

(1950); for Ennius, Risicato (1966); for Horace, Bonfante (1994), Bourciez (1927), Ruckdeschel (1911); for the *Peregrinatio Aetheriae*, Löfstedt (1911), for Persius, Gérard (1897: 81–103); for Petronius, Abbot (1907: 43–50), Boyce (1991), Stefenelli (1962), Petersmann (1977); for Phaedrus, Bertschinger (1921); for Plautus, Happ (1967: 60–114), Povsic (1987: 27–31 and 30–6), Sznajder (1996: 167–90); for Pliny, Brakman (1930: 207–22); for Propertius, Enk (1940: 299–322), Neumann (1925); for Varro, De Saint-Denis (1947: 141–62); for the *atellana* and the mimes, Bonfante (1967: i–xxiv).

[9] This does not entail that all features of Augustine's language are distinctively colloquial. However, when a specific formation in Augustine's work is (a) formed by means of an affix showing particular productivity in colloquial speech and (b) occurs in colloquial sources only, it should be considered to have a colloquial flavour, taking into account the well known tendency of Augustine (especially in his *sermones*) as well as of other Christian authors for often using popular language (cf. Palmer (1954: 202)). For the language of Augustine, cf. also Mohrmann (1932).

(cf. 1.1.13, *nec potest esse architectus grammaticus*), Cato's and Columella's agricultural works, the *Mulomedicina Chironis*, Pliny's *Naturalis Historia*; (ii) by later grammarians compiling glosses and linguistic commentaries, such as the Appendix Probi etc.; (iii) by *diplomata, chartae, documenta*, and legal texts of the Middle Ages, especially from the sixth to the ninth century, as well as by the whole of medieval Latin (sixth century onwards);[10] and (iv) by the reflexes of various linguistic items and phenomena in the modern Romance languages, which stem not from CL but from the vernacular.

Apart from the features of Terence's language which are found in such sources only, and are the ones to be discussed in detail in this book, there are several other linguistic options found in Terentian drama that have often been labelled as colloquial in Terentian as well as in Latin linguistic scholarship in general. Some of these features are given the term colloquial simply for impressionistic reasons, with no rationale at all (especially in commentaries on Terence's plays), others in accordance with the notion of the *Umgangssprache* developed by Hofmann in his *Die lateinische Umgangssprache* and based mainly on a psychological interpretation of the language, that is the affected character of colloquial speech, an outdated approach nowadays. Several of these features, however, have been so closely associated with colloquial speech (e.g. proleptic accusative, indicative in indirect questions) that their absence here, in a book which claims to be a thorough analysis of this linguistic category in Terentian drama, might seem very strange. For these reasons I have opted to list all such features in a table at the end of the chapter.[11] They are not discussed in detail, not because I am unaware of their association with colloquial speech but only because they are not found exclusively in colloquial sources (as set out in the Introduction) but often occur in higher genres as well. Therefore the possible results of such an examination would not be conclusive, since the colloquial

[10] For this cf. in particular Vossler (1954: 69).

[11] Some of the features to be found in table 1 appear only in colloquial and archaising sources, which often draw on the language of EL comedy. What appears in a literary text as an archaism may at the same time be found in the colloquial register (Maltby (1976: 13), Adams and Mayer (1999: 10)). In the case of such features, additional information is given in an explanatory parenthesis.

character of such lexical items/formations/constructions/stylistic options cannot be definitely established.

A further restriction adhered to here must be mentioned at this juncture: only options belonging to the strictly linguistic levels (i.e. phonology, morphology, syntax, semantics) are examined; pragmatic options, i.e. variations depending on type of text/discourse considerations etc. are not listed here, as they cannot properly be held to belong to 'language' itself, to a particular social register, but rather to the specific utterance conditions.

Features occurring in colloquial sources only

Derivation

Before moving to the examination of several colloquial derivatives, an initial methodological remark is in order. The derivative forms to be discussed here are divided into two main categories. Within each category the formations to be discussed comply with the criteria described below:

Category A encompasses derivatives that:

1. are formed by means of affixes which, diachronically within Latin literature, show a particular productivity in colloquial sources only, despite their occasional occurrence in higher genres as well;
2. within EL these affixes are common in comedy and satire but are avoided or used sparingly in tragedy and epic;
3. the specific derivative itself is found in colloquial sources only.

Category B. Under this heading I shall examine words that:

1. are again formed, as is category A, through the medium of affixes which diachronically in the history of Latin appear to a greater extent in colloquial sources; but
2. within EL do not show a particular concentration in colloquial sources only, even though in some cases such affixes are slightly more common in EL colloquial genres;
3. in any case, the specific words to be discussed occur in colloquial sources only.

Category A

Substantives and adjectives

Substantives in *-arius*. Such formations abound in colloquial sources; comedy, especially Plautus (cf. for example *Aul.* 508–16, where sixteen words in *-arius* are heaped together for comic effect), in the Script. RR (especially the neuter forms), satire, technical treatises, Petronius, inscriptions.[12] Even within EL these derivatives, both substantives and adjectives, seem to have acquired a distinct colloquial flavour, as they are avoided by higher literary genres, especially tragedy; they are favoured, on the other hand, in comedy and satire.

In Terence we find in the mouth of the slave Parmeno *palmarium* at *Eun.* 930 *id verost quod ego mi puto palmarium*. The word in the sense of *palma dignus, praestans, eximius* reappears in late Latin authors, e.g. Cassiod. *Var.* 8.9.5 *in palmarii Eugenetis linguae ubertate suffecit*,[13] as well as in inscriptions, e.g. Inscr. Hispan. Ant. Epigr. 4–5, 1953–5, n. 670 *uxor pia viro palmario posu<it>*.

Cetarius in the sense of 'fisher' or 'fishmonger' is found at *Eun.* 256–7 *concurrunt laeti mi obviam cuppedenarii omnes, cetarii lanii coqui fartores piscatores* in the speech of the parasite Gnatho. The word appears also in satire, e.g. Var. *Men.* 209.1 *cetarios*, Script. RR, e.g. Col. 8.17.12 *salsamentorum omnium purgamenta, quae cetariorum officinis everruntur* and in Christian authors, e.g. Aug. *C. Iul.* 2.10.37 *nautae, tabernarii, cetarii, coqui, lani. Cetarius* appears once in Cicero as well, *Off.* 1.150, when he is, however, quoting a line from Terence.

Adjectives in *-inus*. A majority of the adjectives of this termination are derived from the names of animals. These are very common in the *sermo plebeius*. Such formations abound in comedy, especially in Plautus, in the satirists, and in agricultural authors, whereas their use by classical writers is chiefly confined to proverbial expressions, further evidence of their popular character (e.g. Cic. *Fam.* 9.18.3 *pluris iam pavones confeci quam tu pullos*

[12] For the colloquial character of such formations and their distribution in Latin literature, cf. Cooper (1895: 70–4).

[13] For colloquial elements in the language of Cassiodorus, cf. Fridh (1950: 46).

columbinos etc.). The suffix has survived in Romance languages as well, where it has acquired a diminutive force.[14] In EL as well these adjectives abound in comic poets, satirists and agricultural authors.

Terence shows his linguistic purism here once more, restricting himself to just one formation of this kind, in opposition to Plautus, who uses fifteen adjectives in *-inus*. *Mustelinus* occurs at *Eun.* 688–9 *hic est vietus vetus veternosus senex, colore mustelino*, in the speech of a low character, the *ancilla* Pythias. The word reappears in later colloquial sources, e.g. Plin. *Nat.* 30. 124 *ex utriculo mustelino* and Chiron. 686 *ruta<m> mustelinam.*

Diminutive nouns/adjectives. Both diminutive nouns and adjectives are extremely frequent in colloquial sources, especially those in *-culus, -a, -um*, mainly when, having lost their diminutive force, they are equivalent to the simple nouns or adjectives from which they derive. In EL, they abound in the comedy of Plautus, in opposition to Terence, who is more reserved in the use of such formations.[15]

In CL, Cicero uses them mainly in his letters. Elsewhere they occur more often in his court speeches, which are closer to everyday language, than in his state speeches or in his early works, where he often uses linguistic features of a colloquial nature avoided in his later works.[16] Seneca later uses diminutives mainly in his letters. Authors like Caesar, Sallust and Nepos use diminutive forms sparingly.

As for poets, Axelson (1945: 39–45) has remarked that high poetic genres (epic, tragedy etc.) are not fond of such formations. Even though diminutives are common in Lucretius, they are found mainly in colloquial poetic genres: Catullus, Horace mainly in the *Satires, Epistles* and *Epodes*, Vergil in the *Eclogues*, Juvenal, Martial, Propertius, Ovid,[17] Late Latin poetry etc.

Diminutives are also common in technical treatises, Pliny, Cato, Varro, Palladius etc. They also appear in the language of Petronius

[14] For the colloquial character of such formations and extended data on their distribution, cf. Cooper (1895: 139).

[15] For the colloquial character of diminutives even in EL, cf. also Wahrmann (1908: 103).

[16] For this cf. H-Sz 42*, Löfstedt (1911: 13 n.2).

[17] For the more colloquial character of the language of Propertius and Ovid, cf. H-Sz 43*.

and Apuleius, as well as in late Latin vulgar texts (Peregr. Aeth., Greg. Tour.) and Christian authors, especially Augustine and Hieronymus.[18] This does not mean that all diminutive formations are distinctively colloquial. Those discussed here are the ones found in colloquial sources only.[19]

1. *cistella*: the diminutive form of *cista*. The word appears in comedy, e.g. in Plautus, *Rud.* 1109 etc.; in satire, e.g. Martialis 13.36 tit. *cistella olivarum*; as well as in late Latin technical, treatises, e.g. Pallad. 4.10.35 *ficus in cistellis servetur*,[20] and medieval Christian texts, e.g. Pallad. *Hist. mon.* I 23 p. 304[c] *inveni cistellam quae uvas . . . habebat.* The word is found at *Eun.* 753 *cistellam, Pythias, domo ecfer*, in the speech of the *meretrix* Thais.
2. *tardiusculus*: the word appears in Plautus, e.g. *Cist.* 380 *eo sum tardiuscula*, and later in Augustine.[21] In Terence it is found at *Heaut.* 514–15 *videlicet ille Cliniai servos tardiusculust*, in the speech of the rustic *senex* Chremes.
3. *grandiusculus*: this is the reading offered by both Donatus and Eugraphius at *Andr.* 814 *grandiuscula iam profectast illinc.* The diminutive, referring to age, occurs later several times in Augustine, e.g. *Epist.* 27.2, *Serm.* 302.1, *In epist. Ioh.* 9.1 p. 2045, *Epist.* 262.8 etc. The word is used by Crito while addressing the *ancilla* Mysis.

Verbs

Verbs in *-illare*. Such diminutive derivative verbs are productive in colloquial sources (Plautus, Varro) but are rare in higher genres. This is especially the case with those derived from verbal stems, such as *sorbillo*, derived from *sorbeo*.[22] Of the seven verbs of this kind to be found in Cicero none is traced to a verbal stem. The suffix has also survived in the Romance languages, a further proof of its mainly colloquial character. In Terence we find once *sorbillare* at *Ad.* 591 *carpam et cyathos sorbillans* (the reading offerred by Σ vs. *sorbilans* in the Kauer and Lindsay edition) *paullatim hunc*

[18] For detailed distributional patterns, analytical discussion and further bibliography, cf. H-Sz 774–7.

[19] For the colloquial character of such diminutive formations, see also Cooper (1895: 164–94). For diminutives in EL, cf. also Conrad (1930–2: 74–84, 127–48); for diminutives in Terence, cf. also Minarini (1983: 161–73).

[20] For the colloquial character of the language of Palladius, cf. Svennung (1935).

[21] Cf. Cooper (1895: 191 n. 9).

[22] Cf. for this *OLD* s.v., Ernout and Meillet (1951: 1124) 'diminutif familier et affectif'; for the colloquial character of verbs in *-illare*, cf. also Cooper (1895: 243–5).

producam diem, in the speech of the slave Syrus. The verb occurs in comedy and reappears later in the novel of Apuleius, e.g. *Met.* 2.16, 3.14.

Verbs in *-issare*. Such hybrid formations show their colloquial character from EL, being very common in comedy, especially in Plautus.[23] Avoided by the purists of the classical era, Cicero and Caesar, such verbs become common again in medical and Christian authors. The suffix has also remained in the Romance languages.[24]

In Terence we find *patrissare* at *Ad.* 564 *laudo: Ctesipho, patrissas* by the rustic *senex* Demea. The word is restricted to comedy, e.g. also Plaut. *Most.* 638–9 *euge! Philolaches patrissat*, and reappears later in the colloquial language of Apuleius, e.g. *Fl.* 3 *cum in artificio patrissaret tibicinii* (cf. also *pytissare*, found only in comedy, at *Heaut.* 457 by the *senex* Chremes).

Frequentatives. These show a particular productivity in colloquial sources, especially when, having lost their frequentative sense, they are used as equivalents to the simple verbs they derive from.[25] Even in EL the colloquial character of such formations is evident by their frequency in comedy, especially in Plautus, in contrast to Terence, who is here again more reserved. In the later history of Latin, iterative verbs are found mainly in colloquial and archaising authors. They belong to the vulgar linguistic register of Petronius' freedmen[26] and are very productive in Late Latin vulgar authors (Chiron, Vitae patr.). This does not entail of course, as in the case of diminutives, that every frequentative verb is by definition colloquial. The formations to be discussed here occur in colloquial sources only; having lost their frequentative/iterative force, they have sunk to the level of the equivalent simple verb.

Commetare is found at *Heaut.* 444 *commetare ad mulierculam* by Chremes. The verb appears mainly in comedy, in Plautus, e.g. *Capt.* 185 *meus scruposam victus commetat viam* and possibly

[23] For their colloquial character even in EL, see Wahrmann (1908: 94, 103).
[24] For a discussion of the colloquial character of such formations, cf. Cooper (1895: 321).
[25] For frequentatives in colloquial speech, cf. Cooper (1895: 205–16), H-Sz 297.
[26] Cf. H-Sz 297.

at *Men.* 1019 *nimis bene ora commetavi atque ex mea sententia* (*commentavi* according to B²), in Afranius, e.g. *tog.* 344 *quo tu conmetas*, in Nov. *atel.* 7 *commetant lupi*. Apart from comedy, it also occurs in Script. RR, e.g. Var. *R.* 3.5.16 *pisciculi . . . commetant.*[27] The word seems to be an EL colloquialism fitting the general archaising flavour of Chremes' speech.

Category B

Substantives and adjectives

Substantives in *-tor*, *-trix*. These derivatives are agent nouns, e.g. *acceptor* = *is qui accipit*. Even though such derivatives are common in CL as well, popular sources favour them, as is also the case with verbal abstracts in *-tio*, in the sense that every verb was capable of giving its corresponding *nomen agentis*. In EL, it is in Plautus that these forms show a particular concentration (158), whereas in CL Cicero used them mainly in his letters.[28] In Silver Latin, many are also found in Pliny and Martial. These derivatives, however, show a particular productivity in the Christian authors (Tertullian, Augustine and Hieronymus). What is more, the masculine suffix remained in full use in all Romance languages as well.[29]

Extortor appears in comedy and later in Christian authors, e.g. Aug. *C. Gaud.* 2.8.8 p. 264, 22 *crudelis tortor et vilentus extortor*, 1.27.31 p. 229, 19 *Donatistae isti suarum animarum extortores et alienarum tortores*. The word occurs in Terence at *Phorm.* 374 *bonorum extortor, legum contortor*, in the speech of the slave Geta. Similarly, the feminine form *advorsatrix* appears only in comedy, e.g. Plaut. *Most.* 257 *nunc adsentatrix scelesta est, dudum advorsatrix erat*, where we also find *adsentatrix*, another formation eschewed by CL speech and found later as an adjective in a fifth-century Christian author, Prosp. *Epigr.* 88 (85). *Advorsatrix* appears later in the language of the Christian author Tertullian as

[27] At *Schol. carm.* 1.17.1 the text is not sound. *Commodet* is the reading given by all manuscripts; *conmettet* is simply a conjecture by Stowasser.

[28] Cf. Stinner (1879: 6).

[29] For a detailed analysis on the distribution of these forms in colloquial sources, cf. Cooper (1895: 58–70).

well, *Anim.* 31.[30] The word is found in Terence at *Heaut.* 1007 *quin tu in ea re mi fueris advorsatrix* in the speech of the *senex* Chremes.

Adjectives in *-osus*. Although not avoided by higher literary genres, such formations diachronically abound in colloquial sources. They are very frequent in the comic dramatists, especially in Plautus, and show particular productivity in technical treatises, the Scriptt. RR (Cato 16 forms, Varro 13/6 new, Col. 31/18 new, Pliny 48 new) and veterinary or medical writers (new formations: Pelag. Vet. 5, Veg. Vet. 11, Cael. Aur. 24). These adjectives are also very common in Apuleius as well as in African inscriptions. The *Appendix Probi* as well (GLK 199 12–12) censures the use of such formations: *rabidus non rabiosus*. In Romance languages the suffix is still productive.[31]

Cadaverosus appears in comedy and later in the Christian author Ambrosius,[32] e.g. *In psalm.* 118. Cf. also *Serm.* 16.28 *nihil cadaverosum, nihil mortuum ore tuo sumas*. The word occurs in Terence at *Hec.* 441 *cadaverosa facie* in the speech of the *adulescens* Pamphilus, but while he is addressing a low character, namely his slave Parmeno.

Adverbs

Adverbs in *-im*. Adverbs of this kind abound in EL sources where, however, they are not avoided by genres like tragedy and epic. Yet, diachronically, such formations are favoured in colloquial sources (Pliny, Apuleius, Christian authors etc.).[33] Cicero, for example, uses no form in *-im* for which the classical language has a corresponding form in *-e*. *Unciatim* occurs in comedy and later in Pliny's *Nat.* 28.139 *datur et phthisicis unciatim cum vini veteris hemina decocta*. The word occurs in Terence at *Phorm.* 43–4 *quod*

[30] For the colloquial character of Tertullian's language, cf. Cooper (1895: xxxvi).

[31] For the distribution of such forms, cf. Cooper (1895: 122–32).

[32] For Ambrosius as a source of vulgar Latin, cf. Rohlfs (1956: 39).

[33] For distributional patterns suggesting the colloquial character of the suffix, cf. Cooper (1895: 196–200), Wahrmann (1908: 89).

ille unciatim vix de demenso suo suom defrudans genium conpersit miser in the speech of the protatic slave Davus.

Verbs

Verbs compounded with *ad*-. Verbs compounded with *ad*-, as is also the case with *cum*- and *de*- compounded verbal forms, are common in colloquial sources, especially those which have sunk to the semantic level of their equivalent simple verb, since the prefix has lost its intensifying character. Such formations are very common in Plautus, in technical treatises and in Christian authors. They occur very frequently in the Romance languages as well (*arrivare, arriver, arribar*). Within CL, on the other hand, this prefix is not productive at all and gives few new forms.[34]

In Terence we find *apposcere* at *Heaut.* 838 *porro haec talenta dotis adposcunt duo*, uttered by the senex Chremes. Apart from in comedy, the verb occurs later in Horace's *Epistles*, e.g. 2.2.100 *si plus adposcere visus.*

Verbs compounded with *con*-. Such formations are very common in comedy, especially in Plautus, where one can find a large number of *hapax legomena*. Whereas in CL the prefix is not productive, as is evidenced by the reluctance shown by classical authors to add to the extant number of such verbs, it becomes common again in Gellius, probably due to his archaic tendencies, and in Christian authors, especially in Tertullian and the Sardinian Bishop Lucifer Calaritanus.[35]

In Terence *commitigare* occurs at *Eun.* 1028 *utinam tibi conmitigari videam sandalio caput!*, in the sense of 'to soften', i.e. semantically with no difference from its uncompounded equivalent, *mitigare* (cf. *OLD* s.v.). It is uttered by the parasite Gnatho. The word appears once more in this sense, with reference to the human body again, in Aug. *C. Iul.* 3.5.11 *verum etiam capita sandaliis muliercularum commitigentur*. Similarly, *collocupleto* with

[34] For the colloquial character of such formations, cf. Cooper (1895: 258–62), Wahrmann (1908: 95).

[35] For an analytic examination of the distribution of such formations, cf. Cooper (1895: 262–71).

the meaning of the simple *locupleto* (cf. *ThLL* III 1649) appears at *Heaut.* 257–8 *tu interea loci conlocupletasti te, Antiphila* in the speech of the *adulescens* Clinia, in a conversation with the slave Syrus and, what is more, in an emotional outburst, when he is persuaded that his beloved has betrayed him for money. The verb is also found in *Rhet. Her.* 2.28, 2.46.

Syntax

The autonomous partitive genitive *novi negoti* occurs only once in Terence, at *Phorm.* 709–10 *ante brumam autem novi negoti incipere* in the mouth of the slave Geta. It appears twice in Plautus, *Poen.* 640–1 *si quid boni adportatis, habeo gratiam. boni de nostro nec ferimus nec damus, Most.* 1017–18 *mecum ut ille hic gesserit, dum tu hinc abes, negoti.* This construction appears later in Late Latin and Vulgar sources (Chiron, Ven. Fort. etc.) as well. Cf. also Petr. 46. 7 *quod si resilierit, destinavi illum artificii* (the reading of the manuscripts accepted by Löfstedt) *docere, aut tonstreinum aut praeconem aut certe causidicum.*[36]

Lexicon

Nouns and adjectives

lapis The word in the sense of *inutibilis, stultus* is restricted to comedy and Late Latin Christian texts. It is commonly found in Plautus, e.g. *Merc.* 632, *Mil.* 236. In Terence it is found at *Hec.* 214 *tu inquam, mulier, quae me omnino lapidem, non hominem putas* in the speech of the *senex* Laches (the country *senex* of the comedy), at *Heaut.* 831 *quid stas, lapis?* uttered by the slave Syrus and finally at *Heaut.* 917 *ni essem lapis!* by the *senex* Chremes. Later this meaning of the substantive appears in Hier. *Hom. Orig. in Luc.* 22 p. 138.13 (ad. 3, 8).

mastigia This word, with the meaning of *servus flagellis dignus, homo nequam,* is common in Plautus, e.g. *Cas.* 361, *Curc.* 567, *Most.* 1, *Rud.* 1022. It reappears in the satiric poetry of Lucilius 669 and in the Christian author Ambr. *Hel.* 8.24 *ferietur . . . coquorum mastigiarum machaera.* In Terence the word appears once at *Ad.* 781 *non manum abstines, mastigia?* in the speech of the rustic *senex* Demea.

[36] For the colloquial character of the construction, cf. also Löfstedt (1911: 108–9).

Pronouns

quidam Colloquial is the use of *quidam* referring with contempt to a well-known person or someone present at the moment of the utterance.[37] This usage appears in comedy as well as in satire (e.g. Mart. 9.97.1 *rumpitur invidia quidam*). In Terence *quidam* is used in this sense at *Eun.* 483 *neque tibi obstat, quod quidam facit*, by the slave Parmeno.

ipsus/e Colloquial also is the use of *ipsus/e* in the sense of *dominus*, master. This usage appears in comedy, e.g. Plaut. *Aul.* 356, *Cas.* 790, in satire, e.g. Var. *Men.* 47, Juv. 5.30, in Plin. *Nat.* 21.7,[38] Petr. 29.8, in inscriptions, e.g. CIL X 2363 and finally in Late Latin texts, e.g. Cassiod. *Var.* 5.16.4.[39] The usage is confined in Terence to servile speech, cf. *Andr.* 360, 377, 605 by the slave Davus, in v. 415 by the slave Byrria, in v. 265 by the *ancilla* Mysis, at *Eun.* 535 by the *ancilla* Pythias and finally at *Phorm.* 215 and 852 by the slave Geta. Such a usage does appear in the speech of a high character, the *senex* Simo at *Andr.* 598 when addressing his slave Davus.

Verbs

posse The use of *posse* in the sense of 'to be capable of sexual intercourse with' seems also to be colloquial, occurring in comedy and satire, cf. Hor. *Epod.* 12.15 *Inachiam ter nocte potes*,[40] Mart. 3.32.1 *non possum vetulam*, 11.97.1–2 *una nocte quater possum: sed quattuor annis si possum, peream, te Telesilla semel*. In Terence *possum* appears with this meaning at *Eun.* 665–6 *ego amatores audieram mulierum esse eos maxumos, sed nil potesse* in the speech of the *ancilla* Pythias.[41]

crepo This verb, referring to doors in the sense of the Greek ψοφῶ, is another colloquial usage restricted to comedy, epistolography and the colloquial novel, e.g. Plaut. *Amph.* 496, *Aul.* 665, *Bacch.* 1057, *Cas.* 813, *Curc.* 486; see also Sen. *Ep.* 80.1 *non crepabit subinde ostium* [*crepuit* . . . codd.], Petr. 99.5 *cum crepuit ostium impulsum*. Three out of four Terentian instances occur in the speech of low and rustic characters; it is used twice by the rustic *senex* Chremes at *Heaut.* 173–4 *sed quid crepuerunt fores hinc a me?*, 613 *quid est quod tam a nobis graviter crepuerunt fores?* and once by the parasite Gnatho at *Eun.* 1029 *sed fores crepuerunt ab ea*. A fourth instance occurs in the speech of Ctesipho at *Ad.* 264, when addressing the slave Syrus: *quidnam foris crepuit?*.

[37] For the colloquial character of the expression, cf. H-Sz 197.

[38] For the *sermo plebeius* in the language of Pliny the Elder, cf. Cooper (1895: xxxix–xl).

[39] For Cassiodorus' indulgence in colloquialisms, cf. Fridh (1950: 46 and passim).

[40] For colloquial language in Horace's *Epodes*, cf. also Mankin (1995: 12–14).

[41] For the colloquial character of the expression, cf. also Müller (1997: 225), *OLD* s.v. 7b.

emungo This verb, construed with the ablative of separation in the sense of *fraudulenter aliquem aliqua re spoliare, privare*, is also colloquial; it is restricted to comedy, e.g. Plaut. *Bacch.* 1101 *miserum me auro esse emunctum*, and satire, e.g. Lucil. 881. Later it reappears in the epistolography of Sidonius Apollinaris, e.g. *Epist.* 7.2.8, 9.7.1. The verb is used in this sense once in Terence at *Phorm.* 682 *emunxi argento senes* in the speech of the slave Geta.[42]

enico This word, in the sense of *vexando molestias praebere*, occurs only in comedy, e.g. in Plautus, *Asin.* 920–1 *pol me quidem miseram odio enicavit*; see also *Pers.* 48a, 484, *Rud.* 944. It reappears later in Aug. *Soliloq.* 2. 13. 24 p. 896 *loquere iam, hic sum; quid enicas?*, and in *CE* 1870, A. 5 *et suspensos enecant animosque torquent.*[43] In Terence, with the exception of *Andr.* 660, all instances of the verb are found in the speech of low characters or are uttered by high characters when addressing low characters, at *Eun.* 554 *qui me . . . rogitando obtundat enicet* by the ephebe Chaerea, at *Phorm.* 384 *enicas* by Demipho to the parasite Phormio and in v. 856 *enicas* by Antipho to the slave Geta.

scortor The verb is frequent in comedy with the meaning of 'to consort with prostitutes', e.g. in Plautus, *Asin.* 270, *Merc.* 1018, *Pseud.* 1133. Later it reappears in Apuleius, *Met.* 7. 11, where it is used in the sense of 'to behave like a prostitute', 'to act promiscuously' (cf. *OLD* s.v.), see also *Vulg.* II Macc. 6.4. It occurs once in Varro *L.* 7. 84 when, however, discussing the use of the verb in a line of Terence. In Terence the verb appears at *Heaut.* 206 *scortari crebro nolunt, nolunt crebro convivarier* in the speech of the rustic *senex* Chremes and at *Ad.* 101–2 *non est flagitium, mihi crede, adulescentulum scortari neque potari* by Micio when addressing his brother, the rustic Demea.

Iuncturae

The combination *flocci facere* with the meaning of *parvi momenti aestimare* is another colloquial usage, restricted to comedy, e.g. Plaut. *Cas.* 332, *Men.* 423, 994, *Truc.* 606, 769, see also Iuvent. *com.* 5. This construction appears later in Cicero's *Epistles* as well, e.g. *Att.* 1.16.13, 4.15.4, 13.50.3. The syntagm occurs in Terence once, in the speech of the soldier (ephebe) Chaerea, at *Eun.* 303 *tum autem qui illum flocci fecerim.* See also at v. 411 *ego non flocci pendere* by the soldier Thraso.

[42] For the figurative use of *emungere*, cf. also Callahan (1964: 67–78).

[43] For *Carm. epigr.* belonging to the *sermo vulgaris*, cf. Rohlfs (1956: 10); for the colloquial character of this use of the verb, see also *ThLL* V.$_2$ 563 *subest genus quodam hyperbolice dicendi, quale sermoni cottidiano adamatum esse constat.*

Conclusions

This research on the colloquial elements of the language of Terence has yielded surprisingly few entries, in comparison both to the abundance of features to be examined in the following chapters, under the headings of archaism, long-winded speech etc., and many colloquial elements discussed by other scholars and relegated in the present study to table 1, presented at the end of this chapter. The reasons for this scarcity are twofold: the first is the employment of a strict methodological distributional criterion (after Maltby's methodological principles), in order to maximise the value of the analysis; this necessity has led me to reject most of the findings of earlier scholarships not as *wrong*, but as *uncertain*, as *not proven*. The second reason is of a different nature, but not less crucial. It is connected with the choices of the author, Terence, himself. Terence has always been considered to be *a puri sermonis amator*, and indeed the relatively low proportion of popular or colloquial elements in his plays, after a strict comparative and distributional research has been carried out, should be read as confirmation of this.

1. The totality of linguistic elements examined here belong to general categories (such as diminutives, verbal derivatives, etc.) which show great productivity in colloquial sources. Furthermore, only those individual lexical items or constructions which are completely absent from higher genres, even if the general category to which they belong is not, have been taken into consideration. In this way, we may claim with a considerable degree of certainty that the elements discussed in the present section have a more popular character.
2. Colloquialisms, in the sense described above, are found in the speech of low characters, slaves, parasites, *meretrices*, or country *senes*, namely Chremes in *Heautontimoroumenos* and, to a lesser extent, Demea in *Adelphoe* and Laches in *Hecyra*.
3. Colloquial features found in the speech of other characters are mainly used when addressing low and rustic characters, that is, when accommodating their language to the linguistic level of their interlocutors. On the other hand, low and rustic characters use such features without any particular concentration, and with no dependence upon their interlocutors.

Table 1 *Colloquial elements in the language of Terence*

Numbers
- collective/generic singular
- sociative plural
- plural for singular when addressing a person representing his whole family

Cases
- accusative of exclamation
- partitive genitive denoting person after *quid*
- partitive genitive with neuter pronouns and adverbs denoting place
- partitive genitive with *nullus*, *nemo*
- possessive pronoun instead of objective genitive
- ethic dative/reflexive dative
- instrumental ablative with *fio*, *facere*
- *ad* + accusative for dative
- *de* + ablative for genitive

Adjectives/adverbs
- adverbs denoting quality (*bene probe pulchre*) as equivalents to *valde* in combinations with adjectives
- adverb + *esse* syntagms in place of monolectic semantically equivalent verbs

Pronouns/pronominal adverbs
- *ego, tu* etc. as subjects with finite verbal forms
- *suus* in non-self-referential cases
- *hic* for *is*
- combinations of the type *hic – hic, ille – ille*
- repetition of the subject/object of the main clause by means of *is, ibi* etc.
- pronominal adverbs in place of a case of a pronoun

Prepositions
- modal use of *ad* with adjectives
- *ad* denoting hostile attitude
- *apud* for *in*
- concise/adnominal use of *a(b)*
- *in* + ablative for *in* + accusative
- *cum* + ablative in indignant statements

Genera verbi
- impersonal passive for personal active constructions
- simple verbs for their reflexive equivalents

Tenses and moods
- present for future
- future for imperative
- imperfect for events still taking place in the present
- perfect referring to future
- *coepi* + infinitive periphrasis for the ingressive perfect
- pluperfect for perfect
- future perfect for simple future
- perfect as apodosis in conditionals of the unreal
- jussive subjunctive especially of the second person singular
- infinitive of purpose (found commonly in EL/archaising sources)
- infinitive of indignation
- omission of the subject in 'accusativus cum infinitivo' syntagms
- periphrastic verbal forms by means of active present participle
- *non* in place of *ne* + subjunctive of prohibition
- imperatives substituted by question clauses
- gerund as participle

(*cont.*)

Table 1 (*cont.*)

Nominal and verbal ellipsis Negation
– *non* as simple negative particle
– *nihil, numquam, nullus, minime, minus* = *non*
– double negative

Questions
– *quid, quidni, qui* instrumental questions
– omission of introductive interrogative particles
– *ne-* confirmation questions
– question clauses split into two or more smaller interrogative questions

Coordination/subordination
– asyndeton
– repetition in place of relative-clause subordination
– relative pronouns and particles in place of conjunctions and other link particles
– parenthetic clauses
– proleptic accusative
– paratactic subjunctive constructions in place of subordination
– *postulo* + *ut* syntagms
– *etiam* introducing questions denoting impatience
– *at* introducing threats, curses, oaths, requests, exclamations
– repetition of a statement with *autem* in question form
– reassuring *nam* in combination with *pol, hercle*
– the subjunctive without *ut (facias volo*)
– parataxis in place of conditional clauses
– asyndetic parataxis of two contrary presuppositions
– coordination for 'accusativus + infinitivo' syntagms
– coordination for a consecutive clause (only in colloquial sources and in the archaising Sallust)
– indicative in indirect questions
– indicative in consecutive/relative clauses
– confusion between *qui–quis* clauses
– relative clauses without antecedent
– linking of relative clauses by means of *et, que* with or without repetition of the relative
– *dum* = 'since' with the present in place of perfect
– *quia* + subjunctive causal clauses
– interrogative/exclamative *quam* + verbs
– *quam* = *quam ut, si cum, qui*, i.e. omission of the second conjunction in *quam* + comparative syntagms or *tam*
– *secus quam* sequences
– interrogative *ut*
– *tam . . . quam* in the sense of 'as *much as*'
– *ita . . . ut* in oaths and declarations/protestations, *ita* + infinitive
– independent *ut* clauses
– coordination of two *ut* clauses the one being syntactically dependent upon the other
– *ut* giving the standpoint for judging something
– *ut fit* formulaic expressions
– conditional *si* clauses, where the verb in the main clause is either in the optative or the imperative
– *nisi* = *sed, etsi, tametsi, nisi si, quasi si*
– attraction of antecedent

Individual lexemes
– *adiutare* for *adiuvare*
– *aetas* = 'ages'
– *ambulare* for *ire*
– *auscultare* for *audire*
– *abire* = 'get out of this'
– *comedere* for *edere*
– *grandis* for *magnus*
– *narrare* for *dicere*

Table I (*cont.*)

– *omitto* = 'forget'	– *crispus*
– *plorare* for *flere*	– *ilicet*
– *portare* for *ferre*	– *inpendio*
– *reddo* = 'pay back'	– *malum*
– *satius* = *melius*	– *mancupium*
– *sescenti* for denoting a large number	– *mansio*
– *sic* = *talis*	– *ostium*
– *sino* = 'to let a thing pass'	– *praeterhac*
– *suavis* = nice	– *quippe*
– *vivere* = *esse*	– *sex septem*
– *magis* as a reinforcing particle	– *submoneo*
– *hodie* as an intensive particle	– *utique*
– *bellus*	– double forms, e.g. *ubiubi*
– *casa*	– simple answers, e.g. *plane, recte, ita, verum, admodum* etc.
– *colaphus*	
– *commodum*	

CHAPTER 2

ARCHAISMS

Introduction and overall review

Terence stands closer to CL than Plautus. There is, however, a group of lexical, morphological and syntactical phenomena that occur in Terence in both their Early Latin and their classical forms. In these cases the EL equivalent seems to be rather the exception than the rule; it is found rarely, whereas the CL equivalent is the regular form. In Terence one often finds that the EL feature is restricted to specific plays or characters, while all others use the CL form.

Maltby was the first to show that such EL linguistic features are often used by old people (*satias* for the CL *satietas, ai(e)bam* imperfects, *scilcet* + infinitive constructions); such features impart an old-fashioned character to senile speech, differentiating it from the language of all other characters, who opt for the CL equivalent. Even though some of Maltby's conclusions are to be proved correct, his work suffers from some methodological infelicities. In detail:

1. He uses insufficient data, especially on the morphological and lexical level.
2. Several of the examples he adduces do not correspond to the safe criterion set out by him in his introduction for characterising a specific feature as EL, namely that the feature in question should occur in EL sources and disappear from the later history of the language with the exception of archaising authors or genres (e.g. Fronto, Apuleius, epic of the classical era etc.). For example, the *faxo, faxim* forms, although being EL *-sso, -ssim* formations, never cease to exist and are well attested as formulaic or fossilised forms in both CL and PC Latin.
3. In several instances, his remarks on the distribution of a specific feature in Latin literature are false. His claim, for example, that

reduplicated perfect forms of *fero*, i.e. *tetuli* for *tuli*, reappear after the EL period only as an intentional archaism in Lucretius and Catullus (1979: 138 n. 22) is not true. Such forms reappear also in Hieronymus, inscriptions etc. (cf. N-W III 346–8).

4. Although Maltby points out that in Terence's first play, *Andria*, linguistic characterisation by means of archaisms is not so clear cut as in subsequent plays,[1] he fails to notice that it is also absent from *Eunuchus*, a play which differs from the other Terentian comedies in all linguistic aspects.

The above criticism of Maltby's work has, I believe, sufficiently shown the necessity for a new and more thorough examination of the use of archaisms in Terentian drama, based on more secure methodological criteria.

Aims and objectives

In this chapter I shall examine all the EL morphological, syntactic and lexical linguistic features (except those already discussed by Maltby) which also exhibit a CL alternative in Terence. In such cases, the CL equivalent often is the regular form in Terence. My aim is to show how these EL forms are more commonly found in the speech of old people. Secondly, I shall show, following Maltby again, that there is a binary linguistic opposition between the pairs of *senes*: Demea in *Adelphoe* and Chremes in *Heauton-timoroumenos* are more archaic than their respective counterparts Micio and Menedemus.

[1] For *Andria* in particular, Maltby suggests that several archaic forms in that play simply reflect its earlier date. Terence rejects several of these archaic forms in his later plays (e.g. *medicor* for *medeor*, *qui* in place of *ut* with verbs of striving etc.). This lack of restriction of several archaic features to senile speech in *Andria* is due to its immature character in matters of linguistic characterisation. In distributional patterns, *Andria* differs significantly from other Terentian plays, not only on the level of archaisms but also in the matter of long-winded expressions, hellenising lexicon and, up to a point, colloquialisms (see relevant chapters, 3, 4, 1). Apart from those discussed here, for an account of archaisms in *Andria*, cf. also Maltby (1976: 235–6, 1979, especially 139, n. 30 (22 archaisms uttered by or directed to old people vs. 10 by others)). For *Eunuchus*, cf. Barsby (1999: 326 and passim), who, however, characterises forms that regularly occur in CL (*deum*) as archaic. For the distribution of *deum*, cf. N–W I 172–6.

Methodological note

First of all, a terminological remark is necessary: for deciding upon the archaic or old-fashioned character of a specific linguistic phenomenon, five general factors have been taken into account:

1. Order of appearance of a linguistic option in the course of the history of Latin (i.e. older vs. more recent linguistic equivalents).
2. Greater frequency of a specific feature in Early Latin as opposed to scarcity or avoidance in CL (norm vs. exceptional usage, productivity vs. fossilised usage).
3. Literary genres, authors and context of appearance in CL of a specific phenomenon considered to be archaic.
4. Verse position (archaisms tend to be used at the end of the line or just before the caesura for metrical reasons).
5. The testimony of ancient authors (cf. Cic. in *Orat.*), especially grammarians (Donatus, Servius etc.), concerning the archaic flavour of a specific linguistic element at least for their own era.

EL in this study refers to features which are well attested in the preclassical period (mainly Plautus, Cato, Ennius, Naevius, Accius, Pacuvius and other dramatists of the earlier period, Early Latin inscriptions) and are rare in CL/PC or die out altogether, with the exception of random instances occurring mainly (a) in formulaic expressions of the official, legal and sacral language, which often opts for the retention of archaic linguistic elements, or (b) in deliberately archaising authors such as Sallust, Livy and, to a lesser degree, Tacitus,[2] Gellius, Fronto, Apuleius etc. or (c) epic or didactic verse and tragedy as deliberate archaisms (e.g. *duellum* in place of *bellum*, *patrare* instead of *efficere, conficere* etc.).[3]

[2] As for archaism in individual authors: in Catullus, Heusch (1954); in Gellius, Holford Strevens (1988), Marache (1957); in Fronto, Foster (1912), Schuster (1931); in Livy, Riemann (1885); in Tacitus, Adams (1972, 1973), Valmaggi (1891); for Iulius Valerius, Fassbender (1909); for Ausonius, Green (1991); for EL authors, Engelbrecht (1883), Harsh (1940), Smith (1890).

[3] Several archaic features equally in morphology (e.g. first-declension singular genitives in *-ai*), in the lexicon (e.g. *ensis, -que . . . -que*) and in syntax (use of infinitives instead of clausal structures) having been displaced from the prose register of CL are found in poetry. Cf. also Tarrant (1976: 198, 201, 219).

Morphology

Nouns declension

First declension

Genitive singular. The termination *-ai* of first-declension nouns is restricted to EL and archaising sources. Even by the early second century *-a¯i¯* was already archaic. Ennius tends to keep the disyllabic form for the verse end and this is also the case with Lucretius.[4] In Terence this genitive seems obsolete and is used only twice, at *Andr.* 439 *hospitai* by Simo and at *Heaut.* 514–15 *Cliniai* by Chremes.

Second declension

Vocative singular. A further non-classical feature is found in the use of the vocative *puere*[5] instead of the normal CL form *puer*, found three times in Terence's comedies (cf. *Andr.* 84, *Ad.* 940, *Phorm.* 152). In Terence the archaic form is found twice, once in the speech of an old man, the *senex* Laches at *Hec.* 719 *eho puere curre*. Another instance occurs at *Eun.* 624 in the mouth of Dorias.

Genitive plural. Archaic also is the use of the termination *-um* instead of *-orum* (the normal termination in Terence) in the plural genitive of second-declension nouns and adjectives.[6] The termination is usually retained, however, in words for coins and measures and in a number of stereotyped phrases, e.g. *deum, virum, liberum, meum*, accepted even in CL. Terence uses these CL forms at *Phorm.* 393 *talentum*, *Ad.* 411 *maiorum suom*, *Ad.* 793 *nostrum liberum*, *Andr.* 237, *Eun.* 943 *pro deum fidem*, *Andr.* 246,

4 It is also found in Ennius, Lucilius, Plautus, Accius, Pacuvius, Vergil, Cicero only in poetry, Prudentius; for the form as an archaism from the second century BC, cf. Coleman (1999: 41–2), Fordyce (1977: 146), cf. also Quintilian's comment (*Inst.* 1. 7. 19) on the use of the form by Virgil, *amantissimus vetustatis*.

5 For the archaic and archaising character of the form, cf. Barsby (1999: 204), Palmer (1954: 84), Cordier (1939: 36). In Plautus *puere* occurs very frequently: cf. *Asin.* 382, *Bacch.* 577, *Curc.* 75, *Merc.* 912, *Most.* 949, *Pers.* 792, *Pseud.* 170 etc., Caec. *com.* 93, Afran. *tog.* 193.

6 Genitives in *-u(o)m* are also found later as intentional archaisms, e.g. in Vergil (see Austin II 33, Fordyce (1977: 103)). The forms had also survived in official language, in expressions such as *triumvirum, sodium* etc.

Heaut. 61, *Hec.* 198 *pro deum atque hominum fidem, Phorm.* 351 *pro deum inmortalium.* On the other hand, only three really archaic terminations in *-um* occur in Terentian drama. They occur twice in the speech of Lucius Ambivius, the old man in the prologues of *Heautontimoroumenos* and *Hecyra*, *amicum ingenium*, *iniquom* at *Heaut.* 24, 27 respectively. Finally, the EL genitive plural of the third person possessive pronoun *suom* is uttered by the *senex* Demea at *Ad.* 411.[7]

Third declension

Locative singular. Another Early Latin feature can be found in the use of the temporal locative in *-i*, e.g. *luci* at *Ad.* 841 in the mouth of Demea.[8] This is a reading found in the codex Bembinus and the scholia Bembina and accepted by the editors. Donatus remarks: ἀρχαισμός, *nam 'cum primo luci' veteres dicebant.*

Fourth declension

Genitive. The use of *-uis* as termination for the genitive of the fourth-declension nouns is an EL feature (cf. also in Varro *quaestuis, partuis, fructuis, domuis, graduis, anuis*), which occurs in Terence once at *Heaut.* 287 *eius anuis causa opinor quae erat mortua* in the speech of the slave Syrus referring to an old person.

Pronouns

Personal pronouns

vostrarum. This is the archaic form of the second-person plural genitive of the personal pronoun in place of *vestri*,[9] found twice

[7] Cf. on the other hand *quorum* at *Phorm.* 887 by the parasite Phormio. For the archaic character of the form, cf. also Martin (1976: 167–8).

[8] Cf. D-K ad loc. 'die ältere und eigentliche Form des in temporalem Sinne gebrauchten Lokativs'; for the archaic/EL character of the form, see also Holford Strevens (1988: 41). *Luci* is found frequently in Plautus, e.g. *Amph.* 165, *Cas.* 786, *Cist.* 525, *Men.* 1005, *Merc.* 255, *Stich.* 364, as well as in other Early Latin and archaising authors, Atta *tog.* 9, Enn. *Ann.* 423, Com. pall. *inc.* 70, Varro *L.* 6.92, 9.60 (an edict), Gel. 2.29.1, as well as in legal documents: for the distribution of the form, cf. also *ThLL* VII 1906. One instance of the EL combination *cum primo luci* at Cic. *Off.* 3.112 is attributed to the influence of the annalistic tradition; see *ThLL* ibid. *haud dubie veterem quendam annalium scriptorem secutus.*

[9] Cf. Plaut. *Men.* 1085, *Pseud.* 186, *Stich.* 141, Caec. *com.* 146, *Titin. tog.* 56; for the archaic character of the form later in Livy, see also Oakley (1997–8 II: 491).

in the speech of an old person, the *senex* Laches at *Hec.* 216, 240. An exception occurs at *Heaut.* 386 in the speech of Bacchis. Terence, in this case again, stands closer to CL in using these forms sparingly. *Nostrarum* for *nostrum* occurs only once, at *Eun.* 678.

Verbs

Subjunctive

3rd decl. present. Another archaism is found in the use of the subjunctive *creduas* instead of *credas*, otherwise attested only in Plautus (cf. *Bacch.* 476, *Poen.* 747, *Trin.* 606). In Terence we normally find the CL subjunctive type *credas*: *Andr.* 899, *Heaut.* 623, *Eun.* 710, *Ad.* 857, *Heaut.* 591. Just once Terence uses *creduas* at *Phorm.* 993 *cave isti quicquam cred<u>as* in the end of the verse. The form is used by the *senex* Chremes.

Similarly, *duim*, *perduim* forms are early Latin traces of a subjunctive-optative in *-im* which survives mainly in old laws and other formulae, especially in some types of imprecation *di malum etc . . . duint*. Apart from these *duim, perduim* forms, found in imprecations (cf. *Phorm.* 519) which are well attested in the classical period as well (cf. e.g. Cic. *Catil.* 1.22, *Phil.* 10.13), in Terence we find only once the form *duim* at *Phorm.* 713 *ego curabo nequid verborum duit*, in the speech of Demipho.[10]

Apart from the common *faxo, faxim* forms, well attested in CL/PC Latin as well (cf. Cic. *Verr.* 3.81, *Fam.* 14.3.3, Petr. 95.3 etc., for *faxo* in Plautus; see Ashmore (1897)), we find in Terence just two cases of old Latin futures in *-so (xo)* or subjunctives in *-ssim (xi)*. One is found again in the linguistically Early Latin *Andria*, v. 760 *cave quoquam ex istoc excessis loco!*. The other example occurs at *Phorm.* 742 *ne me istoc posthac nomine appellassis* in the speech of the *senex* Chremes.

[10] *Duim* forms, apart from those occurring in formulaic imprecations, are found in Plautus, Cato, Livy, Ulpian, and Gaius drawing on the Twelve tables, Tacitus, Fronto; for the archaic character of the forms, cf. also Ernout and Thomas (1972: 244).

Subjunctive of *sum*

fuam This archaic alternative form of the present subjunctive of *sum* is frequent in Plautus and other EL authors,[11] but did not survive in CL except as an intentional archaism or for metrical convenience (e.g. Verg. *A.* 10.108 *Tros Rutulusne fuat*). These forms reappear later with some frequency only in archaising authors or passages (cf. Apul. *Apol.* 92, Fro. *De Eloq.* 2.10.3 etc.). Simple and compound forms of this archaic subjunctive do not occur in official inscriptions even of the second century; they are relatively more common in tragedy than in comedy; they tend, in both genres, to occur at the ends of iambic and trochaic verses and in formulaic expressions, like *fors fuat*, a further indication of their archaic flavour. In Terence this Early Latin form is found once at *Hec.* 610 *fors fuat pol*, in a formula expressing a wish, in the speech of Sostrata.[12]

siem This is an older form of the present subjunctive of *esse* in place of *sim* and occurs in EL or archaising sources only.[13] It is used in Terence chiefly at the end of the line or half-line *metri gratia*, where its iambic shape is metrically convenient, an indication that even in Terence's time the form may have had an old-fashioned flavour. It occurs within the line only twice, significantly in the speech of old men: at *Hec.* 637 by Phidippus and at *Ad.* 83 (at the beginning of the line) by Demea.

Imperative

3rd conjugation active present. In CL the active present imperatives *dic, duc, fac* drop the final *e*. The same rule holds for the compounds of *dic, duc* and *fer*. In true compounds of *facio* on the other hand (that is, with prepositions in opposition to *bene, male* + *facio* types) the vowel of the root is modified and the imperative is regular, e.g. *perfice*. In Plautus, forms retaining the final *e* are regular in all possible verse positions.

Whereas *face* is attested in the CL/PC period as well, not only in poetry but also in prose (Nepos, Ovid, Valerius Flaccus, Iuvenalis, Ausonius), *duce* and its derivative compounds occur in EL sources

[11] Cf. also Afran. *tog.* 280, Andr. *trag.* 23, Enn. *trag.* 151, Pac. *trag.* 116; for the archaic/EL character of the forms, see also Ernout and Thomas (1972: 244).

[12] The formula occurs in EL/archaising sources: Plautus, Terence, Fronto, Apuleius, Ausonius, Symmachus, Sidonius Apollinaris.

[13] For the archaic character of the form being the older equivalent, cf. Laidlaw (1938: 80), Barsby (1999: 95), Gratwick (1993: 147), Bailey (1949 I: 82); for the form being frequent or productive in pre-Ciceronian Latin and in Lucretius, cf. also *OLD* s.v.

only. The old form *duce* does not occur at all in Terence, who, in accordance with CL, uses in all cases *duc, Andr.* 818, *Eun.* 377, *Heaut.* 432 etc.[14]

As for the compound forms, however, we may note the following:

redduc/redduce. In Terence we normally find the form *redduc*, in both instances before vowels: *Hec.* 654 *redduc uxorem*, 698. At *Hec.* 605, however, Σ gives the EL form *redduce, mi gnate, da veniam hanc mihi, redduce illam*. It is not a coincidence, perhaps, that this non-classical form is found in the speech of the *matrona*, Sostrata, which is often interspersed with archaic linguistic features.

abduc/abduce. The EL *abduce*[15] is used twice by old people: at *Ad.* 482 *hunc abduce vinci* by the rustic Demea and at *Phorm.* 410 *abduce hanc* (A gives us again *abduc*) by Demipho. Cf. also *adduce* at *Phorm.* 309 *atque huc adduce*.

transduc/transduce. The form occurs twice in the speech of the *senex* Demea at *Ad.* 910, 917. Another instance occurs at *Heaut.* 744 in the speech of the slave Syrus.

Infinitive

Present passive. Another archaic feature common in Plautus and Terence is the present passive infinitive in *-ier*. These infinitive forms occur commonly in archaic inscriptions, but their restriction mainly to verse end in Plautus suggests they were already archaic in his time.[16] In Terence again the majority of the instances are found at the end of the verse, where the infinitive gives a short penultimate (*Andr.* 203, *Eun.* 164, *Heaut.* 206 etc.). There are, however, some cases where this archaic infinitive is used in other positions. This is the case at *Hec.* 827 *nescioquid suspicarier mage coepi* in the speech of Bacchis, which again is characterised by a penchant for archaisms. Another instance is *Ad.* 535 *laudarier te audit*, where

[14] *Dice* instead of *dic* is not found at all in Terence.

[15] *Abduce* is found elsewhere in Plautus, *Bacch.* 1031, *Curc.* 693, *Poen.* 1173 etc. See, however, in CL *adduc*, Cic. *Q.fr.* 2.9.4, *Tusc.* 2.37 etc.

[16] Cf. also Coleman (1999: 44–5); for infinitives in *-ier* as deliberate archaisms in the Augustan poets, see also Fordyce (1977: 72); for their use by Cicero mainly in archaising contexts, in poetry and in direct quotations of legal formulas, cf. also Zetzel (1995: 216).

laudarier is found in an extremely unusual initial position. Here it is uttered by the old slave Syrus.

Verb roots

coepi Only perfect stems of the verb are normally used in CL. Present stem forms belong mainly to Early Latin.[17] In Terence we find only once a present stem form of the verb *coepi*, the imperfect subjunctive *coeperet* at *Ad.* 397, uttered by Demea. The verb is found at the end of the verse, a fact which possibly once more indicates that it was felt to be archaic even in Terence's time.

mavolo This is an older form for *malo*, which is the normal equivalent in Terence (cf. McGlynn I 345). The form marks the transition from the archaic *magis volo* to *malo*.[18] The earlier form is found once in Terence at *Hec.* 540 *quamvis causam hunc suspicari quam ipsam veram mavolo* at the end of the line, a further indication of the archaic flavour of the form in Terence's time. This is the only instance of its use in Terence and is found in the speech of Myrrina.

Syntax

Expressions of purpose

Verb of movement + accusative supine

Another Early Latin feature is the use of *eo* + accusative supine construction as a periphrastic future when the notion of purpose is weak.[19] In Terence the supine constructions are common with main verbs of motion. However, there is a decrease in these periphrastic futures with the supine, especially of the intransitive type *accubitum, cubitum, dormitum ire*, which are very frequent in Plautus (44 times). In avoiding this Early Latin construction, Terence again

[17] Cf. *coepio* at Plaut. *Men.* 960, *coepiam* at Cato *orat.* 250 and Caecil *com.* 79, the infinitive *coepere* at *Pers.* 121.

[18] Cf. Sandys (1885: 168), Ernout (1953: 182); The verb seems to have been felt as archaic already in Plautus, because it is used only in certain positions in the verse, Plaut. *Asin.* 835, *Merc.* 421, *Poen.* 301, 303, *Rud.* 1413 etc. The present stem forms of the uncontracted verb occur in EL/archaising authors, namely Plautus, Terence, Iulius Valerius, *Itinerarium Alexandri Magni*. Only the perfect uncontracted form *mavoluit*, not found in any EL or archaising author, appears in Petr. 77.5.

[19] For the EL character of the construction and Terence's standing closer to CL in avoiding it, cf. also Maltby (1976: 18, 26).

stands closer to CL. The few instances of this old-fashioned construction are to be found again mainly in the speech of old people, at *Heaut.* 655 *ea lavatum dum it* by Sostrata, at *Phorm.* 462 *percontatum ibo* by the *senex* Demipho and at *Andr.* 134 *te is perditum* by Simo. One exception occurs at *Heaut.* 315 *is quaesitum*, spoken by Clitipho.

Gerundive expressions of purpose

The use of a dative gerundive to express purpose with certain verbal and adjectival phrases is a feature of Early Latin.[20] This is the only gerundive construction (otherwise so much favoured by classical speech) which is more common in Plautus (fourteen times) than in Terence. Here again Terence anticipates CL usage, where this construction is rare.

In CL dative constructions of this type occur mainly:

1. in legal and official language, which often preserves archaic expressions, e.g. *decemviri sacris faciundis, tresviri Aquileiae coloniae deducundae*[21] etc.;
2. as an intentional archaism, in contexts where other archaic expressions are also to be found, e.g. Hor. *Ep.* 1.2.44–5, where *quaeritur argentum puerisque beata creandis uxor*[22] is coupled with the also archaic *argentum* in place of *pecunia.*[23]

Otherwise in CL the gerundive appears in the dative case not as an autonomous construction, but simply because it agrees in case with its subject, which, for independent reasons such as verbal syntax, happens to be in the dative. Other instances may also be interpreted as ablatives.[24] Dative-gerundive constructions with final sense do not become common again until Tacitus, who probably uses them as a deliberate archaism.[25] In Terence this construction (dative-gerundive syntagms where the dative is not due to verbal syntax) is found only twice. In *Ad.* 545 *nisi me credo huic esse natum rei, ferundis miseriis* is found in the speech of Demea. Here, however,

[20] For the archaic character of the construction, cf. Risch (1984: 32–3).
[21] Cf. Risch (1984: 32).
[22] Cf. Risch (1984: 33) 'einen als altertümlich empfundenen Dativ', Mayer (1994: 119).
[23] Cf. Mayer (1994: 118) 'archaic/poetic'.
[24] Cf. Risch (1984: 32).
[25] Cf. Maltby (1976: 25), Adams (1972: 372) 'archaising dative of purpose'.

the gerundive may be in the dative case due to its apposition to the dative of purpose *huic*. A clearer instance is uttered by Bacchis at *Hec.* 821 *hic adeo his rebus anulus fuit initium inveniundis* (for the archaising or senile character of Bacchis' speech, see also Maltby (1976: 242 and passim)).

Temporal clauses: antequam *and* priusquam

(1) When *antequam* or *priusquam* is used in a pure temporal sense (i.e. 'before this or that happened') referring to a future action, it is normally constructed with

(a) the future, a rare construction avoided in Terence, e.g. Plaut. *Pseud.* 524 *priusquam . . . pugnabo*;
(b) the future perfect, especially in negative clauses, e.g. *Phorm.* 1044–5, *neque ego ignosco neque promitto quicquam . . . priusquam gnatum videro*;
(c) the present subjunctive, e.g. *Ad.* 583–4 *priusquam ad portam venias, apud ipsum lacum est pistrilla*;
(d) the present indicative.

The present indicative in place of the present subjunctive or the future tenses in this type of *priusquam/antequam* construction is also found in CL, where it is restricted, however, to cases where the verb of the main clause is a future, especially to formulaic or fossilised expressions of the type *priusquam/antequam* + present indicative, *dicam* ('before I say this thing I shall say something else', cf. Cic. *Mur.* 2. *antequam pro L. Murena dicere instituo, pro me ipso pauca dicam*); it is found occasionally when the verb of the main clause is a subjunctive expressing a wish (cf. Verg. *A.* 4.24–7).[26]

Outside formulaic expressions the free (without particular restrictions) use of the indicative is regular in the archaic period,[27] where the subjunctive is used only when the main clause is an expression of will or wish, so that the idea of purpose is clear (cf. Plaut. *Merc.* 559). With the exception of *Andr.* 311, all other instances of this EL indicative occur in the speech of, or addresses

[26] Cf. Ernout and Thomas (1972: 368).
[27] Cf. Plaut. *Asin.* 232 *prius quam abis*; for this free use of the indicative as a feature of EL, cf. Bléry (1965: 188).

to, old people.[28] Cf. *Phorm.* 719 *transito ad uxorem meam, ut conveniat hanc priusquam hinc abit* by Chremes, *Phorm.* 1036, 1037 by Phormio to Nausistrata.

(2) *priusquam/antequam* denoting an activity being prohibited by the verbal action in the main clause is regularly constructed, according to CL rules, with the subjunctive, e.g. Liv. 25.18.14 *Badius priusquam opprimeretur parma atque equo relicto ad suos aufugit.*[29] In Terence we find this CL subjunctive construction, e.g. *Eun.* 751 *cave ne prius quam hanc a me accipias*, *Heaut.* 816–17. In addition to instances already stated in the previous paragraph, cf. also *Andr.* 558–60 *priusquam harum scelera et lacrumae conflictae dolis redducunt animum aegrotum ad misericordiam, uxorem demus* in the speech of Simo; *Phorm.* 897–8 *priusquam dilapidat nostras triginta minas ut auferamus* is uttered by Demipho. Two further instances occur at *Phorm.* 1045 by Nausistrata and *Heaut.* 584 by the slave Syrus.

Ut *temporal clauses*

The main use of temporal *ut* in Plautus, Terence and CL is with the perfect indicative referring to a single completed action in the past. Unlike *postquam*, *ut* + perfect in the sense 'since', 'now that' is an EL feature.[30] This construction is more common in Plautus than in Terence, whose only example is found at *Hec.* 751–2 *id pollicerer tibi, Lache, me segregatum habuisse, uxorem ut duxit, a me Pamphilum* in the speech of Bacchis.

Correlatives

Usque adeo as a correlative to a temporal *donec* is also another EL feature,[31] found in Plautus (cf. *Cist.* 583, *Rud.* 812), in Cato (cf. *Agr.* 67.2 etc.) and, later, once in the archaising Lucr. 6. 458. In

[28] *Heaut.* 237 is textually doubtful; *Scias* is the reading of C^2δEF^2υεη. For *Phorm.* 1037, cf. the form *respondeas*, offered by Lυ.

[29] For the EL indicative vs. the CL subjunctive in this type of *priusquam/antequam* constructions, cf. Bléry (1965: 189–91).

[30] Cf. also Maltby (1976: 50, 52–3, 66).

[31] Cf. H-Sz 629. Elsewhere in Terence we find *usque donec* correlative pairs, *Hec.* 125–6.

Terence the syntagm is found once at *Andr.* 662 in the speech of Pamphilus. Outside *Andria*, the construction is found once more, significantly in the speech of an old man, Demipho, at *Phorm.* 589–90 *neque defetiscar usque adeo experirier donec tibi id quod pollicitus sum effecero.*

Causal clauses

Nunc cum

In CL *nunc cum* is constructed with the subjunctive when it has a causal sense, whereas the indicative is the regular mood when *nunc cum* has a temporal meaning. Terentian usage follows the CL rules: the subjunctive in a causal *nunc cum* clause at *Hec.* 658 *nunc quom eius alienum esse animum a me sentiam*, the indicative in a temporal clause at *Heaut.* 448–9 *nunc quom sine magno intertrimento non potest haberi, quidvis dare cupis.* The indicative in a causal *nunc cum* clause is a feature of Early Latin, which is without exception the regular use in Plautus. In Terence, this archaic use of the indicative in a causal *nunc cum* clause[32] is found once at *Ad.* 737–8 *placet tibi factum Micio? Non si queam mutare. nunc quom non queo, animo aequo fero* in the speech of Micio.

Ut *causal clauses*

Ut used in a causal sense as *quoniam* ('given the fact that') with the indicative is an EL feature which dies out after Plautus and Terence.[33] In CL the construction is restricted to clauses of the type *aiunt hominem, ut erat furiosus, respondisse* = 'like the mad man he was . . .' (Cic. *S. Rosc.* 33, see also H-Sz 635). Outside these formulaic expressions the use of *ut* in a causal sense, construed with the indicative, is mainly a feature of EL. Causal *ut* is also found later in late Vulgar Latin texts, but here it is construed, just like *sicut*, with the subjunctive. With the exception of the textually doubtful *Andr.* 738, all other instances occur in the speech of old

32 Cf. also Bléry (1965: 114).

33 Cf. Bléry (1965: 128) 'archaique', Plaut. *Pseud.* 278 *ut occupatus nunc sum*, and later Sal. *Cat.* 59.2, as an intentional archaism; cf. also H-Sz. 635. Hor. *S.* 1.9.42 is textually doubtful as for the use of the indicative. We should read with Lejay *ut contendere durum cum victore.*

people, *Heaut.* 649 *ut stultae . . . sumus* by Sostrata, *Ad.* 749 by Demea, *Phorm.* 638 by Geta.

Object clauses

interdico ne. The use of a periphrasis consisting of *volo* with a perfect instead of a present infinitive after the *interdico ne* expression is an archaic survival of an old legal idiom also found in the *Senatus Consultum de Bacchanalibus*.[34] In Terence the expression is found only once at *Hec.* 563 *interdico ne extulisse extra aedis puerum usquam velis* in the speech of Phidippus. In these archaic periphrases the force of the perfect tense of the infinitive after *volo* is scarcely perceptible. Here *ne extulisse velis* is simply an equivalent to *ne ecferas*.

potin ut/ne. The construction of *potin* with an *ut* complement clause is an EL construction, common in Plautus (Afran. *com.* 202, *Amph.* 903, *Bacch.* 751, *Merc.* 495 etc., *Rud.* 424). In Terence, the construction occurs once at *Ad.* 539 *potin ut desinas* in the mouth of the old slave Syrus. Similarly, the syntagm *potin es/est* is an EL feature (cf. Plaut. *Trin.* 759) which, apart from *Eun.* 101, occurs at *Andr.* 437 in the speech of Simo.

Subject clauses

usus est ut. The use of *usus est* with an *ut* clause is another archaic expression. In addition, even the substitution of *usus* for *opus* in this kind of expression (the regular equivalent in Terence and in CL) is a further EL feature.[35] The expression is found at *Heaut.* 81 *an quoiquamst usus homini se ut cruciet?* in the mouth of Chremes.

Prepositions and prepositional constructions

***clanculum* + accusative.** *Clanculum* is used as a preposition construed with the accusative only in EL. In Terence the construction is found once, at *Ad.* 52–3 *clanculum patres* in the speech of Micio.

[34] For the archaic character of the construction, cf. Allardice (1929: 85), Fantham (1998: 107).

[35] Cf. Plaut. *Epid.* 167, *Mil.* 1132, Bléry (1965: 157), H-Sz 123.

Elsewhere in Terence *clanculum* is used only as an adverb. Cf. *Heaut.* 472, *Eun.* 310, *Phorm.* 873. Terence regularly uses *clam* + accusative prepositional syntagms (cf. McGlynn III 86).

***oro* + *cum* + ablative syntagms.** The combination *oro cum*, in the sense 'to entreat', is another EL feature. In Terence the expression is found once at *Hec.* 686 with an *ut* clause as its complement, *oravi tecum uxorem ut duceres*, in the speech of Laches.[36] Elsewhere Terence uses *oro* + accusative object constructions (cf. *Andr.* 190).

Verbal syntax

***queor* + inf.** The passive (deponent) form of *queo* constructed usually with a present passive infinitive is also archaic and is found again only once in Terence, who otherwise frequently uses the normal CL forms of the verb.[37] The Early Latin *nosci non quitast* is found at *Hec.* 572, in the speech of a *matrona*, Myrrina. Donatus remarks *ab activo queo passivum facit queor et inde participium quita est. sed antique dixit.*

***mitto* + substantivised infinitive.** Another EL construction is found at *Heaut.* 900 in the speech of Menedemus. In *mitto iam osculari atque amplexari*, in the sense 'I say nothing about kisses and embraces', the infinitive has the role of a substantive, direct object of the verb *mitto*.[38]

Lexicon

***occipere* = begin.** In Plautus the word does not seem to have been felt as archaic, and is in fact the most common word for 'begin' (73 times). Though not avoided by Terence, it loses ground to the CL *incipere* and *coepi* (cf. Maltby (1976: 183)). Especially, uses

[36] Cf. Plaut. *Asin.* 662, *Bacch.* 494, *Cas.* 324, etc. Cf. also *ThLL* IX_2 1037.

[37] For the archaic form *quita*, cf. Ashmore (1910: 236); for the also archaic construction of the auxiliary *queo* attracted to the voice of its passive infinitive complement, cf. Ernout and Thomas (1972: 208).

[38] For the EL character of the substantivised present infinitive as an accusative object without any accompanying demonstrative or personal pronoun, cf. Bléry (1965: 30 n.1), H-Sz 343.

of *occipio* without complement are avoided by Terence except for two instances in the Plautine *Eunuchus*[39] vv. 299, 725. Outside *Eunuchus*, it is found only once, at *Ad.* 289 *modo dolores, mea tu, occipiunt primulum* in the speech of the *anus* Canthara. The use of the perfect passive form *occeptus sum* in place of *inceptus sum* is also an EL expression, found exclusively in Plautus and Terence (cf. Plaut. *Pseud.* 919, *Rud.* 776). In Terence the form is found once in *Eunuchus*, v. 22, and once more in the speech of the *senex* Chremes at *Heaut.* 649.[40]

Complex expressions

salvos sies. One of the most typical greeting-formulas in Terence is *salve, salvete*, used with no restriction by all character types in Terentian drama. The formula *salvos s(i)es*, however, in place of *salve* is an archaic greeting, commonly found in Plautus;[41] later it disappears from Latin literature, after three examples in Terence. The formula is used only by or to old people, at *Andr.* 906 *salvos sis Chremes* by the old man Crito, at *Ad.* 890 by the old slave Geta *sed eccum Demeam. salvos sies* and finally at *Andr.* 802 *salvos sis, Crito* by Mysis when greeting the *senex* Crito.

minime gentium. The combination *minime gentium* as a reinforced negation[42] is an EL feature (cf. Plaut. *Merc.* 418, *Poen.* 690) which reappears later only in the archaising Apuleius (cf. *Met.* 9.17.9). In Terence two out of three instances are found in the speech of old people, at *Phorm.* 1033 by the *senex* Demipho and at *Ad.* 342 by the *matrona* Sostrata (cf. also *Eun.* 625).

Correlatives

ea gratia.[43] The use of *ea gratia* in place *of ea causa* as a correlative to a final clause is an EL feature (cf. also *trag. inc.* 168f.) which

[39] Cf. chapter 7.

[40] For the archaic character of the word, cf. also Barsby (1999: 86), Oakley (1997–8 I: 438).

[41] Cf. *Bacch.* 456, 536, *Epid.* 548, 549, *Men.* 776, 910, *Mil.* 902, 1316, *Most.* 718 etc. (twenty times).

[42] For negations in Plautus and Terence, cf. Thesleff (1960).

[43] The ablative *gratia* (lit. 'thanks to', Gr. χάριν), frequent in EL, is avoided in CL and becomes less frequent than equivalent *causa* + genitive syntagms. The exception is again

is found in Terence once at *Andr.* 587–8 *sed ea gratia simulavi vos ut pertemptarem* in the speech of an old person again, the *senex* Simo. It is also uttered by Syrus when addressing Chremes at *Heaut.* 768–9. Donatus ad *Andr.* 433 remarks: *gratia veteres pro causa ponebant.*

Miscellaneous isolated examples

Finally, several other Early Latin words (avoided in CL but used only in the archaic period, especially in Plautus, Cato etc. and later by archaising authors, Gellius, Fronto, Ausonius etc.)[44] are found in the speech of Terence's old people. These lexemes may not be as significant as those features for which there exists a CL equivalent, which is, in turn, more common in Terentian drama. Their concentration in the speech of old people, however, should not be seen as a simple coincidence.

Heautontimoroumenos

1. Chremes: *pultare* at *Heaut.* 410, *postilla*[45] at *Heaut.* 447, *techina* at *Heaut.* 471, *subigito* at *Heaut.* 566, *cautim* at *Heaut.* 870, *advorsatrix* at *Heaut.* 1007, *gerro* at *Heaut.* 1033.
2. Menedemus: *vocivus* at *Heaut.* 90.

Phormio

1. Nausistrata: *distaedet* at *Phorm.* 1011.
2. Geta: *succenturiatus* at *Phorm.* 230, *postilla* at *Phorm.* 347, 705.
3. Demipho: *postilla* at *Phorm.* 1018.
4. Chremes: the EL imperative *inque*[46] at *Phorm.* 919.

found in archaising authors, such as Sallust, where *gratia* gains ground. This CL trend away from *gratia* is anticipated in Terence: whereas *causa* prepositional syntagms occur sixteen times, the equivalent *gratia* expressions occur only twice, at *Andr.* 836 by Simo and at *Hec.* 836 by Bacchis. As for the elevated tone of *gratia* constructions, cf. Jocelyn (1967: 277).

44 For their analytical distribution, cf. *ThLL* s.v., *OLD* s.v., L-S s.v.

45 At *Andr.* 936 by the *senex* Chremes. Cf. also *Eun.* 127 by the *meretrix* Thais.

46 For *inque* cf. Plaut. *Pseud.* 538, for *inquito* Plaut. *Aul.* 788, *Rud.* 1342. A further instance of the EL imperative occurs at *Heaut.* 829. It is spoken by Syrus in the presence of the old man Chremes (cf. also here, in concentration, another feature associated with senile speech, the pleonastic *pleraque omnia*).

Adelphoe

1. Demea: *raptio* at *Ad.* 356, *ganeum* at *Ad.* 359, *patrisso* at *Ad.* 564, *primulum* at *Ad.* 898.
2. Micio: *pultare* at *Ad.* 637, *prolubium* at *Ad.* 985.
3. Canthara: *primulum* at *Ad.* 289.
4. Geta: *proviso*[47] at *Ad.* 889.

Utibilis at *Phorm.* 690 is uttered by Antipho when addressing Geta. The only instances of EL and archaising lexical items that do not follow the distributional pattern described above (of or to old people) are *deamo* at *Heaut.* 825 by Clitipho to Syrus, *incogitans* at *Phorm.* 155 by Antipho to Phaedria and *Phorm.* 499 by Dorio to Phaedria, *pultare* at *Ad.* 633, *Heaut.* 275 by Aeschinus and Syrus respectively.

Conclusions

In the present chapter I have shown that the comparatively rare EL features characterise mainly the speech of old people, whereas the CL equivalents are used by all characters. With the exception of the *Andria* and *Eunuchus*, EL features are used without any particular concentration in the speech of old people, which thus acquires an overall archaic linguistic ring. EL features in the speech of other characters (with the exception of Bacchis in *Hecyra*) are often concentrated in a specific part of the play, mainly when the interlocutor is an old person. Finally, there is a binary linguistic opposition between the pairs of *senes* in *Adelphoe, Heautontimoroumenos*. Chremes (thirteen instances) and Demea (fifteen instances)[48] use more archaisms than their counterparts Menedemus (three instances)[49] and Micio (four instances), respectively.

[47] In *Andria proviso* occurs in v. 957 in the speech of Charinus and at *Eun.* 394 is spoken by Parmeno.

[48] Apart from the instances found in this chapter, cf. *aibas* at *Ad.* 561 and *aibat* at *Ad.* 717; for this, cf. Maltby (1979: 140), *quippe qui* for *quippe quod* or *cum* at *Heaut.* 538 (cf. Maltby (1976: 250)), *scilicet* + infinitive at *Heaut.* 856, 892 (cf. Maltby (1976: 248)).

[49] Apart from the two instances mentioned in this chapter, cf. also *aiebas* at *Heaut.* 924, pointed out by Maltby (1979: 140).

CHAPTER 3

SENILIS ΜΑΚΡΟΛΟΓΙΑ AND ΠΕΡΙΣΣΟΛΟΓΙΑ

Introduction

A second group of linguistic phenomena associated with senile speech, occurring again both at the lexical and syntactical levels, seems to be long-winded forms of expression, marking the language of old persons as slow or ponderous.

Ancient theorists have often remarked on the prolix character of senile speech. Aristotle in the *Rhetoric* (B 1390a6–9) claims that old people are characterised by ἀδολεσχία. Cf. also Demetr. *Eloc.*8 οἱ γέροντες μακρολόγοι διὰ τὴν ἀσθένειαν, Longin. *Sublim.* 9.12 ἴδιόν ἐστιν ἐν γήρᾳ τὸ φιλόμυθον, Cic. *Sen.*55 *senectus est natura loquacior* (see also Isoc. *Panath.* 88, D. Chr. *Euboicus* 1 πρεσβυτικὸν πολυλογία, Maximian 1. 204 *o sola fortes garrulitate senes*).

Donatus often comments on the garrulousness of Terence's old people. Their loquacity, according to the ancient scholiast, results in πολυλογία, μακρολογία, or even περισσολογία, involving the use of more words than are necessary to express a thought. On *Ad.* 68, where Micio says *mea sic est ratio et sic animum induco meum*, Donatus remarks: *senilis* μακρολογία.[1] Furthermore, at *Eun.* 971–3 the *senex* of the play says *Ex meo propinquo rure hoc capio commodi: neque agri neque urbis odium me umquam percipit. ubi satias coepit fieri commuto locum.* Donatus, commenting on the second sentence in the quotation, points out its superfluous character. The first two lines, according to the scholiast, were sufficient to express the idea. He adds, however, *sed hic* ἐνάργεια *est senilis eloquii, faceti et garruli simul.*

Based on the above, as well as on the well-known opinions about the prolixity of senile speech prevalent in antiquity, I shall examine

[1] Cf. also Introduction, p. 5.

how, under what conditions, and to what extent Terence tries, as a stylistic effect, to give his old people a more prolix diction in comparison to other character types.

Brief overview

Maltby was again the first modern scholar to examine the long-winded character of senile speech in Terence. He has shown that in the case of some synonymous words and expressions, the longer forms are the ones favoured by older people in opposition to the shorter forms, used by all other character types (cf. *prohibeo* vs. *veto, sceleratus* vs. *scelestus*), and he has also suggested that a number of other long-winded expressions restricted to old persons, for which there are no exact synonyms in Terence, may also characterise senile speech as ponderous and garrulous.[2] I should add to his catalogue the following instances: the lengthier *propediem* in place of the common *cito*[3] (thirteen times), restricted to the speech of old people, Chremes at *Heaut.* 160, 868 and Demea at *Ad.* 888, the lengthier *omnino* in place of *prorsus, plane*, again exclusively used by old people, at *Andr.* 524 by Simo, at *Hec.* 214 by Laches, at *Hec.* 714 by Phidippus and finally at *Ad.* 990 by Demea.

Maltby's methodological tools, however, are not always safe, and his data are often incomplete. As a result, although his overall conclusions are correct, he is unable to adduce details concerning their relationship to the data; he provides the reader with an over-simplistic description, which does not take into account the particular conditions under which linguistic differentiation is discernible and the limitations operating upon the corpus. In particular:

1. Although the Terentian corpus exhibits dozens of instances of the phenomena under discussion, Maltby examines only some. For example, he suggests that the pleonastic combination *propterea quod*, found twice in the speech of the old man Simo in *Andria* (vv. 38, 584), characterises the old man's speech as long-winded, since in both cases the simple *quod* or *quia* could have been used. However, several similar

[2] Cf. Maltby (1976: 250–4).

[3] Cf. Donat. *Ad.* 888 *propediem adverbium est temporis, ut si diceret 'cito'*.

pleonastic combinations are found in the language of other characters in *Andria*, i.e. combinations of two terms where only one would have been sufficient. A small sample would include: *perparce nimium* (v. 455),[4] *incipit . . . initium* (v. 709),[5] both in the speech of the slave Davus, *praescisse . . . ante* (v. 239),[6] *nisi si* in place of a simple *nisi* (v. 249)[7] by the *adulescens* Pamphilus etc.

2. He does not offer any clear subcategorisation of the long-winded expressions he examines, and is thus unable to fine-tune his analysis to locate the specific levels at which linguistic differentiation operates (pleonasms and synonyms) and the degree to which it is evident at each level.
3. Although he establishes an evolution in Terentian techniques in the matter of linguistic differentiation, and more particularly in the use of archaisms and hellenising lexicon, from the *Andria* to the later plays (excepting *Eunuchus*), he fails to observe the same pattern in the matter of long-winded expressions. Linguistic characterisation by means of pleonastic expressions is absent from *Andria*, as well as from *Eunuchus*.[8]
4. Maltby also ignores the stylistic differences between the senarii and other comic verses (septenarii, octonarii). It has long been established that the longer comic verses, partly due to the necessity of filling up the line, are characterised in both Plautus and Terence by a high proportion of circumlocutions and padded expressions, mainly doublet-synonyms. By examining both the iambic and the longer lines, I shall show that linguistic characterisation on the basis of pleonastic expressions is more clearly detected in the senarii, which, in any case, represent more than the half of all Terentian lines (55. 6 vs. 37. 6 per cent in Plautus). The iambic senarii were spoken lines approximating everyday language[9] and were mainly used in *diverbium* scenes. All other metres were intoned against a musical background (recitative metre rather than song-styled *canticum*). Thus, the distribution of

[4] Cf. also Donat. ad loc. *et 'perparce' et 'nimium', cum sufficeret 'per'; etenim 'per' et 'nimium' vituperatio est.*

[5] For the pleonasm, see also K-S 569.

[6] Cf. K-S 575, Donat. ad loc. *Et 'ante' abundat aut certe 'prae', cum sufficiat 'scisse'.*

[7] For its pleonastic character, cf. K-S 575; see also a similar instance in the speech of the slave Davus in v. 671.

[8] Accumulation of synonyms in *Eunuchus*: vv. 96, 103, 146–7, 175, 193ff., 294, 300, 362–3, 377, 389, 416, 418–19, 427, 484–5, 543, 554, 565, 643, 688–9, 709, 746, 826, 886, 929, 932, 935ff., 962, 966–7, 1039, 1048, 1079; pleonasms in *Eunuchus*: vv. 98, 110, 160, 226–7, 229, 246, 283, 317, 324–5, 352, 370, 436, 469–70, 495, 522, 524, 534, 548, 549, 561, 574, 578, 591, 614, 634, 637, 645, 662, 668, 677–8, 702, 737, 757, 774, 781, 787, 793, 794–5, 797, 866, 884, 895, 902, 934, 945, 975, 996, 1003, 1014, 1032, 1050, 1082.

[9] For iambic lines close to everyday language in Greek, cf. Arist. *Po.* 1449a21ff.

circumlocutionary or long-winded expressions in the Terentian corpus is related both to the metre and the character speaking.

Aims and objectives – methodological tools

In this section, I shall examine the following linguistic categories:

1. accumulation of synonymous expressions
2. pleonastic combinations of two or more lexical items.

These will establish the following features of Terentian drama:

1. Accumulated synonyms as well as pleonastic expressions constitute a permanent feature of senile speech.
2. The few occasional instances of these expressions in the speech of other character types (slaves, young men) often show a particular concentration in specific parts of their speech, namely in repartee with old people, that is when they adapt their language to the linguistic habits of their interlocutor.

A few methodological remarks concerning the terms 'synonym' and 'pleonasm' are in order:

Synonym. In the strictest sense, 'synonym' is a word or expression that has the same meaning as another word or expression. Such complete synonymy, which presupposes the unconditional substitutability of two or more linguistic items in all contexts and refers both to denotative and connotative semantic elements, is very rare, almost impossible, at least in the case of lexemes. In this book, synonym is used in a broader sense, and encompasses two or more words and expressions having overlapping meanings, e.g. in English 'acquire', 'get', 'obtain' etc.[10] In particular, I use the term to cover lexemes that can be substituted in some but not in all contexts depending on their denotative or connotative meaning (e.g. strike or hit a man but only 'strike' a bargain) or lexemes that, although they have the same denotative meaning, have different connotations depending on regional, social or stylistic parameters (e.g. 'money', 'dough', 'bread').[11]

[10] Cf. Lyons (1996: 60–5), Jones (1987).

[11] As basic corroboration of the relative synonymy of two items, full use is made of the standard lexica of Latin, mainly the *ThLL*, which offers 'synonyma' for the lexemes it

Pleonasm. Pleonasm in this book, following the definition of K-S (567–78), is the use of a linguistic element (single word or combination of several words) the meaning of which has already been expressed either through the same or a semantically related linguistic unit, and which, therefore, from both a grammatical and a logical point of view, appears superfluous. Donatus' relevant remarks have also been taken into account, with caution though, since in several instances the grammarian characterises as pleonastic combinations that do not correspond to the criterion spelled out above.[12] In particular, all cases which Donatus characterises as παρέλκον, or where he uses the following expressions – *est productio* (cf. ad *Andr.* 29), *productionis locus est* (cf. ad *Eun.* 393), *abundat* (cf. ad *Andr.* 90, 201 etc.), *suffecerat* (cf. ad *Phorm.* 228), *supervacuum est* (cf. ad *Phorm.* 322) – have been examined in detail.

In order to facilitate comprehension, two frequently used terms are defined here:

1. absolute number: total number of occurrences
2. ratio: percentage obtained from the absolute number of occurrences in the speech of a particular character type in proportion to the number of lines spoken by this character type.[13] An increase of 1–2 per cent may seem small; however, it usually corresponds to dozens of examples.

There are several combinations in the Terentian corpus which are often translated or interpreted as synonymous and pleonastic. In fact, however, we are not dealing with real synonyms or the synonymy is very difficult to establish. These are the following:

contains, and secondarily the *OLD*, which offers phrase-interpretative lemmata. However, it must be emphasised that in most cases personal judgement and interpretation is also involved, as the specific meaning of a linguistic item is heavily context-dependent.

12 For a detailed criticism of Donatus' remarks on pleonastic expressions in Terence, cf. Papadimitriou (1982: 427–42).

13 Attribution of lines according to the Oxford text of Kauer and Lindsay. Shared lines were not simply counted as a half, one-third, a quarter etc., depending on whether two, three or four characters shared them, but according to the portion of the line spoken by a character. E.g. *Phorm.* 111 is shared by Davus and Geta: Davus: *amare coepit*. Geta: *scis quam? Quo evadat vide*. I give to Davus not half of the line but only one-third. Therefore my statistics may differ slightly from previous ones which did not follow the same principle.

1. *Hec.* 152 *pium ac pudicum ingenium narras Pamphili.* The two adjectives here do not seem to have been used simply as synonymous but they rather refer to different persons or situations. More precisely *pium* refers to the conscience Pamphilus shows towards Bacchis, whereas *pudicum* alludes to the sexual continence the young man shows towards his wife, the *virgo* Pamphila (for such a reading of the combination, cf. also Carney (1963: ad loc.)). *Heaut.* 122–3 *animo fere perturbato atque incerto pro aegritudine.* According to the *OLD* s.v. 10 *incertus* here means 'not certain what to think/do', 'hesitant', 'irresolute', whereas *perturbatus* has the more general sense of 'agitated in mind', 'perturbed' (cf. *OLD* s.v. 2).
2. *Heaut.* 810–11 *ut te quidem omnes di . . . cum istoc invento cumque incepto perduint!.* The *ThLL* does not mention the two words as synonymous. As for the *OLD*, it gives the following meanings for the specific line: *inventum* 2 = 'a thing devised', 'a plan' / *inceptum* 1 = 'a thing undertaken or started'. The juxtaposition, in this specific order, of these two words, which are originally passive participles, conveys, in my view, a sense of temporal sequence (first/second) and should be interpreted as having a verbal rather than a nominal aspect. A proper translation therefore should be 'May the Gods punish you Syrus, for having devised this plan and then having put it in action'.
3. *Phorm.* 626 *quid hic coeptat aut quo evadat hodie?. Coepto* has the meaning of 'venture on', 'begin' (cf. *OLD* s.v. 2), whereas *evado* 'means arrive (at) by course of an action, argument', 'end up' (cf. *OLD* s.v. 7). A notion of temporal sequence is also here discernible and we should translate with Martin (1959: ad loc.) 'what is he up to, what will be the outcome?'.
4. *Hec.* 488 *amoque et laudo et vehementer desidero. Desidero* here has, according to *ThLL* (V_1 702), the meaning of *amissum vel absentem requirere*, ἐπιποθεῖν and is not a simple synonym of *amo*. We should, therefore, translate as follows: 'I love my wife, I praise her and I miss her very much.' In any case, these conjoined expressions constitute a clear case of an emphatic accumulation, the aim of which is more likely to express Pamphilus' strong feelings for his absent wife rather than a stylistic device for characterising his speech as long-winded.
5. Finally, I should add two further instances: (a) *Heaut.* 798 *omnes te in lauta et bene acta patre putant* is textually doubtful and is characterised by the K-L edition as *locus desperatus*. Any conclusions based on this line would therefore be unsafe. (b) Although corroborating my argument, in this examination, there have not been taken into consideration the idiomatic and formulaic combinations of *aequum* and *bonum* (cf. *aequi bonique facio*, *aequomst et bonum*), which are extremely common (more than a hundred instances) in the totality of Latin literature

and occur as invariable set phrases. In such cases, due to the extreme frequency and banality of these combinations, it seems that there is no particular conscious choice on the part of the playwright to create a pleonastic combination. It is a matter of language rather than of a conscious stylistic choice. For reasons of methodological consistency, all such instances have not been considered here.

Accumulation of synonyms

All instances of accumulative synonyms are arranged by verse. The symbol '=' denotes synonymy in the sense described above.

Heautontimoroumenos

1. Menedemus: vv. 424–5 *et quanto diutius abest mage cupio tanto et mage desidero*, v. 465 *sumat consumat perdat* (cf. *ThLL* IV 618), v. 926 *abs te petere et poscere* (cf. L-S sub *posco* in the catalogue of synonyms: *flagito, postulo, peto*).
2. Chremes: vv. 61–2 *quidvis tibi aut quid quaeris*?, vv. 152–3 *siquis recte aut commode tractaret* (cf. *ThLL* III 1926), v. 438 *si te tam leni et victo esse animo ostenderis* (cf. *ThLL* VII 1142),[14] v. 460 *relevi dolia omnia, omnis serias* (cf. *ThLL* V_1 1835), v. 912 *quemquamne animo tam comi esse aut leni putas* (cf. *ThLL* III 1788).

Hecyra

Syra: vv. 64–5 *et moneo et hortor ne quoiusquam misereat* (cf. *ThLL* VIII 1410), *quin spolies mutiles laceres* (cf. *OLD lacere* 4 'mangle', *mutilo* 1 'maim', 'damage by cutting or breaking off a part').

Phormio

1. Geta:[15] v. 131 *quod erit mihi bonum atque commodum* (cf. *ThLL* II 2127), v. 226 *iustam illam causam facilem vincibilem* (cf. *ThLL* VI_1 64).
2. Demipho: v. 441 *Quanta me cura et sollicitudine adficit* (cf. *ThLL* IV 1469–70), vv. 443–4 *ut saltem sciam quid de hac re dicat quidve sit sententiae*, v. 894 *Dis magnas merito gratias habeo atque ago*.[16]

[14] 'such a gentle and softened state of mind'.

[15] For Geta's age, cf. Papadimitriou (1998: 286), Austin (1922: 27).

[16] For *gratias habere/agere* belonging to the same semantic field of 'to show gratitude, thanks by word or deed for services rendered', cf. *OLD* s.v. 4, see also 4 c/d.

3. Nausistrata: v. 1008 *pro di immortales, facinus miserandum et malum!*[17]

Adelphoe

1. Micio: v. 45 *parce ac duriter* (cf. *ThLL* V$_{1}$ 2313), v. 59 *haec fratri mecum non conveniunt neque placent*,[18] v. 145–6 *verum si augeam aut etiam adiutor si<e>m eius iracundiae* (cf. *ThLL* II 124), v. 756 *hilarum ac lubentem*,[19] v. 827 *video [eos] sapere intellegere*.[20]
2. Demea: v. 134 *profundat perdat pereat*,[21] v. 789 *quid faciam? quid agam? quid clamem aut querar?* (cf. *ThLL* VI$_{1}$ 124), v. 883 *quid fit? quid agitur?* (twice v. 885) both meaning 'what's going on?', v. 926–7 *quam maxume unam facere nos hanc familiam, colere adiuvare adiungere* (cf. *ThLL* III 1693), v. 930 *proba et modesta*.[22]
3. Syrus:[23] vv. 375–6 *est hercle inepta, ne dicam dolo, atque absurda* (cf. *ThLL* II 225), 390–1 *inepta lenitas patris et facilitas prava* (cf. *ThLL* VI$_{1}$ 76).
4. Hegio: v. 472–3 *venit ipsus ultro lacrumans orans obsecrans fidem dans*,[24] v. 480–1 *non malus neque iners* (cf. *ThLL* VIII 216).

Compared to the instances found in the speech of old people, accumulation of synonyms is rare in the speech of other characters. In the majority of such instances the accumulated synonyms appear when the character in question has as interlocutor an old person. In detail, the following cases occur, at *Heaut.* 521–2 *mulier commoda et faceta haec meretrix* (cf. *ThLL* VI$_{1}$ 42), at *Heaut.* 526 *sed habet patrem quendam avidum, miserum atque aridum*[25] both by the slave Syrus to the *senex* Chremes and finally at *Ad.* 662–3

[17] For *miserandum* here having the sense of *improbum, turpe, pravum*, cf. *ThLL* VIII 1134; for *malum* in the same sense, cf. *ThLL* VIII 219.

[18] For *convenire*, cf. *OLD* s.v. 7 'to be agreed upon'; for *placere*, cf. *OLD* s.v. 5 'to be agreed on'.

[19] For *hilarus*, cf. *ThLL* VI 3 2787 *laetus*, ἱλαρός; for *lubens*, cf. *ThLL* VII 1326 *laetus*, see also *OLD* s.v. 'cheerful' in both instances.

[20] For *sapere* = 'to be intelligent', 'understand', cf. *OLD* s.v. 6, and *intellegere* in the same sense, cf. *OLD* s.v.

[21] For *perdo*, cf. *OLD* s.v. 6 'throw away', 'dissipate', 'waste'; for *profundo*, cf. *OLD* s.v. 8 'throw away', 'squander', 'spend or use wastefully'.

[22] For *proba*, cf. *OLD* 4 b (esp. for women) 'virtuous', 'modest'; for *modestus*, cf. *OLD* 3 (esp. for women) 'seemly', 'modest'.

[23] For the age of Syrus, cf. *Ad.* 562–3, where Syrus describes himself as *senex, non puduisse verberare hominem senem! quem ego modo puerum tantillum in manibus gestavi meis*.

[24] For *oro* here, cf. *OLD* s.v. 1 'pray', 'beseech'; for *obsecro*, cf. *OLD* 1, 3 'beseech', 'pray'.

[25] For *aridus* = *avarus* here, cf. *ThLL* II 568; for *avidus/aviditas* = *avarus/avaritia*, cf. *ThLL* II 1424.

factum a vobis duriter inmisericorditerque (cf. *ThLL* V$_1$ 2313) by Aeschinus to the *senex* Micio.

In the whole Terentian corpus, apart from *inmunda inluvie* at *Heaut.* 295 spoken by the slave Syrus, the only two instances of synonymous doublings which do not follow the pattern described above (senile speech / addressing old people) both occur in the language of the slave Parmeno in *Hecyra*, at vv. 165–6 *pudens modesta incommoda atque iniurias viri omnis ferre* and v. 334 *capiti* atque *aetati illorum.*[26] Crucially, it has already been observed by Donatus that the speech of this slave is characterised by garrulousness (cf. ad *Hec.* 193 *curiosus est Parmeno et idem garrulus: nam per totam fabulam talis inducitur*). Although Donatus cannot always be safely relied upon, the distribution of the data in this case is so clear that it lends credibility to his observations.

Longer lines

In *Heautontimoroumenos* linguistic characterisation by means of accumulated synonymous words or expressions is absent from the longer lines. Both old people and the other characters use almost the same amount of synonyms. The following instances occur:

1. Old people:
   (a) Chremes: v. 633 *te inscientem atque inprudentem dicere ac facere omnia,*[27] v. 950–1 *adeo exornatum dabo, adeo depexum,*[28] v. 966 *ei commisi et credidi* (cf. *ThLL* III 1904).
   (b) Menedemus: vv. 874–5 *ego me non tam astutum neque ita perspicacem esse id scio,*[29] v. 877 *caudex, stipes, asinus, plumbeus,*[30] *sed hic adiutor meus et monitor et praemonstrator,*[31] v. 957 *scio tibi esse hoc gravius multo ac durius* (cf. *ThLL* V$_1$ 2312).

[26] For *caput* = *vita*, as is the meaning of *aetas* here, cf. also *ThLL* III 416.

[27] Cf. *OLD insciens* 1 'not knowing', 'ignorant', 'unaware'; *imprudens* 1, 2, 3 'ignorant', 'unaware'.

[28] 'I shall make him such a pretty sight, such a punchbag'; for *exornare*, cf. Non. 299 M *foedare*, Gloss. IV, 68, 28 *exornatum* = *deformatum*.

[29] Cf. also here the pleonastic use of *id* referring to the infinitive syntagms *astutum, perspicacem esse*.

[30] For all theses words having the meaning of *stupidus*, cf. *OLD asinus* 2, *caudex* 1c, *stipes* 2d, *plumbeus* 2c.

[31] 'This prompter of mine, this teacher, this stage-director, surpasses me in this.'

2. Others to old people:
   v. 956 *quodnam ob facinus? quid ego tantum sceleris admisi miser?* (cf. *ThLL* VI_I 82) by Clitipho to Menedemus, v. 1027 *quod peto aut quod volo*[32] by Clitipho to Sostrata.
3. Others to others:
   v. 226 *habet bene et pudice eductam* (cf. *ThLL* II 2119), v. 227 *meast potens, procax, magnifica, sumptuosa, nobilis*[33] by Clitipho in his monologue, v. 240 *dum moliuntur, dum conantur, annus est*[34] by Clitipho to Clinia, v. 580 *hominis frugi et temperantis* (cf. *ThLL* VI_I 1456) by Syrus to Clitipho, v. 704 *bonam atque iustam rem oppido imperas* (cf. *ThLL* II 2127) by Clinia to Syrus, v. 710 *qui vim tantam in me et potestatem*[35] by Syrus to Clinia, v. 988 *te indulgebant, tibi dabant* (cf. *ThLL* V_I 1673), v. 992–3 *in peccato adiutrices, auxilio . . . solent esse* by Syrus to Clitipho.

One might argue that the higher amount of accumulated synonyms in the speech of old people in the iambic senarii of the play is simply due to the fact that the total number of iambic senarii spoken by all other character types together amounts only to half of those uttered by old people, whereas the longer lines are almost equally distributed between old and other characters. However, the crucial point is not the total number of occurrences, but the proportion of occurrences to lines, which is higher for old people in the iambic senarii. A further indication of how the speech of old people accommodates synonyms in the iambic senarii is that in their speech synonymous expressions show an even distribution, while in the speech of other characters the few instances of accumulated synonyms appear only when addressing old people and not in monologues or when addressing other character types (parasites, slaves etc.), i.e. when their speech is accommodated to that of their interlocutor.

In *Hecyra, Phormio* and *Adelphoe*, however, accumulated synonyms are used more frequently by old people even in longer lines. In the case of *Adelphoe* there is a restriction of such features to

[32] For *peto, volo* having overlapping semantic fields, namely 'to aim at', 'to be after', cf. *OLD* 7, 16 respectively.

[33] Cf. *OLD magnificus* 2 'splendid in outward behaviour', *nobilis* 7b 'impressively grand in manner', 'stately', 'regal'.

[34] Cf. *OLD conor* 1 'to make an effort', *molior* 2 'to make efforts', 'strive'.

[35] Cf. *OLD potestas* 7 'physical/mental power', 'strength', 'capacity'; *vis* 14 'power/capacity to do something'.

the lines spoken by old people. The distribution, in detail, is as follows.

Hecyra

1. Old people:
   - (a) Pamphilus reporting the speech of his mother-in-law Myrrina: v. 387 *si ius si fas est* (cf. *ThLL* VII 296), v. 388 *adversa eius per te tecta tacitaque apud omnis sient*.[36]
   - (b) Laches: v. 761 *facilem benivolumque lingua tua iam tibi me reddidit* (cf. *ThLL* VI1 65), v. 797 *nobilitatem ex eo et rem natam et gloriam* (cf. *ThLL* VI2 2076).
   - (c) Phidippus: v. 457 *salvom atque validum* (cf. *OLD salvus, validus* 1, 2 respectively).
2. Others to old people: v. 472 *quam fideli animo et benigno in illam et clementi fui* (cf. *ThLL* II 1904) by Pamphilus to Laches and Phidippus.

Two further instances of accumulated synonyms occur in the speech of the *meretrix* Bacchis, who, as I have remarked in the chapter on archaisms, uses several linguistic features associated with senile speech, v. 837 *dum illo licitumst usa sum benigno et lepido et comi* (cf. *ThLL* II 1904), v. 860 *morem antiquom atque ingenium obtines*.[37] Accumulated synonyms of this kind appear only once in the speech of the *adulescens* Pamphilus, when addressing his slave Parmeno, v. 841 *ut mi haec certa et clara attuleris* (cf. *ThLL* III 922). It is significant that Pamphilus here gives his slave an order; therefore the adoption of this stylistic feature, strictly associated with senile language, may add to the authoritative character of the utterance.

Phormio

1. Old people:
   - (a) Demipho: v. 767 *dum nimium dici nos bonos studemus et benignos* (cf. *ThLL* II 1904).
   - (b) Nausistrata: v. 1025 *quam ob rem exspectem aut sperem porro non fore*.[38]

[36] 'to keep her hardship concealed and a secret before all'.

[37] Cf. *OLD mos* 5 = 'character', 'disposition'; *ingenium* 1 = 'natural disposition', 'temperament'.

[38] For *exspectare* = *sperare*, cf. *ThLL* V2 1895 and see 1897 for the specific example.

(c) Chremes: v. 1047 *immo vero pulchre discedo et probe*.[39]

2. Others in the presence of old people: v. 497 *adeon ingenio esse duro te atque inexorabili* (cf. *ThLL* V_1 2313) by Phaedria in the presence of Geta.

Only one exception to the pattern described above (by or to old people) occurs in the longer lines of *Phormio*, namely v. 164 *nam tua quidem hercle certo vita haec expetenda optandaque est*[40] by Phaedria to Antipho.

In *Adelphoe* such syntagms appear in the speech of old people only:

1. Demea: v. 861 *facilitate nil esse homini melius neque clementia* (cf. *ThLL* VI 1 74), v. 864 *clemens, placidus* (cf. *ThLL* III 1333), v. 866 *agrestis saevos tristis parcus, truculentus, tenax* (cf. *ThLL* I 1419–20), v. 869 *vitam atque aetatem meam*,[41] vv. 872–3 *illum amant, . . . illum diligunt* (cf. *ThLL* I 1951), v. 953 *bene et sapienter dixti dudum* (cf. *ThLL* II 2127), v. 967 *postremo hodie in psaltria hac emunda hic adiutor fuit, hic curavit*,[42] v. 986 *quod te isti facilem et festivom putant* (cf. *ThLL* VI 1 65), v. 988 *adsentando indulgendo et largiendo* (cf. *ThLL* II 860), v. 991 *effundite emite*.[43]
2. Micio: v. 703 *periit abiit navem escendit*,[44] v. 944 *etsi hoc mihi pravom ineptum absurdum atque alienum* (cf. *ThLL* I 225).
3. Syrus: v. 963 *docui monui bene praecepi semper quae potui omnia*.
4. Geta: vv. 321–2 *te ipsam quaerito, te exspecto*.[45]

Another instance is possibly vv. 602–3 *quae dolore ac miseria tabescit* ('under distress and affliction', cf. *ThLL* V_1 1854) by Hegio. *Dolor*, however, here may also have the meaning of 'pain of childbirth' as it does at *Andr*. 268 and at *Ad*. 289, 486, in which case we are not dealing with synonyms. *Dolor* in the sense of distress, a meaning which is not to be excluded here, occurs also at *Andr*. 831.

39 For *probe* here = *bene, recte*, cf. *ThLL* X, 2 fasc. X 1487. I follow here Bentley and the Loeb edition.

40 'By heaven, man, your present life is a thing you might call out and pray for.'

41 For *aetas* = *totum vitae spatium* here, cf. *ThLL* I 1123; see 1125 for the specific instance.

42 'He was the person who helped, who got it done.'

43 'Squander, spend away.'

44 'Lost, disappeared gone aboard ship.'

45 'I have been looking for you, searching for you.' K-L give *te exspecto* to Sostrata. Most of the editors (Gratwick, Marouzeau, Martin, Sargeaunt), however, give Geta the line.

Pleonasms

Lexical items

adulescens* + *mulier:[46] at *Hec.* 661 by Laches.
nemo* + *homo:[47] at *Phorm.* 591 by Geta.
servus* + *homo:[48] at *Phorm.* 292 by Geta.
quisquam* + *homo:[49] at *Ad.* 716–17 by Demea.
oculis* + *videre:[50] at *Heaut.* 491 by Chremes.
coacta ingratiis:[51] at *Heaut.* 446 by Chremes.
in/cum animo cogitare:[52] at *Ad.* 30 and 818 by Micio, at *Ad.* 500 Hegio.
ades praesens:[53] at *Ad.* 393 by Syrus.
solere* + *plerumque:[54] at *Phorm.* 89–90 by Geta.
opportune* + *in ipso tempore: at *Hec.* 626–7 by Laches.[55]

Pronouns

nemo/nihil* + *quisquam/quidquam/quicquam:[56] at *Hec.* 67 *nam nemo illorum quisquam, scito, ad te venit* by Syra, at *Phorm.* 80 *noster mali nil quicquam primo* by Geta and at *Ad.* 366 *nil quicquam vidi laetius* by Syrus.

ceteri* + *omnes:[57] at *Phorm.* 624 by Geta.

repetition of pronouns:[58] at *Heaut.* 790–2 *sed illud quod . . . dixi . . . id nunc reddendumst illi* by Syrus to Chremes, in his effort to persuade the old man to give the money Clitipho needs for Bacchis, at *Ad.* 357–8 *si illum potest, qui aliquoi reist, etiam eum ad nequitiem adducere* by Demea, at *Ad.* 741 *illud quod cecidit forte, id arte ut corrigas* by Micio, at *Hec.* 14–15 *in is quas . . . didici novas partim sum earum exactus, partim vix steti* by L. Ambivius Turpio, at *Heaut.* 131–4 *sed gnatum unicum, quem pariter uti his decuit aut etiam amplius, . . . eum ego hinc eieci miserum* by Menedemus.

46 For its pleonastic character, cf. K-S 568.

47 For the pleonastic character of the combination, cf. also Martin (1976: ad loc.) and Ashmore (1910: 138).

48 Cf. also K-S 568. 49 Cf. Ashmore (1910: 297). 50 Cf. K-S 568.

51 Cf. K-S 575. 52 Cf. K-S 568. 53 Cf. K-S 575, H-Sz 799.

54 For the pleonastic character of combinations consisting of *soleo* and adverbs such as *saepe, persaepe, plerumque*, cf. H-S 797.

55 Cf. also Donat. ad loc. ταυτολογία.

56 For the pleonastic character of these syntagms, cf. K-S 572, H-Sz 802, Papadimitriou (1982: 430); cf. also Donat. ad *Hec.* 67 *nam nemo quiscquam* παρέλκον *tertium, nam abundat quicquam*, ad *Phorm.* 80 *tertium* παρέλκον, *ut in Hecyra*, ad *Hec.* 400, ad *Ad.* 366.

57 Cf. K-S 572. 58 Cf. H-Sz 802.

repetition of relative antecedent: in a relative clause, the relative pronoun is sometimes pleonastically followed by the noun to which it refers, which normally occurs in the main clause.[59] This lengthy form of expression is again restricted in the speech of old people in Terence, especially to that of Lucius Ambivius in the prologues of *Heautontimoroumenos* and *Hecyra* (two out of three examples): *Heaut.* 20–1 *habet bonorum exemplum, quo exemplo sibi licere [id] facere* and *Hec.* 10–11 *sinite exorator sim eodem ut iure uti senem liceat quo iure sum usus adulescentior*. The last example is spoken by Micio at *Ad.* 854 *i ergo intro, et quoi reist, ei rei [hilarum] hunc sumamus diem.*

Adverbs

comparative adverbs: words with comparative connotation are occasionally emphasised by the use of comparative adverbs.[60] This is mainly the case with inchoative verbs, e.g. *magis augesco, magis adgravesco*. In Terence such an expression is found in the speech of Menedemus at *Heaut.* 423 *augescit magis*.

tandem* + *aliquando:[61] at *Hec.* 683 by Laches.

solum* + *unum:[62] at *Ad.* 833 by Micio.

semper* + *adsidue: at *Heaut.* 37–9 by Lucius Ambivius.

denuo* + verbal compounds with *re-: at *Hec.* 38 *refero denuo* by L. Ambivius[63] and at *Hec.* 691 *revolutum denuo* by Laches.

rursum* + verbs compounded with *re-:[64] at *Phorm.* 922 *rursum . . . rescribi* by Demipho, at *Ad.* 71 *rursum . . . redit* by Micio.

***una* + *cum* prepositional syntagms**: *nobiscum una* at *Ad.* 753, *cum illa una* at *Ad.* 851 by Micio, *una . . . cum Aeschino* at *Ad.* 356, *una . . . mecum* at *Ad.* 843 by Demea.

adverbs denoting place (*hinc, huc* etc.) with prepositional combinations denoting place:[65] *in proxumo hic* at *Heaut.* 54, *sed quid crepuerunt fores hinc a me* at *Heaut.* 173–4 by the *senex* Chremes, *hic viciniae* at *Phorm.* 95, *petam hinc unde a primo institi* at *Phorm.* 604 by Geta, *hic prope adesset* at *Ad.* 453 by Demea, *ego huc ad hos proviso* at *Ad.* 889 by the old slave Geta.

***saepe* + frequentative verb**:[66] at *Ad.* 60 *venit ad me saepe clamitans* by Micio. *Clamito* here has, according to *OLD* s.v. 1, its frequentative meaning to 'shout repeatedly'.

foras* + verbs with elative meaning *(egredior, exeo* etc.*):[67] *esse elatum foras* at *Phorm.* 958 by Demipho, *foras egressum* at *Heaut.* 426 by

[59] Cf. K-S 569. [60] Cf. also Allardice (1929: 3), H-Sz 798.
[61] Cf. K-S 574, H-Sz 799. [62] Cf. K-S 571.
[63] Cf. Donat. ad loc. *aut 're' abundat aut 'denuo'*. [64] Cf. K-S 575.
[65] Cf. K-S 574, Allardice (1929: 92). [66] Cf. H-Sz 797.
[67] Cf. Papadimitriou (1998: 27), Barsby (1999: 105).

Chremes, *egreditur foras* at *Ad.* 923 by Demea, *eiecisset foras* at *Ad.* 109 and *excludetur foras* at *Ad.* 119 by Micio, *exirem foras* at *Hec.* 36 by the old man L. Ambivius Turpio.

***primo* + *coepi* + infinitive syntagms**:[68] at *Phorm.* 75 *coepi advorsari primo* by Geta.

Conjunctions[69]

Quasi* + *ad: at *Heaut.* 145 *quasi talenta ad quindecim coegi* by Menedemus.

Utrum* + *ne* + *an: at *Ad.* 382 *utrum studione id sibi habet an laudi putat* by Demea. Double questions are normally introduced either with *utrum-an, ne-an* or simply . . . *-an*. In our case, since the question is introduced with *utrum*, *ne* in *studione* seems to be pleonastically used or vice versa.[70] The construction is found in the speech of the *senex* Demea.[71]

at* + *tamen:[72] at *Heaut.* 88 by Chremes, at *Phorm.* 630 by Geta, at *Ad.* 830 by Micio.

ergo* + *propterea:[73] at *Hec.* 63 by Syra.

All the above do not mean, of course, that we do not occasionally find some pleonasms in the speech of other characters. Their number, however, is proportionally low in comparison to the amount of pleonasms found in senile speech. What matters again is not the individual features themselves, but their relative accumulation in the speech of specific character types and their relative absence from the language of others. In addition, as is the case with accumulated synonyms, several of these pleonasms occur

[68] Cf. K-S 570.

[69] I did not include in my examination the combination *quia enim*, since it is not clear whether the syntagm is pleonastic or not. *Enim* does not have always the value of a causal conjunction. It can have the function of a simple assertive particle (cf. Papadimitriou (1982: 442)).

[70] Cf. Papadimitriou (1982: 434). Donatus ad loc. remarks *Utrum studione aut ordo est utrumne aut est* παρέλκον *tertium*.

[71] Different is the case at *Phorm.* 659–60 *utrum stultitia facere ego hunc an malitia dicam*, uttered by the *adulescens* Antipho, on which Donatus remarks again *utrum stultitia facere* παρέλκον *tertium idem enim valet 'utrum' quod 'an'*. It seems that here we do not have two pleonastically used synonymous interrogative particles in the same sentence, as Donatus appears to believe, but the normal use of an *utrum. . . an* particle introducing an elliptical double question *utrum stultitia facere ego (hunc) dicam an malitia (facere hunc) dicam*. Cf. also *Eun.* 721 *utrum . . . an . . . ne* by Pythias.

[72] Cf. K-S 575.

[73] For the pleonastic character of the syntagm, belonging to the same group as *ergo igitur, itaque ergo*, cf. K-S 575, H-Sz 525.

when a particular character has as his interlocutor an old person (cf. *pleraque omnia* at *Heaut.* 830 by Syrus to Chremes; *iterum ut reddant* at *Phorm.* 404 by Phormio to Demipho; *tum postea* at *Ad.* 649 by Aeschinus to Micio). In particular, apart from the examples already mentioned, the following instances of pleonasms are found in the speech of other characters (not old people): *numquam . . . umquam* at *Heaut.* 559,[74] *egreditur foras* at *Heaut.* 561 by the slave Syrus; *erunt egressi foras* at *Phorm.* 892 by the parasite Phormio; *mecum una* at *Hec.* 131, 433 by the slave Parmeno and the *adulescens* Pamphilus respectively; *hic intus* at *Hec.* 98, *cum virgine una* at *Hec.* 138 by the *meretrix* Philotis; *huc raro in urbem commeat* at *Hec.* 175 and *nondum etiam* at *Hec.* 192 by Parmeno.

What is more, all these instances belong to pleonastic subcategories which are also to be found in senile speech, where the ratios of occurrence are much higher. No pleonastic combination occurring in the speech of other, non-old characters is absent from senile language. When there is restriction of specific pleonastic categories to the speech of a character type, this type is always the old people.

Longer lines

The following distributional patterns are observable.

Heautontimoroumenos

1. Old people:
   (a) Chremes: v. 953 *viduae mulieri.*
   (b) Menedemus: v. 874 *ego me non . . . perspicacem esse id scio*, v. 903 *huc est intro*, v. 907 *mecum una simul.*
   (c) Sostrata: v. 651 *una cum puella*, v. 652 *expers partis.*
2. Others: v. 241 *cum Syro uno* by Clitipho to Clinia, v. 385 *mecum in animo considero*, v. 391 *nisi si* by Bacchis to Antiphila, v. 604 *hanc secum huc adduxit, ea quae est nunc apud uxorem tuam* by Syrus to Chremes, v. 722 *exit foras* by Syrus to Clinia, v. 744 *huc ad vos* by Syrus to Bacchis, v. 994 *profer palam* by Syrus to Clitipho, v. 1000 *exit foras* by Syrus.

[74] Cf. K-S 574.

Hecyra

1. Old people:
   (a) Laches: v. 215 *crebro soleo*, v. 249 *quod tu si idem faceres, magis in rem et vostram et nostram id esset*, v. 273 *tecum una*, v. 607 *procul hinc stans*, v. 733 *huc foras*, v. 738 *magis cautius*, v. 745 *nondum etiam*, v. 754 *huc intro*, v. 762 *quoque etiam*.
   (b) Phidippus: v. 543 *quoque etiam*, v. 551 *intro ad amicam, quid tum postea*.
   (c) Sostrata: v. 236 *cum matre . . . una*, v. 337 *mage morbus adgravescat*, v. 341 *in proxumo hic*.
   (d) Pamphilus recounting the words of Myrrina: v. 400 *nil quicquam*.
2. Others: v. 281 *nemini . . . homini* by Pamphilus, v. 291 *rursum . . . restitues* by Parmeno to Pamphilus, v. 348 *hoc intro*, v. 351 *ortumst initium* by Parmeno to Sostrata, v. 363 *perspexi hisce oculis*, v. 364 *eduxi foras*, v. 371 *propere praecucurrit* by Pamphilus in his monologue. Four further instances occur, however, in the speech of Bacchis, who shares several linguistic features with old people: v. 734 *quoque etiam*, v. 793 *huc intro*, v. 808 *propere curre*, v. 863 *meis oculis . . . videram*.

Phormio

1. Old people:
   (a) Geta: v. 250 *nil quicquam*, v. 484 *exit foras*, v. 864 *intro ad eram*, v. 878 *huc egreditur foras*.
   (b) Demipho: v. 794 *adulescens mulier*.
   (c) Chremes: v. 741 *concede hinc a foribus*, v. 808 *homo nemost*.
   (d) Nausistrata: v. 1041 *homo adulescens*.
2. Others to old people: v. 538 *rursum . . . reddere*, v. 556 *una tecum*, v. 877 *atque . . . quoque* by Antipho to Geta. The only exception to the pattern described above (by or addressed to old people) is v. 172 *plerique . . . omnes* uttered by Phaedria to Antipho.[75]

Adelphoe

1. Old people:
   (a) Micio: v. 594 *nisi si*, v. 687 *at . . . tamen*, v. 970 *huc ad me*.
   (b) Demea: v. 541 *praeterea autem*, v. 949 *hic sub urbe*, v. 990 *prorsus . . . omnino*.
   (c) Syrus: v. 224 *praeterea autem*, v. 264 *exit foras*, v. 562 *hominem senem*, v. 579 *rursum redi*, v. 973 *una mecum*.

[75] *At contra* in v. 173 has the meaning of *e contrario*, see *ThLL* II 1003, and is not simply a pleonastic combination of *at and contra*.

(d) Geta: v. 306 *quem neque fides neque iusiurandum neque illum misericordia repressit*,[76] v. 315 *tum autem Syrum inpulsorem, vah, quibus illum lacerarem modis!*, v. 329 *hisce oculis egomet vidi*, v. 339 *palam proferimus*.

(e) Hegio: v. 598 *una mecum*.

2. Others to old people: v. 222 *mallem auferre potius* by Sannio to Syrus, v. 525 *revorti . . . iterum* by Ctesipho to Syrus. The only exceptions to the pattern (by or addresses to old people) occur in v. 169 *hic propter huc* by Aeschinus to Sannio, v. 180 *ante aedis . . . hic* by Aeschinus to Sannio, v. 259 *hominem neminem* by Ctesipho.

As in the iambic senarii, in the longer lines the pleonasms occurring in the speech of non-old people are those which are evenly distributed, i.e. which do not show any particular concentration according to character type, even though their frequency of appearance is often higher in the speech of old people (*foras* + *ex*-compounded verbs, *rursum* + *re*-verbal compound, *una* + *cum* + ablative syntagms). When there is restriction as well as a particular concentration of specific pleonastic categories in the speech of a character type, this type is always the old people.

Conclusions

It is obvious from the above that senile speech in Terence is characterised by its penchant for wordiness. This does not entail that other character types avoid using occasional long-winded expressions. Again, it is not the individual features themselves that are important, but their relative accumulation and variety in the speech of specific character types, and their relative absence from the language of others. Some long-winded expressions, namely the accumulated synonyms, in the speech of other characters (i.e. non-old people) are often not freely interspersed throughout their language, but show a particular concentration in a specific part of their speech when they have an old man as their interlocutor, whereas such features are avoided when addressing other people.

[76] Cf. Donat. ad loc. παρέλκον, *nam abundat 'illum'*.

More specifically, in the iambic senarii old people tend to use many pleonastic combinations on the level of lexemes[77] consisting mainly of two words, phrases etc., where one is adequate in sense, as is evidenced from the speech of other characters (i.e. not old people). This is the case with combinations of adverbs (*magis* + words of comparative notion etc.), conjunctions (*at* + *tamen)* and many other lexical items (*nemo* + *homo* etc.). Pleonasms always occur in higher ratios in the speech of old people (*Heaut.* 2.7% vs. 2.16%; *Hec.* 6.67% vs. 2.59%; *Phorm.* 2.76% vs. 1.06%; *Ad.* 4.52% vs. 2.17%).

Accumulation of synonymous expressions also shows a particular concentration in senile speech. As with pleonasms, accumulated synonyms occur in higher ratios in the speech of old people (*Heaut.* 2.03% vs. 1.62%; *Hec.* 1.3% vs. 0.86%; *Phorm.* 1.51% vs. 0%; *Ad.* 3.14%[78] vs. 2.17%). More importantly, however, with the exception of the two instances in the speech of the garrulous Parmeno in the *Hecyra*, all other (few) instances of accumulated synonyms in the speech of non-old characters occur when addressing old people. It must be noted that some of the cases of synonymy adduced above are not as clear-cut or striking as others; however, they have been mentioned both because a more complete picture is thus offered and because, even if they are only near-synonymous (and, as already mentioned, synonymy depends on context and subjective judgement), they still impart a rambling or long-winded character to the speech of old people, where they are concentrated.

An evolution in the Terentian technique of characterisation through the medium of long-winded expressions is also discernible. In *Andria* such features are not favoured in the speech of old people. In the iambic senarii: eight pleonasms[79] by old people, six by other characters,[80] eight accumulated synonyms by old

[77] Not on the syntactic level, e.g. correlatives, appositional syntagms, dativus ethicus of pronouns, syntagms consisting of a *verbum dicendi* or *putandi* + *esse* in place of equivalent finite forms, appositional negations etc.

[78] The high percentage in this case is due to a single instance (addressed to an old man) divided, however, by a small total number of verses.

[79] Cf. vv. 55, 63, 81, 90–1, 107, 174, 543, 807.

[80] Cf. vv. 455, 671, 726, 734, 755–6, 759.

people,[81] seven by others[82] (ratios, respectively, 2.95% vs. 2.65% and 2.95% vs. 3.09%). This is also the case with *Eunuchus*, which is completely different in matters of language in general and stylistic techniques in particular.[83] Linguistic characterisation by means of prolix diction starts with *Heautontimoroumenos*. This technique of characterisation becomes perfected in Terence's final drama, *Adelphoe*, in which one finds not just a high accumulation of the features in question in senile language and discourse addressed to old people, but a complete restriction of these features to the diction of, or addresses to, old people.

Linguistic characterisation by means of long-winded or pleonastic expressions is also evident in the Terentian prologues. These senile linguistic features are to be found in the prologues of *Hecyra* and *Heautontimoroumenos*, which are both spoken by the old man L. Ambivius Turpio, in opposition to all other Terentian prologues, uttered by other (not *senes*) actors: the pleonastic repetition of a pronoun at *Hec.* 15, the repetition of a relevant antecedent at *Heaut.* 20 and *Hec.* 10–11, the pleonastic combinations *exirem foras* at *Hec.* 36, *refero denuo* at *Hec.* 38, *semper . . . adsidue* at *Heaut.* 37–9.

In other lines linguistic characterisation by means of long-winded features is not as clear-cut as in the iambic lines. As for accumulated synonyms, they tend to be used more frequently in senile speech in *Hecyra, Phormio* and *Adelphoe*,[84] where both the absolute number of instances and the ratios are higher in the speech of old people (*Hec.* 1.87% vs. 1.80%, *Phorm.* 1.19% vs. 1.10%, and more importantly *Ad.* 5.58% vs. 0%, *Heaut.* 3.33% vs. 3.61%). What is more, the synonyms found in the speech of other characters occur mainly when their interlocutor is an old person, or are found in the speech of Bacchis, whose linguistic behaviour

[81] Cf. vv. 62, 74, 132, 137, 404, 560–1, 809, 886.

[82] Cf. vv. 139, 274, 277–8, 279–80, 291, 296, 723.

[83] Cf. note 3 of this chapter.

[84] *Hecyra* is believed to have been produced in 165 BC. Hence, chronologically, it should be placed between *Andria* (166 BC) and *Heautontimoroumenos* (163 BC). However, in the matter of linguistic characterisation by means of long-winded speech in longer lines, *Hecyra* stands closer to *Phormio* (161) and *Adelphoe* (160) than to *Andria* and *Heautontimoroumenos*. This could be put down to an improvement of the play by Terence in the time between 165 and the second and third (finally successful) performance in 160 BC.

is often similar to that of old people. The same also applies to pleonasms (ratios of old people vs. others: *Hec.* 5.9% vs. 4.95%, *Phorm.* 3.16% vs. 2.21%, *Ad.* 5.95% vs. 3.38%, *Heaut.* 2.86% vs. 2.89%). In *Andria* senile speech is not characterised by its penchant for long-winded features. In particular, five pleonasms by old people,[85] fourteen by others:[86] four accumulated synonyms by old people,[87] twelve by others;[88] ratios, respectively, 4.03% vs. 4.23% and 3.22% vs. 3.62%.

[85] Cf. vv. 201, 205, 580, 828, 910.
[86] Cf. vv. 239, 249, 315, 355, 483, 507, 636, 709, 711, 712, 713, 851, 900, 963.
[87] Cf. vv. 823, 831, 836, 921.
[88] Cf. vv. 206, 236, 238–9, 248, 257, 304, 312, 509, 603, 608, 625, 979.

CHAPTER 4

HELLENISMS

It has long been recognised that lower-class characters in the plays of both Plautus and Terence use words of Greek origin in greater numbers than do upper-class characters.

Tuchaendler was the first to examine the distribution of Greek loan words in both Plautus and Terence, concluding that '*maximam insignium tralatorum partem in ore hominum inferioris ordinis maximum servorum esse*'. Hough (1947: 18–21), examining the question anew, arrived at the same conclusion. Furthermore, he claimed that the tendency of both dramatists to put Greek words into the mouths of lower-class characters increased as their careers progressed. Gilleland (1979: 84 ff.) argued for a common pattern in Roman comedy, underlying the striking similarities between the figures for Greek words in Plautus and Terence. Both dramatists agree in giving more words than average to the *servus*, *parasitus, miles* and *leno*, and fewer than average to the *senex, adulescens, matrona, meretrix*.

More recently, the subject has been reexamined by Maltby (1985), who again reaches the same conclusion. Maltby, however, unlike all his predecessors, makes a distinction between Greek words that would have had a real Greek flavour in Terence's time and those which had been borrowed early into Latin, or at least had become well integrated in the language by Terence's time, and would no longer have retained their foreign colouring for the author. Curiously enough, in his later study of the distribution of Greek words in Plautus, Maltby abandons this methodological differentiation, claiming that in both Plautus and Terence there is little difference in the distribution of these two types of Greek words.

Much scholarly work has been dedicated to the study of hellenisms in the vocabulary of comedy. The corresponding field of syntax, however, has almost been ignored, and it is this lacuna that I intend to fill.

In this chapter, I shall show that Terence has a tendency to use hellenisms not only on a lexical but also on a syntactic level in order to differentiate the speech of his characters. Grecisms, just like colloquialisms, most often characterise the language of male characters of low social status or rustic characters. Other characters use hellenising syntagms mainly when addressing low or rustic characters. More specifically, in this chapter I shall deal with syntactic phenomena of the Latin language which, according to modern scholarship, are attributable to Greek influence, since in most cases no native Indo-European origin can be traced.

Methodological remarks

I must first briefly mention several cases of mistakenly diagnosed hellenisms in Roman comedy, i.e. constructions which, although attributed by many scholars to Greek influence, have been proven by later research to constitute native elements of the Latin language. Consequently, these constructions will not be taken into consideration in my survey.

Genitive of purpose with gerund. An example occurs at *Ad.* 270 *ne id adsentandi mage quam quo habeam gratum facere existumes* ('you might take it for flattery else instead of gratitude'), spoken by Ctesipho. Some modern scholars think that this Latin construction is a grecism.[1] The construction, however, is an archaic idiom common to the Italic languages, as is evidenced by some parallels in Umbrian (e.g. *Ig.* 6a8 *ocrer pihaner = montis piandi*) as well as in some religious inscriptions from Rome (CIL 6 2065 col. 2. 19–20 < A.D. 87 >), where it is difficult to claim Greek influence.[2] As for the Terentian example at *Ad.* 270, Terence simply changes construction in mid sentence. The *ne* clause begins as if a second gerund with e.g. *causa* were going to occur instead of the present

[1] Cf. Brenous (1895: 113–18), Löfstedt (1956: I 169–71).
[2] Cf. Coleman (1975: 129).

quo clause.[3] A second example, at *Rud.* 1374, is more likely to be a dative than a genitive.

Accusativus Graecus. In both Plautus and Terence we find perfect participles of verbs with the sense 'to clothe' or 'to equip' constructed with the accusative, e.g. *indutum . . . pallam* (Plaut. *Men.* 511–12), a construction which has often been explained as an imitation of the Greek equivalent εἱμένος χιτῶνα. In these cases, however, the verbal form is simply middle in sense, an obsolete verbal aspect in Latin, which also has parallels in Umbrian.[4] Only the extension of the construction to finite verbs and other lexemes could be attributed to Greek influence. Whereas the expression is often found in Plautus (cf. *Men.* 190, 511–12, 514–15, *Rud.* 207), it is avoided in Terence, and is found exclusively featured in his more EL and linguistically Plautine *Eunuchus* vv. 1015–16 *ubi vestem vidit illam esse eum indutum* (cf. also Turpil. *com.* 76).

Genetivus Graecus. Genitive in place of the accusative is sometimes constructed with verbs of desiring, scorning and fearing. Examples include *vereor* at *Phorm.* 971 *neque huius sis veritus feminae primariae*. The foregoing usages are not to be regarded as the results of Greek influence. They belong rather with the use of the genitive with verbs of feeling (*miseret, pudet*).[5] It is plausible to hold that *cupio, fastidio, studeo* followed the analogy of *cupidus, fastidiosus, studiosus* etc., and *veretur* with the genitive seems to be attributable to the analogical influence of *pudet* and similar verbs.

***ne* + imperative.** Donatus comments upon *ne me obsecra* in place of *ne obsecres* at *Andr.* 543: τῷ ἑλληνισμῷ. The construction, however, seems to be a common EL feature, found eight times in Roman comedy.[6] No other grammarian, when referring to similar constructions (cf. Serv. *A.* 6.95, 7.202), calls them grecisms.

[3] Cf. also Donat. ad loc. *antiqua* ἔλλειψις *deest enim 'causa'*; for a possible contamination here cf. also H-Sz 75.

[4] Cf. Coleman (1975: 123–5).

[5] Cf. Bennett (1910–4: II 99).

[6] Cf. Mayer (1999: 164 n. 2).

***non umquam* combinations.** Servius remarks on *non umquam* at *A.* 2. 247: *Graeco more*. The syntagm, however, seems to be native to both Greek and Latin (K-S I 827–8).

Neuter plural in place of neuter singular in impersonal verbal expressions (e.g. *mira sunt for mirum est*). Servius remarks on *nota tibi* at A. 1.669: *Graeca figura*. This plural is frequent in Greek with verbal adjectives, see *S. A.* 677ff. In the case of the Latin examples, however, Löfstedt (1956: 158–60) interprets these neuter plurals as involving some notion of collectivity.

Syntactic hellenisms in Terence

Let us now examine the instances of probable Greek influence in Terentian syntax. I shall first treat the cases for which there exists a relative consensus among scholars as to their Greek origin.

Nominal syntax

Adverbs or prepositional complements used as adjectival modifiers

The Greek language had the ability to use freely an adverb or even a prepositional complement as a modifier of a substantive in cases such as ἡ ἐν Σαλαμῖνι ναυμαχία, ὁ τότε πόλεμος, usages facilitated by the existence of the article. At *Andr.* 175–6 in *eri semper lenitas verebar quorsum evaderet*, the adverb *semper* may refer to *lenitas* and not to the verbal action of the clause *verebar*, a hellenising construction frequently found later: cf. Verg. *A.* 1.198 *neque enim ignari sumus ante malorum* (= τῶν πρόσθεν κακῶν), Liv. 22.42.9 *primo Punico bello . . . clades* (= ἡ ἐν τῷ πρώτῳ πολέμῳ ἧττα[7]). If so, here *semper lenitas* is equivalent to *perpetua lenitas* in analogy to the Greek ἡ ἀεὶ εὔνοια. The hellenising expression is uttered by the slave Davus.

[7] For the hellenising character of similar constructions, cf. Ernout and Thomas (1972: 191–2).

Verbal syntax

Case usage

Ablative of respect + accusative denoting person. The construction of *conscindere* with an ablative of respect *capillo* and an accusative of the person *ipsam* at *Eun.* 646 *ipsam capillo conscidit* seems irregular, since the normal Latin construction requires the dative: *ipsi capillum conscidit.* The syntax seems to have been influenced by common equivalent Greek constructions with the accusative of respect.[8] Once more, this element of Greek syntax is found in the speech of a character who also uses many Greek words, the *ancilla* Pythias.

***incipere* + partitive genitive.** A strange use of the partitive genitive is found after *incipio* in *novi negoti incipere* at *Phorm.* 709–10 *ante brumam autem novi negoti incipere*. This construction is nonstandard in Latin, where *incipere* is normally construed with the accusative (cf. *Andr.* 724, 772, *Ad.* 227, 237 etc.) or the infinitive (*Heaut.* 495), and has often puzzled scholars, who have postulated a lacuna after *initium*.[9] As Allardice (1929: 22) points out, however, the construction is perhaps to be attributed to an influence of the construction of the Greek equivalent ἄρχεσθαι with the genitive, possibly occurring in the Greek original. If it is indeed to be analysed thus, it would not be a coincidence again that this conceivably Greek construction is found in the speech of the slave Geta, who, as Maltby has shown, also uses the majority of the Greek words in the play, a characteristic which gives his speech a distinct colloquial colour.[10]

***est* + infinitive.** The use of *est* with an infinitive like the Greek ἔστι, ἔχεστι (= 'it is possible that . . .') is a hellenising construction often found later in Vergil (cf. *A.* 6.596 *cernere erat*) and Horace. A similar case is found at *Heaut.* 192 *miserum? quem minus crederest?*[11] ('miserable? Whom could you fancy less so?'), which is

[8] Cf. Tromaras (1994: 211). [9] Cf. McGlynn I 280.

[10] For another interpretation of the construction, cf. chapter 1, p. 37.

[11] Cf. Maurach (1995: 89, 1983: 123), H-Sz 349, Allardice (1929: 91). See also Servius ad *A.* 8.676 *Graeca figura.*

uttered by the *senex* Chremes. Another instance at *Ad.* 828–9 *scire est liberum ingenium atque animum* is uttered by Micio when speaking to the rustic Demea.

Tense and mood usage

Gnomic aorist. The use of the aorist in a gnomic sense is common Greek and the only parallel adduced for this Greek usage is in Serbian.[12] Hence, the Latin examples should not be seen as survivals of an inherited use. They should, instead, be put down to Greek influence.[13] Furthermore, when found in Latin, this use of the gnomic aorist in Latin is mainly confined to hellenising registers (cf. Verg. *G.* 4.212–14, Sen *Ep.* 82.14).

A gnomic use of the perfect is found at *Ad.* 855 *Numquam ita quisquam bene subducta ratione ad vitam fuit*, uttered by the *senex* Demea, whose speech is also characterised by a penchant for Greek vocabulary. The gnomic character of the perfect, approximating the value of a Greek aorist, is furthermore evidenced by the present sequence of tenses which follows *fuit* (*aliquid adportet novi* and *aliquid moneat*). Another possible instance of gnomic aorist is found at *Hec.* 309[14] *quom de eadem causast iracundus factus inimicissimus*, spoken by the slave Parmeno.

Indirect questions

The use of *si* in place of *num* or *ne* for introducing indirect questions seems to be influenced by similar uses of the Greek particle εἰ.[15] This seems to be especially the case with *nescio si* syntagms in place of *nescio an*, probably calqued on the Greek equivalent οὐ γὰρ οἶδα syntagms. One instance of such a construction occurs at *Hec.* 321 *id si forte est nescio* in the mouth of the slave Parmeno.[16]

dare bibere. Latin grammarians seem to have considered this usage as a grecism. Pompeius (GLK V 213 12–5) insisted that

[12] Cf. Coleman (1975: 134).
[13] Cf. also Ernout and Thomas (1972: 224), Maurach (1983: 119).
[14] Cf. Carney (1964: 63) vs. Allardice (1929: 67).
[15] For the hellenising character of similar constructions, cf. Ernout and Thomas (1972: 320) ‘une influence du grec est en même temps possible’.
[16] For the specific example, cf. Bléry (1965: 58): ‘à moins qu’il ne faille dire que c’est un double hellénisme’.

the usage was not Latin but an *elocutio Graeca*. For Servius, too, the infinitive with *do* comes from Greek syntax (cf. *A*. 5.248 *Graecum est duo verba coniungere, ut paulo post, sed hoc datur poetis*). Among modern scholars, Heraeus (1937: 195–6 n. 3) approves the doctrine of the Roman grammarians that *dare bibere* was a grecism. The construction is found once in the Terentian corpus, at *Andr*. 484 *quod iussi dari bibere*, once more in the speech of a low character, the *obstetrix* Lesbia. In Plautus a similar construction occurs at *Pers*. 821 in the mouth of the slave Toxilus.

Conclusions

It is evident from the above that Terence uses not only Greek words but also hellenising constructions to differentiate the speech of low and rustic characters. These constructions are not evenly distributed between the low characters in Terence but are to be found in the speech of those who also use many Greek words as well (Geta in *Phormio*, who accounts for half of the occurrences of Greek words in the play, Davus in *Andria*, with three Greek words *eugae* v. 345, *opsonium* v. 360, *opsonor* v. 451 followed by the hellenising *semper lenitas* construction). As for female speech, with the exception of the *ancilla* Pythias in *Eunuchus*, whose speech has a distinct hellenising colouring (*techina* v. 718, *ephebus* v. 824, *apage* v. 904, *moechus* v. 957), female speech lacks grecising linguistic features.

It seems that there was a general linguistic trend among educated members of the upper class of the Roman society in the second century BC of avoiding Greek in their speech. This was the attitude of the Scipiones, to whom Terence was attached.[17] There are several testimonies to the negative attitude towards Greek of those supporting *sermo purus*.[18] If so, it is not surprising that several Greek and grecising expressions are assigned by Terence to the speech of his low and rustic characters.

[17] Cf. Petersmann (1999: 297). For Terence and the Scipionic circle, cf. Grimal (1953: 149), Gruen (1993: 197–202).

[18] Cf. Cic. *Off.* 1.111 *sermone eo debemus uti, qui notus est nobis, ne ut quidam Graeca verba inculcantes iure optimo rideamur*, *Tusc*. 1.15 *scis enim me Graece loqui in Latino sermone non plus solere quam in Graeco Latine*.

CHAPTER 5

MARKERS OF ELEVATED LANGUAGE

The mode of speech normally used in epic as well as in tragedy had from the beginning a character artificial and remote from that of everyday life. As the second century advanced, the language of comedy – especially in Terence – moved away from that of tragedy and approached the common language.[1] The language of tragedy and epic, on the other, displayed an increasing tendency to become more elaborate and artificial. Three sources have been suggested for the types of elaboration in early Republican drama: modes of speaking practised by Roman politicians, orators and officials,[2] the Attic τραγικὴ λέξις and formulae of law and religion.[3]

Methodological framework

It is very difficult indeed for a modern scholar to isolate features in the remains of Early Latin tragedy and epic, and label them as peculiarly tragic or epic. Roman critics (Hor. *Ars* 86ff., Gel. 2.23.21) often bewailed the lack of the sharp Attic distinctions of language between comedy and tragedy. Nevertheless some words, phrases, syntactical constructions and specific stylistic options can be shown, from their comparative frequencies in the tragic and comic scripts and the contexts as well as the metrical units in

[1] On Terence and his avoidance of tragic language, cf. Evanth. *de Com.* 3.5 *tam illud est admirandum* (scil. *in Terentio*) *quod et morem retinuit ut comoediam scriberet et temperavit affectum ne in tragoediam transiliret, quod cum aliis rebus minime obtentum et a Plauto et ab Afranio et Appio et multis fere magnis comicis invenimus*. Cf. also Sheets (1983: 209).

[2] Cf. Norden (1898: 839, 889), Leo (1913: 34–40), Eckstein (1921: 173).

[3] Cf. Fraenkel (1960: 338–53).

which they belong, to have possessed a more elevated tone than others.[4]

In this study elevated language will refer to features that:

1. are often found in high literary genres (tragedy, epic) but are comparatively rare in comedy;
2. often belong to specialised registers found mainly in stylised ritual, legal[5] and formal-official language;
3. when appearing in comedy, especially in Plautine drama, are used in contexts which may be characterised as solemn or mock-solemn (ritual settings, imprecations to Gods, formal supplications etc.), official or mock-official (parody of military, oratorical and public official vocabulary and manners of speech)[6] or paratragic, often marked by highly stylised and rhetorically embellished language.

These features are not usually found in the spoken verses but appear in concentration mainly in the musically accompanied verses in a context of linguistic or stylistic elaboration (heavy alliteration and assonance, constant parallelism of clauses with balance of individual words and phrases, rhetorical questions, repetitions, verbal echoes etc.).[7] Such features are usually followed by several other devices of a similar kind, the concentration of which in specific parts of the play heightens the formal character of the contextual setting. In the later history of Latin many of these features, while avoided in colloquial genres like satire and epistolography, reappear more frequently in the higher literary genres (mainly epic) of Augustan poetry.

In this chapter I shall examine how these features, having acquired an elevated character (as described above)[8] in the literary

[4] For musically accompanied verses vs. less elaborate trimeters, especially in Plautus, cf. Haffter (1934: passim), Jocelyn (1967: 41), Lindholm (1931: 94–100), Fraenkel (1928: 93 n.1). For a comparative examination of EL comic, tragic, epic language, cf. Ploen (1882).

[5] For legal language in the Terentian prologues, cf. Focardi (1972: 55–88).

[6] E.g. the use of ablative absolutes with temporal sense, a distinct feature of official language in the second century; for parodying generals' reports of their achievements, see Jocelyn (1967: 400). For parody in Plautus, cf. also Blänsdorf (1996: 133–51), Hoffmann (1980–1: 207–18); for religious language in Plautus, cf. also Piccaluga (1991: 9–22); for tragic diction in Plautus, cf. also Thierfelder (1939: 155–66) and Danese (1985: 101ff.). For tragic language in New Comedy, cf. also Hunter (1985: 114ff.).

[7] For Plautus' approximating tragic style in musically accompanied lines, cf. also Jocelyn (1972: 73–4).

[8] By elevated language I do not mean simple legal, military, or religious terms (e.g. *mancupium*) but features that, as I said, can be shown from their frequency in higher genres

registers of the second century BC, are related in Terentian drama to specific characters as well as to the contextual setting. I shall demonstrate that, on both a lexical and a syntactic level, they are in Terence favoured in the speech of high characters, such as *adulescentes, matronae, virgines* but mainly *senes*. When used by low characters, these features are found mainly in the speech of old slaves, e.g. Geta in *Phormio*, who often use features commonly found in the speech of *senes* or *matronae* of a higher social level, or are found in elevated contexts (e.g. Gnatho's speech at the end of *Eunuchus*).

When discussing archaisms and long-winded and pleonastic expressions as key elements of senile speech, I drew attention to several features of a more elevated language. These are repeated here for the sake of completeness, without details of distribution however, since they have already been examined in detail – but from a different viewpoint – in chapter 2. Next, I discuss lexical choice in Terence, collecting (in alphabetical order) lexical elements which can be shown to have an elevated ring. My examination concludes with similar choices on the morphological and stylistic level.

Archaic and long-winded expressions of an elevated character

Morphology. A possible case in point is genitive terminations in *-ai*, often found in epic, less frequently in tragedy and only occasionally in formulaic and stylised passages in Plautus.[9]

Syntactic options. The use of *gratia* + genitive in place of *causa* + genitive.[10]

(epic, tragedy) as well as in high-style thematic contexts in comedy to have acquired a more elevated flavour.

9 Cf. Jocelyn (1967: 364); for this kind of genitive forms see also Leumann (1945: 253 n.37), (1947: 121); for *gratia* in comedy, cf. also Collart (1978: 293–7); for such genitive forms in Plautus, cf. Hodgman (1902: 295).

10 For the loftier tone of *gratia*, cf. Jocelyn (1967: 277).

Circumlocutions and pleonasms

1. Accumulation of synonymous words, expressions in bi-membered oppositions where the second part of the combination repeats the first, usually in a longer form.
2. Relative clauses repeating the antecedent noun, often found in Latin legal texts.[11]

Lexical choice

Single words

atrox The word, as Lindsay remarks (1900: 250), belongs to the diction of tragedy rather than comedy (cf. Pac. *trag.* 47, 369, Acc. *trag.* 46), and the unique use in Plautus at *Capt.* 539 is considered to be paratragic. In Terence the expression is uttered once at *Hec.* 377 by the *adulescens* Pamphilus, in his passionate monologue, *incredibili re atque atroci percitus.*

derepente* vs. *repente *Derepente* seems to be the elevated equivalent.[12] Tragedy favours the compounded form, which appears 4 times, while the simple form appears only once. Comedy on the other hand prefers *repente* (thirteen times). The compound adverb is found twice in Terence's least farcical play, *Hecyra*, in vv. 518, 554 uttered by two old people, Myrrina and Phidippus respectively.

flamma* vs. *ignis *Flamma* appears to have been a word of elevated tone,[13] being favoured by high literary genres. It occurs ten times in tragedy whereas its synonymous *ignis* occurs 26 times in comedy and only once in tragedy. Similarly, the derived verb *inflammari* is found only in tragedy (Enn. *trag.* 92 and Acc. *trag.* 14), whereas comedy prefers the synonymous *incendere* (13x). In Terence, apart from the standardised proverbial expression at *Eun.* 491 *e flamma petere . . . cibum*, the word occurs as synonymous with *ignis* once at *Andr.* 130 *ad flammam accessit inprudentius* in the speech of the *senex* Simo.

gradus *Gradus* in the sense of 'act of taking a step' occurs in tragedy (cf. Enn. *trag.* 6–7 *gradum regredere conare*) and in all Plautus' instances the word seems to be a parody of military or tragic contexts.[14] In Terence the word is found once at *Phorm.* 867 *suspenso gradu placide ire perrexi accessi astiti.* The expression is uttered by the slave Geta, who often uses features associated with senile speech.

limen The word has many solemn associations for the Roman mind and is to be found in tragedy, Acc. *trag.* 531 *ab limine caeli*, as well as in

[11] Cf. Kroll (1910–12: 8–10). [12] Cf. Jocelyn (1967: 210).
[13] Cf. Jocelyn (1967: 199). [14] Cf. Jocelyn (1967: 173).

some solemn contexts in Plautine drama, such as *Cas.* 815, Pardalisca's monody, *sensin super attolle limen pedes*, a comic parody of formulaic ritual, official and tragic diction.[15] The derived verb *eliminare* also occurs exclusively in tragic scripts (cf. Acc. *trag.* 448, 592, Enn. *trag.* 238, Pac. *trag.* 134). In Terence the word is found once, at *Hec.* 378 *ut limen exirem*, uttered by the *adulescens* Pamphilus.

luctus The word seems to be elevated in tone, as it is favoured by tragedy (nine times) and avoided by comedy. In Terence it is found once, at *Hec.* 210 *filio luctum paras*, in the speech of the *senex* Laches.

quadrupes* vs. *animal Tragedy has *quadrupes* commonly for animals.[16] The word is also found in Plautus at *Capt.* 814, in a tragically styled parody of a praetor's edict. The adjective, preferred in tragedy, is found once in Terence, at *Andr.* 865, in conjunction with an EL future imperative, which has a highly formal tone even in the early second century,[17] *quadrupedem constringito*, in the speech of the old man Simo again.

satias* vs. *satietas The EL *satias* has in Plautus an elevated tone, and is used in mock-official contexts, i.e. in comic imitation of religious and possibly legal language. In particular it occurs: (1) at *Pseud.* 334, in the context of formal ritual language by the *adulescens* Callidorus; (2) at *Cist.* 502, in a legal context. The word is also found in didactic poetry (Lucretius) and later in Tacitus as a conscious archaism. In Terence it is used by high characters, Sostrata at *Hec.* 594 and Chremes (Laches) at *Eun.* 973. The elevated character of the word, favoured by high literary genres, seems to be a further reason, apart from its EL character,[18] for its being assigned to old people.

uspiam The word had an elevated colouring already in Plautus, being used mainly in mock-epic passages (cf. *Mil.* 597).[19] In Terence this word is found twice in the speech of the old man Micio, at *Ad.* 28 and 37.

[15] Several elevated features appear in concentration at *Cas.* 815ff.: cf. *nova nupta, sospes-superstes* alluding to Enn. *trag.* 246 *ut sospitent superstitentque*, *potior pollentia* alluding to *trag. inc.* v. 175 *quis plus pollet potiorque est patre*, the separation of *limen* from its preposition *super* giving a further ritualistic flavour to the language, and the bi-membered asyndeton *quaerunt volunt*, favoured in official and tragic diction; for the elevated character of the context in discussion cf. Fraenkel (1960: 342), MacCarry and Willcock (1976: 190); for the formal and elevated colouring of the word in Republican drama, cf. also Jocelyn (1967: 377).

[16] Cf. Naev. *trag.* 25, Enn. *trag.* 157, *Ann.* 236, Pac. *trag.* 2, Acc. *trag.* 315, 381, cf. also *quadrupedantes* Enn. *trag.* 169, Acc. *trag.* 603 *quadripedantum sonipedum*, the first attestation of the calque of Hesiod's καναχήπους.

[17] For the formal character of the imperative in *-to*, cf. Jocelyn (1967: 278).

[18] For the archaic character of the expression, cf. Maltby (1976: 237–8).

[19] For the elevated character of the word, cf. also Maltby (1976: 243).

Expressions

extra aedis* vs. *extra portam Whereas comedy favours *extra portam* vs. *ex aedibus*, in tragedy we find the combination *extra aedis* (cf. Enn. *trag.* 238). It is found once also in a paratragic line of Pomponius (*atel.* 33) *eleminabo extra aedis coniugem.* In Terence the expression is found once, at *Hec.* 563 *interdico ne extulisse extra aedis puerum usquam velis*, uttered by the *senex* Phidippus. What is more, the periphrasis *ne extulisse . . . velis*, consisting of *volo* with a perfect for a present infinitive, an archaic survival of an old legal idiom,[20] adds further to the formal character of Phidippus' utterance, which here apes the style of public edicts.

ferte opem* vs. *ferte auxilum *Ferte opem* probably originates in sacral language. It is found in tragedy (cf. Enn. *trag.* 42 *ferte opem, trag. inc.* 241) as well as in elevated/paratragic contexts in Plautus (cf. *Rud.* 617).[21] In Terence the expression is found twice in the speech of two *virgines*, Glycerium and Pamphila, at *Andr.* 473 and *Ad.* 487, respectively, in formal imprecations to Juno *Iuno Lucina, fer opem! serva me obsecro!*.

paucis* = 'in a few words' vs. *ad pauca Maltby (1976: 242–3) has plausibly claimed that the ablative expression *paucis* had developed by Terence's time into a high-register feature, being used in mock-official contexts, as is the case with *Eun.* 1067–8 *prius audite paucis: quod quom dixero, si placuerit, facitote*, where the use of parallel subordinate clauses introduced by *quom* and *si* as well as the EL imperative *facitote* calls to mind ancient legal language.[22] This line in *Eunuchus* is uttered by Gnatho. *Paucis* is later found with this meaning (= 'in a few words') in high genres like epic (e.g. Verg. *A.* 4.116 *paucis . . . docebo*) in contrast to *pauca* / *ad pauca*, which occurs in more colloquial genres (in the satires of Horace *S.* 1.6.61, Juv. 5.107). The expression is again uttered by high characters, Simo at *Andr.* 29, Laches at *Hec.* 510, L. Ambivius Turpio at *Heaut.* 10 and finally Micio at *Ad.* 806. The colloquial form *ad pauca*, on the other hand, is found in the speech of two slaves, Parmeno at *Hec.* 135 and Geta at *Phorm.* 648 *ut ad pauca redeam.*

pedem efferre* vs. *domo abire Of the two equivalents, *pedem efferre* is the one more elevated in tone, as is also the case with similar circumlocutions with *pes* often found in tragedy (cf. Enn. *trag.* 215 *nam numquam . . . domo efferret pedem*). In Plautus the expression is again

[20] Cf. Allardice (1929: 85).

[21] Here Trachalio rushes out of the temple and yells for help, parodying tragic and oratorical diction in eight-beat trochaics full of heavy alliteration. For this, see also Fay (1983: 138); for the claim that the scene has been modelled on *O.C.* 884ff., cf. Marx (1959: 142); for the elevated character of the expression in comedy, cf. also Jocelyn (1967: 215).

[22] Cf. Leg. XII tab. VIII 12 *si non furtum faxsit, si im occisit, iure caesus esto.*

found in formal contexts, cf. *Bacch.* 423 *digitum longe a paedagogo pedem ut ecferres aedibus*, where the expression appears in a highly rhetorical context, a condemnation of the new education in comparison to the old by the pedagogue Lydus.[23] *Domo abire* on the other hand is the usual expression in comedy (Plaut. *Amph.* 502–3, *Epid.* 46, *Merc.* 12, *Stich.* 29, *Trin.* 1010, Ter. *Eun.* 661 etc.). In Terence the expression *pedem (ef)ferre* is found once at *Andr.* 808 *nam pol, si id scissem, numquam huc tetulissem pedem*, uttered by the *senex* Crito. The archaic reduplicated perfect form *tetulissem* here in place of the simple and normal *tulissem* could add further to the elevated and formal character of the utterance.

templa caeli The expression, found once at *Eun.* 590 *templa caeli summa sonitu concutit*, often appears in epic and tragedy, especially in Ennius (cf. *Ann.* 1.48 *ad caeli caerula templa*, 54–5), having its counterpart in the Greek τέμενος αἰθέρος, A. *Pers.* 365.[24] Donatus as well claims that the expression is derived from tragic diction (*tragice*). The expression is uttered by the *adulescens* Chaerea when referring to the story of Danae, which must already have been known to the Roman audience through Latin adaptations of Greek tragedies.[25]

prudens sciens Cicero quotes the expression from tragedy (*Fam.* 6.6.6).[26] The expression is uttered by the *adulescens* Phaedria at *Eun.* 72–3.

Morphological choice

Compound adjectives of the type *damni-ficus, falsi-dicus*. Compound adjectives of this kind are mostly favoured in authors of Republican epic and tragedy, in an attempt to coin new Latin equivalents for similar Greek poetic compounds, which constitute a regular feature of Greek epic and choral lyric style.[27] In CL these formations occur in high genres, mainly in the *Aeneid* and

[23] Lydus uses here a stylised and rhetorically embellished language which consists of: (1) various stylistic effects such as verbal antithesis, parallelism of clauses, verbal echoes, repetitions, alliterative pairs, assonance, set speech with interruptions, reminiscent in tone and form of the typical Aristophanic ἀγών (cf. Cassio (1979: 1–22), Barsby (1986: 132, 133–4); for the elevated character of the expression, cf. also Jocelyn (1967: 355)); (2) tragic diction, v. 426 *hoc etiam ad malum accersebatur malum* (see E. *Alc.* 557 καὶ πρὸς κακοῖσιν ἄλλο τοῦτ' ἂν ἦν κακόν), followed by *et discipulus et magister perhibebantur inprobi* (cf. also *Ph.* 94); for the tragic diction here cf. Leo (1966: 135).

[24] Cf. Skutsch (1985: 201). [25] Cf. Andr. *trag.* 19, Naevius *trag.* 3–13.

[26] For the tragic or elevated flavour of the diction here, cf. also Barsby (1999: 96), Flury (1968: 58–9).

[27] Cf. also Coleman (1999: 61).

in Ovid's *Metamorphoses*.[28] Plautus seems to exploit the elevated tone of non-CL compounds of this kind, making them suitable for characterising the language of gods, pompous old men and *adulescentes* in love.[29] Similar compounds, usually coinages by Plautus, are also found in the speech of low characters, often in mock-official and mock-tragic contexts (cf. *Asin.* 33ff.).[30]

In Terence, one non-CL compound is uttered by a high character, Pamphilus at *Andr.* 294 (*morigera*) in a very formal context, when imitating Chrysis' speech on her death-bed. The elevated character of the adjective fits, according to Maltby (1976: 211), the highly stylised language, with its balanced phrases (vv. 288–90 *et ad pudicitiam et ad rem tutandam, per . . . dexteram et genium / per . . . fidem perque . . . solitudinem*) and the repeated *si . . . sive . . . seu* clauses at 292ff. adding further to the formal effect of the utterance. Another instance is found in the speech of the slave Geta at *Phorm.* 213 *ne te iratus suis saevidicis dictis protelet* (cf. also the assonance), who, as often claimed, usually adopts a more elevated style, imitating features associated with high characters, mainly old people.[31]

Stylistic options

Disjunction of *per* from its object. *Per* disjoined from its object by the pronominal subject and/or object of the verb of supplication had an archaic ring, being already old-fashioned in tone from the early second century. It has its parallels in Greek tragedy (cf. E. *Andr.* 892–3 πρός σε τῶνδε γουνάτων οἴκτιρον ἡμᾶς) and is later used in epic poetry (Luc. 10.370, Sil. 1.658). Whereas this type of construction is often found in tragedy (cf. Enn. *trag.* 3–4 *per ego deum sublimas subices umidas*), it does not occur in comic oaths and is rare in comic supplications. The construction occurs twice in Terence, in the formula *per (ego) te deos oro* at *Andr.* 538 and 834. Both instances are found in the speech of the old man

[28] Cf. Hor. *Ars* 97–8 speaking about *sesquipedalia verba* as the norm for tragedy from which Telephus or Peleus might depart *si curat cor spectantis tetigisse querella.*

[29] Cf. Maltby (1976: 208).

[30] Cf. Maltby (1976: 207), speaking about 'spurious elevated tone'.

[31] For compound adjectives in EL poetry, cf. also Coulter (1916: 153–72). See also Sideri Tolia (1988: 205–21), Stein (1971: 598–606).

Simo. See also two further instances of the phenomenon, outside the formula, *Andr.* 289 *per hanc te dexteram [oro]* and *Andr.* 694 *per omnis tibi adiuro deos numquam eam me deserturum* by the *adulescens* Pamphilus.

***dicam* + accusative + infinitive.** The use of *dicam* + accusative + infinitive in direct and indirect questions is found in tragedy (cf. Enn. *trag.* 300 *quemnam te esse dicam qui* in place of the usual equivalent *quis tu es qui*; in Greek tragedy, E. *Rh.* 38–9 τί σε φῶ νέον ἀγγέλλειν, fr. 1 Nauck ποίαν σε φῶμεν γαῖαν ἐκλελοιπότα πόλει ξενοῦσθαι τῇδε etc.), and in solemn and mock-solemn (official/tragic) contexts in comedy, *Curc.* 1 *Quod ted hoc noctis dicam proficisci foras*, in a scene which is a parody of *Choephoroi*.[32] In Terence the expression is uttered once by the *adulescens* Antipho at *Phorm.* 659–60 *utrum stultitia facere ego hunc an malitia dicam . . . incertus sum.* Cf. also *quid dotis dicam te dixisse filio?* at *Heaut.* 937 by the *senex* Menedemus, *id qua causa clam me habuisse dicam non edepol scio* at *Hec.* 519–20 by the *matrona* Myrrina, *dicam fratris esse hanc?* at *Ad.* 625 by the *adulescens* Aeschinus. One exception occurs at *Hec.* 434 *vovisse hunc dicam?* by the slave Parmeno.

Perfect or present + future of the same verb in paratactic construction in a verse. The figure is frequent in Attic drama (cf. E. *Tr.* 467 πάσχω τε καὶ πέπονθα κἄτι πείσομαι, 499 οἵων ἔτυχον ὧν τε τεύξομαι). It is also found in Roman tragedy (cf. Enn. *trag.* 270 *dixi et dicam*) as well as in elevated contexts in comedy, *Bacch.* 1087 *Quiquomque ubi sunt, qui fuerunt quique futuri sunt*, where we have Nicobulus' lament in anapestic long verses.[33] The construction, frequently found in official public inscriptions, seems

[32] Cf. Collart (1979: 25) 'un démarquage amusant du thème plastique des Choéphores'. The scene displays ritual (*pompa* etc.) and stylised legal language (bi-membered asyndeton of two past participles in *status, condictus*, an archaic accusative *ted* etc.); for the formal context here see also Wright (1981: ad v. 5); for the elevated character of the expression in Republican drama, cf. also Jocelyn (1967: 423).

[33] The scene displays an elaborately structured language (sentence with a series of seven alliterative synonyms, clause-balance, alliteration, assonance) and parodies similarly stylised laments of contemporary Roman tragedy (cf. Gestri (1940: 237–60), Barsby (1986: 183)).

to be exploited by the dramatists as an imitation of the magistrates' manner of speech.[34] The figure is found twice in the speech of old people, Phidippus at *Hec.* 722 *iamdudum dixi idemque nunc dico* and Laches at *Hec.* 739 *nam si id facis facturave es.* It is also found once, however, in the speech of Pythias at *Eun.* 1009 *vidi nec videbo.*

***o* + vocative apostrophe to the three elements.** *O* + vocative is confined to persons. The triple apostrophe with anaphora of *o* at *Ad.* 790 of the three elements, earth, sea and sky, *o caelum, o terra, o maria Neptuni!*, is a feature of elevated language.[35] The line is spoken by Demea. In Roman Republican drama this mainly triple anaphora of *o* + vocative combinations is found in tragedy (cf. Enn. *trag.* 87 – *o pater, o patria, o Priami domus*) as well as in paratragic contexts in Plautus (cf. e.g. *Bacch.* 933 in the great Troy *canticum*). A similar triple apostrophe to earth and air is found in Menander at *Sam.* 325–6 ὦ πόλισμα Κεκροπίας χθονός, ὦ ταναὸς αἰθήρ, ὦ – τί, Δημέα, βοᾷς; based on tragic diction again, Euripides.[36] This is the one feature of elevated language found in the speech of the *senex* Demea, as opposed to several examples uttered by his urbane brother, Micio.

Conclusions

The language of Terence's high characters appears to be differentiated not only in a negative way, i.e. in that it lacks colloquialisms, but also in a positive manner, i.e. in that it favours features elevated in tone on a lexical, syntactic and stylistic level. Among the high characters, it is old people again who employ the majority of these features, especially Simo, the *senex* of *Andria*. In most cases, the elevated language old people adopt has at the same time a distinct archaic or long-winded ring, much favoured in senile speech. This seems to be the case with relative clauses repeating the antecedent noun (long-winded character), *satias* in place of *satietas*, the prepositional use of *gratia* instead of *causa*, genitive

[34] Cf. Jocelyn (1967: 400). [35] Cf. also Martin (1976: 212).
[36] Cf. also Gomme and Sandbach (1973: 577), Zagagi (1994: 52).

in *-ai* (EL or archaic character). When used by low characters, these features are occasionally found in the speech of those who, in general, use features associated with senile language, e.g. *gradus* in the sense of 'act of taking a step' and possibly the non-CL nominal compound *saevidicus* by Geta in *Phormio*. Sometimes they occur in thematically elevated contexts along with several other features of the kind in concentration (cf. Gnathos' speech at the end of *Eunuchus*).

Micio's speech in *Adelphoe* is characterised in a negative way by its relative lack of colloquialisms, archaisms and hellenisms, which mark the speech of his counterpart Demea. The less colloquial, archaic, hellenising *senex* is also characterised in a positive way, in that his speech presents several features of elevated language, avoided on the other hand in the language of the rustic Demea (only one example at *Ad.* 790). This is the case with *paucis* vs. *ad pauca, uspiam, pepulisti.*[37] To this may be added the use of the copula *que . . . et* at *Ad.* 64 *praeter aequomque et bonum* in place of *et . . . et*, which is often found in tragedy (Ennius, Accius, Pacuvius) but rarely in comedy.[38] A similar technique, however, does not appear in the case of the pair Chremes–Menedemus in *Heautontimoroumenos*, a fact which may indicate that *Adelphoe* – Terence's last play – constitutes a final stage in the evolution of the playwright's techniques of linguistic characterisation.

[37] Cf. chapter 6, p. 110.

[38] For the relatively more elevated character of the combination, cf. Jocelyn (1967: 166). The syntagm is found even in EL at the end of the line, an indication that it was already felt to be archaic. The combination is common as an archaism in poetry, mainly in the high poetic style, Vergil, Tibullus, Horace (cf. H-Sz 515 'in der Dichtung ist *que . . . et* als Archaism . . . dem höheren Stil angemessen'). For *et . . . et, que . . . et, que . . . que* in Terence, cf. also Elmer (1887: 327).

CHAPTER 6
IDIOLECT

Introduction

Methodological framework

I have so far considered Terence's ability to differentiate the language of his characters by means of colloquial, archaic or elevated features and long-winded speech. There are, however, several other linguistic features which, without having any particular character – either colloquial, EL or elevated – are associated with the speech of specific characters or character types and are avoided by others. This is especially the case with overlapping linguistic options, both on a lexical and a syntactical level. In these cases it seems that specific characters or character types have a penchant for one of the overlapping lexical or syntactical equivalents. The rather vague term 'penchant' may be translated as either absolute use without exceptions or use in overwhelming majority – usually only one exception, often justified by the demands of the contextual setting.

By the term overlapping I understand synonymous or alternative words or expressions and constructions having the same syntactical function. Capitalising again on Maltby's methodology, my main linguistic tools for evaluating the equivalence or differentiation of lexical items and constructions have been:

1. *for vocabulary*: the *OLD*, the *ThLL*, McGlynn's *Lexicon Terentianum*, Maltby's seminal work;
2. *for syntax*: mainly the Latin grammars by Kühner and Stegmann and Leumann, Hofmann and Szantyr, Bennett's *Syntax of Early Latin* and Bléry's and Allardice's work on Terentian syntax.

In both fields, my personal detailed examination of the context of appearance has offered valuable insights.

Maltby again was the first to point out that certain linguistic features of the kind examined below are restricted in Terence's plays to specific character types. In particular, several linguistic features seem to be restricted to the speech of old people (e.g. the use of the imperative form *ades*, the words *adiungo, adsidue, clemens, consuefacio, obsequor, tantisper, impetro, obiurgo* etc.). Synonymous equivalents of many of the above word options, favoured in senile speech, are either evenly distributed to all character types or show a particular concentration in the speech of other linguistic groups (cf. *impetro* vs. *exoro*).[1] Other words or expressions, on the other hand, are favoured in the speech of low characters (slaves, parasites, prostitutes, soldiers, e.g. *in mente esse* constructions, *praecipio* etc.).

Studies on Menander's language have established that the Greek comic playwright explored techniques of characterisation by having his characters use personal idiosyncrasies of expression. As for Terence, Donatus observes the Roman playwright's ability to follow his Greek predecessor, e.g. his remarks on the use of the possessive pronoun in forms of address as an idiosyncratic feature of Thais' language, *velut peculiare verbum esse Thaidis* etc.[2] Maltby observed that 'pet' words or expressions of the kind favoured in Menandrian comedies are to be found in Terence as well. This is the case, for example, with *propterea quod* instead of a simple *quod* or *quia*, favoured by the *senex* Simo at *Andr.* 38 and 584, *ut tempus est diei* found twice in the speech of the *senex* Chremes at *Heaut.* 168 and 212, the EL and PC *inpuratus* used as a term of abuse only by the old man Demipho at *Phorm.* 669 and 962, *vostro (meo) inpulsu* spoken three times by Laches at *Hec.* 242 (twice) and 687. Another idiosyncratic feature of Laches' language seems to be his penchant for the adverb *adeo* found in his speech seven times in 60 lines, between 201 and 261 (vv. 201, 220, 221, 240, 248, 259, 261). The slave Geta's speech in the *Phormio* is also characterised by its penchant for the word *modo* (vv. 59, 68, 93, 95, 109, 142, 149, 198, 566, 624, 773, 859, 865).

[1] Cf. Maltby (1976: 257–8). [2] Cf. ad *Eun.* 95, Introduction, p. 5.

Aims

The subject, however, needs to be examined in greater detail. More specifically, this chapter has as its object to pursue further Maltby's remarks by investigating the following cases:

1. Lexical items possessing more than one meaning in Terentian drama. It would be interesting to determine whether any of these submeanings, for which there often exists a semantically overlapping lexeme in Terence, show a particular concentration in the speech of specific characters or character types; and I will show that several lexical items of this kind, often without any particular archaic, colloquial or elevated character, are favoured in the speech of specific characters or character types.
2. Several other linguistic features on a syntactical and pragmatic level are also favoured in the speech of specific character types (old people, low characters etc.).
3. Several 'pet' expressions and constructions constitute an idiosyncratic linguistic feature of specific characters (the term 'pet' as used by Maltby (1979), i.e. lexical and syntactic options either found in Terentian drama only in the speech of a specific character – cf. the syntagm *propterea quod* twice by Simo – in opposition to the equivalent options found in the speech of all other character types, or used in a specific play only or in overwhelming majority by one character – cf. *modo* by Geta).

Within each subsection in the paragraphs following, alphabetical order is observed.

Distributional patterns

Vocabulary of old people

Nouns

commoditas for *commoda, bona*: at *Andr.* 569 by Simo and at *Phorm.* 841 by the pedagogue Geta.

homo for *quis, quivis, aliquis*: at *Heaut.* 666 *non licet hominem esse saepe ita ut volt* by Chremes, at *Ad.* 431 *ut homost ita morem geras* by the old slave Syrus and finally at *Ad.* 821–2 *multa in homine . . . signa insunt* by Micio.

Verbs

adsum in the figurative sense *animum attendo, animum advorto*: outside the prologue-formula *adeste aequo animo*, the verb is exclusively used by old people: *ades dum: paucis te volo* at *Andr.* 29 by Simo, *ades, audi paucis* at *Hec.* 510 by Laches, *adeste quaeso* at *Phorm.* 350 by Demipho (cf. also once in the Terentian prologue the formulaic *adeste aequo animo* at *Heaut.* 35 by the old man Lucius Ambivius Turpio).

evomere in a figurative sense expressing anger or indignation: at *Hec.* 515 *atque in eam hoc omne quod mihi aegrest evomam* by Laches, at *Ad.* 312 *ut ego iram hanc in eos evomam omnem* by the old slave Geta, at *Ad.* 510 *ibo ac requiram fratrem ut in eum haec evomam* by Demea.

omitto with the meaning of *desino*: at *Phorm.* 861 by the pedagogue Geta, at *Eun.* 989 by the senex Chremes/Laches.

prodo with the meaning of *desero*: at *Hec.* 672 by Laches,[3] at *Ad.* 692 by Micio, at *Heaut.* 639 by Chremes.

puto with the meaning of *existimo, iudico*: at *Heaut.* 485 by Chremes, at *Heaut.* 900 *id nil puto* by Menedemus.

servo in the sense of *teneo, habeo*: at *Heaut.* 1040 by Chremes, at *Ad.* 241 by the old slave Syrus and finally at *Phorm.* 212 by the pedagogue Geta.

Adverbs

prope in place of *paene, ferme*:[4] at *Heaut.* 98, 104 by Menedemus and at *Hec.* 22 by Lucius Ambivius Turpio.

recte in place of *iure, iuste, merito*: at *Andr.* 766 by Chremes, at *Hec.* 559 by Myrrina, at *Ad.* 951 by Demea and finally at *Ad.* 997 by Micio. A last example is uttered by the *meretrix* Bacchis at *Hec.* 862, whose diction exhibits many features otherwise favoured by senile speech. The single exception is *Eun.* 981, spoken by the slave Parmeno to an old person, the *senex* Chremes/Laches. The same also applies to the use of *recte* for *prospere, feliciter, ex sententia*, at *Andr.* 804 by Crito, at *Heaut.* 159 by Chremes, at *Ad.* 289 by the old *anus* Canthara and finally at *Ad.* 884 by Syrus. Similarly, *recte* in the sense of *ita ut convenit* occurs at *Hec.* 531 in the mouth of Phidippus and once more at *Hec.* 399 by Pamphilus when reporting, however, Myrrina's speech.

ultro for *prius*: at *Hec.* 609[5] by Laches, at *Ad.* 596 by Micio.

[3] Cf. Donat. ad loc. *deseremus, proiciemus, porro dabimus.*

[4] For the paradigmatic option, cf. McGlynn II 54, the adverb being otherwise normally used in Terence for denoting local and temporal immediacy.

[5] According to FL.^{2}, Ty.

Obsolete lexical features

Another group of linguistic features associated with senile speech consists of certain lexemes or constructions which, although they cannot be termed archaic according to the criterion set out in chapter 2, since they occasionally appear in CL, nevertheless possess a certain old-fashioned or obsolete character; this character was probably the cause of their restriction to senile speech in Terence, and so this group of lexical items should not be viewed as a simple idiolectal feature of old characters. The term 'old-fashioned' or 'obsolescent' applies to words, expressions, syntactic options that are common in the literature before Terence, especially in Plautus, but lose ground in the younger dramatist to more modern common CL equivalents. Such features are present in classical literature to a greater extent than features discussed in the chapter on archaisms, but even in these cases their much greater frequency in the more archaic prose writers (such as Sallust, Livy etc.), coupled with the fact that, chronologically, in the history of the Latin language, they often appear before their binary equivalent, have led several scholars to consider them as having an archaic flavour in CL.

Verbs

Verbs of thinking

reor The CL *puto* gains ground in Terence (59x) at the expense of *reor*, found only twice, at *Hec*. 581 uttered by the *matrona* Sostrata and in v. 819 by Bacchis.[6] *Censeo* and *opinor* become less frequent in Terence, especially in parenthetic phrases of the type *ut censeo, ut opinor*, which are found frequently in Plautus. At *Phorm*. 951, *Hec*. 545, *ratus* is used as an adjective in the sense of *fixus, certus, stabilis*.

censeo, opinor *Arbitror, existimo* and *iudico* all gain ground in Terence at the expense of *censeo, opinor*. This is especially the case with *ut* + *censeo*/*opinor* syntagms, which are restricted to the speech of old people: *ut censeo* is found once in the mouth of the *senex* Demipho at *Phorm*. 776, whereas *ut opinor* is uttered by the *senex* Simo at *Andr*. 179, the *matrona* Sostrata at *Hec*. 598 and the *senex* Micio at *Ad*. 648, the pedagogue *Geta* at *Phorm*. 555.

[6] For *reor* having an archaic or obsolete colour in CL, cf. Fordyce (1977: 142), Axelson (1945: 64). Apart from the past participle *ratus*, the verb is rare in CL. It is not found in Cicero's speeches or Caesar. Furthermore, with the exception of Vergil and Ovid, it is also rare in Classical verse.

Verbs of asking With verbs of asking there is in Terence a movement away from *interrogo* (1x), *exquiro* (3x) towards the simple *quaero* (72x).

exquiro It is used twice by old people, Simo at *Andr.* 186 and Laches at *Hec.* 783, and the last example is found in the speech of Bacchis at *Hec.* 773.

interrogo Although frequent in Plautus (cf. *Amph.* 438, *Aul.* 161, *Curc.* 340, *Epid.* 250, *Men.* 916, *Poen.* 730), the verb is found in Terence once, at *Eun.* 981 by Parmeno to the *senex* Laches/ Chremes.

Adverbs

repente This is the older form for 'suddenly' and is the only word used in Plautus, who never uses *subito*. In verse *repente* is preferred with some frequency by Lucretius only, which, according to Maltby (1976), suggests that it was felt to be archaic and may have commended itself for this reason to archaising writers such as Sallust and Tacitus. In Terence we find a movement towards *subito*. Whereas *subito* is used by all character types (e.g. *Phorm.* 180, 842 by the slave Geta, 534 by the *adulescens* Phaedria), with the exception of the textually doubtful *Hec.* 368, all the instances of *repente* are found in the speech of old people, *Hec.* 356 Sostrata, *Heaut.* 23 L. Ambivius, *Ad.* 302 the old slave Geta, *Ad.* 984 Micio.[7] Similarly, the compound *derepente* is twice used by old people, Myrrina and Phidippus at *Hec.* 518 and 554, respectively.

Complex expressions

infitias eo The fact that this phrase is well attested in Plautus but absent from the prose of the first century BC (apart from Livy and Nepos) shows, according to Oakley (1997–8: I 699), that it was archaic in late Republican and Augustan times and it may have been obsolescent for Terence as well. It reappears later in archaising authors such as Gellius and Apuleius. Terence again here stands closer to CL in avoiding the expression with the exception of two instances, both uttered by old people, the old slave Geta at *Ad.* 339 and the *matrona* Sostrata at *Ad.* 347.

[7] For the use of *repente* in CL as an archaism, cf. Axelson (1945: 32–3), 'wohl auch etwas altertümlicheres Gepräge', Austin II 160 'an archaism'.

Vocabulary of low characters

Pronouns

noster, nostra The use of the possessive pronoun with the meaning of 'master', 'mistress' is restricted to the speech of slaves: *Phorm.* 66, 80, 110, 117 by Geta, *Hec.* 188 by Parmeno, *Heaut.* 712 by Syrus, even in direct address at *Phorm.* 398 *eu noster, recte* by Geta to Demipho and at *Eun.* 154 *eu noster, laudo* by Parmeno to Phaedria.

Verbs

frigeo in a figurative sense, mainly of failure and indifference: at *Eun.* 268 *nimirum hic homines frigent* by the parasite Gnatho, at *Ad.* 233 *refrixerit res* by the *leno* Sannio (cf. also *Phorm.* 994 *si non totus friget, me enica* by the parasite Phormio in the sense 'to be terrified'). Another example is uttered at *Eun.* 517 *ubi friget* by the rustic *adulescens* Chremes.[8]

nego with the meaning of *recuso/abnuo*: at *Andr.* 379, 384 by the slave Davus, at *Phorm.* 113 by the slave Geta, at *Eun.* 619 by the *ancilla* Dorias, at *Hec.* 120 by the slave Parmeno.

teneo in the sense of *intellego*: the verb is found mainly in the speech of slaves, at *Andr.* 86 Sosia, at *Andr.* 300 Mysis, at *Andr.* 498 Davus, at *Phorm.* 214 Geta and at *Heaut.* 778 Syrus. In two cases this usage is also found in the speech of two *adulescentes*, Charinus at *Andr.* 349 and Clitipho at *Heaut.* 700, when, however, addressing slaves, Davus and Syrus respectively. Another instance occurs in the speech of the soldier Thraso at *Eun.* 406.

Adverbs and particles

vel construed with the imperative as equivalent to *si tu vis, quantum ad me attinet*: at *Andr.* 680 by the slave Davus, at *Phorm.* 143 by the slave Geta, at *Phorm.* 989 by the parasite Phormio.

verum enim at *Phorm.* 555 by the slave Geta, at *Eun.* 742 by the *meretrix* Thais and at *Ad.* 201 by the *leno* Sannio.

Interjections

heus Syrus in *Heautontimoroumenos* has a penchant for adding the interjection *heus*[9] whenever addressing other characters, v. 313 *heus*,

[8] On the rustic character of the young man, cf. also Donat. ad *Eun.* 507. Cf. also v. 732 *sine Cerere et Libero friget Venus* by the rustic *adulescens* Chremes.

[9] Cf. Donat. ad *Andr.* 636 *'heus' significatio est modo nominis ad intentionem considerationemque revocandi*; for *heus*, cf. also Watt (1963: 138–43).

v. 369 *sed heus tu*, v. 550 *at heus tu* (combinations used only in the speech of slaves in Terence), 743 *heus, Dromo*. Apart from being restricted mainly to Syrus' speech in *Heautontimoroumenos*, the interjection is used in all cases by male characters. It is found once in the speech of a female character, the *ancilla* Dorias at *Eun*. 624, reporting, crucially, the speech of the soldier Thraso. The interjection might have a colloquial flavour, since it is frequently found in Republican comedy but is avoided in high genres such as tragedy.[10]

Individual features

Chremes. Apart from its common use as equivalent to *fero, tolero* and *sustineo, patior* is also often used in Terence in the sense of *sino, permitto*.[11] With this meaning the word, constructed with a.c.i., is favoured in the speech of the *senex* Chremes in the *Heautontimoroumenos* (six times), *Heaut*. 443, 486, 532, 761, 913, 1037. *Video*, in the sense of *intellego, cognosco, scio, sentio* (cf. the English 'I see') is, again, mainly associated with Chremes' speech (six times), vv. 211, 869, 871, 962, 1023, 1053. Furthermore, Chremes has the tendency to interrupt his interlocutor's narration using the formulaic *quid tum*, asking for the next step in an argument or in a narrative, *Heaut*. 800–1 *in eum suspiciost translata amoris / quid tum?*, 846–7 *invenisti hodie filiam / quid tum?*, 602, 605. Ἀποσιώπησις, that is, the breaking off of utterance, is also frequent in Chremes' speech (cf. vv. 780, 913, 918–19, 1041).[12] He also uses *comparo* in the sense of *paro, coemo* (cf. vv. 778, 855). Chremes also has a penchant for using simple *ne* + present imperative combinations for expressing a negative imperative (in place of *noli* + infinitive, *ne* + singular subjunctive constructions etc.), cf. v. 84 *ne lacruma*, v. 85 *ne retice, ne verere*, v. 89 *ne labora*, v. 564 *ne nega*, v. 975 *ne te admisce*.[13]

[10] Cf. Hofmann (1951: 15). [11] Cf. McGlynn II 10.

[12] For ἀποσιώπησις, cf. also Bardon (1943–4: 102–20), Papadimitriou (1994: 77–113).

[13] This construction is favoured in the speech of old people. With the exception of *Andr.* 384 and *Eun.*95, all other instances of such a usage are associated with senile speech: at *Andr.* 543 and 868 by the *senex* Chremes; at *Phorm.* 664 by the *senex* Chremes; at *Phorm.* 803 by the matrona Sostrata; at *Ad.* 279 by the old slave Syrus; at *Ad.* 802 by Demea. Another example occurs at *Heaut.* 1052 *age quaeso, ne tam offirma te* in the mouth of Menedemus. The syntagm is accompanied here by a reinforcing *age quaeso* (for *ne* + imperative constructions accompanied by reinforcing expressions in comedy

Davus. Davus in *Andria* has a penchant for referring frequently to his master by using the demonstrative pronoun *ipsus*, vv. 360, 377 and 605. He also uses *accipio* in the sense of *suscipio* (cf. vv. 367, 397) and *otiosus* for *securus, tranquillus* (cf. vv. 398, 842). Finally, he often uses the oath *hercle* (seven times), vv. 194, 225, 440, 495 505, 597, 774.

Demea. Demea in *Adelphoe* has a predilection for calling upon Juppiter (vv. 111, 366 *pro Juppiter*, 757 *o Juppiter)* and a tendency not to give a direct answer but to repeat simply the question he was asked in echo-questions (cf. vv. 84 Micio *quid fecit?* Demea *quid ille fecerit*?, 374, 396, 733, 753, 803). Demea's speech is also characterised by the paucity of his vocabulary in expressions of graciousness after his decision to change character. He just repeats the phrases *lubens bene faxim* in vv. 887 and 896. He also repeats in vv. 959, 982 the phrase *frugi homo*. This is due, according to Martin (1976: 227), to the fact that he is acting *praeter naturam*.

The rustic Demea, unlike his urbane brother Micio, often uses expressions associated with rustic activities in a figurative sense, *gannire* in v. 556 *quid ille gannit?* in the sense of 'what's she yapping about?', a verb otherwise normally used for the bark or yelp of a dog or a fox,[14] *olfecissem* in v. 397,[15] *perreptavi* in v. 715, a word also applicable to reptiles and plants, in order to say that he has hobbled all over the town. He also uses financial imagery, especially terms drawn from accounting, in a figurative sense, appropriate, according to Fantham (1972: 69), to Demea's materialistic values, v. 796 *rem ipsam putemus*, v. 855 *subducta ratione*.

Geta. The use of *homo* in place of a simple demonstrative pronoun, *hic, is, ille* or *iste*[16] is frequently found as an idiolectal peculiarity in the speech of the slave Geta in *Phormio* (seven times), v. 135

cf. Bennett (1910–14: I 362)). *Ne* + imperative constructions are common in EL and later are used mainly as archaisms, especially in poetry (see H-Sz 340). The syntagm may have sounded obsolescent even in Terence's time (13 instances in Terence against 73 in Plautus).

14 Cf. Martin (1976: 185), Fantham (1972: 56).

15 Cf. Fantham (1972: 62).

16 Cf. McGlynn I 254.

persuasit homini, v. 252 *sed quid cessas hominem adire*, vv. 592, 598, 620, 632, 845.

Gnatho. The parasite in *Eunuchus* is the only character who uses the figurative expression *uro hominem* in the sense 'that's hurt him' (vv. 274, 438 *te . . . urat*).[17]

Mysis. She favours the oath *pol*, found eight times in her speech, *Andr.* 229, 459, 770, 778, 788, 790, 803 and 817. She also uses the full form *edepol* in v. 692, oaths favoured in the speech of another *ancilla*, Pythias in *Eunuchus* (cf. vv. 665, 719, 731, 883, 903, 941, 1009). When formulating a request, Mysis almost always modifies it by means of *obsecro*, found six times in her speech at vv. 232, 721, 725, 747, 781, 800.

Micio. *Autem* often stands as an expletive after the word it emphasises, lending a note of indignation. In these cases, a sentence-echo usually follows where there is no shift to the subjunctive but the clause retains the indicative mood. Micio in *Adelphoe* has the habit of adding this expletive *autem* in questions expressing anger, vv. 934 Mi: *me ducere autem?* De: *te*, 935, 940, 950. He is also the only character to use the combination *fores pellere*[18] (vv. 638, 788) in place of the regular *crepare* or *pultare*, the normal words to express a door making a noise, or someone knocking on a door. According to Donatus, the expression has an elevated character: *Ad.* 638 *pepulisti elatum verbum et tragico coturno magis quam loquelae comicae accommodatum.* If so, the expression adds further to the general elevated flavour of Micio's speech.

Parmeno. The slave Parmeno in *Eunuchus* frequently uses military imagery or language for describing the conflicts of love, vv. 53–5 *infecta pace . . . eludet ubi te victum senserit*,[19] vv. 60–1 *suspiciones, inimicitiae, indutiae, bellum, pax rursum*, v. 74 *ut te redimas captum*. This is also the case with Syra in *Hecyra*,

[17] Cf. Donat. ad *Eun.* 274 *dolere cogo.*

[18] For *pellere* in EL, cf. Maniet (1966: 28–36).

[19] Cf. Fantham (1972: 28), see also Donat. ad *Eun.* 55 *eludere proprie gladiatorum est, cum vicerint.*

v. 65 *spolies mutiles laceres*, v. 70 *hiscin tu amabo non contra insidiabere?*, v. 73 *aut qua via te captent eadem ipsos capi?*.[20]

Syrus. *Modo*, just like *dum*, is a modal particle often associated with the imperative, with the meaning 'no more than', 'just,' 'only', lending a note of insistence to the imperative.[21] *Modo* as a modal particle in this sense is favoured in the speech of the slave Syrus in *Adelphoe*, e.g. v. 280 *tace modo ac sequere hac*, v. 538 *fuge modo intro*, v. 982 *reddam hercle; da modo*. Finally, *praecipere* in place of *iubere, monere* occurs in vv. 424, 434, 963.

Syntax

In Terence there are several overlapping constructions, that is, syntagms having the same functions (e.g. expression of cause), irrespective of context or grammatical rules (such as the one stating that a causal sentence is introduced by *si* only when depending on specific verbs like *miror*). It seems, again, that certain of these overlapping constructions are favoured in the speech of specific character types and avoided by others, as is also the case on the lexical level.

Syntax of old people

Conjunctions

si with adversative sense as equivalent to *etsi, etiamsi* or *quamvis:* at *Heaut*. 632 *si tu neges, certo scio* by the *senex* Chremes, at *Ad*. 103–4 *haec si neque ego neque tu fecimus, non siit egestas facere nos* by Micio, 299–300 *si omnia omnes sua consilia conferant . . . auxili nil adferant* by the old slave Geta, 733–4 *si non ipsa re tibi istuc dolet, simulare certe est hominis* and 950–1 *si multumst, tamen faciundumst* by the *senex* Demea.

Quia *and* quod *clauses*

***quia* and *quod*.**[22] *Quia* and *quod* regularly introduce adverbial clauses stating the reason for an action or state described in the

[20] For military language in Terence, cf. also Durry (1940: 57–64), Nougaret (1945: 70–4).
[21] Cf. Martin (1976: 148).
[22] For *quia* and *quod* clauses, cf. Maltby (1976: 78–97).

main clause. They can also introduce subject or object clauses, either with a pronoun antecedent in the main clause or not. As for subject clauses, whereas in Plautus these sentences in their majority develop in apposition to a preceding pronoun in the main clause (thirty times), this is no longer the case in Terence, who, following again the trend of CL, prefers the non-appositional constructions (cf. *Andr.* 905 twice, *Heaut.* 400, 613, *Eun.* 146, 559, 979, *Phorm.* 546, 998, *Ad.* 305, 307, 954). One example of the type *quid* + pronoun + *est* + *quod* is, significantly, found at *Eun.* 642 *sed quid hoc quod timida subito egreditur Pythias?*, i.e. in the play whose more Plautine linguistic character will soon be demonstrated. The other two examples are found in the speech of old people at *Hec.* 236–7 *non signi hoc sat est, quod . . .* by Laches and at *Andr.* 526–7 *illud . . . maxumst . . . quod . . .* by Simo.

Temporal clauses

***priusquam* + subjunctive.**[23] Except in one example, where the subjunctive is used in generalising statements with the second person of arbitrary reference, at *Ad.* 583–4 *prius quam ad portam venias . . . est pistrilla*, subjunctives in *priusquam* clauses do not usually exist in their own right in Terence, but are attributable to attraction of the subordinate clause into the mood of the main sentence or to *oratio obliqua*. This seems to be the regular case in Terence, e.g. *Eun.* 751 *at enim cave ne prius quam hanc a me accipias amittas* (cf. e.g. also *Andr.* 378, *Ad.* 397, 525). All cases of *priusquam* clauses not attracted into the subjunctive mood of the main clause are found in the speech of old people, at *Andr.* 558–9 by Simo, at *Phorm.* 719 by Chremes, at *Phorm.* 897 by Demipho.

Complements

***ut/ne* clauses.** With the exception of verbs of fearing, where the accusative + infinitive construction is never found, self-referring verbs (e.g. verbs of wishing, striving, resolving) are normally construed either with the infinitive, when the subject of the infinitive is the same as the subject of the main verb, or the accusative + infinitive when the subjects are different or even when the subject

[23] For *priusquam* clauses in Plautus and Terence, cf. Maltby (1976: 36).

is the same both of the main and the subordinate verb in passive infinitives and forms of the verb *esse*. *Ut/ne* clauses can also be used in place of the infinitive constructions.

When there is an overlap in the use of the infinitive and *ut/ne* subjunctive constructions, the second is favoured in senile speech: *opto ut*, at *Heaut.* 756 *optabit . . . ut abeat* by Chremes, at *Ad.* 874 *ut vivat optant* by Demea; *exspecto ut*, at *Hec.* 280 *exspecto ut redeat* by Sostrata; *volo ut*, at *Hec.* 396 *volo doque operam ut clam partus eveniat* by Pamphilus quoting his wife's mother, at *Andr.* 550, 165–6 by Simo, at *Phorm.* 151 *ut bene sit tibi (volo)* by Geta, at *Phorm.* 322 by Phormio to Geta; *studeo ut*,[24] at *Ad.* 868–9 *studeo illis ut quam plurimum facerem* by Demea; *postulo* (= demand) *ut*, at *Andr.* 190 *postulo sive aequomst te oro . . . ut redeat*, 823–4 *abs te postulo atque oro . . . ut . . . comprobes*, 550 *ita volo itaque postulo ut fiat* by Simo (in all instances coupled with an almost synonymous verb, a further marker of senile speech). A last example of a *postulo ut* construction is found at *Eun.* 1058–60 *postulo ut mihi tua domus te praesente absente pateat, invocato ut sit locus semper* in an intentionally elevated passage by Gnatho where we find in concentration several senile linguistic features and elevated linguistic options.[25]

[24] *Studere* + infinitive is the regular equivalent in Terence. The *ut/ne* construction is occasionally found in CL (cf. e.g. *B. Alex.* 1.4), but the infinitive is more usual. The construction, which belongs mainly to EL (cf. also Bléry (1965: 21)), might have been felt as obsolescent in Terence's time and may therefore have been assigned to senile speech. This seems also to be the case with *postulo ut/ne* syntagms.

[25] This happens in a context where Gnatho uses in concentration several other features which have a distinct elevated character and/or are otherwise associated mainly with senile speech. These include: the use of the ablative *paucis* in the sense of 'a few words' (at *Andr.* 29 by Simo, at *Ad.* 806 by Micio, at *Hec.* 510 by Laches, at *Heaut.* 10 by Lucius Ambivius Turpio); the EL imperative form *facitote* in parallel subordinate clauses introduced by *quam* and *si*, reminiscent of ancient legal language (cf. Leg. XII Tab VIII 12; see also Maltby (1976: 243)); *ut* + indicative in place of *quoniam* in the sense of 'given that', 'taking into account that', at vv. 1073–4 *tu hercle cum illa, Phaedria, ut lubenter vivis . . .* (cf. also at *Ad.* 749 by Demea, *Heaut.* 649 by Sostrata); the use of *impetro* as equivalent to *exoro*, a usage once more favoured in senile speech (cf. *Andr.* 544, 832 by Chremes, *Andr.* 422, 528 by Simo, *Hec.* 52 by L. Ambivius Turpio, *Hec.* 729 by Laches, *Phorm.* 452 by Cratinus, *Ad.* 490 by Hegio); and, finally, the accusative gerundive, used predicatively in agreement with the object of the main verb for expressing purpose at v. 1087 *hunc comedendum vobis propino et deridendum*, a construction favoured mainly in senile speech (cf. also similar accusative gerundives denoting purpose at *Heaut.* 630, 650 by the *matrona* Sostrata, at *Ad.* 463 by Hegio, at *Andr.* 865 by Simo).

***opus est* constructions.** When it is an action that needs doing, *opus est* is followed by an ablative neuter singular of the past participle passive. More rarely the ablative supine is used instead. This construction is restricted to the speech of old people, Chremes at *Heaut.* 941 *dictu*, Micio at *Ad.* 740 *iactu*.

Syntax of low characters

Expressions of cause

***de*.** In cases of overlap between causal *de* and other causal prepositions (*ex, ob, propter*),[26] *de* is always used by low characters, at *Eun.* 457 by Thraso, at *Hec.* 727, 741 by Bacchis, at *Ad.* 253, 405 by the slave Syrus (so too the formulaic combination *de causa* is used at *Phorm.* 900 by the parasite Phormio, at *Hec.* 309 by the slave Parmeno, at *Hec.* 757 by the *meretrix* Bacchis).

***quod* clauses.** In *quod* clauses of general reference with a meaning 'as to the fact that' the regular mood is the indicative. In Terence, just as in Plautus, however, in several well-defined contexts the subjunctive is found in these clauses. *Quod* still has the meaning of 'as to the fact that', but in all the examples it has a real concessive force. This use of *quod* is again associated with the speech of low characters, at *Andr.* 395–6 *nam quod tu speres* in a solemn warning by Davus,[27] at *Heaut.* 671–2 *nam quod de argento sperem aut posse postulem me fallere nil est* in a mock-official scene by Syrus, at *Eun.* 785 *sane quod tibi nunc vir videatur esse hic, nebulo magnus est* by Thais, at *Ad.* 162–3 *quod te posterius purges hanc iniuriam mi nolle factam esse, huius non faciam* by the *leno* Sannio in a legal context. It is also found in the speech of those characters who usually adopt many features favoured otherwise in slaves' and parasites' speech, mainly but by no means exclusively of a colloquial character, like the soldier Chaerea in *Eunuchus*. Cf. v. 1064 *quod dicas mihi* in a deliberately formal declaration.[28] In

[26] Cf. Maltby (1976: 174), McGlynn I 114.

[27] For the solemn character of the scene, cf. Shipp (1960: 155).

[28] For the formal character of the context and the use of military or official language, cf. Barsby (1999: 284). A gives *scin . . . periisti* to Chaerea. Σ gives the lines to Phaedria.

Plautus the construction is used in a mock-official scene, the mock-contract by a low character, the parasite at *Asin.* 751ff.[29] Terence seems here to follow his predecessor in assigning this construction mainly to his low characters, in contexts, again, of mock-official, mock-legal flavour.

Expressions of purpose

Supines. In cases where there is an overlap between an *ut/ne* clause denoting purpose with the verb *eo* and an accusative supine + object construction, the supine equivalent is found only in the speech of low characters: at *Phorm.* 838 *ancillulam emptum* by the parasite Phormio, at *Eun.* 892 *nutricem accersitum* by the *meretrix* Thais, at *Hec.* 77 *percontatum adventum* by the slave Parmeno (cf., on the other hand, *ut/ne* clauses at *Heaut.* 211, *Ad.* 632, 706 etc.).

Individual features

Chaerea. The ephebe has a particular propensity for rhetorical questions (vv. 305, 318, 326, 327–8, 334, 366, 389) and very frequently uses alliteration and assonance, often linked to verbal repetition (vv. 555, 556, 568, 571, 574, 575, 579, 605).

Chremes. *Etsi* + indicative combinations, *etsi* having the function of a simple coordinating conjunction restricting a preceding affirmation, are not infrequently used in Terence as equivalent to similar *quamquam* constructions. This particular use of *etsi* + indicative is favoured in the speech of the *senex* Chremes in *Heautontimoroumenos*, where it is found four times, in vv. 119–20 *ambo accusandi; etsi illud inceptum tamen animist pudentis signum et non instrenui*, vv. 410–12 *cesso pultare ostium vicini... etsi adulescentem hoc nolle intellego*, vv. 470–1 *falli te sinas techinis per servolum; etsi subsensi id quoque*, v. 752 *etsi scio, hosce aliquot dies non sentiet.*

[29] Cf. Maltby (1976: 93).

Geta. The combination of *pergere* with *ire* as a future periphrasis, where *pergere* has the sense of *incipio, insisto*,[30] is an idiolectal feature which is found only in the speech of the slave Geta in *Phormio* v. 194 *domum ire pergam*, v. 847 *ad lenonem hinc ire pergam*, vv. 866–7 *ad fores suspenso gradu placide ire perrexi accessi astiti*. In his speech we also find the only examples in *Phormio* of the use of *ut* in place of the common *postquam* for describing a single past completed action (cf. vv. 617, 859).

Simo. *Praeter* with a comparative sense,[31] in place of the commoner *prae* or *magis quam*, is an idiolectal feature of Simo's speech in *Andria*, vv. 58–9 *horum ille nil egregie praeter cetera studebat*, vv. 121–2 *lamentari prater ceteras visast*,[32] vv. 122–3 *et quia erat forma praeter ceteras honesta*. He is also the only character to use *postulo ut* constructions in place of a.c.i., where *postulo* is coupled with another synonymous verb, vv. 190, 550, 823–4.

Thraso. The soldier Thraso in *Eunuchus* has a tendency to use the historic infinitive instead of the common simple imperfect or historic present even in direct questions, cf. v. 391 *Magnas vero agere gratias Thais mihi?*, a very rare usage.[33] The following historic infinitives also occur in his speech: v. 402 *credere*, v. 410 *invidere*, v. 411 *mordere*, *pendere*, v. 412 *invidere*.

Pragmatics and discourse analysis

Dialogue signals

Greeting formulas. The long formula *iubeo salvere* in place of a simple *salve* is found exclusively in the speech of old people, at *Ad.* 460–1 by Demea, at *Andr.* 533 by Simo, interrupted though by an impatient Chremes, who does not even return the greeting.

[30] Cf. McGlynn II 19. [31] Cf. McGlynn II 43.
[32] Cf. Donat. ad *Andr.* 121 *plus quam ceterae*.
[33] Cf. also Petr. 62. 8, H–Sz 368. For the historic infinitive in *Eunuchus*, cf. also Calboli (1991: 599–632); for the historic infinitive in Latin verbal system, cf. Dressler (1965: 191–6).

Formulaic expressions of the type *est ipsus de quo agebam*, used for drawing attention to the approach of somebody,[34] are found in the speech of old people, *Ad.* 78 by Micio, at *Phorm.* 355 by Demipho, at *Hec.* 455 by Laches.

***o* + repeated vocative combinations.** This type of direct address, expressing strong emotion, is associated with the speech of *adulescentes*: *o frater, frater* at *Ad.* 256 by Ctesipho; *o Mysis, Mysis* at *Andr.* 282 by Pamphilus; *o Thais, Thais* at *Eun.* 91 by Phaedria. Redoubling in direct addresses is a favourite in the speech of *adulescentes* with *heus* as well: *heus heus Syre* at *Ad.* 281 by Ctesipho; at *Heaut.* 348 by Clitipho (for repeated *heus* favoured in the speech of *adulescentes* as a whole, cf. also *Ad.* 634 (Aeschinus), *Eun.* 337 (Chaerea), 530 (Chremes)).[35]

Oaths

di boni/immortales vs. introductory morpheme + ***di boni/ immortales.*** It seems that the use of a morpheme depends on the social status of the speaker. Plain oaths are to be found in the speech of low characters, mainly slaves, whereas their equivalents, accompanied by an interjectional complement, are uttered by high characters; thus: *di boni* at *Andr.* 338 by Davus, at *Heaut.* 254 by Syrus, at *Eun.* 225 by Parmeno, but *o di boni* by the *senex* Demea at *Ad.* 440; *di immortales* at *Eun.* 232 by the parasite Gnatho, but *pro* + *di immortales* at *Phorm.* 1008 by the *matrona* Nausistrata, at *Ad.* 447 by the *senex* Hegio.

Affirmative or negative responses

In Terence there is a variety of forms having the function of an affirmative answer or response (simple repetition of the main verb of the question or order; use of simple particles like *scilicet, sane, certe, probe, oppido, admodum, vero, ita, verum, factum, sic*; use of verbs denoting wanting, such as *cupio*; formal expressions like *ita faciam, fiet, sic res est* etc.).[36] Some of these types of affirmative

[34] For the function of these formulaic expressions, see also Martin (1976: 111–12).
[35] For gemination in Terence, cf. also Johnston (1905: xliv).
[36] Cf. Müller (1997: 190–201).

answer in Terence seem to be favoured in the speech of some specific characters or character types.

certe. Plain *certe* as affirmative answer is associated mainly with slaves' speech, at *Andr.* 617 by Davus, at *Hec.* 843 by Parmeno, at *Ad.* 488 by Geta (cf. also *Heaut.* 431 by Chremes, whose speech, however, just like rustic Demea's in the *Adelphoe*, exhibits many other linguistic features, especially colloquial ones, favoured in slaves' and parasites' speech).

faciam, fiat, fiet as formulaic affirmative answers. Compliance with an order or request is expressed by a slave through the use of the indicative future: (a) *faciam*, Pythias at *Eun.* 724, Parmeno at *Eun.* 207; (b) *fiet*, Parmeno at *Eun.* 208ff. (twice). A free person, on the other hand, prefers the subjunctive form *fiat*, e.g. *adulescens* Phaedria at *Eun.* 100, *senex* Demipho at *Phorm.* 811. Donatus (*ad Eun.* 500) remarks on the appropriateness of *fiat* as an affirmative answer by a free person *tamquam et ipse iubet sibi.*

ego vero[37] + predicate or object with no verbal complement, in place of a positive answer. It is found exclusively in the speech of slaves, at *Andr.* 186 *ego vero istuc*, at *Andr.* 337 *ego vero ac lubens* by Byrria. The full equivalent, on the other hand, is to be found in the speech of high characters, *ego illud vero ita feci* at *Eun.* 591 by the *adulescens* Chaerea, at *Ad.* 925 *ego vero iubeo* by the *senex* Demea, at *Heaut.* 538 *ego vero laudo* by the *senex* Chremes.

Conclusions

Several linguistic features on a lexical, syntactic and pragmatical level, often with no particular colloquial or archaic flavour, seem to be favoured in the speech of specific character types. This is especially the case with overlapping paradigmatic options (synonymous words, expressions, syntactic constructions). The number and variety of examples falling into this category and following the above distributional pattern point to the non-fortuitous character of the phenomenon. All these do not entail, of course, that Terentian characters do not occasionally use linguistic features favoured by a linguistic group to which they do not belong, often, however, for specific reasons, brought up by the demands

[37] For the possibly colloquial character and the linguistic function of the combination, cf. Müller (1997: 70).

of the context. What matters, again, is not the individual features themselves but the relative accumulation of a specific linguistic option in the speech of a specific character or character type and its relative absence from the speech of another.

In certain cases linguistic features which, according to percentages of usage, belong to a certain linguistic group or individual are used by characters belonging to a different group only when addressing characters of the first group or the specific individual, which shows the importance of the addressee in Terentian drama (e.g. *teneo* in the sense of *intellego* etc.). This is especially the case with linguistic features associated with senile speech, used by other characters only when addressing old people.

In Terentian drama there are some characters who, although they belong to a specific linguistic group exhibit in their speech as a whole, and with no particular concentration, several linguistic features favoured in a linguistic group to which they do not belong. This is especially the case with the *meretrix* Bacchis in *Hecyra* and the *adulescens* Chaerea in *Eunuchus*. When examining archaisms, long-winded expressions, features of elevated language, I pointed out here and there the tendency of the *meretrix* Bacchis in *Hecyra* to use several of these features, otherwise favoured by senile speech. This seems also to be the case with several further features, which, though they have neither a particular archaic or elevated nor a long-winded flavour, are again otherwise restricted to senile speech (e.g. *recte* for *iure, iuste* at *Hec.* 862, *de* in causal function at *Hec.* 727 etc.). Terence is known for introducing the type of the *bona meretrix*,[38] to which Bacchis in *Hecyra* also seems to belong. Dignity of character appears also to be reflected in dignity of speech. The linguistic features which Bacchis shares with the speech of old people overwhelm the few linguistic options (mainly of colloquial character) that she occasionally shares with other low characters. In the case of the soldier Chaerea in *Eunuchus*, however, we meet the inverse phenomenon. When examining colloquialisms, I observed that the soldier Chaerea frequently uses, more than any other Terentian *adulescens*, colloquial features otherwise associated mainly

[38] Vs. Gilula (1980: 142–65), who argues that all Terentian prostitutes are 'wicked'. For a discussion on Plutarch's division of Menandrian prostitutes and scepticism about the use of the term 'good prostitutes', cf. Brown (1990: 241–66, especially 247, 258).

with the speech of low characters, even though he belongs to the linguistic group of high characters. The fact that he is at the moment doing his military service may account for this penchant for colloquial features. Chaerea's penchant to assimilate linguistic habits favoured in slave and parasitic speech, however, is not restricted to colloquial linguistic options, but also includes a further feature which, although it has no particular colloquial flavour, is again favoured in the speech of low characters (i.e. *quod* + subjunctive with concessive sense in mock-official contexts).

In several cases the words of a specific character are reported by another person who often does not belong to the same linguistic group or subgroup as the character whose speech is being reported. This is especially the case with Pamphilus' stating his mother-in-law's speech at *Hec.* 382ff. The young man recounts the speech of Myrrina by using linguistic features favoured in senile speech (not only of EL or long-winded character, e.g. *volo ut* constructions), which, interestingly enough, are otherwise avoided in the rest of his lines.

As for personal idiosyncratic features, I have also identified several phenomena on a lexical (e.g. *video* in the sense of *intellego* by Chremes in *Heautontimoroumenos* etc.), syntactical (Thraso's penchant for historic infinitive constructions in *Eunuchus* etc.), or pragmatical level (Demea's penchant in *Adelphoe* for echo-questions), as well as on the level of imagery (Demea's use of rustic and financial figurative language). Furthermore, in the case of Sostrata and Laches in *Hecyra*, Maltby has pointed out that the couple have some linguistic options in common (e.g. *derepente*).[39] This seems also to be the case with the use of the oath *ita me di ament* (vv. 233, 258, 642, 206, 276, 579) and the expression *dis gratiam habeo* (vv. 346, 653).[40]

[39] Cf. Maltby (1976: 259).

[40] Cf. also Papadimitriou (1998: 215, 220).

CHAPTER 7

PLAUTUS IN TERENCE: THE CASE OF *EUNUCHUS*

Introduction

Studies on Terence's style, structure, motifs and characterisation[1] have shown that he stands outside the main tradition of the Roman *palliata* as exemplified by writers such as Naevius, Caecilius and, most importantly, Plautus. As for Plautus and Terence in particular,[2] it has been argued that these two poets are about as different as two poets working in the same genre can be.[3] This is true up to a point, but there are contexts in which it can be shown that Terence does adopt a more Plautine or traditional style. This seems to be especially so in the case of *Eunuchus*.

In this chapter, after setting out the generally accepted thematic and structural similarities between *Eunuchus* and the Plautine corpus, we turn to the possibility of a *rapprochement* between the two authors on the linguistic and stylistic plane as well in this specific work.

[1] Cf. Wright (1974: 127–51), Maltby (1983: 27–41).

[2] Some of this contrast is, of course, due to the Greek originals Terence and Plautus chose to work with; yet, as Wright (1974: 136) rightly remarks, it must not be forgotten that the Roman playwrights were responsible for their choice. Several dramatic techniques, character types, specific thematic structure etc., although they appear in Greek New comedy, are in Roman Republican drama associated mostly with one of the two playwrights and seem to be avoided by the other (for a similar approach, cf. Duckworth (1952: 176)). But much of this contrast is the work of Plautus and Terence themselves (cf. Wright (1974: 136)). It is significant enough that Plautine comedies based upon Menandrian originals display a greater variety of theme and structure than do the four Menandrian plays of Terence (cf. Duckworth (1952: 176)).

[3] Cf. Wright (1974: 127), Duckworth (1952: 331–60), Palmer (1954: 74–94), Barsby (1999: 20–7).

Structural and thematic similarities

Eunuchus is considered by most scholars as Terence's most Plautine play in both context and structure.[4] Apart from its more farcical character, in the *Eunuchus* we also find several techniques, which, while being very common in Plautus, are, on the other hand, avoided or sparingly used in Terence's plays. This is the case with:

Long inorganic speeches. Unlike Terence, Plautus is fond of including long inorganic speeches, i.e. scenes not closely integrated with the action which hold up the plot. This is mainly the case with the self-introductory monologues of Plautus' parasites (cf. *Capt.* 69–109, 461–97, *Men.* 77–109, *Pers.* 53–80, *Stich.* 155–233). Gnatho's overheard entrance monologue in the *Eunuchus* (vv. 232ff. – the monologue lasts for thirty-six lines) is also an *extra causam* narration, detached from the action, and is much more in the Plautine tradition.[5]

Incongruous romanisms. This is the case with vv. 256–7 *concurrunt laeti mi obviam cuppedenarii omnes, cetarii lanii coqui fartores piscatores*, where we encounter Roman terminology in a Greek context, a technique aiming to increase, according to Donatus (cf. ad loc. σχῆμα *comicum, nam in palliata Romanas res loquitur*), the comic effect (cf. also references to *clientela* in v. 1039). This kind of romanism (especially references to Roman gods and place names, Roman officials, Roman dress and contemporary events) is common in Plautus, especially in the speech of his parasites,[6] but is avoided in Terence. The incongruous romanism, traditional in the *palliata*, is followed here by two Plautine or traditional linguistic patterns as well:

1. the asyndetic quintuplet (the longest list in Terence, cf. also *Eun.* 373ff.), normally avoided in Terence, who is usually content with asyndetic triplets at the most, in contrast to Plautus, who

4 Frank (1930: 121–2) claims that in the *Eunuchus* Terence for once shifts to the Plautine manner, restricting his play chiefly to buffoons, impostors and ludicrous situations. Duckworth as well adds that the foreshadowing of Pamphila's recognition early in the play (in opposition to the common Terentian techniques of suspense and surprise (cf. also Barsby (1999: 99)) also contributes to this view (for similar viewpoints on the Plautine character of *Eunuchus* cf. also Barsby (1999: 15, 20–7), 'Terence's most Plautine play', Tromaras (1994: 16), when accurately remarking: 'Terenz gerade bei diesem Stück dem Plautus nahekommt, indem er viele komische Szenen schafft.')

5 Cf. also Duckworth (1952: 392), Barsby (1999: 127).

6 Cf. Ergasilus in *Capt.* 90, 489, mentioning both the Triple Gate of Rome and the oil market in the Velabrum; see also Barsby (1999: 132), Prescott (1920: 269–70, 1942: 5), Hough (1940: 194–7).

is very keen on accumulating long lists of synonyms or other parallel items;[7]

2. the use of non-CL nouns and adjectives in *-arius* for dramatic effect, a characteristic feature of Plautus' lexicon, avoided, on the other hand, by Terence.[8] Apart from *iocularius*, all other non-CL forms in *-arius* in Terence occur in *Eunuchus: palmarius* (v. 930), possibly an intentional coinage of Terence for the normal *palmaris, cuppedenarius, cetarius* (vv. 256–7).

Other individual thematic features. Concentration of mythological references within one play[9] (three out of five instances of mythological citations in Terence appear in *Eunuchus*, *Eun.* 1027–8, 1085),[10] references to painting (*Eun.* 584ff.),[11] the only example in Terence (*Eun.* 454ff.) of a character entering from a house in response to a voice heard on stage (see, on the other hand, Plaut. *Aul.* 727, *Cist.* 543, *Rud.* 259–60, *Trin.* 1093).

Linguistic and stylistic similarities

Previous research and methodological tools

Does the language of *Eunuchus*, generally considered to be Terence's most Plautine comedy from the point of view of plot, motifs and structure, share some linguistic similarities with Plautine drama as well?

Maltby was the first modern scholar, again, to argue for the more Plautine linguistic character of Terence's *Eunuchus*, by bringing forth several linguistic similarities between Plautine drama and the *Eunuchus* (1976: 232ff.). This seems to be the case with the following: the *nil moror* expression; the elliptical *mirum ni*; the EL use of *si, nisi, quasi, nisi quia* for *nisi quod* (*Eun.* 736); *adsimulare quasi* (*Eun.* 461), the only purpose infinitive, a common feature of Plautus' language, outside the *it . . . visere* type, i.e. *misit . . . orare* at *Eun.* 528 in place of a regular *ut* clause; the use of *amabo* with

[7] Cf. *Aul.* 508–16, *Bacch.* 1088, *Capt.* 770–1 etc.; see also Barsby (1999: 23), Wright (1974: 75), Duckworth (1952: 340); for similar techniques in Caecilius, cf. *com.* 201–2; for Naevius, cf. *com.* 55; for asyndeton in Terence, cf. Bini (1981: 115–22).

[8] Cf. Maltby (1976: 232).

[9] Cf. Barsby (1999: 196).

[10] A further instance occurs in the last act of the *Heautontimoroumenos*, cf. *Heaut.* 1036. See also Radke (1951: 73–5).

[11] For references to painting in Plautus and Terence, cf. Knapp (1917: 143–57). See also Tromaras (1985: 268–77).

an *ut* clause as its complement; the use of the diminutive *adulescentulus* with no semantic distinction, as a simple equivalent for *adulescens*; the higher concentration of substantive diminutives, of the type most favoured in Plautus and in colloquial genres in general.[12]

Maltby's brief overview of the subject suffers, however, from several methodological slips. In particular, his data are incomplete; he examines only a few of the examples present in the Terentian corpus. Moreover, since no clear subcategorisation of the linguistic features examined is offered, it is impossible to discover the specific linguistic or stylistic levels at which Terence's *Eunuchus* is closer to the Plautine linguistic tradition and the degree to which this is evident at each level. Only an examination of the totality of features belonging to a specific category allows one to draw such conclusions. For example, Maltby rightly remarks that the expression *adsimulare quasi*, common in Plautus (*Amph.* 115, *Epid.* 195, *Mil.* 1170, 1181, *Poen.* 600, *Stich.* 84), appears only once in Terence's *Eunuchus*, v. 461. This, however, does not prove the affinity of *Eunuchus* with Plautine language in contrast to all other Terentian plays. Similar complex expressions and phrases, *hapax* in Terence but common in Plautus, occur in other plays as well, e.g. *nusquam . . . gentium* at *Ad.* 540 (see also Plaut. *Amph.* 620, *Cas.* 70, *Men.* 262, *Merc.* 606, *Pseud.* 402, 405).

The subject therefore needs to be examined further on a better methodological footing. In particular, several studies dealing with the language of Roman comedy[13] have shown that the language of the two playwrights differs mainly in their use of the following linguistic features: colloquialisms, terms of abuse, grecising expressions, archaic or EL and non-CL features, interjections, figurative phrases, formulaic locutions, specific terms of endearment and some other individual linguistic or stylistic devices (long lists of synonymous or parallel items in asyndeton etc.);

[12] Cf. Cooper (1895: 164–95).

[13] Cf. Barsby (1999: 19–27), Duckworth (1952: 331–60), Palmer (1954: 74–94), Lilja (1965: 78–85), Hofmann (1951: 9–39), Wright (1974: 19, 40 and passim), Müller (1913: passim), Fantham (1972: passim).

these are used by Plautus far more frequently than by Terence. By exhaustively examining such features I shall show that the proportion of them in *Eunuchus* is higher than in all other Terentian comedies.

Terence seems to be using linguistic features and stylistic devices taken from the earlier tradition of Roman comedy, mainly Plautus, in passages where we know he was altering his original, either inventing new material himself or adding it from another play. Maltby has convincingly shown that this is the case with the last scene of Terence's *Heautontimoroumenos*, where Terence deviates from his original, reworking his material in a more traditional and Plautine way.[14] I shall show that this is also the case with a few other scenes where Terence deviates from his original again, e.g. the Sannio scene in the *Adelphoe*.[15]

Non-CL formations by means of colloquial affixes

Terence, unlike Plautus but in accordance with CL again, normally avoids formations by means of affixes which are productive in colloquial sources, or restricts himself to those few accepted in CL. Several exceptions, however, seem to be concentrated in *Eunuchus*. Maltby again has observed that in *Eunuchus* we find the only non-CL noun in *-ura* in Terence, *curatura* at *Eun.* 316, a rare meaning for *cura* or *curatio*. This is another feature, in Maltby's view, of the style of *Eunuchus*, bringing it closer to Plautine language. In Plautus, on the other hand, these non-CL formations are quite frequent (cf. *Asin.* 327, *Stich.* 688 etc., cf. also Cooper (1895: 28–9)). The imagery technique here also has a Plautine ring,

[14] Cf. Maltby (1983). The scene displays in concentration many linguistic features which, while avoided elsewhere in the Terentian corpus, are on the other hand associated with well-established Plautine usage (e.g. the idiomatic use of *dabo* + past participle, the *ut . . . meminerit semper mei* formula, *depecto* and *exorno* in the sense 'to beat' etc.).

[15] For the scene from Diphilus, cf. also Drexler (1934: 1–40), Fantham (1968: 196–216), Ludwig (1968: 171–2), Lloyd-Jones (1973: 279–84), Marti (1963: 72–9), Rieth (1964: 34–59), Webster (1970: 160). In this book, 'Sannio scene' refers to the Aeschinus–Sannio dialogue (vv. 155–96), i.e. the scene from Diphilus, as well as to Sannio's monologue vv. 197–208, where, as Gratwick (1987: 239) remarks, Terence does not follow Diphilus or Menander but seems to extemporise.

reddunt (sc. virgines) curatura iunceas (i.e. *tam graciles quam iunci*), where *iunceus* is used in the metaphorical sense 'thin as a reed'. In Terence, just as in Menander, the commonest form of imagery is the single-word metaphor, mostly conveyed by a verb. The figurative use of adjectives, on the other hand, as Fantham has observed (1972: 80), is a common Plautine imagery technique, which is not favoured in Terence (cf. also a further instance at *Phorm.* 964).

This is also the case with several other unclassical formations by means of affixes, productive in colloquial sources. These Terentian *hapaxes* show a concentration in *Eunuchus*:

substantives in *-tudo* (Plaut. *Trin.* 874, *Rud.* 524, *Epid.* 609 etc.), *habitudo* at *Eun.* 242;
adjectives in *-inus* (Plaut. *Pseud.* 319, *Rud.* 533, *Cas.* 973 etc.), *mustelinus* at *Eun.* 689;
nouns in *-arium* (Plaut *Merc.* 490, *Poen.* 202, *Truc.* 480 etc.), *palmarium* at *Eun.* 930.

All these do not mean of course that we do not occasionally find examples in other plays. This is the case with *subtristis* at *Andr.* 447, *patrocinari* at *Phorm.* 939. What matters again is not the individual features themselves, but their relative accumulation and variety in one play and their relative absence from the others.

As for non-CL forms in general, we may observe the following: Terence, unlike Plautus, is characterised by restricting himself to formations or constructions which were later to be used regularly in CL. Nevertheless, several EL and non-CL forms are to be found in Terence as well. Their distribution, however, as Maltby rightly remarks (1976: 213), argues against Wahrmann's assertion that the presence of such formations in Terence simply reflects the state of the language at the time the playwright was writing, for in this case they would be either evenly distributed or slightly more common in the earlier plays. This is not the case, however. *Eunuchus*, Terence's fourth play, again has the highest proportion of non-CL features (202), approximating in this case Plautine ratios, whereas these forms are least frequent in *Hecyra*. Hence, the higher proportion of non-CL forms in *Eunuchus* seems to have a stylistic motivation.

Terms of abuse

One of the most striking differences in the language of the two playwrights is their handling of terms of abuse.[16] In this subsection I shall examine all the cases where a specific term of abuse in Terentian drama either appears *hapax*, in opposition to its repeated occurrence in Plautus, or its frequency of appearance in Plautus is higher than in Terence. Most of the terms of abuse of this kind are found only or in overwhelming majority in *Eunuchus*:

v. 23 ***fur*** This is the most common of terms of abuse referring to stealing. Apart from slaves, cooks are abused as *fures*. The term is common in Plautus (*Asin.* 421, 681, *Aul.* 322, 326 <twice>, *Cas.* 720, *Pseud.* 365, *Stich.* 766). In Terence, the only two examples are restricted to the *Eunuchus* (vv. 23, 776).

v. 71 ***scelestus*** This is the most common term of abuse in Plautine comedy (51 times, e.g. *Amph.* 348, *Asin.* 149, *Bacch.* 784). Terence, on the other hand, prefers far more often the corresponding abstract noun *scelus*, which is not so common in Plautus.[17] Whereas *scelus* is evenly distributed in Terentian drama, *scelestus* shows in Terence a particular concentration (six out of its ten occurrences) in *Eunuchus* (vv. 71, 668, 709, 817, 832, 944; isolated examples at *Ad.* 159, *Andr.* 790, *Heaut.* 312, 970). What is more, two out of the four instances where *scelestus* appears outside the *Eunuchus* are found in scenes where Terence deviates from his original, namely the Sannio scene in *Adelphoe* and the last scene of *Heautontimoroumenos*.

v. 152 ***pessuma*** *Pessumus* is a very common term of abuse in Plautus (22 times, e.g. *Asin.* 214, *Aul.* 64, *Bacch.* 1122). It is the superlative of *malus*, a further very common Plautine term of abuse (27 times). In Terence the word is found only twice, significantly at *Eun.* 152 by the *adulescens* Phaedria of the *meretrix* Thais and at v. 1017 in the altercation between Parmeno and Pythias.

v. 425 ***inpudens*** This is another term of abuse common in Plautus (eighteen times, e.g. *Amph.* 818, *Aul.* 746, *Cas.* 97), found twice in *Eunuchus* (vv. 425, 856). It occurs once more at *Andr.* 710, where Terence deviates once more from his original in introducing the characters of Byrria and Charinus.[18]

[16] Cf. also Barsby (1999: 20).

[17] Cf. Lilja (1965: 22, 36–7, 57), Barsby (1999: 96). For terms of abuse in Roman comedy, cf. also Müller (1913: 492–502). See also Opelt (1965).

[18] Cf. Donat. ad *Andr.* 301. *has personas Terentius addidit fabulae, – nam non sunt apud Menandrum.*

v. 604 ***fatuus*** As a term of abuse already found in Plautine drama (*Amph.* 1026, *Bacch.* 1088), *fatuus* is restricted in Terence to *Eunuchus*, vv. 604 and 1079.

v. 616 ***insanus*** This term of abuse is common in Plautus (eight times, e.g. *Curc.* 19, *Men.* 336, *Mil.* 371, *Most.* 450). In Terence it is again restricted to *Eunuchus*, vv. 616 (*ancilla* Dorias), 861 (*meretrix* Thais).

v. 648 ***veneficus*** As a term of abuse *veneficus* is common enough in Plautus (eight times, e.g. *Amph.* 1043, *Epid.* 221, *Most.* 218). In Terence it is found only in vv. 648 and 825. The sequence of the four terms of abuse here in asyndetic quadruplet (*scelerosus, impius, scelus, veneficus*) also has a Plautine ring.

v. 696 ***monstrum hominis*** The combination noun (*monstrum*) + genitive is a *hapax legomenon* in Terence, at *Eun.* 696. Noun + definitive genitive combinations functioning as terms of abuse, although avoided elsewhere in Terence, occur very frequently in Plautus (*deliciae popli, scelus viri, flagitium hominis, frustum pueri, hallex viri, populi odium* etc., cf. a combination with *monstrum* at *Poen.* 273 *monstrum mulieris*). In any case, this is the only instance of an appositional or epexegetic genitive (*genetivus definitivus*) in Terence, otherwise common in the rest of the *palliata*.[19]

v. 754 ***odiosus*** A term of abuse that is found only here in Terence. Plautus, on the other hand, uses the word as a term of abuse twice (*Men.* 884, *Truc.* 619) and the abstract substantive *odium* ten times.

v. 803 ***canis*** This is the only example of *canis* as a term of abuse in Terence. *Canis* is frequently found in Plautus in an abusive sense (*Bacch.* 1146, *Cas.* 320, *Curc.* 598, *Men.* 714, 837). In general Plautus uses animal names as terms of abuse (*bestia, lupa, pecus, simia, pithecium, ovis, mula* etc.) much more freely than Terence, who has only *asinus* (*Eun.* 598), *belua* (*Eun.* 704), *lepus* (*Eun.* 426) and *canis* found significantly in concentration only in the *Eunuchus*.

Conclusions on terms of abuse

Many terms of abuse are common to both Plautus and Terence, though the handling of abuse is otherwise quite different in the two playwrights.[20] It seems, however, that in *Eunuchus* Terence opts to depart from his own reserved handling of abuse and approximates to a greater extent than in any other comedy to common Plautine

[19] Cf. Plaut. *Asin.* 473, *Aul.* 703, *Cas.* 155, 552, *Men.* 489, 709, *Merc.* 755, *Pers.* 204, *Pers.* 848, *Poen.* 1310, Caec. *com.* 246 *nomen virginis*, Afran. *tog.* 57 *novercae nomen*.

[20] For differences between Plautus and Terence in this matter, cf. Lilja (1965: 78–85, 90–4), Barsby (1999: 20–1), Miniconi (1958: 159–75).

techniques. Hence I may conclude that in Plautus the relative frequency of terms of abuse is far higher than in Terence.[21] *Eunuchus* is the only exception and has nearly twice as many examples of abuse as any other of Terence's plays. The percentage of terms of abuse in *Eunuchus* is 5.9 per cent, a proportion approximating Plautine usage[22] and giving a distinct colloquial flavour. What is more, in *Eunuchus* Terence displays not only a higher percentage of terms of abuse in the Plautine manner but also opts for a finer variety. Most of the terms, more common in Plautine comedy than in Terence, either occur exclusively in *Eunuchus* (*insanus, pessumus, veneficus*, terms of abuse derived from the animal kingdom – *canis* etc.) or appear in this play in overwhelming majority (*scelestus, furcifer, impudens*). Finally, whereas Terence usually uses no more than one term of abuse at a time (as is also the case in Menandrian comedy),[23] in *Eunuchus* he often piles up terms and creates whole scenes of abuse (vv. 668–70 *exi foras, sceleste. at etiam restitas, fugitive? prodi, male conciliate . . . carnufex*, 825ff., 1079 *fatuos est, insulsus, tardus*) in the Plautine way.[24]

All this does not entail that terms of abuse which occur either *hapax* in Terence or in higher frequency in Plautus than in Terence cannot be found in other plays. What matters, again, is the relative accumulation of these features in a specific play and their relative absence from others. Additionally, in most cases, these terms of abuse occur in scenes where Terence deviates from his original, probably reworking his material in a more Plautine way. Apart from the instances already dealt with above, this is also the case with *periurus*[25] at *Ad.* 189 in the Sannio scene, imported by Terence from Diphilus' *Synapothnescontes*, *stultus* (35 times in Plautus) at *Eun.* 837, *Heaut.* 1009 (the last scene of *Heautontimoroumenos*), *Ad.* 218 (the Sannio scene), *verbero* (21 times in Plautus) at *Phorm.* 684, where Terence brought Antipho back early,[26] creating two scenes with four speakers. The only exceptions to the distributional pattern described above are *improbus*

[21] Cf. Lilja (1965: 80). [22] Cf. Lilja (1965: 78–81). [23] Cf. Lilja (1965: 90).

[24] For Plautine techniques of this kind, see also Lilja (1965: 82–5), e.g. *Pseud.* 794 *multiloquom, gloriosum, insulsum, inutilem, Bacch.* 1088 etc.

[25] For *periurus* as a term of abuse, cf. also Plaut. *Capt.* 57, *Mil.* 1066a, *Pers.* 562, *Poen.* 575 etc.

[26] Cf. Lowe (1983a: 41).

at *Hec.* 383, *mastigia* at *Ad.* 781, *stultus* at *Ad.* 724, *Heaut.* 585, *verbero* at *Phorm.* 850.

Interjections and Greek expressions

One of the most evident differences between Plautus' and Terence's language is their handling of interjections.[27] Terence has a penchant for interjections, especially primary ones (*ah, au, eho, hem, hui* etc.),[28] which are three times as frequent as in Plautus. While prolific in using interjections, Terence seems to avoid several specific interjections, mainly Greek ones (*apage, attat, eu, euge, heia, papae pax*), which are, on the other hand, far more common in Plautine drama.[29] Here again *Eunuchus* has the greatest concentration of these interjections among all Terence's plays (eleven out of 29). Some of them are found exclusively in *Eunuchus*. This is the case with the following:

v. 229 ***papae*** The interjection, like *attat*, while common enough in Greek tragedy (S. *Ph.* 792 παπαῖ etc.) as an expression of pain, is in Roman literature almost entirely confined to comedy. This distinctively colloquial interjection,[30] although found several times throughout the Plautine corpus (*Bacch.* 207, *Cas.* 906a, *Epid.* 54, *Men.* 918, *Rud.* 1320, *Stich.* 425, *Truc.* 507), in Terence shows a particular concentration in *Eunuchus* (four examples in vv. 229, 279, 317, 416, three of them spoken by the slave Parmeno). It is avoided in all other Terentian plays.

v. 756 ***apage*** This is a Greek colloquialism frequent in Plautus (27 times, e.g. *Amph.* 310, *Bacch.* 73, *Capt.* 209), but occurring only twice in Terence, only in *Eunuchus*. The word is used here, just as in Plautus, in a quasi-stereotyped way, to convey a firm rejection of an idea, person or event previously referred to.[31] What is more, in v. 904 there occurs *apage te*, a frequent and stereotypical combination in Plautine drama (*Pseud.* 653, *Trin.* 258, 266, *Cas.* 459, *Amph.* 580).

As for Greek words in general, Terence seems again to assimilate common Plautine techniques in *Eunuchus*. *Eunuchus* is the only play of Terence to attain the same frequency of Greek words as that

[27] For interjections as a marker of linguistic difference between the two playwrights, cf. Barsby (1999: 21–2), Hofmann (1951: 9–39).

[28] For the term and examples, cf. Hofmann (1951: 9–39).

[29] Cf. Barsby (1999: 22).

[30] Cf. Hofmann (1951: 24), Barsby (1999: 125).

[31] Cf. also Zagagi (1980: 100).

found in Plautus' plays (1:37:5). What is more, *Eunuchus* displays exclusively nine Greek words (*astu, propino, riscus, sandalium, cetarius, cistella, comissor, elephantus, stomachor*), many of them (e.g. *propino*) commonly found in Plautine drama. *Hecyra*, on the other hand, displays the lowest ratio (1:247: 3).[32]

The following subsection is concerned with data collected from the viewpoint of stylistics, and contains such features as metaphors, rhetorical and metrical devices, etc. and not purely linguistic choices.

Figurative language[33]

Plautus and Terence share a number of figurative uses (metaphors concerning fire and storm, heat and cold, sickness and health, teacher and pupil, hunting and fishing, theatre). Many of these figurative expressions find precedents in Greek New Comedy (*comedere* for wasting or squandering = κατεσθίειν, καταφαγεῖν). These metaphors do not show any particular concentration in Terence, but are evenly distributed in all Terentian comedies.

Several metaphorical expressions, however, are independent of known Greek metaphors and occur for the first time either in Plautus or, less frequently, in Terence. While figurative language occurring for the first time in Terence is evenly scattered throughout the whole Terentian corpus (as is also the case with metaphors well attested in Greek New Comedy), figurative expressions, independent of known Greek models, attested for the first time in Plautus and often related to well-established Plautine language, often occur in Terence only as *hapax* expressions.[34] These last cases (*hapax* instances) show a particular concentration in *Eunuchus*. This does not entail, of course, that individual cases are not to be found in other plays (*derivare* at *Phorm.* 323, possibly *ferire* at *Phorm.* 47, referring to someone stung or touched for money, *macula* at

[32] For the percentages, cf. Maltby (1985: 120).

[33] For the characterisation of a specific usage as figurative, I follow mainly *OLD*, which uses the abbreviations 'fig.' [= figurative(ly)], 'transf.' [(in) transferred (sense)]. For figurative language in Roman comedy, cf. also Corbett (1964: 52–69).

[34] Identifications of humans with animals, figurative uses associated with warfare and single combat, agricultural images.

Ad. 954, a higher number in *Heautontimoroumenos, bolus, obsaturare, deperire, provincia, depectere*). These are often associated (*bolus, depectere*), however, with scenes where Terence is believed to depart from his original, and to rework his material in a more traditional or Plautine way. This is especially the case with the last scene of *Heautontimoroumenos*.

What matters, again, is not the individual features themselves but their relative concentration within one play. What is more, in *Eunuchus* we find some distinctively Plautine imagery techniques otherwise avoided in Terence, as is the identification technique (v. 426), as well as the most extended figurative use in the Terentian corpus (vv. 103–5, 121).

Some particular examples:

v. 79 ***nostri fundi calamitas*** An agricultural image, 'blight on our estate'. Metaphors from plants and agriculture are common in Plautus but are avoided in the comedies of Terence.[35] Three out of four instances of agricultural imagery in Terence are found in *Eunuchus: nostri fundi calamitas* (v. 79), *pannis annisque obsitum* (v. 236), *istaec in me cudetur faba* (v. 381). In this instance again, Terence deviates from his practice of using simple verb metaphors. Once more he uses a noun metaphor at *Eun.* 85 *ignem hunc*, where the courtesan Thais is compared to a fire. Commenting upon the use of the metaphor by the slave Parmeno, Fantham (1972: 9) remarks 'a touch of fantasy more characteristic of Plautus than Terence'.

vv. 103–5, 121 ***plenus rimarum . . . perfluo*** Parmeno compares himself to a leaking vessel. The image starts in v. 103, where *contineo* means to 'hold my contents' and is found again at v. 121 (*effluet*). Terence does not usually prolong his images to this length. A lengthy comparison of life to a game of dice is found at *Ad.* 739ff. It is not on the same scale as in *Eunuchus*, however. Prolonged images, on the other hand, are common in Plautus (*Aul.* 229–35, *Trin.* 28–33, 675–9 etc.), where most images are developed in detail.[36]

vv. 383–4 ***crux*** *Illis crucibus, quae nos . . . semper omnibus cruciant modis*. For similar figurative uses of *crux*, cf. also Plaut. *Aul.* 522, *Pers.* 795.

v. 406 ***exspueret miseriam ex animo*** *Exspuere* is used here in the sense of 'spew out' troubles. Terence elsewhere uses the similar verb *evomere* (*Hec.* 515, *Ad.* 312, 510). *Evomere* in this figurative sense is common

[35] For agricultural images differentiating the language of the two playwrights, see Fantham (1972: 76), Barsby (1999: 154).

[36] Cf. Fantham (1972: 73).

in Republican literature and is found not only in Plautus but also in Ennius (*Ann.* 275). Terence deviates from his common practice of using *evomere* for anger and other emotions and employs *exspuere* only in the *Eunuchus*. The only contemporary use of *exspuere* is found in Plautus, *Pseud.* 76 *non queo lacrumam exorare* (sc. *oculos*) *ut exspuant unam modo*.[37]

v. 426 ***lepus tute' s, pulpamentum quaeris?*** This is the only example of the identification technique in Terence, a common feature in Plautine drama (*Merc.* 361 *muscast meus pater, nil potest clam illum haberi, Cas.* 360–1 *stimulus ego nunc sum tibi, fodico corculum, Pseud.*747 *anguillast, elabitur* etc.).[38] The Plautine technique regularly consists of three parts:

(A) the subject of the identification (e.g. in Plaut. *Merc.* 361 *pater*)
(B) the object, an animal with which the subject is identified (e.g. *musca*)
(C) the explanation of the identification, the point which (A) and (B) have in common (*nil potest clam illum haberi*).

Terence avoids this pattern, adopting it but once here in *Eunuchus*, according to the following schema:

(A) animal object (B) ⇒*lepus*
(B) subject of identification (A) ⇒*tute*
(C) explanation (C) in asyndeton ⇒ *pulpamentum quaeris*

A similar example of this technique is found in Caecilius *com.* 34–5 *<Est> haec caterva plane gladiatoria cum suum sibi alius socius socium sauciat*, even though in this case the explanation does not follow in asyndeton.[39] What is more, the identification technique is also followed here by a Roman allusion (*caterva gladiatoria*) within a Greek setting.

v. 560 ***quid taces? o festus dies hominis! amice, salve*** The use of *festus dies hominis* as a term of endearment, possibly equivalent in sense to *festivus homo* (*Ad.* 983), is unparalleled in the whole of extant Latin literature with the exception of Plaut. *Cas.* 137, where a bailiff imagines his bride-to-be addressing him as *meus festus dies*.[40] What is more, *festus dies* here is followed by a genitive of definition, *hominis*, of the same type as *monstrum hominis*, a very common stylistic feature in Plautine comedy but avoided elsewhere in Terence with the exception of *Eunuchus* (cf. above).

[37] Fantham (1972: 52) remarks: 'use . . . vulgar and facetious'.
[38] Cf. Fraenkel (1960: 21–54), Fantham (1972: 80).
[39] For the Plautine ring of this line in Caecilius, cf. also Fraenkel (1960: 44).
[40] Cf. Barsby (1999: 192), 'redolent of Plautus'.

Another possible reading here is the one accepted by both Bentley and Ashmore: *o festus dies! o meus amicus! salve*. Even in this case, however, we encounter a further linguistic feature, common in Plautus (83 times) but avoided elsewhere in Terence, namely the use of the nominative *meus* in a vocative function. This usage is avoided later with the exception of archaising authors, as in Gellius, 15.7.3 *Ave, mi Gai, meus asellus iucundissimus*, Fronto, Apuleius.

v. 712 ***exsculpere*** The figurative use of *exsculpere* at *Eun*. 712b *possumne ego hodie ex te exsculpere verum* has its equivalent in Plautus, e.g. *Cist*. 541. The metaphor is found nowhere in Greek literature, whereas in Latin the verb is otherwise always used in its literal sense only.

Further linguistic and stylistic features

In the following paragraphs a list of additional individual features is given which, while they have no great value on their own, nevertheless serve to strengthen the point made if taken in conjunction with all the linguistic particularities examined above.

Formulae

v. 305 ***unde is?*** The use of various formulaic expressions (in prayers, greeting scenes, returning-traveller scenes etc.) is, according to Wright (1974: 147–51), one of the most striking differences in style between Plautus and Terence. Terence frequently opts for their reduction or even elimination. A common conventional greeting formula in Plautus is *unde is?* (*Cas*. 245, *Cist*. 776, *Most*. 547, 785, *Stich*. 319 etc.). The formula is avoided in Terence, except for the *Eunuchus* example.

v. 377 ***age eamus*** Another common formulaic combination in Plautus (*Poen*. 491, 717, 1422, *Rud*. 1179), found only once in Terence, in *Eunuchus*. What is more, the singular *age*, used as a simple interjectional expression by a speaker addressing more than one person,[41] is quite common in Plautus (*Cas*. 488, *Mil*. 928, *Stich*. 221) but exceptional in Terence.

v. 530 ***heus heus, ecquis hic?*** This is a common door-knocking formula in Roman comedy, frequently found in Plautus (*Amph*. 1020, *Bacch*. 582, *Most*. 899, *Poen*. 1118; see also a variant at *Capt*. 830) but avoided in Terence with the exception of *Eun*. 530.

vv. 918–19 ***eccum Parmenonen incedere video*** This is a variation of the formula *eccum incedit*, common in Roman comedy for referring to

[41] For this function of *age* in place of *agite*, see also Müller (1997: 115).

an entrance from the wings. It is frequently found in Plautus (*Aul.* 473, *Bacch.* 403, *Curc.* 676, *Epid.* 608, *Mil.* 1281, *Most.* 1120, *Poen.* 470, *Pseud.* 410–11, *Rud.* 492 etc.) but occurs only once here in Terence.

Further individual linguistic and stylistic features

As Martin (1995: 139–51) rightly observes, examining several cases of *hapax legomena* in Terence, in an author whose total oeuvre is less than 6,000 words, some words will necessarily appear once only; whether in a given case a *hapax* is significant or not requires careful consideration, with due account being taken of speaker, context and common Terentian linguistic techniques. Thus, as he suggests, it is surely a matter of chance that *acqua* appears only once in Terence, whereas, e.g. taking into account Terence's avoidance of coarse language, the *hapax* use of a distinct colloquial term of abuse, commonly found in the Plautine drama, may have a specific stylistic effect. In this section, following Maltby's methodological tools, I shall examine several words and expressions having either a distinct EL or colloquial character (and thus avoided elsewhere in Terence) or which are simply associated with a well-established Plautine usage. It is often the case that these formations in Terence either have a different meaning, with the exception of *Eunuchus* where the playwright opts for the regular Plautine meaning,[42] or are formations for which Terence has different equivalents, with the exception of *Eunuchus* again, where the playwright opts once more for the Plautine common usage.

Lexical option

Nouns and adjectives

v. 244 ***ridiculus*** The word here is equivalent to 'parasite'. This is the regular meaning of the word in Plautus (Plaut. *Capt.* 477 *neque ridiculos iam terrunci faciunt*, *Stich.* 171 *nunc si ridiculum hominem quaerat*

[42] I.e. the unique Plautine equivalent or the one whose ratio is by far higher in Plautus than in Terence, in the sense described and used above, when examining other linguistic features.

quispiam, 217, 221, 382, 389, 637 etc.), but is avoided in Terence except for here. Elsewhere in Terence the word has its common negative sense 'ridiculous', 'absurd' (*Heaut.* 353, *Ad.* 676, *Andr.* 371).

v. 260 ***famelicus*** It is an EL expression, commonly found in Plautus with the sense of 'starveling', derived from *fames* = hunger (cf. Donat. ad loc. *famelicus a fame et ab edendo dictum est quasi famedicus*, see also *ThLL* Vi 227, 79ff., *Cas.* 130, *Rud.* 311, *Stich.* 575). The word, which disappears later in CL, appears in Terence only at *Eun.* 260 *ille ubi miser famelicus videt mi esse tantum honorem* in the speech of the parasite Gnatho.

v. 274 ***mancupium*** This is a legal term, very common in Plautus for referring to slaves (*Capt.* 954, *Epid.* 686, *Rud.* 930, 1395 etc.). In Terence the term with this sense is avoided, with the exception of two instances in the *Eunuchus* vv. 274 and 364.

v. 456 ***meum savium*** Terence normally avoids *savium*, a distinct colloquial term having sexual associations (cf. Donat. ad loc. *savia libidinum vel amorum*, Serv. ad *A.* 1.256 *savium voluptatis*). This *vox blanda* at *Eun.* 456, found in the speech of the soldier Thraso, is a *hapax legomenon* in the Terentian drama, where lovers usually employ *anime* as a term of endearment (*Eun.* 95, *Heaut.* 406 etc.). *Savium* as a term of endearment between lovers, on the other hand, is more frequent in Plautus (*Poen.* 365ff. *mea salus, meum savium*).

Pronouns

v. 79 ***sed eccam ipsa egreditur*** *Eccam* here is due to correction. All the manuscripts, however, have the reading *ecca*, a form found elsewhere only in Plautus (*Cas.* 163, *Men.* 180, *Rud.* 1174.). The form *ecca* here has been rejected on the ground that it is found only once in Terence. It is not a coincidence, however, that this form occurs significantly in the *Eunuchus*, where we find many other Plautine linguistic features.

vv. 677–8 ***nostrarum*** This genitive plural of the first-person pronoun (cf. also Donat. ad loc. 'ἀρχαισμός' *est figura pro 'nostrum'*) is found only here in Terence (cf. also, on the other hand, in Plautus, *Amph.* fr. xiv, *Poen.* 540, 861).

Verbs

v. 254 ***adventamus*** (reading accepted by Umpfenbach, Dziatzko, Fabia, Barsby) The verb is often used in Roman comedy with no frequentative sense, as a simple equivalent of *advenio* (cf. *ThLL* I 83547 ff.). This colloquialism is avoided in Terence, with the exception again of *Eun.* 254 (cf. on the other hand, Plaut. *Aul.* 145, *Poen.* 561, *Truc.* 402).

v. 271 ***impertire*** The verb, construed with the accusative of person and the ablative of thing shared, is found in its active form, as is always the case in Plautus, only here at *Eun.* 271. Otherwise the verb is deponent in Terence (*Ad.* 320).

v. 387 ***culpent*** The EL use of *culpo* in the sense 'to blame' is common in Plautus (*Asin.* 510, 718, *Bacch.* 397, *Curc.* 503, *Mil.* 736, 756, *Most.* 180, *Pseud.* 828, *Trin.* 210, *Truc.* 349). Terence, in accordance with CL usage once more, uses the verb only once, at *Eun.* 387, in conjunction with the usage, also common in Plautus, of *rescisco* in place of *scio, quod qui rescierint, culpent.* Elsewhere Terence uses the regular (in CL) *reprehendo* (*Ad.* 994) or *vitupero* (*Andr.* 15, *Phorm.* 465; see also Nonius 39 M *vituperare dictum est vitio dare, tamquam culpae vel displicientiae*).

v. 432 ***emoriri*** The fourth-conjugation form (*moriri* for *mori*) is found in Terence only here; cf. Engelbrecht (1883: 77), who remarks: 'Infinitivus "moriri", quem solum novit Plautus semel legitur apud Terentium, contra quater forma volgaris exstat.' Plautus has *emoriri* at *Pseud.* 1222 and *moriri* at *Asin.* 121, *Capt.* 732, *Rud.* 684. Donatus (ad loc.) claims that here Terence, just like Plautus, attributes defective words to his soldier. The defective word is, according to the scholiast, the form *emoriri* in place of *emori*, which also occurs in Terence, in the speech of a high character though, the Attic young man Clitipho in *Heautontimoroumenos*.

v. 666 ***potesse*** Plautus frequently uses the lengthened form of the infinitive *potesse* in place of *posse* (*Bacch.* 559, *Most.* 1015, *Pseud.* 26, 1302, *Rud.* 55, *Truc.* 90), whereas Terence has only this one example, where the verb has the sense 'to be capable of sexual intercourse'.

v. 827 ***occidi*** The verb is used within Terentian drama as a simple interjectional exclamation of despair (*Andr.* 592, *Eun.* 701, 993, *Phorm.* 641). Its use in a full sentence, not just as a simple equivalent of an interjection of despair, is common enough in Plautus but is avoided in Terence with the exception of *Eun.* 827–8 *hem misera occidi, infelix, siquidem tu istaec vera praedicas*.[43]

v. 912 ***supposivit*** The form in *-ivit*, common in Plautus (Plaut. *Pseud.* 1281, *Trin.* 145, *Truc.* 460, 804) in place of *supposui*, is not preserved by the manuscripts here, but is required by the metre.

v. 972 ***percipit*** The verb is used here in the sense of 'to take hold of' (see *OLD* 8b); the compound *percipere* is found only in this sense elsewhere in Plautus (*Amph.* 1118, *Cas.* 879, *Men.* 921, *Stich.* 341, *Truc.* 467). This EL and regular meaning of the word within Plautine drama is avoided in Terence except for v. 972. Elsewhere in Terence the word has the regular sense *comprehendo, cognosco* (e.g. *Hec.* 363).

43 For this exceptional use of *occidi* here, cf. also Barsby (1999: 240).

v. 975 ***praestolare*** The verb is commonly used in Plautus in place of *expectare*, *opperiri* or *manere* (Nonius (161 M), *Cas.* 578, *Epid.* 217, 221, *Most.* 1066, *Poen.* 1173). The verb is rare in the classical period (when it is constructed with the dative case) and becomes common again only in Apuleius. Terence, on the other hand, avoids the word in this sense except for here and v. 977. Donatus suggests an etymological connection with the adverb *praesto*, which means 'to be ready, waiting on the spot'.

v. 1074 ***victitas*** Plautus frequently uses the frequentative verb *victitare* (*Rud.* 764, *Capt.* 83, *Most.* 153, *Most.* 321, *Truc.* 315, 347) in the sense of the Greek διαιτῶμαι; the frequentative, used in this sense in place of the simple *vivere*, appears only here in Terence.

Adverbs, interjections and prepositions

v. 301 ***praeut*** *Praeut* in the sense of 'in comparison to' is an EL feature, common in Plautus, where it introduces clauses of comparison (*Amph.* 374 *perii: parum etiam, praeut futurumst praedicas*, *Bacch.* 929, *Men.* 935, *Merc.* 470, *Mil.* 19–20). In Terence the word is used once at *Eun.* 301 *praeut huius rabies quae dabit*.[44] After Terence, the word is found only once, in Fronto, who is well known for his archaising tendencies.[45]

v. 427 ***facete lepide laute nil supra*** A particular combination of three adverbs found once more at Plaut. *Mil.* 1161 *lepide et facete, laute ludificarier*. Furthermore, only here in Terence do we find *lepide*, a common colloquialism mainly of Plautus' *meretrices* (see in Plautus, *Bacch.* 1181, *Cist.* 10, *Mil.* 739, *Most.* 318, *Pseud.* 949, *Rud.* 408, *Stich.* 685 etc.). *Lepide* is used here in an alliterative combination, *lepide . . . laute*, as is also the case in Plautus (*Bacch.* 35, *Mil.* 241, 615, *Poen.* 666, 697, 861 *Pseud.* 743).

v. 493 ***poste*** *Poste* is used here in place of *post. Poste* is restored to the text from one of the ancient glossaries; the manuscripts have *post, postea*, or *post huc*, of which only the last can scan. *Poste* is a common form in the Plautine comedy (*Amph.* 797, *Asin.* 915, *Bacch.* 966, *Cist.* 525, *Men.* 545, *Merc.* 220, *Most.* 290, *Rud.* 755, *Stich.* 380, *Truc.* 910 etc.).

v. 709 ***vae mihi*** *Vae* is an interjection expressing dismay and is always followed by dative. Terence has always the formulaic combination *vae misero (miserae) mihi* (*Andr.* 302, 743, *Heaut.* 250, *Hec.* 605, *Ad.* 301, 383). The formulaic *vae mihi*, on the other hand, without an inserted *misero (miserae)*, common enough in Plautus (*Amph.* 1080,

44 Terence opts for other conjunctions introducing comparison clauses, on this cf. Bennett (1910–14: I 106–19).

45 Another instance in Symm. 1.50.1 is textually doubtful, cf. *ThLL* X 373 16.

1109, *Asin.* 410, 924, *Merc.* 616, 722, *Most.* 367), is found only once here at *Eun.* 709 in Terence.

Composite expressions and formulaic combinations

v. 232 ***di immortales*** The combination without a preceding contact-morpheme, e.g. *pro* (*Phorm.* 1008, *Ad.* 447), is found only once here in Terence. In Plautus, on the other hand, this oath is very frequent (*Aul.* 785, *Capt.* 195, 242, *Epid.* 13, *Pseud.* 905, 936, *Rud.* 1161 etc.).

v. 254 ***scitum hercle hominem*** This is the only case in Terence of the accusative of exclamation used in combination with a reinforcing *hercle* (Plaut. *Bacch.* 999 *malum quidem hercle magnum, Epid.* 212 *hercle rem gestam bene*).

v. 492 ***iamne imus?*** *Iam* or *iamne* construed with the present indicative in deliberative questions is well attested in Plautus (Plaut. *Cas.* 503, *Curc.* 132, *Men.* 176, *Mil.* 1400). In Terence these combinations are found only in *Eunuchus* (vv. 492, 814 *iam dimitto exercitum?*). The same also applies to *quam mox* + present indicative combinations, v. 788 *quam mox intuimus?* (also in Plaut. *Bacch.* 775, *Men.* 135, *Mil.* 1406).

v. 644 ***facinus facere*** This is one of Plautus' most favoured figures (*Aul.* 220, *Bacch.* 641, *Cist.* 231, *Curc.* 24, *Men.* 447, *Mil.* 309, *Most.* 459, *Poen.* 308 etc.). Whereas Plautus has over a dozen examples of the *figura etymologica facinus facere*, this is Terence's only example.

v. 732 ***sine Cerere et Libero friget Venus*** A metonymy in which the names of gods are used for the things with which they are associated. This is the only instance in Terence where *Liber* is used in a metonymy, as equivalent to *vinum* (for *vinum, Hec.* 823, *Heaut.* 458, 568, *Ad.* 470, *Eun.* 727). In Plautus, on the other hand, the metonymic use of *Liber* is common enough (*Cas.* 640, *Cist.* 127 etc.).

v. 801 ***faciam ut huius loci dieique meique semper memineris*** The line spoken by the *senex* of the comedy is almost identical with Plaut. *Capt.* 800, where the parasite Ergasilus is threatening any bystander who gets in his way.

v. 834 ***era mea*** Servants in Terence address their mistresses in the vocative *era*, alone. The use of the possessive pronoun with the vocative is more common, on the other hand, in Plautine comedy (e.g. *Cas.* 632, 646, *Trin.* 1072). The use of the vocative with the possessive pronoun is found only here in Terence, uttered by the *ancilla* Pythias, *era mea, tace tace, obsecro*.

v. 923 ***quid* + *rerum* (partitive genitive) + *gero*** Formulaic combinations of this type, where *quid* . . . *rerum* is equivalent to *quasnam res*,[46]

[46] Cf. Barsby (1999: 257).

are common in Plautus (*Aul.* 54, 117, *Capt.* 376, *Men.* 789, *Mil.* 397, *Pers.* 513, *Pseud.* 1063, *Rud.* 897, 1068). The combination is found only once in Terence, at *Eun.* 923 *quidnam Chaerea . . . rerum gerat* ('how is Chaerea getting on?').

Syntactical options

v. 280 ***fortasse tu profectus alio fueras*** In several instances in Latin the perfect forms of the verb *esse*, namely *fui, fueram, fuerim*, are used with the perfect participle of a specific verb in place of the present or imperfect forms of *esse*. *Profectus fueram* is used here with the meaning of *profectus eram* as is also the case with *mercatus fuerat* in place of *mercatus erat* at *Eun.* 569 *eunuchus quem mercatus fuerat frater Thaidi*. Such a construction, common enough in Plautus, is avoided in Terence with the exception of these two instances in *Eunuchus*. For Plautus, see *Pseud.* 171 *oblitus fui* in place of *oblitus sum*, *Pers.* 380 *surrepta fueris* for *surrepta sis, Trin.* 850 *natus fuerit* for *natus sit, Most.* 487 *oblitus fueram* for *oblitus eram, Merc.* 232 *mercatus fueram* for *mercatus eram* etc.

v. 288 ***facete dictum: mira vero militi qui placeant?*** ('very smart, as sayings must be to delight the Captain'), *Mira (sunt)* here is equivalent to *mirum est* (cf. Barsby (1999: 138). This is the only Terentian example of the plural form used in place of the normal impersonal expression in the singular (*Heaut.* 1, *Phorm.* 848). The plural form is quite common in Plautus (*Amph.* 283, 432, *Bacch.* 450, *Capt.* 805, *Epid.* 553, *Men.* 1046, *Pseud.* 1216, *Trin.* 861).

v. 405 ***requiescere ubi volebat, quasi . . . nostin?*** This is the only instance in Terence of the temporal *ubi* with the imperfect indicative, exhibiting here iterative force (see, on the other hand, Plaut. *Bacch.* 685, *Mil.* 856, *Trin.* 503, fr.26).

v. 594 ***exspecto* + *si* clauses** *Si* clauses are often construed with verbs of waiting in Plautus (33 times). This is an El feature, avoided in Terence, who opts once more for the CL equivalent construction *dum* + subjunctive. One example of this Plautine usage is found in *Eun.* 594 *sto spectans si quid mi imperent*.

v. 735 ***nil, nisi abiens mi innuit*** Simple *nisi* in place of *nisi quia* is avoided in Terence with the exception of *Eunuchus* again (vv. 735 and 826–7 *nescio; nisi amasse credo Pamphilam*. This usage is more common in Plautus and is scattered throughout the Plautine corpus with no particular concentration (*Cist.* 676 *ubi ea sit nescio, nisi . . . loca haec circiter excidit*, *Bacch.* 324, *Epid.* 281, *Poen.* 649–50, *Rud.* 750–1).

v. 736 ***nescibam id dicere illam, nisi quia correxit miles*** This is the only example in Terence of the combination *nisi quia* in the sense of 'except for the fact that' introducing a substantive causal clause. The *quia* clause is an object of a *scio* to be supplied after *nisi*. In Plautus, on the other hand, these combinations are frequent (*Cist.* 223, *Pers.* 546, *Pseud.* 107, 568, *Trin.* 937, *Truc.* 786).

v. 803 **threatening verb + *ego* + object** The use of a postponed *ego* followed by a noun object or a pronoun (usually demonstrative) after a threatening verb, placed at the head of the clause and not vice versa (e.g. *Heaut.* 730 *ego pol istos commovebo*), is a common Plautine structure (*Bacch.* 571 *tollam ego ted*, *Bacch.* 766 *vorsabo ego illunc*, *Most.* 1168). In Terence this type of word order is found only once, at *Eun.* 803 *diminuam ego caput tuum hodie, nisi abis*.

v. 875 ***quid si*** This is the only instance in Terence of *quid si* introducing a conditional clause with the protasis in the perfect indicative, *quid si hoc quispiam voluit deus?* (see, on the other hand, Plaut. *Epid.* 599 *quid si servo aliter visum est?*, *Amph.* 701, *Pseud.* 286, 539).

v. 891 ***iam frater ipse hic aderit virginis*** The use of the pronoun *ipse, -a, -um* in the adverbial sense of *coram*, as here, is the only instance in Terence. See, on the other hand, in Plautus *Amph.* 71, 88, *Men.* 969, *Pers.* 654.

v. 956 ***equidem*** *Equidem* is normally construed with a first-person verb. This is always the case in Terence with the exception of *Eun.* 956 *atque equidem orante ut ne id faceret*, where *equidem* is construed with a third-person verb. This colloquial usage (construction of *equidem* with second- or third-singular verb) is, on the other hand, very frequent in Plautus (*Aul.* 138, *Bacch.* 974, 996, *Cas.* 208, *Curc.* 211, *Epid.* 16, 99, 378, 603, *Mil.* 158 etc.).

Overall conclusions

Terence's language in *Eunuchus* is much more in the Plautine tradition than in all his other comedies on many linguistic levels. This is evident from the first line of the play with the construction *ita me comparem non perpeti meretricum contumelias?* (vv. 47–8), where *ita* creates the expectation of a following *ut* clause. The colloquial infinitive construction, although avoided by Terence with this exception, occurs in other comic dramatists of the *palliata* and the *togata*, i.e. Titinius (*tog.* 57), Turpilius (*com.* 100). This seems like a statement of purpose: Terence from the first line of his play hints at the traditional and more colloquial character of this comedy.

By examining the main linguistic differences in the language of the two playwrights we may conclude the following:

Use of Greek. Terence, in contrast to Plautus, is more reserved in using Greek words, especially interjections. *Eunuchus* is, again, the exception and has the largest concentration of Greek words and expressions, approximating in this way ratios encountered in Plautine drama (cf. Maltby (1985: 120)). The proportion of Greek words in the *Eunuchus* is 1: 37.5.

Early Latin and non-CL formations. Eunuchus has, again, the highest proportion of non-CL features (202), approximating in this case Plautine ratios. What is more, many of the features involved seem to be colloquial in nature. This is the case, for example, with several *hapax* unclassical formations in Terence, by means of colloquial affixes unproductive in CL but common in Plautine drama. Such formations, again, show a particular concentration in *Eunuchus*.

Use of terms of abuse. The play not only displays the highest proportion and a finer variety of Plautine terms, but also exhibits piling up of abuse in the Plautine manner. In particular, terms of abuse such as those discussed above, which have a significantly higher ratio in Plautus than in Terence (unlike those which have the same ratio in the two playwrights or whose proportion is higher in Terence than in Plautus), show, in their totality, a particular concentration in *Eunuchus*.

Imagery. Whereas imagery common in the Greek originals or imagery found for the first time in Terence is scattered throughout Terentian drama without any particular concentration, imagery independent of known Greek usage, often associated with a well-established Plautine usage, shows a particular concentration in *Eunuchus* (*nostri fundi calamitas, annis pannisque obsitum, iunceus, miseriam expuere, iugulare, lepus, exsculpere verum* etc). What is more, imagery techniques common in Plautus (identification, lengthy metaphors, conundrum forms, use of comic adjectives, noun metaphors etc.) are to be found mainly in *Eunuchus* as well.

Individual cases. In *Eunuchus* we also find in concentration several individual stylistic features associated with a well-established Plautine usage but avoided elsewhere in Terence: (i) formulaic expressions, e.g. the *unde is* greeting formula, the door-knocking formula *heus ecquis hic?* etc.; (ii) several further stylistic devices, e.g. long lists of synonyms or other parallel items in asyndeton; the additional use of the genitive of definition with terms of abuse, e.g. *monstrum hominis*; terms of endearment, e.g. *festus dies hominis*; *figura etymologica* of the type *facinus facere*; forms of hyperbaton etc.; (iii) particular lexical or syntactic options, e.g. *mira sunt* for *mirum est* in v. 288; *culpo* in the sense of 'to blame' in v. 387.

Many of these features occur in accumulation, i.e. in the same or in adjacent verses, thus intensifying the overall effect (cf. vv. 255–7, the incongruous romanism + asyndetic quintuplet + non-CL formations in *-arius* for dramatic effect, v. 316, etc.).

Several of the features discussed above occur in scenes where Terence deviates from his original (last scene of *Heautontimoroumenos*, the Sannio scene in *Adelphoe*). There is an important difference, however, in the distribution of these features between the *Eunuchus* and the other plays. While concentrated in specific scenes in other comedies, in *Eunuchus* these Plautine linguistic elements are scattered throughout the play without any particular concentration, giving the comedy an overall Plautine ring. It seems, however, in general that when the farcical element of a play is heightened Terence adopts a more traditional and Plautine linguistic style.

A final remark: as is evident from Terence's prologues, the playwright had been accused of plagiarism (*furtum*) by Luscius Lanuvinus, an accusation that he rejects in his prologues. This is the case in the *Eunuchus* (cf. *Eun.* 23ff.), as well as in the scene with the *leno* at *Adelphoe*, act 3 scene 2 (cf. *Ad.* 1ff.). It has been shown in these two cases that Terence seems to adopt to a greater extent common Plautine–traditional techniques, linguistic peculiarities and favourites. Could that be just a coincidence?

PART 2

LINGUISTIC AND STYLISTIC UNITY IN ROMAN COMEDY

Introduction

The purpose of part II is to investigate the language of the *comoedia palliata*, *togata* and *atellana* in order to uncover any possible linguistic or stylistic relations between them. The ultimate aim is to establish that a certain unity in Roman comedy exists, from which Terence, the main object of this book, stands out, with the exception of his more traditional play *Eunuchus* and those scenes of his other plays in which he differentiates himself from his Greek model (last scene of *Heautontimoroumenos*, the Sannio scene in *Adelphoe*, the *advocati* scene in *Phormio*). In these he is apparently reworking his material in a more traditional way.

Part II constitutes the first complete comparative analysis of the language of Roman comedy. Some initial steps in this direction were taken by Wright, whose study was based mainly on stylistic features rather than purely linguistic ones. His is the only work examining the totality of the *palliata*; there exist also a certain number of smaller studies, exploring the language and style of individual authors without offering an overall comparative approach (references and criticism will be found in the introduction to each chapter below). Although some of Wright's final conclusions agree with the results of my investigation, they have several shortcomings. First, the data he examines are very limited, insufficient for any valid conclusions. Wright does not offer a comprehensive linguistic survey in that he restricts himself mainly to stylistic or lexical options, failing to give a full account of the range of linguistic features involved in a comparative analysis. In addition, no clear-cut categorisation of the data or the results is offered.

Unfortunately, the data are actually *false* in several cases, for example, his claim of a linguistic relationship between Naevius and Plautus relies on the presence in both of a certain stylistic device, namely the repetition of *alius* forms (cf. Wright 1974: 38), which however is also present in Terence, and therefore cannot be used as proof of any special affinity between the two earlier authors. Similar defects are also to be found in the shorter studies dealing with the language of the *palliata*, the *togata* and the *atellana*.

Methodological tools

The present study attempts to examine the whole of the *palliata* and the *togata*, taking into consideration the full distribution of all available data. The following methodological procedure was adopted.

Work-procedure

(1) The extant text of all authors of both the *palliata* and the *togata* is scrutinised word-by-word, in order to establish whether any linguistic item is present in Plautus and the other authors of the *palliata, togata* and *atellana* but absent from the Terentian corpus.

From such linguistic features, i.e. features which, while avoided in Terence, are found in both Plautus and one or more of the other comic authors, only the cases where Terence presents an alternative synonym, i.e. had the opportunity to use the linguistic item in question but consciously opted not to do so, are considered valid evidence. For example, the absence of the word *scriblitarius* (a specialised cook making a sort of sweet without honey) from the Terentian corpus as opposed to its presence in both Titinius and Plautus does not constitute evidence of any linguistic similarity between Plautus and Titinius in contrast to Terence, simply because in the Terentian comedies there was never the opportunity, thematically, for this specialised term to be employed. Only when Terence had the opportunity to use the word in question, but instead systematically preferred a synonymous or nearly synonymous alternative, is one justified in talking about conscious avoidance.

Apart from those linguistic features for which there is no alternative option in Terentian drama, another set of linguistic items were also excluded, namely those for which no synonym or alternative (literal) expression in the Latin language exists. For example, the presence of the word *testamentum* ('will') in all authors of the *palliata* is insignificant, as there was no alternative way to express this notion.

A third exemption is made in the case of linguistic items which are present in more than one author of the *palliata* (e.g. Plautus and Caecilius vs. Terence), but which have different meanings in each author. For example, the verb *suscito*, present in both Plautus and Caecilius, does not prove any linguistic affinity between the two authors since in Plautus the verb means to 'wake up', 'to rouse from sleep or unconsciousness' (*Mil.* 33, 690, *Most.* 372, 382, *Rud.* 922), whereas in Caecilius it is used with the meaning of 'stir up a war' (*com.* 277). On the contrary, if the other authors (Plautus, Caecilius, Naevius etc.) have the item with the same meaning, and only Terence exhibits a different usage, the item is examined, because it shows a particularity of Terence.

(2) A classification based on generally accepted linguistic categories is constructed, i.e. linguistic particularities are classed as belonging to the domains of morphology, syntax, lexicon and style. In each category, several subcategories are distinguished (derivation, verbal complementation, figurative usages etc.) in order to determine in more detail the levels at which linguistic affinities between authors are discernible.

(3) The specific position of each linguistic item with respect to CL is examined, i.e. an effort is made to determine whether it has any particular archaic, colloquial, or simply unclassical character, so as to establish the degree to which Terence is closer to classical language.

(4) All *hapax* linguistic usages in Terence are examined for which, as in (1), and for the same reason, an alternative option within the Terentian corpus exists, in order to determine whether this *hapax* is actually the option preferred in the other authors of the *palliata* or *togata* and *atellana* and whether, in this case, it exhibits any particular distribution, i.e. concentration in specific comedies or scenes of a comedy. This will show that such *hapax* usages are concentrated in *Eunuchus* and in those scenes of other plays where the authors deviate from the Greek original (e.g. the *advocati* scene

in the *Phormio*, the Sannio scene in the *Adelphoe*, several scenes with four speakers etc.). From this investigation are exempted those linguistic items which are present both in Terence (as a *hapax* here) and in more than one other author of the *palliata* or *togata* and *atellana*, but which have a different meaning in each author. For example, the word *stilus* means writing instrument in Plautus (cf. *Bacch.* 996), spine used as weapon in Naevius (*com.* 53), and style in Terence (cf. *Andr.* 12); therefore, no affinity between any of these authors can be proved from the use of this word. As in (1), if it is only Terence who exhibits a different meaning or usage versus the unified practice of the other comic authors, then the item in question is discussed.

(5) The few cases of linguistic items which are present in Terence and another author of the *palliata, togata* and *atellana* but are absent from Plautus are also collected, in order to give a complete picture of the distributional pattern of all linguistic items. As in (1), from this collection are excluded those linguistic items (a) for which no alternative or synonym expression in Plautus is found, i.e. Plautus did not have, thematically, the opportunity to use the item found in both Terence and one or more than one of the other comic authors and (b) the meaning of which is different in Terence and the other comic authors. For example, *silicernium* means in Caecilius funeral feast (Caec. *com.* 122), but in Terence it is used as a term of abuse for an old man (*Ad.* 587).

Reservations

Before embarking on the detailed examination of the language of the *palliata, togata* and *atellana*, an important reservation must be expressed, valid for most authors of Roman comedy with the exception of Plautus and Terence: the extant corpus of their work is very limited, amounting to a few hundreds verses, and is of a very fragmentary nature, consisting mainly of verses quoted by ancient grammarians in order to exemplify a specific linguistic point. Inevitably, therefore, it is impossible to achieve certainty about the total picture of their language. However, the frequency of appearance of the features under investigation is such that it allows us to be confident about making some generalisations concerning the general linguistic trend they are following.

The fragmentary nature of the evidence is in several instances an obstacle to linguistic analysis, as the absence of context makes the determination of the specific meaning/usage of a linguistic item difficult. The few cases where this happens are exempted from investigation. For example, the meaning of the word *vestimentum* at Tit. *tog.* 31 (garment or bed-clothing?) cannot be clarified from the context and any conclusion based on that would be insecure.

Research tools

The main instruments employed for the linguistic investigation of Roman comedy are as follows. Apart from standard reference textbooks of Latin grammar and syntax (Kühner and Stegmann, Hofmann and Szantyr, Ernout and Thomas etc.), of particular use was the *Thesaurus Linguae Latinae*, providing as it did the history and the full range of usages of each linguistic item, but also the personal investigation of each quotation in its context. For the examination of the history of those linguistic items not covered by the *ThLL*, i.e. words beginning with N and those after *progenies*, the main sources of information were the *OLD*, the LS, the *Lexicon Mediae et Infimae Latinitatis*, the PHI-#6 CD-ROM of the Packard Humanities Institute, and the two first CD-ROMs of the *Patrologia Latina* database. Even in the case of items covered by the *ThLL*, additional checking and information was provided by these other electronic and dictionary sources.

CHAPTER 8

TERENCE, PLAUTUS AND THE *PALLIATA*

Turpilius

The dramatic activity of the comic playwright Sextus Turpilius[1] is dated to the second half of the second century BC, according to the testimony of Hier. *ad ann. Abr.* 1914 *Turpilius comicus senex admodum Sinuessae moritur*. More specifically, some scholars[2] place him well after Terence, whereas others believe that the two playwrights might have been contemporaries.[3] Cf. also the testimony of Petrus Crinitus in his *De poetis latinis*: *invenio apud veteres grammaticos hunc Turpilium summa benevolentia coniunctum fuisse Pub. Terentio et iisdem ludis utriusque fabulas aliquando actas*.

It has been argued that Turpilius must be placed in the line of Terence.[4] The main arguments for this opinion are the following:

1. Turpilius tends to use Greek titles.
2. He avoids Roman allusions.
3. He depends heavily on Menandrian originals.
4. His plots, like those of Terence, appear to have stressed the sentimental element more than is common in Plautine drama.[5]

It has been shown, however, that Turpilius, mainly as far as characterisation, staging, metre and, up to a point, language are concerned, is much closer to the comic tradition as exemplified by authors such as Livius, Naevius, Caecilus etc., but above all Plautus, rather than Terence, who stands apart.[6]

[1] For reservations about the *praenomen* Sextus, attested only by the Italian humanist Petrus Crinitus, cf. Rychlewska (1971: VII), Wright (1974: 153).
[2] Cf. Bardon (1952–6: 132), Duckworth (1952: 68).
[3] Cf. Rychlewska (1971: VII), Wright (1974: 153–4).
[4] Cf. Beare (1964: 116).
[5] For a discussion of these views, cf. Wright (1974: 153 –81).
[6] Cf. Wright (1974: 153 –81, Bigot (1948: 1428 –30).

The present chapter offers the first thorough examination of the language and style of Turpilius' fragments. This will show that

1. Turpilius' language and style is close to the comic tradition (i.e. to the language of its main representatives, Plautus, Caecilius etc.), in opposition to Terence's language and style, which stands apart from the linguistic unity of comedy as a genre.
2. Linguistic and stylistic usages common in both Plautus and Turpilius but found *hapax* or rarely in Terentian drama are mainly found: (a) in *Eunuchus* and (b) in some specific scenes in other plays where Terence deviates from his original (scenes with four characters etc.), reworking again his material in a more traditional way, as is shown by the accumulation of such traditional, mainly Plautine, features, elsewhere again avoided by him. This would entail that Turpilius opted to imitate Terentian linguistic and stylistic peculiarities found mainly in his plays or parts of plays that show a particular traditional linguistic and stylistic flavour, or vice-versa that Terence chose to imitate Turpilian techniques only when assimilating the previous comic tradition to which Turpilius demonstrably belongs.

Before we begin, a note on the text is necessary: the edition used is that of Rychlewska (1971).

Morphology

Gender of nouns

v. 180 ***uterum cruciatur mihi!*** The use of *uterum* in the neuter gender, in place of the CL masculine *uterus*, is also found in a similar expression in Plautus, *Aul.* 691 *uterum dolet.*[7] The form appears also in Afran. *tog.* 345 *Consedit uterum.* An alternative explanation would be that *uterum* here is a direct object accusative depending on a passive impersonal verb *cruciatur*.[8] The construction, which is rare in the whole Latin literature, does not occur in Terence but is found on the other hand in Plautus, *Mil.* 24 *epityra estur insanum bene.*[9]

v. 219 ***glabrum tapete*** The neuter gender *tapete* is an EL feature as is also the use of *glaber* in the sense of *tonsilis.*[10] The same combination occurs at Caec. *com.* 272.

[7] For variations of gender in Plautus, cf. Hodgman (1901: lxxxiii–lxxxv).

[8] Cf. Bennett (1910–14: II 261).

[9] For the expression, cf. also Rosén (1970: 135–47).

[10] Cf. *ThLL* VI 2 1999.

Derivation

v. 29 ***homo unica est natura ac singularia*** The form *singularius, -a, -um* in place of CL *singularis, -is, -e*, is an EL form found elsewhere in Plautus, *Capt.* 112 *is indito catenas singularias.* It reappears later as an archaism in Gellius, 9.4.6, 17.9.2.

vv. 110–11 ***differor: tu mihi . . . suavitudo***[11] *Suavitudo* for *suavitas* has its parallels twice in Plautus, *Stich.* 755 *age, mulsa mea suavitudo, salta, Bacch.* 18 *mel meum, suavitudo, cibus, gaudium*. In both these instances, the word belongs to the *sermo amatorius* as a term of endearment, as is also the case with the example in Turpilius. In both Plautus and Turpilius the equivalent form *suavitas* is used in quite different contexts (v. 191, Plaut. *Asin.* 179, *Poen.* 242). Turpilius, approaching Plautus, exhibits some strictly EL *-tudo* derivatives that disappear in the later history of Latin (also *orbitudo* v. 213).[12] Terence, on the other hand, exhibits formations in *-tudo* which recur in later Latin (especially CL) literature.[13] As for *differor* used, as here, in the context of love, see also *Poen.* 156–7 *differor cupidine eius*, *Mil.* 1163. In Terence the verb is used only for physical pain, *Ad.* 486, in the sense of *disturbare, in diversum ferre, Andr.* 408, or as equivalent to *divulgo, dissemino, Heaut.* 16.

v. 171 ***meritissimo*** The superlative form of *merito* is an unclassical formation.[14] Avoided in Terence, it is found both in Plautus *Epid.* 430 and Caec. *com.* 16, Turpil. *com.* 171.

vv. 206–7 ***non est mediocris res neque vulgaria fallacia haec*** *Vulgarius, -a, -um* in place of *vulgaris, -is, -e* occurs also once in Afran. *tog.* 263 and once in Nov. *atel.* 99. The form reappears later with some frequency in the archaising Gellius (e.g. 3.16.18, 12.2.1 etc.). Adjectives in *-arius* belong mainly to colloquial speech.[15] Turpilius uses such forms twice (also *singularius* v. 29). Plautus exhibits several formations of this type, *catapultarius Curc.* 689, *manifestarius Trin.* 895 al. (found later in the archaising Gellius 1.7.3), *polentarius Curc.* 295, *praesentarius Most.* 361 (found later both in Gellius 7.4.1. and Apuleius, *Met.* 2.25), *ridicularius Asin.* 330, *sectarius Capt.* 820 etc. Terence once more in this case avoids EL and archaising formations in *-arius* and restricts himself mainly to those used later also in CL, e.g. *temerarius, primarius*, in opposition to the rest of the Roman comic tradition. In two instances he also uses adjective forms that are not used

[11] Cf. also Traina (1969: 156).

[12] Cf. lists for Plautus in Sblendorio-Cugusi (1991: 284–6).

[13] Cf. *habitudo, vicissitudo, aegritudo* for *tristitia, fortitudo* for *vigor, sollicitudo* for *trepidatio, solitudo, consuetudo* for *mos, familiaritas, amor, solitudo* with a moral sense or equivalent to *vastitas, longitudo*; for their distribution cf. Sblendorio-Cugusi (1991: passim).

[14] It appears only once in CL, Cic. *de Orat.* 1.234.

[15] Cf. Cooper (1895: 147–55).

in CL but crop up in the literature in the PC period (*iocularius*[16] and *argentarius*[17]).

Cases

v. 37 ***veteri exemplo amantium*** The ablative *veteri* for *vetere*, the regular equivalent in Terence (*Hec.* 37), appears also in Plautus, *Stich.* 768. Although not absent from CL, the *-i* ending is not as common as its *-e* equivalent formation. In Cicero as well as in Livy, for example, in most cases of a variant reading *veteri*, the best manuscripts read *vetere.*[18] Terence once more here opts for the more common equivalent in CL.

Syntax

Case syntax

v. 33 ***meos parentes careo*** *Careo* construed with the accusative in place of the ablative is also found in Plautus, *Curc.* 136 *id quod amo careo, Poen.* 820.[19] The CL construction is that with the ablative, found three times in Terence, *Heaut.* 137, 257, *Hec.* 663. The accusative object equivalent is found only once in Terence, at *Eun.* 223 *ego illam caream.*

v. 67 ***scies ea, quae fuisti inscius*** In this line we encounter a rare construction, namely the accusative as object of a periphrasis consisting of an adjective + *esse* (either explicitly used or easily understood), equivalent to a simple transitive verb construed with the accusative (*inscius fui* = *non scivi, ignoravi*). Such syntagms, also found in other EL sources,[20] while avoided in Terence, occur twice in Plautus, *Most.* 100 *gnaruris vos volo esse hanc rem mecum* by analogy with *novisse, Amph.* 878 *uno fetu et quod gravida est*, by analogy with *concepit.*[21] In CL the construction is avoided, appearing only once in the archaising Sallust. *Hist.* 3.88 *facta consultaque eius quidem aemulus erat*, by analogy with *aemulabatur.* The fragment, however, is textually doubtful and there is an alternative reading with the participle *aemulatus*. Terence again in this case, as opposed to both Plautus and Turpilius, anticipates later CL usage in avoiding such constructions, which gain ground only in Late Latin texts.

16 Cf. Pompon. Porph. *Comm.* 2.2.60.4.

17 Apic. 2.2.10; Vitr. 5.1.2.

18 Cf. N-W II 86.

19 It reappears later in the archaising Fronto, probably by analogy with *desidero*, cf. H-Sz 83.

20 Cf. S. C. Bacch. *sententiam scientes essetis.*

21 Cf. H-Sz 34.

v. 104 ***fastidit mei*** The construction of *fastidio* with the genitive in place of the accusative is regular in EL. It occurs in Plautus, *Aul.* 245 *fastidit mei* and possibly at *Stich.* 334 *mein fastidis*, with Lipsius' emendation. It is also found once in Titin. *tog.* 94 *mei fastidis*. The verb *fastidio* occurs once more in Turpilius at v. 102 *ille insolens autem ut fastidit carnifex.* This verb[22] belongs to a group consisting of verbs that acquire the genitive construction by analogy with the similar genitive constructions of adjectives derived from their stem, thus *fastidiosus* for *fastidio, cupidus* for *cupio, studiosus* for *studio.* In Plautus as well, there are examples of such constructions, apart from *fastidio* examples, with *cupio* in *Mil.* 963 *cupiunt tui*. With *studeo*, Caec. *com.* 191 *qui te nec amet nec studeat tui*. In Terence no such construction is found; in such cases the accusative is the only possible case option in his plays.

v. 128 ***voti condemnata est*** *Condemnare* construed with the genitive denoting the crime in place of the ablative, in the sense of 'to doom to the fulfillment of a vow in granting a request', belongs to sacral language.[23] In literary texts it appears elsewhere only in Titin. *tog.* 156 *nunc eius voti condemnatust: immolavit hostiam.*

v. 154 ***praestolabo illi*** *Praestolo/or* is mainly an EL verb, common in Plautus, which is found twice in Terence only in *Eunuchus.* The verb is construed either with the accusative or the dative, as here *preastolabo illi*. Terence opts twice to construe the verb with the accusative, *Eun.* 975 *quem praestolare* and similarly *quem praestolare* in an echo-question in v. 977. The dative construction, on the other hand, occurs in Plautus, *Epid.* 217 *ego illam illi video praestolarier.*[24]

v. 158 ***meminisse illius formam*** The use of the accusative (not neuter pronoun accusative) in place of the genitive as a direct object of *memini* has its parallels in Plautus, *Cist.* 381 *meminere officium suom, Men.* 45, *Merc.* 1011, etc. In Terence the verb is construed with the accusative normally only with neuter pronoun objects (*Andr.* 943, *Phorm.* 387, *Eun.* 216). Otherwise it is construed with the genitive, in the case of direct object nouns or pronouns (*Heaut.* 951, 1026, *Eun.* 801), the a.c.i. (with the accusative clearly denoted or easily understood, *Andr.* 429, *Phorm.* 74, *Hec.* 822), or indirect interrogative clauses (*Phorm.* 224). A full noun as a direct object in the accusative does not appear at all.

v. 159 ***expars malitiis*** The construction of *expars, expers* with the ablative in place of the genitive is common in EL writers. In comedy, apart from Turpilius, it is also found in Plautus, *Asin.* 44 *dono te ob istuc dictum, ut expers sis metu, Amph.* 713, *Pers.* 509. In Terence we encounter only the genitive construction, *Heaut.* 652 *ne expers partis esset de nostris bonis.*

22 Cf. also Bennett (1910–14: I 99).

23 Cf. *OLD* s.v. 1, c.

24 Unless *illi* is an adverb in Plautus and Turpilius. For whether *illi* is an adverb or a pronoun, cf. also *ThLL* X, 2 fasc. VI 993.

v. 161 ***oculi ex longa intercapedine adpetunt cupide intui*** *Intueor* in absolute use in the sense of *aspicere, oculos dirigere* is also found in Plautus, *Bacch.* 1130 *viden limulis, opsecro, ut intuentur*. In Terence such a construction does not appear. The verb is constructed with an accusative object (*Heaut.* 403) or is used in the sense of *deorsum intueri pro tristem, animo demissum esse, Eun.* 580.

v. 166 ***amicos utor primoris viros*** The use of a noun accusative (and not gerundives and/or neuter pronouns) as a direct object of *utor* seems to be a colloquial usage, common in colloquial sources, such as comedy, with the exception of Terence again, Cato, Lucilius' satire, Varro and later Latin texts, sources of Vulgar Latin.[25] As for comedy in particular, such a usage occurs in Titinius, *tog.* 99 *item uti eum oportet libertatem, qui sapit*, Novius, *atel.* 69 *quod res vis hunc privari pulchras quas uti solet*, 99 *atqui facilitatem, video, <haut> uteris vulgariam.* The presence of such a usage in Plautus has been denied by Langen (1886: 293, 388), Steinthal (1918: 50) and H-Sz (123), who consider such usages as interpolation. Guardì (1985: 143), however, rightly remarks that in at least two cases the use of the noun in the accusative as a direct object is well documented in the manuscript tradition, *Poen.* 1088 *uteris, ut voles, operam meam, Rud.* 1240–1 *qui . . . astute cavet, diutine uti bene licet partum bene.* At *Mil.* 799a *auris utor*, Lodge (s.v.) also accepts such a usage, a reading found only in the Ambrosian Palimpsest but not in the Palatine codices, which Leo has changed into *aurib' utor*, whereas at *Epid.* 263 *si placebit, utitor consilium* Leo, Lindsay and Buckworth try to avoid the accusative construction by punctuating after *utitor* and at *Stich.* 450a the line seems to be interpolated.[26]

In Terence, on the other hand, there is no such *utor*-construction. The verb is normally construed with the ablative (*Eun.* 168, *Heaut.* 217, *Hec.* 837 etc.), a relative clause (*Andr.* 14 in conjunction here with *transfero*), or the accusative of the neuter pronoun (*Ad.* 815).

But even in this last case (*Ad.* 815, *mea, quae praeter spem evenere, utantur sine*), an alternative explanation can also be put forward; Donatus remarks ad loc. *aut deest 'his', ut sit; his utantur, aut 'mea utantur' antique locutus est.* In this case we could have *mea* attracted to *quae* in a kind of mild anacoluthon, suitable to the colloquial speech of the rustic Demea, where we also found several other colloquial features. At *Heaut.* 133 *utor* is used in a passive gerundive construction *quod illa aetas magis ad haec utenda idoneast.*

v. 173 ***oblita . . . es eius . . . mansiones*** *Oblivisci* is here construed with the accusative in place of the genitive. The accusative construction is common in Plautus, *Trin.* 1013–14 *satin in thermopolio condalium es oblitus?*, 1017, *Bacch.* 790, *Cas.* 104. The accusative construction

[25] Cf. H-Sz 123. [26] Cf. Guardì (1985: 143).

occurs also with neuter pronouns, *Poen.* 40 *quod paene oblitus fui, Asin.* 226. Also Caec. *com.* 56, *qui, homo ineptitudinis cumulatus, cultum oblitus es?*. In Terence only the genitive construction is found, *Eun.* 306 *sum oblitus mei.* See also infinitive syntagms at *Andr.* 841, indirect questions at *Heaut.* 848–9.

v. 197 ***epistula excidit mi!*** *Excidere* is construed here with the 'dative of separation'.[27] This is the regular construction of the verb in Plautus, *Bacch.* 668, *Cist.* 677, *Most.* 732. In Terence the verb is construed with the ablative of separation, *Andr.* 423 *erus . . . uxore excidit.*

Verbal complements

vv. 36–7 ***est iratus pater, quia se talento argenti tetigi*** The construction of *irascor* with a *quia* clause denoting cause appears three times in Plautus as well, *Capt.* 715–16 *qur ergo iratus mihi es? quia illi fuisti quam mihi fidelior, Cist.* 101–2, *Merc.* 923–4. Within Terentian drama the cause with *irasci* is denoted either by means of the *dativus incommodi, Andr.* 664, *Hec.* 623, or prepositional syntagms, *Hec.* 780, *Heaut.* 990 etc.

v. 181 ***deliberatum est me illis obsequi*** The use of *deliberare* in the sense of *statuere, constituere* in the impersonal third singular, construed with the a.c.i., is also found in Afran. *tog.* 274 *deliberatum est non tacere <me> amplius.* The verb is used in Terence only in normal CL functions, either in absolute use or with an accusative object (*Hec.* 508, *Ad.* 196) or as a gerundive complement (*Phorm.* 457).

Tense and mood syntax

vv. 22–3 ***antehac si flabat aquilo aut auster, inopia tum erat piscati*** Here we encounter a conditional sentence rare in the *palliata* and *togata* (eight examples in the whole corpus), namely the use of the imperfect indicative, *flabat*, in a *si* clause. Terence avoids this construction, which is on the other hand frequent enough in Plautus, *Asin.* 143 *ea si erant, magnas habebas omnibus dis gratias, Mil.* 1326, *Poen.* 525, *Pseud.* 286, 798, 800, *Truc.* 748. In Terence *si* clauses are found only in the present, future, perfect, pluperfect and future perfect indicative.

vv. 27–8 ***nam si iceris me posthac . . . credas mii velim*** We have here a conditional sequence, quite rare in both *palliata* and *togata* (nine instances), where the protasis introduced by *si* and followed by the future perfect indicative *iceris* has for apodosis an independent subjunctive *credas velim.* The construction, avoided in Terence, is well established in Plautine comedy, *Amph.* 671–2 *si situlam cepero, numquam . . . creduis, Asin.* 782–3, 854–5, *Cist.* 499, *Rud.* 789–90. In

[27] Cf. Bennett (1910–14: II 148–50).

Terence such *si* clauses are followed by a present indicative apodosis, often having a future force (*Heaut.* 437–8 etc.), a future indicative (*Phorm.* 637–8 etc.), a future perfect indicative (*Heaut.* 478ff. etc.), or an imperative apodosis (*Heaut.* 550–1 etc.).

v. 175 ***dum ego conixi somno, hic sibi prospexit vigilans virginem*** *Dum* in the sense of 'while' is regularly construed in Terence with the present indicative. In several cases the *dum*-clause with the present indicative is equivalent to a present perfect, while the main clause is either a present perfect or a present with the force of a perfect.[28] Otherwise the *dum*-clause can also be construed with the historic present; this is the case with all instances in Terence's comedies.[29] The use of a real perfect tense in a *dum*-clause denoting 'while', as here with *conixi*,[30] is unparalleled in Terence. There are, however, six examples in Plautine drama, *Amph.* 599–60 *omne, uti quidque actum est, dum apud hostis sedimus, edissertavit, Mil.* 504, *Capt.* 925, *Stich.* 628, *Truc.* 380.

Voice

v. 83 ***proficisceret*** The active form in place of the deponent *proficisci* is found elsewhere only in Plaut. *Mil.* 1329 *prius quam proficisco?.* In Terence the verb is always deponent (*Andr.* 329, 600, *Ad.* 224).

Lexicon

Nouns and adjectives

v. 11 ***spissum est iter*** *Spissus* in the sense of *tardus* is a common word in Roman comedy. It is used by Plautus, e.g. *Cist.* 75 *Spissum istuc amanti est verbum, 'veniet', nisi venit* etc. but also by several other comic writers of both the *palliata* and the *togata*, Caec. *com.* 22, Naev. *com.* 61, Titin. *tog.* 59, Afran. *tog.* 196.

v. 12 ***testamentum ergo celabis? <logi!>*** *Logus* is a Greek word equivalent to the Latin *verbum, sermo*. The word is used here in a derogatory sense,[31] also found in Plautus, *Pers.* 394 *dabuntur dotis tibi inde sescenti logei* as well as in Terence, *Phorm.* 493 *feneratum istuc beneficium pulchre tibi dices: logi!*, in a scene, however, where Terence deviates from his original.[32]

28 Cf. Bennett (1910–14: I 95–7); for *dum*-clauses, cf. H-Sz 612–13.

29 For a *dum*-clause as equivalent to a present perfect with the main clause in the present perfect, cf. *Heaut.* 242, 257; for a *dum*-clause equivalent to a present perfect with the main clause in the present having the force of a present perfect, *Heaut.* 240; for a *dum* clause with a historic present, *Heaut.* 272, *Eun.* 341, *Ad.* 541 etc.

30 For the perfect tense of the verb, cf. also Prisc. GLK II 478 11–12.

31 Cf. *ThLL* VII 1613 *cum respectu vanitatis*; Non. 63 M *dicta ridicula et contemnenda.*

32 Cf. Lowe (1983a: 430–1), Büchner (1974: 330–5, 338–41, 347–50, 454–7).

v. 29 ***homo unica est natura*** *Unicus* with the meaning of 'having no match', 'singular', 'unique' occurs also at Plaut. *Asin.* 748 *tu poeta es prosus ad eam rem unicus*, Afran. *tog.* 15 *quis tam sagaci corde atque ingenio unico?*. In Terence *unicus* always has the sense of 'one and only', 'sole', 'only son/daughter', *Andr.* 100, 540, *Heaut.* 93, 131, 540, *Hec.* 118, *Phorm.* 646.

v. 30 ***delenificam mulierem!*** *Delenificus* for *blandus, demulcens* appears also in Plautus, *Mil.* 192. This is an EL–archaising and PC usage,[33] avoided completely in Terence.

v. 47 ***iudicia, litis, turbas, tricas, contiones maxumas*** *Tricae* in the sense of *impedimenta* (the word used by Terence at *Andr.* 707), *implicationes*, is often used by Plautus, *Pers.* 530–1 *nil mi opust litibus neque tricis, Curc.* 613, *Most.* 572, *Rud.* 1323. The derived verb *intricare* in the sense of *impedire, morari* is also found in Afranius, *tog.* 113 *ita intricauit huius hanc rem temeritas*, also Plaut. *Pers.* 457 *nunc ego lenonem ita hodie intricatum dabo*. The expression, either in the sense 'difficulties' or with the meaning of 'trifles', 'nonsense',[34] occurs, apart from comedy, in later colloquial sources as well, such as epistolography (Cic. *Att.* 10.8.9, *Fam.* 8.5.2), satire (Mart. 14.1.7) or PC colloquial sources (Petr. 53.12). Terence once more shows his purism in avoiding this colloquial form.

v. 135 ***domicilium hoc contulit*** *Domicilium* as synonymous with *aedes, domus, casa, tectum, habitatio, mansio, sedes*[35] appears also in Plaut. *Mil.* 451 but not in Terence.

v. 137 ***litteras misi ad senem*** *Litteras* here is equivalent to *epistulam*, the regular equivalent in Terence. This use of the noun occurs, on the other hand, in Plautus, *Amph.* 70 *seu per scriptas litteras, Bacch.* 389. *Litterae* appears once in Terence, at *Eun.* 476–7 *fac periclum in litteris, fac in palaestra, in musicis*, where *litterae*, however, has the meaning of grammar or literature.

v. 149 ***in lustris lates*** *Lustra* for *lupanaria* is also found in Plautus, *Asin.* 867 *is apud scortum corruptelae est liberis, lustris studet, Cas.* 242. It also occurs once in Afran. *tog.* 242 *scias abesse ab lustris ingenium procul*. Such an expression does not occur in Terence. In Terentian drama we find instead the word *ganeum, Ad.* 359, which can also be used in the sense of *lupanar*.[36]

v. 202 ***coronam, mensam, talos, vinum*** *Mensa* here is a metonymy for *convivium, cena*. This metonymic use of *mensa* appears also in Plautus, *Mil.* 51 *communicabo . . . te mensa.*

[33] Also found in Fronto, Fulgentius, Ausonius, Symmachus, Ennodius.

[34] Terence uses *nugae* in this sense.

[35] For these words as synonymous with *domicilium*, cf. *ThLL* V_1 1873–7, OLD s.v.; for words denoting 'house' in Latin, cf. Ernout (1931: 40–1), (1932: 297 –314).

[36] For this meaning of *ganeum*, cf. Schol. Schlee p. 155, Schol. Bembina ad loc., L-S s.v.

v. 206 ***non est mediocris res*** *Mediocris* is used here in the sense of the Greek μέτριος. This usage appears also in Plautus, *Bacch.* 425 *haud mediocris poenas, Curc.* 537. In Terence the adjective is used in the sense of *indole, Ad.* 966.

v. 208 ***utinam istuc perpetuum itiner sit tibi!*** *Itiner* in place of *iter* as a nominative or accusative singular is a form[37] common in EL which also occurs in Plautus, *Merc.* 913 *inceptum hoc itiner perficere exsequar*, 929. In Terence, on the other hand, the *iter* form is the only equivalent both for the nominative (*Phorm.* 66) and the accusative (*Hec.* 194, 415, *Eun.* 1065).

v. 209 ***nobilitate, factione fretus interdicere*** *Factio* in the sense of *opulentia, abundantia, nobilitas* is also found in Plautus, *Aul.* 167 *istas magnas factiones, animos, dotes dapsiles.* It is also used in the same sense by Caec. *com.* 166 *nam opulento famam facile occultat factio*, as well as by Titinius, *tog.* 111–12 *Qui ex tanta factione atque opibus adgredi eam sum ausus.* Furthermore in Titinius the word is combined with *opes*, a frequent doublet in Plautus, *Cist.* 493–4, *Trin.* 497.

Verbs

v. 2 ***tuburcinatur*** The verb in the sense of *raptim manducare, vorare*[38] is also found in Plaut. *Pers.* 122 *tuburcinari de suo, si quid domist* and in Titin. *tog.* 82 *tuburcinari sine me vultis reliquias.* This is an EL verb, which reappears later as a reminiscence of comic language in Apul. *Met.* 6.25,[39] where, however, it is used in a passive sense. It seems to be a colloquial verb, being restricted to comedy and avoided by high literary genres, formed by analogy with verbs such as *sermocinor, lenocinor* etc.[40] Terence, on the other hand, uses the synonymous *vorare, Eun.* 939.

v. 24 ***in acta cooperta*** The verb in the sense of *velare, contegere, obtegere* is avoided in Terence, but appears in Plautus, fr. 176 *linna cooperta est + textrino Gallia +.*

v. 27 ***iceris*** *Icere* in the sense of *percutere* is common in the comic dramatists with the exception of Terence again. See Plaut. *Truc.* 601 *icit femur, Cas.* 849, *Mil.* 28, 205, *Pers.* 846, *Vid.* 92. See also Caec. *com.* 24 *si . . . vidit quem catapulta aut balista icerit*, Afran. *tog.* 307 *offendit fregit rupit icit poculo.* This verb is not found in Terence, with one possible exception at *Eun.* 178 *labascit ictus*, in a textually doubtful line however. Modern editions (cf. Barsby ad loc.) prefer the equivalent reading *victus.* For *percutere, Andr.* 125. Furthermore, as

37 Cf. also Acc. *trag.* 457, 500, Enn. *trag.* 289, Pacuv. *trag.* 44–5, 121, 226.

38 Cf. Non. 179 M.

39 For reminiscences of comic language in Apuleius, cf Callebat (1968: passim).

40 For its colloquial character, cf. Ernout and Meillet (1951: 1247).

for verbs denoting 'to beat', in Turpilius we also find *offendere* used in this sense, v. 176 *caput [ut] offendi*.[41] A similar use of the verb appears in Plautus, *Curc.* 282 *ne quem in cursu capite aut cubito aut pectore offendam aut genu, Capt.* 798, also Afran. *tog.* 307. In Terence the verb is used only in the sense of *invenio, reperio, reprehendo, Hec.* 325, *Heaut.* 365, *Phorm.* 758 etc. Terence restricts himself to *percutere.*

v. 34 ***<iurata es?> non sum iurata*** Periphrastic forms of *iuro* consisting of the past participle *esse* also occur in Plautus, *Curc.* 458 *quid quod iuratus sum?,* 566, *Pers.* 401, *Rud.* 1372, 1398. This is a rare construction, possibly of colloquial flavour, found also in *Rhet. Her.* 2.41, Cic. *Inv.* 2.126 and reappearing later in PC Latin, in the archaising Gell. 6.18.18 and in Hyg. *Astr.* 2.15. In Terence only monolectic forms of the verb appear.

v. 145 ***comperce verbis velitare*** The verb, as well as the derived noun *velitatio* in the sense of *contentio*, are also found twice in Plautus, *Men.* 778 *nescioquid vos velitati estis inter vos duos, Rud.* 525. Also Afran. *tog.* 267. According to Nonius Marcellus (3 M) the word *velitatio* was also used by Caecilius in *Pausimacho*, but there is a lacuna in the text of the grammarian and therefore the relevant line is missing. Such a usage for 'bickering', 'wrangling', 'dispute', well established in the comic scripts, does not occur in Terence.[42] The use of *comperce* with an infinitive as its complement has its parallel in Plautus, *Poen.* 350.[43]

v. 151 ***subduxi cum hac me*** The reflexive use of the verb, *me subducere*, in the sense 'to withdraw' is also found at Plaut. *Asin.* 912. In Terence this usage occurs at *Eun.* 795 *et cum eo clam te subduxti mihi?*. See also *Eun.* 628.

v. 165 ***ego supersederem nuptiis*** *Supersedeo* in the sense of *se amovere*, 'to abstain', construed with an ablative complement, occurs at Plaut. *Poen.* 414 *supersede istis verbis.*

v. 198 ***inter tuniculam ac strophium conlocaram*** *Collocare* in the sense of *statuere, ponere*, appears also in Plautus, *Men.* 986 *postquam in tabernam vassa et servos collocavi.* The verb appears once with this sense in Terence at *Eun.* 593 *deinde eam in lecto illae conlocarunt.* Elsewhere in Terence the verb is used figuratively, *Heaut.* 689, 695. Once, at *Phorm.* 759, it is also used with reference to the *sponsalia.*

v. 213 ***cesso occupare*** *Occupare* here has the sense of *praevenire* construed with the infinitive. This is a common usage in EL texts, especially in comedy, with the exception again of Terence, Plaut. *Most.* 566 *occupabo adire, Poen.* 320, *Pseud.* 921, *Rud.* 248, *Stich.* 89. The word occurs with this meaning once at Titin. *tog.* 146–7 *ergo occupa*

[41] Cf. Non. 358 M *offendere est percutere.*

[42] Cf. in his comedies the use of equivalent or synonymous *alterco* syntagms, *Andr.* 653. For *alterco/or* = *contendo, disputo*, cf. McGlynn I 38, L-S s.v., *OLD* s.v.

[43] Cf. also Löfstedt (1912: 184).

foras exire. In Terence, on the other hand, the verb has once the sense of *subito invadere, Andr.* 297, but it is mainly equivalent to *distineo, impedio, distringo* construed in active syntagms with a direct object accusative, *Hec.* 4–5. For passive uses, see *Phorm.* 502, *Andr.* 829.

Adverbs

v. 25 ***nec recte dici*** According to Festus (158), *nec* in this line of Turpilius is equivalent to a simple *non*. This is an EL feature, found in Plautus as well, *Asin.* 471, which has survived later mainly in legal and sacral language[44] or as an intentional archaism in repudiating formulaic expressions, e.g. Verg. *Ecl.* 9.6 *quod nec vertat bene*.[45] In Terence *nec* is always used with a paratactic disjunctive function. The formulaic word group *nec recte dicere* is often found in Plautus, *Asin.* 471, *Bacch.* 119, *Most.* 240, *Poen.* 516, *Pseud.* 1085. As for the combination *iam dudum audio*, see also Plaut. *Merc.* 953 *iam dudum audivi*.

v. 35 ***nimis numero*** *Numero* in the sense of *cito*,[46] found also once more at Turpil. *com.* 151, occurs frequently in the comic poetry with the exception of Terence, see Plaut. *Amph.* 180, *Cas.* 647, *Men.* 287, *Mil.* 1400, *Poen.* 1272. The word is used in this sense also once at Caec. *com.* 5 *Numero uenit* and three times by Afranius, *tog.* 270, 312, 320 *perfalsum et abs te creditum numero nimis*. This last example exhibits the combination *numero nimis*, which is elsewhere found only at Turpil. *com.* 35. Terence normally uses *cito*, *Andr.* 255, *Heaut.* 375, *Ad.* 443 etc.

v. 41 ***modice atque parce eius serviat cupidines*** *Modice* in the sense of *moderate, modeste, parce* is also found in Plautus, *Mil.* 1214, *Pers.* 346.

v. 97 ***sensim celox*** *Sensim* in the sense of 'gradually', 'slowly', 'little by little' is not found in Terence but is common in Plautus, *Cas.* 815 *sensim super atolle limen pedes, Most.* 1070. Terence, on the other hand, quite often uses *paul(l)atim* in the same sense,[47] *Heaut.* 870, *Hec.* 169, *Ad.* 591, 898.

v. 105 ***num illum illaec pudet?*** *Num* as an introductory particle in direct questions has the following functions:[48] it is used in sentences which challenge the hearer to acknowledge something which the dialogue or the action makes evident, in this case to deny, i.e. its most frequent use occurs when the speaker expects a negative answer. It is also used in cases where the question is asked clearly for information, or, rarely,

[44] Cf. e.g. Cic. *Leg.* 3.6 *nec oboedienem*, Gaius, *Inst.* 3.184 etc.

[45] For the archaic or colloquial character of the feature, cf. H-Sz 448–9.

[46] For this meaning, cf. Non. 352 M.

[47] For *paulatim* = 'gradually' as a synonymous word for *sensim*, cf. L-S s.v., *OLD* s.v.

[48] For *num* in direct questions, cf. also Shackleton Bailey (1953: 120–5).

in sentences in which the context shows that the speaker could not possibly have held the negative opinion or have expected a negative answer, as is the case here.[49]

Whereas the first two functions of the particle are quite common within *palliata, togata* and *atellana* (38 and 33 instances, respectively), the last is relatively rare (only six examples in the whole corpus). In Terence's comedies we frequently find examples of the two first usages,[50] whereas *num* having the third function is not found. Such a usage, on the other hand, is attested several times in Plautine drama, *Amph.* 620, 709, 753, *Aul.* 242, *Men.* 413.

v. 149 ***foede dum in lustris lates*** *Foede* is used here as synonymous with *turpiter, cum infamia, sceleste.* This use of the adverb, avoided in Terence, appears in Plautus, *Pers.* 230 *ne . . . foede semper servias.*

v. 160 ***equidem amorem intercapedine ipsa lenivit dies*** *Equidem* not construed with the first person singular, as here, appears several times in Plautus, *Aul.* 138 *decet tequidem vera proloqui, Bacch.* 974, *Epid.* 16, 603, *Mil.* 650, *Poen.* 1240 etc. In Terence this construction appears once at *Eun.* 956 *conligavit (eum)? – atque equidem* (the reading of codd.) *orante ut ne id faceret Thaide.* At *Heaut.* 518 *quid tu istic?– recte equidem, istic sum* or *me habeo* can be understood after the *recte equidem* syntagm.[51]

v. 161 ***adpetunt cupide*** *Cupide* for *valde, acriter, vehementer* occurs also in Plautus, *Cas.* 267 *quid istuc tam cupide cupis?, Most.* 73. In Terence the word appears at *Ad.* 209 *cupide accipiat faxo*, where Terence deviates once more from his original, importing a scene from Diphilus' *Synapothnescontes.*

Style

Word combinations

v. 32 ***sandalio innixa digitis primoribus*** The formulaic combination *digiti primores*, denoting the tips of the fingers, is also found twice in Plautus, *Bacch.* 675 *sic hoc digitulis duobus sumebas primoribus?, Poen.* 566. See also the use of the same adjective to describe the extreme part of the nostrils at Afran. *tog.* 384 *diram tuam animam in naribus primoribus.*[52] The Greek word *sandalium*, in place of *solea, calceus* or *crepidula*, found once more at Turpil. *com.* 147, also occurs at *Eun.* 1028.

49 For this categorisation and examples, cf. Bennett (1910–14: I 473–4).
50 Cf. *Phorm.* 411, 524, *Andr.* 477, 496, 578 and *Andr.* 438, *Eun.* 756, *Phorm* 846, *Ad.* 488 respectively.
51 Cf. also McGlynn I 167.
52 For *primor* = *primus*, avoided in Terence, cf. also Plaut. *Trin.* 910, *Amph.* 204.

vv. 107–8 ***ne me attigat! atque aufer manum!*** According to Rychlewska (1971: 33), the fragment belongs to a scene in which a young girl tries to keep away a man who wants to caress her. The word group *aufer manum* recurs in a similar situation in Plautus at *Men.* 627–8 *aufer manum / sic datur* when Menaechmus II tries to soothe and caress his wife. See also here the use of the formulaic colloquial combination *sic datur* found also at *Pseud.* 155, *Truc.* 634, Turpil. *com.* 71.

v. 114 ***cum illa limassis caput*** *Limare* in the sense of *coniungere*, especially in the formulaic combination *limare caput* ('to kiss'[53]), is common in the comic dramatists with the exception of Terence again, see Plaut. fr. 112 *nam pater tuos numquam cum illa etiam limavit caput, Bacch.* 15, *Merc.* 537, *Poen.* 292. It also occurs once in Caec. *com.* 131. Terence on the other hand uses the common *osculari, Heaut.* 900.

v. 170 ***subductis cum superciliis*** *Supercilium* in pregnant use for 'stern looks', 'severity' occurs also in Plaut. *Rud.* 317–18 *senem . . . tortis superciilis, contracta fronte.*

v. 177 ***malam aetatem*** The use of the combination in place of *senectus/senecta* is also found in Plautus, *Men.* 756–8 *consitus sum senectute, onustum gero corpus, vires reliquere: ut aetas mala est! merx mala ergost.* It also occurs in Afran. *tog.* 382 *mala aetas nulla delenimenta invenit.* Such a periphrasis is avoided in Terence, who uses simply either *senectus* (*Heaut.* 521, *Phorm.* 575, 1023 etc.) or *senecta* (*Ad.* 954).

Further individual word combinations or collocations also point to Turpilius' linguistic and stylistic affinity with Plautus rather than with Terence.

1. nominal *iuncturae*: *quaestus(i) causa* (Turpil. *com.* 44, Plaut. *Poen.* 95), *magnus ignis* (Turpil. *com.* 125, Plaut. *Capt.* 844, *Rud.* 767).
2. verbal *iuncturae*: *sapientiam a(di)pisci* (Turpil. *com.* 11 *spissum est iter (ad sapientiam); adipisci (apisci Rib.) haut possem*, Plaut. *Trin.* 367 *ingenio apiscitur sapientia*, where *apiscere* has the sense of *discere, discendo vel cogitando acquirere*), *foras excitare* (Turpil. *com.* 55, Plaut. *Rud.* 260), *fores exurere* (Turpil. *com.* 201, Plaut. *Pers.* 569), *deos venerari* (Turpil. *com.* 75, Plaut. *Poen.* 950), *sermonem interrumpere* (Turpil. *com.* 68, Plaut. *Trin.* 1149), the alliterative combination *vitam vivere*, where *vitam* is the direct object of the verb (Turpil. *com.* 143, see also Plaut. *Merc.* 473, *Mil.* 628, 726, *Pers.* 346, 494–5), *sermonem sublegere* (Turpil. *com.* 6, Plaut. *Mil.* 1090), *docta dicere* (Turpil. *com.* 39, Plaut. *Poen.* 216, *Trin.* 380, *Truc.* 453), *ultro sectari* (Turpil. *com.* 101, Plaut *Mil.* 91), *foras progredi* (Turpil. *com.* 155,

[53] Cf. L-S s.v. *limare*. *Cum* in these syntagms denotes mutuality or reciprocity, cf. Waters (1902: lxxvi).

Plaut. *Bacch.* 611, *Most.* 686–7, *Pers.* 682), *(ad) cenam condicere* (Turpil. *com.* 188, Plaut. *Stich.* 432–3, 447), *aetatem degere* (Turpil. *com.* 59, Plaut. *Cist.* 77, Ter. *Phorm.* 417), also *extorrem facere* (Turpil. *com.* 96, Titin. *tog.* 72–3).

3. phrases: *hoc . . . orare . . ut* syntagms where the *ut* clause is used in apposition to *hoc* (Turpil. *com.* 213, Plaut. *Bacch.* 494, Ter. *Eun.* 1084).

Figurative usages

v. 26 ***etiam me inrides, pessime ac sacerrime?*** *Sacrum* used here as a term of abuse has the meaning of *scelestum, detestabile*,[54] found once more in Turpil. *com.* 134–6 *abhinc triennium sacerrimum domicilium hoc quidam contulit leno*.[55] The word in this sense is also found in Plautus, *Poen.* 88–90 *vendit eas omnis, et nutricem et virgines, praesenti argento – homini, si leno est homo, quantum hominum terra sustinet sacerrumo.* It also occurs once in Afran. *tog.* 185 *o sacrum scurram et malum!*. This usage, common in the comic scripts, does not occur in Terence, who normally uses synonymous expressions, e.g. *scelestus* (*Heaut.* 970, *Ad.* 159 etc.). Furthermore, *pessimus*, as a term of abuse, is common in Roman comedy, in Plautus, *Cas.* 645, *Men.* 488, 1061, *Pers.* 221, *Stich.* 245, *Truc.* 120, Naev. *com.* ex inc. 20 *pessimorum pessime.* In Terentian drama this usage appears twice, in *Eunuchus* only, *Eun.* 152–3 *pessuma, egon quicquam cum istis factis tibi respondeam?*, 1017.

v. 37 ***quia se talento argenti tetigi veteri exemplo amantium*** The figurative use of *tangere* in the sense of *circumvenire*,'to take in', 'trick', 'dupe', is common in Plautus, *Pseud.* 120 *si neminem alium potero, tuom tangam patrem*, 1238, *Epid.* 705, *Poen.* 1286. It also occurs once in *inc. com.* 45 *sentin senem esse tactum triginta minis?*. Another instance of such a figurative use of the verb is found in Turpil. *com.* 131–2, according to the testimony of Nonius (408 M), *quasi alias [res] vini cado, <tangam>*. In Terence a figurative sense of *tangere* is found at *Eun.* 420–1 *quo pacto Rhodium tetigerim in convivio, numquam tibi dixi?*. The meaning here, however, is quite different, 'sting or nettle' somebody by something said.

v. 48 ***apertae surae*** *Apertus* here is used in the figurative sense of *nudatus, nudus*.[56] The word is used with this sense referring to several parts of the human body. It occurs in Plautus, *Capt.* 475 *ipsi de foro tum aperto capite ad lenones eunt*, as well as in Afran. *tog.* 106 *aperto*

[54] Cf. Non. 397 M.

[55] Cf. also here the formation *domicilium*, found in poetry once more only in Plaut. *Mil.* 451.

[56] Cf. Non. 236 M.

capite. This formulaic figurative usage is not found in Terence, where *aperio* is used either in its regular sense 'to open' (*Heaut.* 276, etc.) or in a figurative sense for *prodere animum, Andr.* 632, *patefacere, detegere Hec.* 628, or *explicare, expediri, Ad.* 23. See, on the other hand, *Phorm.* 106 *capillus passus, nudus pes.*

v. 60 ***sperabam consilia nostra dividiae tibi*** *Dividia* here is used in the sense of *taedium.*[57] Such an ante-classical usage in the formulaic combination *mihi dividiae est* is not attested in Terence, who uses synonymous expressions (*taedet, aegre esse* constructions etc.). The word is found with this sense several times in Plautus, *Bacch.* 770 *Nimio illaec res est magnae dividiae mihi, Cas.* 181, *Merc.* 619, *Stich.* 19. This EL combination resurfaces later, possibly as an intentional imitation of comic speech, in the archaising Apuleius, *Apol.* 28.

v. 105 ***viden ut osculatur cariem?*** *Caries* in the sense of *vetustas, putrilago* is also found in Afran. *tog.* 250 *nemo illa uiuit carie curiosior*, where, as here, it is used in a figurative sense, as a term of abuse; it is probably a colloquial usage *Priap.* 57.1 and is avoided in Terence.

vv. 112–13 ***istam tibi tristitiam exorbebo*** The verb is used similarly in a figurative sense in Plautus, *Bacch.* 868–9 *nunc nisi ducenti Philippi redduntur mihi, iam illorum ego animam amborum exorbebo oppido.*

v. 133 ***invitavit [viri] plusculum hic sese in prandio*** *Invitare* in the sense of *replere* occurs also in Plautus, *Amph.* 283 *mira sunt nisi invitavit sese in cena plusculum, Rud.* 362. It also occurs in Turpil. *com.* 73. This figurative usage is not found in Terence. In his plays the verb has only the regular meaning 'to invite', *Eun.* 619, 622, *Heaut.* 185.

v. 147 ***misero mihi mitigabat sandalio caput*** The most striking parallel to this line is *Eun.* 1028 *utinam tibi commitigari videam sandalio caput. Commitigari*, lit. 'be softened', in the sense of 'beaten up to a pulp', has its parallels, apart from Turpilius, in Plautus as well, where *mitis* is sometimes used in this sense, *Mil.* 1424 *mitis sum equidem fustibus.* A similar usage occurs also in Afran. *tog.* 67.

vv. 163–4 ***hanc meretricem, quae te . . . studuit perdere, detegere, despoliare*** *Detegere* (= *retegere, nudare*), used literally in the sense of *tecto privare*, especially for a storm wind carrying away the roof,[58] is used here in a figurative sense, occurring in Plautus as well, *Epid.* 65 (according to P) *detegetur corium de tergo meo* ('my back is going to lose its skin roof'), also *Most.* 139–40 *haec verecundiam mi et virtutis modum deturbavit detexitque a med ilico.*[59] Such a figurative usage does not appear in Terence. In the whole of Latin literature, it is restricted to Plautus and Turpilius.[60]

[57] Cf. Non. 96 M. [58] Cf. e.g. Plaut. *Rud.* 85 *detexit ventus villam.*

[59] Cf. here the alliterative homoioarcton combination *deturbare – detexit*, as in Turpilius' line.

[60] Cf. *ThLL* VI 792–3 under *detegere = retegere, nudare.*

vv. 200–1 ***nemo umquam vidit ebrium ire interdiu neque turbam facere neque foras exurere*** The figurative use of *exurere* in the expression *exurere foras*, 'burn down the doors', is also found in Plautus, *Pers.* 569 *at enim illi noctu occentabunt ostium, exurent fores.* Here we have a description of the typical behaviour of a young man in New Comedy. The language Turpilius uses is quite in the traditional or Plautine manner, also for *ebrium ire interdiu*, a similar line in Plautus, *Pseud.* 1298 *quae istaec audaciast te sic interdius cum corolla ebrium incedere*,[61] as well as the expression *turbam facere.* Similar expressions of the kind *turbam/as dare* or *facere*, with the meaning 'to create turmoil', are avoided in Terence, with the exception of *Eunuchus* again, vv. 653, 616, 744. Otherwise it is well attested in the *palliata*, Plaut. *Bacch.* 357, *Curc.* 651, *Pers.* 729, 852, Caec. *com.* 98.

Conclusions

The present study has shown that Turpilius stands much closer than Terence to the linguistic and stylistic tradition of the *palliata*, as exemplified by authors such as Naevius, Caecilius Statius etc. and principally Plautus. There are very few instances of a linguistic usage found in Turpilius and Terence but avoided in other comic authors, namely *mansio* in the sense of *commoratio* in v. 173, *Phorm.* 1012, *saevitia* for *saevitudo* (Turpil. *com.* 91, Ter. *Eun.* 854), *gracilis* (Turpil. *com.* 14, Ter. *Eun.* 314), the *iunctura clamem et (aut) querar* (Turpil. *com.* 148, Ter. *Ad.* 789), *antiqua consuetudo* (Turpil. *com.* 94, Ter. *Hec.* 92), *curae est aliquis alicui* (Turpil. *com.* 118, Ter. *Ad.* 129) *heu me infelicem* (Turpil. *com.* 119, Ter. *Hec.* 282). In particular:

1. Several EL options on the morphological, syntactical or even lexical level, which are common in Plautus but avoided in Terence, are found in Turpilius' fragments. This is the case, for example, with several archaic formations in *-tudo*, or *-arius*, EL active verbal forms in place of CL equivalent ones, the use of *nec* in place of *non* etc. In opposition to Terence, who stands closer to CL in avoiding such EL features, Turpilius opts for archaic forms, words and constructions, favoured in comic dramatists such as Plautus, Caecilius etc.
2. Some colloquial options, mainly on the lexical and syntactical level, common in Plautus and other comic dramatists, but again avoided by Terence, are also to be found in Turpilius' plays. This is the case

[61] Cf. Rychlewska (1971: 53).

for example with *tuburcinari* in place of *vorare, tricae* in place of *impedimenta* or *nugae*, the use of an accusative noun as direct object of *utor* etc.

3. Specific features on the morphological, syntactical and lexical level, with no particular colloquial and/or archaic character, also demonstrate Turpilius' adherence to the previous comic tradition, from which Terence distances himself. This is the case with equivalent morphological, syntactical and lexical alternatives. In such cases Turpilius opts for the one common in Plautus and other comic dramatists and not for the one used by Terence. Characteristic examples are the use of *obliviscor* with the accusative in place of the Terentian genitive construction, the use of *expa(e)rs* with the ablative instead of the genitive attested in Terentian drama, *sacer* as equivalent to *scelestus* etc.
4. Particular figurative usages (imagery) common in the comic tradition are also found in Turpilius. Some of these figurative usages are restricted to comedy in the whole of Latin literature, e.g. the figurative use of *detegere.* Further examples include the use of *tangere* in the sense of 'to trick', *caries* as a term of abuse for an old person etc. These figurative usages, common in the previous comic tradition, especially Plautus, are absent from the Terentian corpus.
5. Certain other stylistic and lexical options, like the use of specific *iuncturae*, word groups, common in the comic tradition again but avoided in Terence, occur in Turpilian drama, e.g. the use of *limare caput* for *osculari, mala aetas* for *senectus/a*, the expressions or formulaic combinations *ad cenam condicere, sermonem sublegere, docta dicere* etc.

Several linguistic and stylistic options common in the comic tradition and/or in Turpilius as well are occasionally found in Terence. In these cases, however, these features are found mainly in *Eunuchus* or in some specific scenes in other plays where Terence deviates from his original. This is the case e.g. with *careo* construed with the accusative etc.

All these do not mean of course that *hapax* linguistic usages in Terence, present in Plautus and other comic dramatists, do not occasionally occur outside the *Eunuchus* or the scenes traditional from a linguistic point of view in *Adelphoe, Heautontimoroumenos*, or *Phormio.* This is the case with the *iunctura odio esse* in v. 43 (Plaut. *Capt.* 1035, *Curc.* 501, *Poen.* 51 and Ter. *Hec.* 343), formulaic combinations of *pudet* and *piget* (Turpil. *com.* 19, Plaut. *Pseud.* 281–2, Ter. *Ad.* 392). What matters again here is the relative accumulation of such features in a specific play or specific scene of a play and their relative absence from another.

Caecilius Statius

Caecilius Statius (ca. 230/220–168 BC)[62] was an Insubrian Gaul, probably from Mediolanum. As a result of a war between Rome and Gaul (223–2 or 200–194) he was brought as a slave to Rome, where he was freed by a Caecilius.[63]

Unlike both Naevius and Ennius, Caecilius devoted himself exclusively to the *fabula palliata*. In antiquity, his work was highly appreciated. Among others, Volcacius Sedigitus (ap. Gell. 15.24) ranked him first among Roman comic playwrights.[64] Caecilius has been seen as a forerunner of Terence, mainly in retaining a large proportion of Greek titles, in avoiding Roman allusions and in adapting largely Menandrian comedies (sixteen plays). From his work some forty-two titles and 177 fragments with 279 lines survive, which show, however, especially the three passages of the *Plocium* quoted by Gellius (2.23) together with Menander's original, that his style is similar to that of Plautus rather than Terence.[65]

In this section I shall examine in detail the language of Caecilius in comparison to that of all other comic dramatists. This will show the following:

1. Caecilius' language, as a whole, is closer to the traditional linguistic pattern of Roman comedy than to the innovative Terence.
2. Which features of Caecilius' language avoided in Terence should simply be attributed to the historical development of the Latin language,

[62] Cf. Hieron. *chron. a. Abr.* 1838 assigning his *floruit* to 179 BC, Guardì (1974: 9), Duckworth (1952: 45), Wright (1974: 87–8), Albrecht (1997: 206 –14).

[63] Cf. also Guardì (1974: 11).

[64] Cf. Var. *Men.* 399, *L.* 10, Cic. *Cato* 24ff., *de orat.* 2.257, Hor. *Ars* 53ff. etc.

[65] Cf. Wright (1974: 87–126), Duckworth (1952: 47–8; for Caecilius' dramatic style in comparison to Plautus and Terence, cf. Ritschl (1965: 145), Leo (1913: 220–1), Duckworth (1952: 46–9), Bardon (1952–6: 39, 43), Faider (1908–9: 289–313). For Caecilius' life, work, dramatic style, cf. also Argenio (1937: 359–68), Faider (1908–9: 5–35), Gamberale (1967: 162–4), Haffter (1953: 7–8), Oppermann (1939: 196–7), Pociña (1981–3: 63–78), Riedweg (1993: 133–59), Robson (1938: 301–8), Skutsch (1897: 1189–92), Traina (1957–8: 385–93).

and which EL features are deliberately used as archaisms by Caecilius and other comic dramatists, except Terence.

3. Terence is closest to the language of both Caecilius and Plautus in *Eunuchus* and those individual scenes of other plays where he reworks his material in a more traditional way.

Morphology

Nouns and adjectives

v. 50 ***Quid illud est pulchritatis!*** In Caecilius we find several unclassical formations in *-tas* for CL *-tudo, -tia, -edo* equivalents. This is the case with *pulchritas* for *pulchritudo, dulcitas* for *dulcedo* (v. 207), *opulentitas* for *opulentia* (v. 177), also found in Plautus, *Mil.* 1171. Such unclassical alternative formations in *-tas* are not found in Terence, who again restricts himself to those later used in CL, *largitas* (*Ad.* 985, *Heaut.* 441) or always prefers the CL equivalent *pulchritudo* (*Phorm.* 105). Even though the use of such formations is not avoided in Plautus (see *opulentitas* above), it seems to be an idiolectal feature of Caecilius' language, see also *luculentitas* v. 61.

v. 87 ***nam ista quidem noxa muliebre est magis quam viri*** According to Nonius (224 M), in this case the neuter *muliebre* could be used in place of *muliebris* due to the following *est.* Such a construction, according to the ancient grammarian, is also found in Titin. *tog.* 36 *formicae pol persimilest rusticus*, Naev. *com.* 57 *pol haut parasitorum aliorum simile est!*, Nov. *atel.* 62 *tu pueri pausilli simile es*, as well as in Plautus.[66] Several scholars do not agree with such an explanation,[67] arguing that the final *-s* of the masculine is elided and therefore the short *-i* is swallowed by the *e* of *est*, an explanation, however, seriously doubted by Lindsay (1922: 76 and 129–33).[68] Such instances are not found in Terence, who uses regularly the *-is* form before *es/est, tristis est* at *Hec.* 352, *lenis est* at *Heaut.* 45, *tristis est* at *Heaut.* 620, *vilis est* at *Phorm.* 558 etc.

v. 162 ***pudebat credo commemoramentum stupri*** As for formations in *-mentum*, it has been argued that they are characteristic mainly of a less elevated style of writing, since, for example, comedy shows 52 examples of new forms but tragedy only three, compared to equivalent

[66] For an account of possible instances of such a phenomenon in Plautus, cf. Leo (1966: 286).

[67] Cf. Leo (1966: 285–7), Skutsch (1892: 113).

[68] For an explanation by analogy with forms such as *necess(e), pot(e)* used for all the genders, cf. Sommer (1914: 293).

-men derivatives.[69] Terence again here shows his purism in avoiding such formations and restricting himself to those commonly used later in CL; even the form *salsamentum* at *Ad.* 380 is found later in Cicero (*Div.* 2.117). In contrast to Terence, unclassical formations of this kind are common in earlier comic writers,[70] and they are often found elsewhere in the EL or archaising and/or colloquial register of Latin. In Caecilius we also find *peniculamentum* in v. 118 *peniculamentum ex pallio datur*, common in colloquial genres, Lucil. 565 *peniculamento vero reprehendere noli*, reappearing later in the archaising Arnobius.

v. 245 ***quantum amantum in Attica est*** The consonant-stem genitive plural *amantum* in place of *amantium* is also to be found in Plautus, *Most.* 171 *sententiasque amantum* and in Turpilius *com.* 203. In Terence we encounter only the normal CL form in *-ium, amantium, Andr.* 218 *inceptiost amentium, haud amantium, Heaut.* 570 *novi ego amantium animum.* As for consonant-stem genitives in *-um* of participles or adjectives (not substantives) in *-ent-*, Terence avoids these formations, but they are common in Plautus, *apsentum* at *Stich.* 5, *gerentum* at *Truc.* 223, *precantum* at *Rud.* 260.

v. 248 ***grammonsis oculis ipsa atratis dentibus*** *Atratus* is an adjective formed on the model of participles from denominative verbs in *-are.* Such formations are common in colloquial genres and are normally eschewed by the purists of the classical period.[71] Plautus exhibits several adjectives of this kind, *aculeatus, aleatus, caesariatus, columnatus, eburatus, hostiatus, impluviatus, ingeniatus* etc. They appear also in Titinius, *fimbriatus* at *tog.* 115, as well as in Pomponius, *coleatus* at *atel.* 69. Terence once more shows his purism in avoiding such formations.

Pronouns

v. 8 ***med*** EL formations of the type *med, ted* in place of the accusative or ablative *me, te*, are completely absent in Terence, but occur in Plautus, where they are found sporadically without any clear functional oppositions with regular CL equivalent forms, *Asin.* 632, *Men.* 820, etc.[72]

v. 26 ***sentire ea aetate eumpse esse odiosum alteri*** *Eumpse* in place of *ipsum* is an EL masculine accusative singular of the demonstrative pronoun *ipsus.* In CL *ipse* was no longer regarded as consisting of two elements (*is + pse)*, but was declined regularly according to the second declension. This is also the case in Terence, where no such EL formation is to be found; on the other hand, in Plautus we find *eumpse*

[69] Cf. Cooper (1895: 84–8).

[70] Cf. in Plautus *deliramentum, explementum* etc. Afranius *delenimentum* in *tog.* 378, 382.

[71] For their colloquial character, cf. Cooper (1895: 134–8).

[72] Cf. also Fay (1909).

at *Most.* 346, *Pers.* 603, *Trin.* 950, *Truc.* 114, 133, 890, 891, *eampse* at *Aul.* 815, *Poen.* 272, *Rud.* 1278, *Trin.* 800, *Truc.* 133, *eopse* at *Bacch.* 815, *eapse* at *Curc.* 534, *Epid.* 254, *Trin.* 974.

Verbs

v. 4 ***actutum, voltis, empta est; noltis, non empta est*** Non-periphrastic forms of *nolo*, such as *noltis* in place of *non vultis*, are also found in Plautus, *nevis* for the CL *non vis* at *Curc.* 82, *Merc.* 150, *Most.* 1176 etc. As for *nevolt* for *non vult*, also *Epid.* 42, 586, *Most.* 110, *Trin.* 361, 364. See also Titin. *tog.* 108 *ipsus quidem hercle ducere sane nevult.* Such forms are found, already in Plautus, at the end of the line or just before the caesura, an indication that even in Plautine drama, as well as in Titinius, such forms must already have been felt as archaic. In contrast to several comic dramatists, Terence does not include such forms in his archaising register. In his comedies only the regular CL forms are to be found.

v. 79 ***ere, obsecro, hercle, desine, mane; coepiam*** The use of active forms of the present tense of the verb *coepi* is an EL feature which is often found in Plautus as well, *Men.* 960 *neque ego litis coepio, Truc.* 232 *quaestum coepiat*, also *Pers.* 121 *coeperest.* In Terence we normally find the CL form *coepi/isse.* The single instance of an active form from the imperfect *coeperet* occurs at *Ad.* 397. There, however, it seems to be used for stylistic effect in the speech of an old person, Demea, in whose mouth we find several other EL features.

v. 114 ***reperibit*** The EL future form *reperibo* for *reperiam* occurs also at Plaut. *Epid.* 151, Pompon. *atel.* 9. In Terence we find instead only the CL future, *reperies* at *Hec.* 843, *reperiam* at *Phorm.* 235, *reperient* at *Phorm.* 234.

v. 170 ***patiere quod dant, quando optata non danunt*** The third plural of the present *danunt* is an EL form for the CL *dant.*[73] It is also found, apart from Caecilius, in several lines in Plautus, *Capt.* 819, *Merc.* 226, *Most.* 129, 561, *Pers.* 852, *Poen.* 1253, *Pseud.* 767, 770, *Rud.* 1229, *Truc.* 245. Even in EL writers, however, the form seems to have been felt as archaic, since it is restricted to line end or just before the caesura. Such an intentional archaism is not included, however, in the archaising register of Terence. In his comedies we find instead only the regular CL form *dant, Phorm.* 675 *si illam dant.*

Adverbs

v. 204 ***noenu volt*** *Noenu* is an archaic equivalent of *non* which is often regarded as derived from it. This form does not appear in Terence,

73 For a morphological examination of the form, cf. also Sommer (1914: 490–1), Leumann (1977: 514).

who always uses the regular form *non*, but is found in Plautus, *Aul.* 67 *noenum mecastor quid ego ero dicam meo.*

Syntax

Voice and mood usage

v. 15 ***nil fore opino inter me atque illum*** *Opino* is the EL form for *opinor* which is also found in Plautus, *Bacch.* 487 *ut opino.*[74] The form reappears later in the Itala *Psalm.* 49, 21. In Terence, on the other hand, we encounter only the regular CL deponent form *opinor Heaut.* 287, 678, *Eun.* 563 etc.

vv. 94–5 ***surdo mihi suadet ut eam quisquam dormitum?*** According to Guardì (1974: ad loc.) these lines are probably to be attributed to a young man, *adulescens*, addressing his slave. In this line we encounter the combination *eo* + supine, i.e. *eam dormitum*, in the function of a simple periphrastic future. Such an EL usage is common in Plautus, especially in formulaic combinations of the type *accubitum, cubitum, dormitum ire* (44 examples). Such a usage in Terentian drama seems to belong to the archaising register of the author, used for stylistic effect, since these constructions are markers of senile speech, along with several other EL and archaising features in concentration, at *Heaut.* 655 *ea lavatum dum it* by the *matrona* Sostrata, at *Phorm.* 462 *percontatum ibo ad portum* by the *senex* Demipho and at *Andr.* 134 *quor te is perditum* by Simo.

Case syntax

v. 28 ***itanest inmemoris*** The adjective in absolute usage, as here, appears also at Plaut. *Pers.* 168. In Terence *immemor* is always construed with a genitive complement, *Andr.* 44, 477.

v. 218 ***hospes est mi adulescens*** The construction of the syntagm *hospes est* with the possessive dative (*mi*) occurs also in Plautus, *Poen.* 120, 1050–1. In Terence it appears once at *Ad.* 529 *hospes nemost vobis*, possibly as an intentional archaism in the speech of the old slave Syrus. The construction occurs elsewhere in the archaising Livy, 21.12.7. At CIL II. 5346, dated to the time of Augustus, the dative *senatui Augustobrigensi* could depend upon the expression *donum dat* as its complement and not on the *hospem esse* expression.

v. 246 ***nomen virginis . . . deintegravit*** In *nomen virginis* we encounter a quite rare construction, namely the so-called appositional or epexegetic

[74] Cf. *ThLL* IX 2 722, Enn. *trag.* 146, Pac. *trag.* 101.

genitive (*genetivus definitivus*[75]). This construction is common in Plautus, *deliciae pueri* at *Pers.* 204, *satis scitum filum mulieris* at *Merc.* 755, *flagitium hominis* at *Asin.* 473, *Cas.* 155, 552, *Men.* 489, 709, *frustum pueri* at *Pers.* 848, *hallex viri* at *Poen.* 1310, *hominum mendicabula* at *Aul.* 703, *monstrum mulieris* at *Poen.* 273, *nomen servitutis* at *Pseud.* 1107–8, *scelus viri* at *Curc.* 614, *Mil.* 1434, *Truc.* 621, *scelus pueri* at *Pers.* 192, also in Afranius *novercae nomen* at *tog.* 57 and *nominis matronae sanctitudinem* at *tog.* 326. In Terence the construction is avoided, with the exception of the more traditional *Eunuchus* again, *Eun.* 696 *monstrum hominis.*

v. 259 ***tantam rem dilabare ut pro nilo habuerit*** The use of the prepositional combination *pro* + ablative of *nihil, pro nihilo/nilo*, in the sense of 'to hold for nothing', is also found in Plautus, *Pers.* 637 *omnes ego pro nihilo esse duco quod fuit quando fuit.* This notion of *nullius preti aestimare* is expressed on the other hand in Terence only by means of the genitive case, *Ad.* 167 *ceterum hoc nihili facis*, *Eun.* 94.

Verbal syntax

v. 12 ***ad amicos curret mutuatum*** *Currere* construed with the supine, appears also in Plautus, *Merc.* 857 *illum curram quaeritatum.* This is an unclassical construction, possibly of colloquial flavour. It reappears later in Petr. 71.9 *cacatum currat*, also Claud. 15.377, but is avoided completely in Terentian drama.

v. 126 ***edepol voluntas homini rarenter venit*** *Venio* here is construed with the dative of the indirect object, found in Plautus, *Capt.* 550 *isti qui sputatur morbus interdum venit, Pseud.* 69–70. Terence usually employs an *ad*-complement to denote the person or thing to which somebody or something comes (cf. McGlynn II 263–4).

v. 148–9 ***quod ego . . . effeci, paelice ut meum privarem virum*** *Efficere* construed with a complement *ut*-clause occurs also in Plautus, *Mil.* 936–7 *hoc si ecficiam plane, ut concubinam militis meus hospes habeat hodie*. In Terence, *efficio* is used either absolutely (*Hec.* 123) or with an accusative object (*Eun.* 1058) or even with a *qui* + subjunctive clause (*Andr.* 334).

Clause syntax

v. 31 ***iamne adeo?*** According to Bennett (1910–14: I 23), *adeo* here is a present indicative of the verb *adeo* and not the adverb. In this case we have here a deliberative question in a present indicative, introduced by

[75] For this term, given to genitives denoting the same entity as the governing noun and its application, cf. Bennett (1910–14: II 68).

the particle *iam.* Such constructions are common in Plautus, *Men.* 176 *iam fores ferio?, Cas.* 503, *Curc.* 132, *Mil.* 1400. In Terence such constructions are restricted to *Eunuchus, Eun.* 814 *iam dimitto exercitum?,* 492 *iamne imus?.*

vv. 57–8 ***quid tibi aucupatiost argumentum aut de meo amore verbificatiost patri?*** Interrogative combinations of the type *quid* + *tibi* + abstract noun in *-tio* + *<est>*, as here, are very common in Plautus, *Amph.* 519 *quid tibi hanc curatio est rem, verbero, atque muttitio?, Asin.* 920 *quid tibi hunc receptio ad te est meum virum? Aul.* 423 *quid tibi nos tactiost?, Cas.* 406, *Curc.* 626, *Most.* 34, *Men.* 1016, *Poen.* 1308, *Rud.* 502, *Trin.* 709, *Truc.* 258, 622, 623. In Terence the only example of such a construction is found significantly at *Eun.* 671 *quid huc tibi reditiost? quid vestis mutatio?.* What is more, here, in contrast to the Terentian example, the *quid tibi est* syntagm in the Caecilian line is followed by a verbal abstract in *-tio, aucupatio*, upon the verbal notion of which a direct accusative complement depends, *argumentum.* Such accusative object constructions of verbal abstracts in *quid tibi est* syntagms occur elsewhere in Plautus only.[76]

v. 125 ***Quaeso, ne ad malum hoc addas malum*** The use of *quaeso* with *ne* + subjunctive occurs once more in Caecilius in v. 78 *quaeso ne temere hanc rem agas ne iracunditer.* The construction is also to be found in Plautus, *Aul.* 210 *quaeso . . . ne id te pigeat proloqui, Bacch.* 1013 *quaeso . . . ne me . . . deseras* etc. In the case of a request of a negative type with *quaeso*, Terence uses only the *ne* + imperative construction following the verb in direct speech, *Heaut.* 1052 *age quaeso, ne tam offirma te, Chreme.* The subordination of the request with *ne* is avoided absolutely in Terentian drama.

v. 216 ***praesertim quae non peperit lacte non habet*** *Praesertim* is construed here with a relative clause, a combination which also appears in Plautus, *Poen.* 820 *servire amanti miseria est, praesertim qui quod amat caret, Cist.* 241, *Rud.* 291. This construction does not appear in Terence, where *praesertim* occurs either in nominal constructions, *Ad.* 784 or in *praesertim cum* (*Eun.* 863, *Hec.* 531, 705)/*praesertim ut* (*Phorm.* 55) combinations.

Word order

v. 88 ***ego illud minus nihilo exigor portorium*** Such a reverse word order in the common combination *nihilo minus* is also attested in Plautus, *Vid.* 50 *minus operis nihilo faciam.* In Terence, on the other hand, only the commoner *nihilo/nil minus* word order appears, *Heaut.* 667 *olim nil minus, Eun.* 435, 535.

[76] Cf. Rosén (1981), 88.

Lexicon

Nouns and adjectives

vv. 20–1 ***ne tibi me esse ob eam rem obnoxium reare*** *Obnoxius* in the sense of *subiectus, obligatus*, because of a specific debit, financial obligation etc. is also found in Plautus, construed with the dative denoting the person to whom the obligation is due, *Poen.* 1191 *omnia faciet Juppiter faxo, nam mihi est obnoxius et me metuit.* In Terence, the word is used in a figurative sense denoting moral duty because of a favour received, *Hec.* 302–3 *uxori obnoxius sum: Ita olim suo me ingenio pertulit, tot meas iniurias, quae numquam in ullo patefacit loco.*[77]

vv. 54–5 ***quid narras barbare cum indomitis moribus, inlitterate inlex?*** *Inlex* as a term of abuse is not found in Terence, but occurs in Plautus, *Pers.* 406–8 *oh lutum lenonium, commixtum caeno sterculinum publicum, inpure, inhoneste, iniure, inlex, labes popli.*

v. 65 ***garruli sine dentes iactent*** *Garrulus* here has the meaning of *multum loquens*, which is also found in Plautus, *Curc.* 477 *confidentes garrulique et malevoli.* In Terence the word has a more specific meaning, namely *qui secreta prodit*, a quite rare usage in Latin literature,[78] *Ad.* 624.

vv. 69–70 ***quin machaera licitari*** *Machaera* is used here as equivalent to *ensis, gladius*. The word appears in this sense also in Plautus, *Bacch.* 68 *capiam pro machaera turturem* v. 887, *Curc.* 424, 567, 574, 632, *Truc.* 506 etc.

v. 90 ***resupina obstipo capitulo sibi ventum facere tunicula*** The diminutive form *capitulum* (*caput hominum*) is also found in Plautus, *Curc.* 293 *operto capitulo calidum bibunt*, metonymical uses at *Asin.* 496. In Terence, the word appears only once, at *Eun.* 531 *o capitulum lepidissimum!*.

v. 93 ***duc me ad patrios fines decoratum opipare!*** Both the adjective *opiparus/a/um* (also *-is, -is, -e*) and the adverb *opipare*, in the sense of 'splendid', 'sumptuous' and 'splendidly', 'sumptuously' respectively, are found in Plautus as well, *Capt.* 768–9 *auges opes, maxumas opimitates opiparasque offers mihi, Mil.* 107, *Poen.* 132; for the adverb, *Bacch.* 373 *instructa domus opime atque opipare.* Terence employs instead synonymous expressions such as *sumptuosus* at *Ad.* 760 *domus sumptuosa*,[79] *magnificus/e, largus/e* (*Eun.* 1078). As for *decorare*, used here as equivalent to *ornare, illustrare*, cf. also Plaut. *Mil.* 1048, *Trin.* 39.

77 For the meaning of the adverb and the difference between the Plautine and the Terentian usage, cf. also *ThLL* IX 2 124–9.

78 Cf. also Hor. *Ep.* 1.18.69, Ov. *Am.* 2.2.44; 2.2.60, *Ars.* 2.606, Mart. 10.5.16, Quint. *Decl.* 10.13, Symm. *Epist.* 1.31.1.

79 Similar reference to *domus* is also found in Plautus with *opipare* at *Bacch.* 373.

v. 104 ***modo fit obsequens*** *Obsequens* in the sense of *officiosus*, used predicatively with the copulative *fio*, as here, appears in Plautus as well, *Pers.* 181 *ut erae opsequens fiam.* Such a usage is avoided in Terence. The form is normally used in his comedies as a predicate with forms of the verb *esse, Hec.* 247, 459.

v. 146 ***fuit integra aetatula*** *Aetatula* has here the meaning of *adulescentia*; the word appears with the same sense in Plautus, *Most.* 217 *dum tibist nunc haec aetatula* (opp. *in senectute), Cist.* 49.

v. 151 ***morosane uxor*** *Morosus* in the sense of *importunus, molestus*, while avoided by Terence, appears in both Plautus, *Poen.* 379 *novi ego huius mores morosi malos* and Afran. *tog.* 372 *dum <me> morigeram, dum morosam praebeo.*

v. 152 ***taedet mentionis*** *Mentio* in the sense of *commemoratio* also occurs in Plautus, *Bacch.* 252, *Rud.* 1289, *Truc.* 195. In Terence the word appears once, significantly in *Eunuchus*, v. 437.

v. 163 ***is demum infortunatust homo*** *Infortunatus* as equivalent to *mala fortuna affectus, infelix* occurs also in Plautus, *Bacch.* 1106 *homo miser atque infortunatus*, 1107. In Terence the word appears only once, in *Eunuchus*, v. 298 *o infortunatum senem?.* What is more, in the Caecilian and Plautine examples, the same *iunctura* occurs, namely *homo infortunatus.*

v. 181 ***cur depopulator? Gerrae!*** *Gerrae* being initially equivalent to *genitalia* acquired with the passing of time the meaning *nugae, ineptiae*, cf. Engl. 'bollocks'. The word is used here in this sense, cf. Nonius (118 M) *gerrae, nugae, ineptiae.* With this meaning the word often occurs in Plautus, *Asin.* 600 *gerrae, Epid.* 233 *gerrae maxumae, Poen.* 137 *gerrae germanae.*

v. 190 ***parentem habere avarum inlepidum*** *Inlepidus* in the sense of *invenustus, rudis, molestus* occurs in Plautus, *Bacch.* 615 *inamabilis, inlepidus vivo.*

vv. 197–9 ***nec quem dolum ad eum aut machinam commoliar . . . fallacias praestrigias praestrinxit commoditas patris*** In this passage we encounter two terms for trickery, namely *machina* and *praestrigia*, commonly found in Plautus for *machina, Bacch.* 232–3 *aliquam machinabor machinam, unde aurum ecficiam, Pers.* 785, *Pseud.* 550, for *praestrigia, Capt.* 524 *operta quae fuere aperta sunt, patent praestigiae*, also *Aul.* 630, *Poen.* 1125, *Truc.* 134. Terence uses other terms for trickery,[80] but avoids these two completely.

v. 225 ***o infelix, o sceleste!*** *Infelix* is used here in the sense of *scelestus, malus, impius, horrendus.* This meaning is found both in Plautus, *Mil.* 300 and in Terence at *Phorm.* 427–8 *itan es paratus facere me advorsum omnia, infelix?*, in the *advocati* scene. Elsewhere in Terence the

[80] Cf. Brotherton (1921).

adjective is used as equivalent to *non fortunatus, miser,* ἀτυχής, *Andr.* 245, *Eun.* 244, 828, 943, *Phorm.* 175, *Hec.* 282, 444, *Ad.* 540, 667.

v. 256 ***si confidentiam adhibes, confide omnia*** *Confidentia* has here the meaning of *fidentia, fiducia.* See Plaut. *Amph.* 1054 *neque ullast confidentia iam in corde, quin amiserim, Pers.* 231, *Pseud.* 763. In Terence *confidentia* is used only *in malam partem,* as equivalent to *nimia audacia, superbia, impudentia, Eun.* 839.

v. 267 ***nimis audacem nimisque bardum barbarum*** *Bardus* as a term of abuse is found in Plautus as well, *Bacch.* 1087–8 *qui fuerunt quique futuri sunt posthac stulti, stolidi, fatui, fungi, bardi, blenni, buccones, Pers.* 169 *me quidem pro barda et pro rustica reor habitam esse aps te.*

v. 269 ***vallata gulla*** *Gulla* in the sense of 'gullet' appears also in Plautus, *Men.* 970–1 *tergum quam gulam, crura quam ventrem oportet potiora esse, Stich.* 639. Terence uses only *fauces* in the sense of 'gullet', *Heaut.* 673 *crucior bolum tantum mi ereptum tam desubito e faucibus.*

Verbs

v. 10 ***tu iam callebis, ille festus desidet*** The use of *calleo* in the sense of *callum habere, indurescere* is a quite rare usage which is also found twice in Plautus, *Pseud.* 136 *ita plagis costae callent, Pers.* 305 *magis calleo quam aprugnum callum callet.* Such a rare meaning appears in the whole of Latin literature only twice elsewhere, *Aetna* 261 and Plin. *Nat.* 11.211. In Terence the word appears with its regular meaning *scire, calidum/peritum esse*, either with an accusative direct-object construction, *Ad.* 533 *ego illius sensum pulchre calleo*, or with a following interrogative clause, *Heaut.* 548 *quo pacto id fieri soleat, calleo.*[81]

v. 17 ***ait hic vicinus se eas peperisse et vobis datum*** According to Nonius (464 M), the verb is used here of a man. A similar usage, in a figurative sense though, is found in Plautus, *Amph.* 785–6, where Sosia says to Amphitruo: *tu peperisti Amphitruonem <alium>, ego alium peperi Sosiam; nunc si patera pateram peperit, omnes congeminavimus*, or *Stich.* 165–6, where the parasite Gelasimus utters *uteri dolores mi oboriunt cottidie, sed matrem parere nequeo.* In Terence *parere* is regularly always used of a female person, *Hec.* 414, 527, *Phorm.* 47, *Ad.* 290 etc.

v. 31 ***Manta!*** *Mantare* is the frequentative of *manere* used here in the sense of simple *manere.*[82] See also Plaut. *Most.* 115–17 *si quid nummo sarciri potest, usque mantat neque id faciunt donicum parietes ruont, Poen.* 264, sometimes in the imperative mood as here, *Pseud.* 254–5 *vah manta!,* 283, *Rud.* 439. The verb is used once more by

[81] Cf. Eugraphius ad loc. *calleo: peritus et doctus sum.*

[82] Cf. Nonius 105 M, *mantat pro manet*, Festus 118 *Mantare saepe manere. Caecilius in Epistola.*

Caec. *com.* 84. Terence, on the other hand, avoids this formation and uses instead *manere* or *morari.*

v. 37 ***non haec putas, non haec in corde versantur tibi?*** *Putare* here is used, according to Nonius (369 M; see there examples from Ennius and Plautus), in the sense of *animo disputare*, 'haven't you a thought for all this?', 'Don't you turn it over and over in your heart?'. A similar use of the verb is found in Terence as well, but, crucially, only once, in *Eunuchus*. The relevant example occurs in vv. 632–3 *dum haec puto, praeterii inprudens villam*, a line upon which Schol. Schlee comments *revolvo in animo.* Another instance is possibly found at *Ad.* 208, in another scene where Terence demonstrably reworks his material in a more traditional way, v. 208 *frustra egomet mecum has rationes puto.* Otherwise the verb in Terence is used in the sense of *tractare, discutere, Ad.* 796, *disputare Phorm.* 718,[83] as synonymous with *arbitror, opinor, censeo* (in absolute use *Phorm.* 545, *Hec.* 379 etc., or with the accusative as direct object *Andr.* 671 etc.), with the a.c.i., *Andr.* 330, *Heaut.* 151 etc., or as equivalent to *existimo, iudico* (*Heaut.* 900). For the *iunctura in corde versari*, see also *Poen.* 196 *quamquam Cupido in corde vorsatur.*

v. 67 ***prodigere est cum nihil habeas te inriderier*** For the meaning of the verb *prodigere* here, Festus 254 *prodigeris, consumpseris, perdideris.* The verb in the sense of 'to waste', 'to squander', is well attested in Roman comedy: Naevius *com.* 81 *ante parta patria peregre prodigunt?*, Plaut. *Aul.* 380–1 *festo die si quid prodegeris, profesto egere liceat*: Pompon. *atel.* 162. The verb is avoided in Terence, where we find several synonymous expressions, such as *effundere*, cf. *Ad.* 991 *effundite emite, facite quod vobis lubet, profundere, perdere*, cf. *Ad.* 133–4 *si tibi istuc placet profundat perdat pereat; nil ad me attinet.*[84] For *perdere* in this sense, *Heaut.* 465, 964, *Ad.* 410. Similarly, *didere* in the sense of 'to waste', 'to squander' appears in both Caecilius and Plautus, respectively *com.* 232 *dide ac disiice, Merc.* 56–8 *ratione pessuma a me ea quae . . . invenisset . . . diffunditari ac didier.*

v. 106 ***vertit prosumiam*** *Vortere* in the sense of 'to cause to revolve', 'turn', 'spin' occurs also in Plaut. *Epid.* 49, *Poen.* 754, *Pseud.* 1317. In Terence the verb is used with the meaning of 'to turn or betake oneself to someone for help or protection' (*Hec.* 516), 'to turn or direct oneself' (*Heaut.* 946), 'to take a given turn' (*Ad.* 191), 'to give a favourable outcome' (*Hec.* 196), or 'to translate' (*Eun.* 7).

v. 110 ***subpilat vestem atque ornamenta omnia*** According to Nonius (12 M), *suppilare est involare vel rapere.* Such a usage is common in Plautus, *Men.* 739–41 *pallam atque aurum meum domo suppilas tuae uxori et tuae degeris amicae, Truc.* 566 *haec quom video fieri, suffuror,*

[83] Cf. Donat. ad loc.

[84] Cf. Schol. Schlee p. 151 *prodige expendat*, CGL, p. 538 *prodigat, multum eroget.*

suppilo, Asin. 815, 888. Another instance is found in Pomponius, *atel.* 162 *alter amat potat prodigit, patrem suppilat semper.* The verb has a colloquial flavour[85] and is found in the Romance languages, a further indication of its more popular character, *pigliare* in Italian or *piller* in French. In Terence, we find instead synonymous expressions, e.g. *intercipere* with the meaning to 'rob', see *Eun.* 80 etc.

v. 123 ***res delicat*** *Deliquo(-co)-are* meaning *decolare, liquidam facere* can be used in a figurative sense, as equivalent to *declarare, explanare.*[86] This is an EL usage, Plaut. *Mil.* 844 *ut tu ipse me dixisse delices*, Titin. *tog.* 80–1 *tibin comoediam, quae sciam, non delicem?*, 103 *quid istuc est aut quid istic sibi vult sermo? Mater, delica.* In all instances the word is used at the end of the line, an indication that it was already considered archaic in the comic dramatists. Terence again does not include such an archaism in his archaic vocabulary. In his comedies we find instead several synonymous expressions, *explanare, Phorm.* 380 *quem amicum tuom ais fuisse istum, explana mihi, declarare, Heaut.* 284 *quae (consuetudo) quoiusque ingenium ut sit declarat maxume.*

v. 142 ***ea me clam se cum mea ancilla ait consuetum; id me arguit*** *Arguere* is used here in the sense of *accusare.* This meaning of the verb is also common in Plautine drama, with the reason for the accusation either clearly expressed or unexpressed, *Mil.* 190 *qui arguat se, Amph.* 882–3 with the genitive, *Men.* 813, *Mil.* 244, 337 with the infinitive construction, or *Amph.* 885 *quae neque sunt facta neque ego in me admisi, arguit, Men.* 940, with a neuter accusative pronoun, as here. Terence uses instead synonymous expressions such as *accusare, obiurgare, culpare.*

v. 166 ***facile occultat factio*** *Occultare* in the sense of *abdere* is found also in Plautus, *Aul.* 277. In Terence the verb appears once, in the last act of *Hecyra*, v. 869 *qui hoc occultari facilius credas dabo.* In this scene Terence deviates again from his original in having Parmeno fetch Pamphilus. Parmeno was not present in the final scene in Apollodorus' Greek original, and the dialogue between Pamphilus and Parmeno in vv. 841–53 replaces an entrance monologue of Pamphilus.[87] Donatus remarks on Terence's reworking of the scene (ad *Hec.* 825) *brevitati consuluit Terentius, nam in Graeca haec aguntur, non narrantur.* As for syntax, however, in both the Caecilian and the Plautine example *occulto* is used transitively, with a direct accusative object; in Terence the verb occurs in passive constructions only.

v. 185 ***destituit omnes servos ad mensam ante se*** *Destituere* here has the meaning of *statuere, collocare.* See also Plautus, *Rud.* 823 *ita duo*

[85] For its colloquial character, cf. Ernout and Meillet (1951: 897).

[86] Cf. also Nonius 98 M *Delica, explana, indica.*

[87] Cf. Lowe (1983: 490).

destituit signa hic cum clavis senex, Naev. *com.* 54 *in alto navem destitui iubet ancoris.*

v. 208 ***ager autem stet sentibus*** According to Nonius (391 M), *stare* here is equivalent to *horrere*, a rare usage also found in Titinius, *tog.* 141 *atque illud ante partum comedet, fundi stabunt sentibus.*

vv. 209–10 ***egon vitam meam Atticam contendam cum istac rusticana Syra?*** The verb *contendere* is used here with the meaning *conferre, comparare.*[88] This use of the verb is also found in Plautus, *Rud.* 752 *contende ergo uter sit tergo – verior.* In Terence such meaning of the verb is not attested. He employs instead synonymous expressions, *conferre* at *Ad.* 94 *si conferendum exemplumst*, or *comparare, Eun.* 681 *ne comparandus hicquidem ad illumst.*

v. 224 ***nunc meum cor cumulatur ira*** *Cumulo* here is used in the sense of *afficio, dono*. See also Plautus, *Mil.* 1383.

vv. 228–9 ***cur in vicinitatem istam meretriciam te contulisti?*** Here *se conferre* is equivalent to *ire, proficisci, confugere.* This usage appears also in Plautus, *Most.* 931 *nunc ego me illac per posticum ad congerrones conferam*, Turpil. *com.* 213. In Terence, *Hec.* 298 is textually doubtful. *Se* is attested only by A and is not adopted in modern editions.

v. 232 ***dide ac disiice*** *Didere* is used here in the sense *of distribuere, dividere.* See also Plaut. *Merc.* 58 *amoris vi diffunditari ac didier, Mil.* 707.

v. 237 ***versaris atque illuseris lautissine*** *Verso* in the sense of 'to influence a person insidiously for one's advantage', 'to manipulate' occurs also in Plautus, *Pers.* 795–6 *quando me hodie vorsavisti, ut me in tricas coniecisti, Bacch.* 766. This is an EL and archaising usage (its distribution: Plautus, Fronto). In Terentian drama *verso* is either used with the meaning of 'to keep turning round', 'to spin' (*Eun.* 1085), or as equivalent to *impeditus/occupatus/situs sum* (*Andr.* 649).

v. 265 ***tu quid mi oscitans hietansque restas?*** *Hietare* is a synonym for *oscitare.* It is also found in Plautus, *Men.* 449 *ubi* (i.e. *in contione*) *ego dum hieto, Menaechmus se subterduxit mihi.* Terence uses the synonymous *oscitare* only, *Andr.* 181 (vs. *interoscitantis* in K-L). *Restare* with the meaning of 'to remain where one is', 'stay put', occurs also in Plautus, *Most.* 851 *at etiam restas? est! abi istinc.* In Terence the verb has the sense of *reliquum esse* (*Andr.* 166, *Heaut.* 1066 etc.) or of *resistere, advorsari* (*Heaut.* 1009).

v. 273 ***si non sarciri quitur*** For *sarcire* in the sense of *reficere, reparare*, 'to mend/repair' see also Plaut. *Most.* 147, *Epid.* 455.

Adverbs

v. 9 ***vigiliis transactis duco desubito domum*** *Desubito* as equivalent to the simple *subito* is well attested in the *palliata*, cf. Plaut. *Bacch.* 79,

[88] For such a meaning of the word here, *ThLL* IV 669–70.

Capt. 62, *Most.* 411, *Stich.* 721; the *togata*, Afran. *tog.* 101, Titin. *tog.* 79; and the *atellana*, Pompon. *atel.* 102, 124, Nov. *atel.* 89. In Terence, the word is found with this meaning at *Heaut.* 673, in a scene where Terence once more deviates from his original, as is evidenced also by the distinct Roman military phraseology of the passage.[89]

v. 113 ***manete ilico!*** The use of the adverb *ilico* in a local sense in absolute function with no accompanying reinforcing adverbs denoting place, as here, is a rare usage, found in Plautus as well, *Bacch.* 1140, where we encounter a similar iunctura, namely *ilico ambae manete, Most.* 887a *manesne ilico, impure parasite.* In Terence the adverb is used in a local sense only with accompanying reinforcing local adverbs (normal CL usage), *Ad.* 156. Otherwise the adverb is used in Terence in a temporal sense as equivalent to *statim, confestim, sine mora*, either on its own or in correlation with temporal particles, *ubi* at *Ad.* 203, *Heaut.* 616, *postquam* at *Hec.* 367.

v. 175 ***publicitus defendendum est*** *Publicitus* is used here in the sense of 'publicly', 'as a public or state concern', as in Plautus as well, *Bacch.* 313, *Pers.* 509. Terence, on the other hand, does not use the unclassical *publicitus*[90] to denote 'publicly'. It is found once in Terentian drama at *Phorm.* 978, with the meaning, however, of 'at public expense'. The CL alternative *publice* in the sense of 'at public expense' appears for the first time in Cicero, *Ver.* 5. 90; therefore it seems probable that the use of *publicitus* for 'at public expense' by Terence should be attributed to the linguistic practice of his era. On the other hand, when there is an option between unclassical and classical formations, as is the case with *publicitus/publice* in the sense of 'publicly', both attested in the literature of the era, Terence opts for the one which becomes the CL equivalent.[91]

Style

Figurative uses

v. 1 ***oram reperire nullam qua expediar queo*** *Ora* is used here in a figurative sense, signifying the opening of a play. Such a figurative usage of *ora* in the sense of *initium*,[92] used literally for denoting the extremities of instruments, bodies, weapons, parts of lands etc., is also found in Plautus, *Mil.* 883 *postquam adbibere aures meae tuam oram orationis.* Terence always employs *initium, Hec.* 351, 821, *Andr.* 709 etc.

[89] For Terence's expanding on the Menandrian original here, cf. Brothers (1988: 206).
[90] Also found in Ennius, comedy, Gellius, Apuleius, Florus, Sidonius Apollinaris.
[91] For *publice* in the sense of 'publicly' in Terence, cf. Rosen (1999: 59, 61).
[92] Cf. also Festus 196 *usus est pro initio rei.*

v. 141 ***dum ego eius mortem inhio*** The figurative use of *inhio* in the sense of *nimis/avide cupere* is also found several times in Plautus, *Aul.* 194 *inhiat aurum ut devoret, Mil.* 715 *bona me inhiant*, 1199, *Stich.* 605. Terence, on the other hand, prefers synonymous expressions, e.g. *nimis cupere, vehementer desiderare* or *cupere, avidus esse* syntagms and other verbs denoting desire accompanied by reinforcing modifiers, *Ad.* 522, *Eun.* 938 etc.

v. 213 ***subfarcinatam vidi*** *Suffarcinatus* in the sense of 'person stuffed by padding out his clothes' appears also in Plautus, *Curc.* 289. This is an EL or archaising meaning; its distribution: comedy, Apuleius. At Cassiod. *Inst. div.* 28 the word has the meaning of 'to deck', 'to adorn', 'to enrich'. The word appears once in Terence's first play, at *Andr.* 770, as a possible archaism in a setting with an old person.

v. 241 ***quem in morbum inici*** *Morbus* used figuratively for *amor, libido* has its parallels in Plautus, *Cas.* 810 *illo morbo quo dirrumpi cupio, non est copiae, Cist.* 71, *Mil.* 1272. An instance of this usage in Terence appears at *Eun.* 225–6 *di boni, quid hoc morbist? adeon homines inmutarier ex amore ut non cognoscas eundem esse!*.

Expressions, schemes and combination of words

v. 71 ***habitabat in tuguriolo pauperculo*** (Rib.) This is an interesting feature of Latin, the redundant addition of diminutive suffixes to both nouns and their modifying adjectives, where the force of the diminutive adjective serves to strengthen the diminutive idea of the substantive. Such a usage is common in colloquial sources (e.g. comedy, Lucilius, Varro, Catullus, Auct. *B. Afr.*, Vitruvius, Martialis, Plinius Caecilius Secundus in the *Epistles*). In Cicero it occurs frequently in the colloquial style of his *Epistles*, e.g. *Att.* 16.11.1 *cerulas enim tuas miniatulas*.

This usage, common in Republican comedy but not in the contemporary higher genres (tragedy, epic), reappears later as an intentional archaism in deliberately archaising authors, such as Gellius, 2.29.8 *pulli . . . trepiduli*, 4.11.6 *porculis quoque minusculis* etc., Apuleius, *Met.* 1.11, *Grabatulus alioquin breviculus* etc. This usage is found in many comic writers of the *palliata* and the *togata*, in Plautus, *Cas.* 848 *papilla bellula, Cist.* 306 *muliercula exornatula, Poen.* 270, *Pseud.* 68, *Rud.* 1156. This is also the case with Titinius *tog.* 142 *togula obunctula*, Afranius *tog.* 224–5 *bacillum . . . corneolum*, 386–7 *inscitulam ancillullam*, Naevius *com.* ex inc. 7 *viridulo adolescentulo.* Terence once more stands outside the main comic tradition in avoiding this colloquial feature.

v. 109 ***ut te di omnes infelicent cum male monita memoria!*** This is an imprecation formula or curse, common elsewhere in Plautus, *Cas.* 246 *di me et te infelicent, Merc.* 436 *hercle illunc di infelicent, Rud.* 885 *di te infelicent!, Epid.* 13 *di immortales te infelicent, Poen.* 449

Di illum infelicent omnes, where *infelicere* is equivalent to *infelicem redere, perdere.* In Terence we find only the more common *di* + object + *perdant/perduint* imprecation formula, *Eun.* 431 *at te di perdant!, Hec.* 441, 469, *Phorm.* 123. See also *di tibi malefaciant* at *Phorm.* 394.

v. 145 ***sermonem serit*** This is a *figura etymologica* found in Plautus, *Curc.* 193 *mihi polluctus virgis servos sermonem serat?, Mil.* 700.

v. 159 ***consequitur comes insomnia*** Statistics have shown[93] that apart from alliterations of [p], which are equally common in both comic writers, Plautus has a penchant for alliterative combinations of [k], [m] and [l], whereas Terence opts more frequently for an [i] or [r] alliteration. Even though we possess only 300 lines from Caecilius, it is interesting that apart from the universally common alliterative combinations of [p],[94] the bulk of all other instances in the Caecilian corpus belong to the [k] or [m] group, the one favoured by Plautus. For [k], apart from here, *ibi consilium claudeat* v. 29, *cum Mercurio capit consilium* v. 3, *si confidentiam . . . confide omnia* v. 256; for [m] *in eadem mantat malitia* v. 84, *malum in mundost* v. 264, *cum male monita memoria* v. 109, *ita quod laetitia me mobilitat, maeror molitur metu* v. 182, *machinam commoliar* v. 197; and for [l] also *quae te lactat largitas* v. 80, *incessi omnibus laetitiis laetus* v. 254.[95]

Individual iuncturae

Several individual *iuncturae*, i.e. specific word combinations or collocations, also indicate a stylistic and linguistic affinity between Caecilius and Plautus rather than Terence. In particular:

nominal *iuncturae*: *cor/animus* in combination (Caec. *com.* 224, Plaut. *Capt.* 387, *Pseud.* 44, 321, 1272a, *Trin.* 650, *Truc.* 455), *ballista/catapulta* collocations (Caec. *com.* 24, Plaut. *Capt.* 796); *nil pecco* (Caec. *com.* 154, Plaut. *Pers.* 630); *rem paternam* (Caec. *com.* 38, Plaut. *Trin.* 13); *foedis factis*[96] (Caec. *com.* 227, Plaut. *Amph.* 1085[97]); the formulaic combination *aurum et vestem* (combinations of the two words by means of *et* vs. *atque/ac*, asyndeton (Caec. *com.* 100, *Curc.* 348, 435, 488); *imperitus rerum* (Caec. *com.* 239, Plaut. *Stich.* 104, Ter. *Andr.* 911, in a scene, however, where Terence introduced Pamphilus early, producing a scene with four

93 Cf. Oniga (1994; 117–34).

94 Cf. *percutias pavidum* v. 194, *petit potitur* v. 105, *plebem pergitur* v. 175, *prolato pede* v. 243, *percutias pavidum; postremo a parco patre* v. 194, *perdo populatim* vv. 124–5.

95 Cf. also Boscherini (1999: 114–15). For alliteration in Plautus, cf. also Baske (1834), Spencer (1906).

96 Cf. also Lee (1965: 954).

97 For *foedus* in the sense of *improbus, turpis, flagitiosus, inhonestus*, as in the Caecilian and Plautine collocation, cf. also Ter. *Eun.* 943.

speakers and transforming an exit monologue of Simo into a dialogue, 952–6[98]); the alliterative combination *laetus laetitia* (Caec. *com.* 254, Plaut. *Merc.* 844, *Pseud.* 1062); *venerius* + substantive combinations where *venerius* means 'of or related to love' (Caec. *com.* 243, Plaut. *Rud.* 624 etc.).

verbal *iuncturae*: *contra constat* (Caec. *com.* 44, Plaut. *Truc.* 538); *in corde vo(e)rsare* (Caec. *com.* 37, Plaut. *Trin.* 223); *male moneo* (Caec. *com.* 109, Plaut. *Pers.* 593, *Pseud.* 1305); *saltum obsaepire*, where *saltus* has the meaning of *vagina mulieris* (Caec. *com.* 60, Plaut. *Cas.* 922); *oppono pignori* (Caec. *com.* 101, Plaut. *Pseud.* 87 and Ter. *Phorm.* 661[99]); *domum advenio* (Caec. *com.* 153, Plaut. *Amph.* 654, 759, *Stich.* 422); *domum fugio* (Caec. *com.* 5, Plaut. *Epid.* 452, *Men.* 850); *diu vivere* (Caec. *com.* 169, Plaut. *Capt.* 792, *Trin.* 65, Naev. *com.* 38); *sonitum facere* (Caec. *com.* 18, Plaut. *Mil.* 1377); *tutelam gero* (Caec. *com.* 176, Plaut. *Trin.* 870, 1058, *Truc.* 254); the uncontracted *nihil ago* syntagm as opposed to equivalent contracted *nil ago* forms (*Ad.* 935) in the sense of *nihil proficio/consequor, irritus sum* (Caec. *com.* 62, Plaut. *Epid.* 112, *Merc.* 459); *savium dare* (Caec. *com.* 153–4, Plaut. *Asin.* 891[100]); *paulisper opperior* (Caec. *com.* 45, Plaut. *Aul.* 805, *Bacch.* 486).

adverbial *iuncturae*: *ubi . . . extemplo* (Caec. *com.* 153, Plaut. *Aul.* 613, *Capt.* 559, *Cist.* 121–2, *Epid.* 423–4[101]); pleonastic syntagms consisting of *hic* + *intus* + prepositional (*in/apud*) combinations denoting place (Caec. *com.* 36, Plaut. *Rud.* 689).

phrases: *mi(hi) hospes est* (Caec. *com.* 218, Plaut. *Poen.* 955); *quassanti capite incedere* (Caec. *com.* 266, Plaut. *Asin.* 403[102]); *in mundo malum* (Caec. *com.* 264 Plaut. *Asin.* 316); the address *mulier quisquis es* (Caec. *com.* 247, Plaut. *Cist.* 610); *decimo mense parere* (Caec. *com.* 157, Plaut. *Aul.* 798); *si linguas habeam decem . . .* (Caec. *com.* 121, Plaut. *Bacch.* 128); the expression *nisi mirum est* (Caec. *com.* 246, Plaut. *Pseud.* 1213); syntagms consisting of *age/age* + imperative + a form of address (Caec. *com.* 93 *age age i puere*, Plaut. *Pers.* 606–7 *age, age nunc tu, . . . vide*); phrases in which the same substantive is repeated in alliterative combinations modified by the adjective *alius* (Caec. *com.* 35 *cum suum sibi alius socius socium sauciat*, Plaut. *Men.* 961 *salvos salvos alios video, Epid.* 323–4 *per illam tibi copiam copiam parare aliam, Merc.* 101, *Most.* 648, *Poen.* 500, *Pseud.* 813, Pompon. *atel.* 114).

98 Cf. Lowe (1983: 41). 99 Cf. Lowe (1983: 41).

100 Here *savium* is used for an erotic kiss, in opposition to Terence *Eun.* 546, where the word is a term of endearment.

101 In Terence, on the other hand, only *quom . . . extemplo, postquam . . . extemplo* combinations occur.

102 For *quasso* = 'to shiver', 'to shake repeatedly', cf. also Naev. *com.* 101.

In addition, there are several other word collocations that Caecilius shares with comic poets such as Naevius, Afranius, Titinius etc. who are in the linguistic and stylistic line of Plautus rather than of Terence, *et homines et pecua* (Caec. *com.* 89, Naev. *com.* 56), *amatores habeo* (Caec. *com.* 129, Afran. *tog.* 379), *inibi esse* as equivalent to *in eo esse* (Caec. *com.* 179, Afran. *tog.* 208).

Conclusions

The present study has shown that Caecilius stands much closer to the traditional linguistic trend of the *palliata*, as exemplified by writers such as Naevius, Ennius, Turpilius, Plautus, than to the innovative Terence. The only similarities between Caecilius and Terence that are avoided in Plautus are the use of *postquam* with the pluperfect indicative in vv. 38–9 *si illi, postquam rem paternam amiserant, iactati forent*, found also in Terence, *Andr.* 177, *duriter* in the sense of *severe, stricte, crudeliter* (Caec. *com.* 40, Afran. *tog.* 251, Ter. *Ad.* 662), *singulatim* (Caec. *com.* 83, Ter. *Phorm.* 1032), *commoditas* in the sense of 'complaisance', 'obligingness' (Caec. *com.* 199, Ter. *Ad.* 710 vs. Plautus, where the word has the meaning of 'opportuneness', 'timeliness'), *difficilis* with the meaning of *durus non affabilis* (Caec. *com.* 191, Afran. *tog.* 252, Ter. *Heaut.* 535, 933), the *iuncturae ad restim reddere*, i.e. 'there is nothing for it but to die' (Caec. *com.* 205, Ter. *Phorm.* 686), *male audio* (Caec. *com.* 21, Ter. *Phorm.* 359).

Several EL features either on the morphological or the syntactical and lexical level, common in several comic dramatists, especially in Plautus, but avoided by Terence, are found in Caecilius' lines.

1. In several cases these features can be attributed simply to the historical development of Latin, as is the case with forms frequently found in comic dramatists before Caecilius (Ennius, Naevius, Plautus) but avoided after him or used as intentional archaisms only, e.g. the accusative and the ablative of the personal pronoun ending in *-d, med* in v. 8, or the EL form *eumpse* for *ipsum* in v. 26. In several cases these EL features are found in Terence as well, but used by him for stylistic effect and restricted to his archaising register, as proved by their position at the end of a line or a half line, their restriction to senile

speech etc. This seems to be the case, for example, with the vocative form *puere* in place of *puer* in v. 93 etc.

2. This is not always the case, however. Several features seem to have been used as intentional archaisms even by Plautus and other comic dramatists anterior to Caecilius, as is shown for example by their restriction to the end of the line and/or half line. This is the case, for example, with *danunt* in place of *dant* in v. 170. Such formations, already felt as archaic by Plautus, Caecilius etc., and used by them (and in many instances by later contemporary comic dramatists or those posterior to Terence as well) as archaisms, are avoided by Terence, who in contrast to these dramatists does not include these features in his archaising register.
3. Sometimes a feature already avoided by Plautus and replaced by a CL equivalent or restricted by him only to his archaising register appears in regular use in Caecilius. This is the case, for example, with the non-periphrastic forms of *nolo*, EL formations in *-tas* in place of CL *-tudo, -tia, -edo* equivalents etc. This is connected with the general archaising trend of Roman comedy, apparent not only in Caecilius, but also in Turpilius, Titinius, Afranius etc., but not in Terence, who regularly anticipates the CL usages. In these cases we are not dealing with features whose distribution is determined simply by the historical development of the language, since their absence from authors prior to Caecilius and their substitution by CL equivalents show that these formations had already begun to disappear in the language in Caecilius' time. In these cases, it seems that we have a conscious choice on the part of the author for the archaic or earlier equivalent, although it has already lost ground to the later equivalent.

Some colloquial options common in Plautus and other comic writers, but avoided in Terence, are also to be found in Caecilius' plays. This is the case for example with *subpilare* for *rapere* in v. 110, the redundant addition of diminutive suffixes to both noun and modifying adjective, in v. 71 *habitabat in tuguriolo pauperculo* etc. In contrast to several other comic dramatists, Terence chose not to include such features in his colloquial register.

Individual features on the morphological, syntactical and lexical level, especially unclassical formations or constructions etc. (EL/PC) with no particular colloquial and/or archaic or archaising character, point also to Caecilius' proximity to the comic tradition from which Terence stands aside. This is the case with equivalent morphological, syntactical and lexical alternatives. In such cases Caecilius opts for the one common in Plautus and the other comic dramatists and not for the Terentian equivalent. This is the case, for example, with the use of *quaeso* with *ne* + subjunctive dependent clause in v. 125 in place of a *ne* + imperative construction following the verb in direct speech, *mantare* for *manere* in v. 31, *gerrae* in place of *nugae, ineptiae* in v. 181 etc.

Certain other stylistic and lexical options, such as the use of specific word groups, figurative usages etc., common in Plautus and other comic dramatists but avoided in Terence, are again to be found in Caecilius, e.g. the *figura etymologica sermonem serit* in v. 145, the formulaic expression *quassante capite* in v. 266, the identification technique in vv. 34–5, the preference of Caecilius for alliterative combinations of [k], [m] etc.

Terence adopts linguistic or stylistic features having the sanction of both Caecilius and Plautus mainly in *Eunuchus* and in some other traditional scenes in other plays where, distancing himself from his original, he reworks his material in a more traditional line. This is the case for example with the appositional or epexegetic genitive in v. 246, the use of the present indicative in a deliberative question in v. 31, the interrogative combination *quid* + *tibi* + abstract verbal noun in *-tio* + *est* in vv. 57–8, etc. Only few linguistic features, while present in both Plautus and Caecilius, appear as *hapax* in Terentian drama and do not follow this distributional pattern (*Eunuchus* or Terentian scenes deviating from the original). See the *iuncturae in tenebris* (Caec. *com.* 36, Plaut. *Asin.* 768, *Pseud.* 981, Ter. *Hec.* 572), *nequiquam volo*, where *nequiquam* = 'in vain' (Caec. *com.* 227, Plaut. *Trin.* 440, 565, Ter. *Heaut.* 344).

Naevius

Naevius put on his first plays not long after those of Livius Andronicus, namely in AUC 519, which can be interpreted either as 235 BC or as 231 BC. We possess thirty titles and around 130 lines of his comedies.[103]

[103] G. D' Anna (1955: 301–10), favouring the second alternative. For Naevius' life and work, cf. also Frank (1927: 105–10), Hartman (1923: 152–3), Jocelyn (1969: 32–47), Kroll (1931: 469–72), Marmorale (1950: 15–181), Mattingly (1960: 414–39), Rowell (1949: 15–34), Sabbadini (1935: 7–34), Skutsch (1951: 174–7); for *Tarentilla* in particular, cf. Wright (1972: 239–42), Barchiesi (1978).

Naevius' comedies display a distinct Roman colour.[104] Several Roman or Italian allusions are to be found (e.g. reference to favourite Roman pork dishes, *com.* 104, Italian funeral mourners, *com.* ex inc. 11–12, jokes about Praeneste and Lanuvium, *com.* 22–6 etc). Furthermore, certain titles of his comedies are partly latinised in the Plautine way, namely by the addition of the Latin suffix *-aria*, possibly derived from Roman legal terminology:[105] *Corollaria, Carbonaria, Nervolaria, Testicularia, Tunicularia.*

Fraenkel (1935: 622–40) and Wright (1974: 33–59) have pointed out several individual similarities between Plautine and Naevian comic drama, especially on the stylistic level, e.g. the *iunctura arte colligor* in v. 8 alluding to *Epid.* 694 *arte colliga*, the formulaic imprecation *ut illum di perdant, qui primum holitor protulit caepam* in vv. 18–19, alluding to the possibly Plautine *ut illum di perdant, primus qui horas repperit* in *Boet.* fr. 1.1, the combination *at enim* at the beginning of a trochaic septenarius in v. 61 as in *Stich.* 129 etc.[106] The subject, however, needs to be examined further.

In this section, I shall examine in detail the language of Naevius' comic fragments. This will show that Naevius' language, on a purely linguistic level, is much closer to Plautus, Caecilius and Turpilius than to Terence. This linguistic affinity is evident not only in the frequent use of several EL features avoided in Terence or used by him only as intentional archaisms, a frequency which could simply be attributed to the historical development of Latin, but particularly in the use of several colloquial features common in many other comic writers but not included by Terence in his colloquial register. This affinity is also evident in the use of a series of overlapping linguistic binary options, with no particular EL or archaising and/or colloquial flavour on the morphological and syntactical or lexical level. The one avoided in Terence (mainly the unclassical equivalent) is, on the other hand, favoured in writers such as Caecilius, Ennius, Turpilius and Plautus. I shall also show

104 Cf. Albrecht (1997: 123).
105 Cf. Fraenkel (1935: 632). For titles in *-aria*, cf. also Beare (1930: 168).
106 For similarities between Naevius and Plautus, cf. also Duckworth (1952: 41–2).

that Terence is again closer to the language and style of both Plautus and Naevius in his most traditional play, *Eunuchus*.

The text used here is the most recent one, provided by Warmington in the Loeb Classical Library (1967). Ribbeck's edition *Scaenicae Romanorum Poesis Fragmenta* (1873), as well as the one by Marmorale (1950), have also been taken into account.

Morphology

Noun declension and composition

ex inc.v. 8 ***ea licet senile tractet retritum rutabulum?*** Substantives in *-bulum*, like *rutabulum* here, are favoured by comedy in contrast to high literary genres.[107] Whereas unclassical formations of this kind are avoided altogether in Terence, they are common in Plautine drama, *dentifragibulum, desidiabulum, exorabulum, mendicabulum, nucifrangibulum, prostibulum, sessibulum*, and are often found later in the colloquial or archaising register of PC Latin as well. Terence once more stands closer to CL usage.

ex inc. v. 20 ***pessimorum pessime audax ganeo lustro aleo!*** *Nomina personalia* in *-o, -onis*, such as *lustro, ganeo* here, are common in colloquial sources.[108] The early comic writers, the satirists, and Late Latin colloquial sources abound in formations of this kind. Their vulgar character even in this EL period is proved, as Wahrmann (1908: 78–9) points out, by their absence from tragic and epic scripts. In contrast again to Terence, who avoids such formations and restricts himself to those regularly used later in CL (*helluo, homincio, nebulo, verbero)*, we find in many other comic dramatists, especially in Plautus, a number of unclassical formations of this kind, e.g. in Plautus *bucco, calcitro, congerro, esurio, legirupio, pellio, phrygio, saturio, silo, sublingio, trico*, in Afranius *flagrio, tenebrio*, in Pomponius *baso, manduco, particulo*, in Laberius *adulterio, appeto*, in Caecilius *truo.* In Naevius we also find the colloquial formation *aleo* in *com.* ex inc. 20, attested also as a title of a comedy by Pomponius, namely *Aleones*, and later used as a term of abuse in Catullus, 29.2, 29.10 *es impudicus et vorax et aleo*.

The only formation of this kind in Terence, not sanctioned by classical speech, is *gerro* in the last act of *Heautontimoroumenos*, v. 1033.

ex inc. v. 22 ***risi egomet mecum cassabundum ire ebrium*** As Cooper has remarked (1895: 92–6), adjectives in *-bundus*, like *cassabundus* here, largely belong to the *sermo plebeius* of the earlier period,

[107] Cf. Cooper (1895: 89–91). [108] Cf. Cooper (1895: 53–8), Gaide (1988).

and reappear with some frequency as archaisms later, in archaising writers such as Livy, Apuleius, Gellius etc. Formations of this kind are common in Plautine drama, *deplorabundus, lixabundus, verberabundus*. A similar formation reappears also in the mimes of Laberius, *amorabundus*. Here again Terence anticipates later CL usage in avoiding unclassical formations of this kind.

Pronouns and adverbs

v. 91 ***domos patris patriam ut colatis potius quam peregri probra*** *Peregri* is the original locative form. An equivalent form *peregre* also exists, on the analogy of the normal adverb ending *-e*. Either form may mean 'abroad' or 'from abroad'. Attempts to distinguish between them seem illusory, in spite of Charisius' remark (GLK I 212 18ff.) *peregre cum abit quis dicimus in locum . . . peregri autem, cum in loco est*. The unclassical form *peregri*,[109] which is rarer than the equivalent *-e* form, is occasionally found in Plautus as well, e.g. *Amph.* 5. In Terence, on the other hand, we encounter only *peregre, Phorm.* 243 *peregre rediens*, 970 *ubi quae lubitum fuerit peregre feceris.*

Syntax

v. 27 ***tibi servi multi apud mensam astant; ille ipse astat quando edit***: The use *of quando* in a temporal clause with the achronic present, as here in *quando edit*, is a quite common construction in Plautine drama, avoided on the other hand completely by Terence, Plaut. *Amph.* 123 *vorsipellem se facit quando lubet*, 862, *Asin.* 289, 301, 323, *Men.* 78, 303, 926, *Stich.* 201, 217, *Trin.* 671, *Truc.* 241. A similar example is also found in Titinius, *tog.* 125 *quando fervit.* Temporal *quando* in general is mainly an EL or colloquial feature which reappears later in the colloquial and/or archaising register.[110]

Terence never uses temporal *quando*.[111] Temporal *quando* occurs in Plautus not only in achronic general expressions but also in several other constructions, with the real present indicative, with the present indicative referring to the future and with the imperfect, future, pluperfect or future perfect indicative.[112]

[109] Cf. also Prud. *Perist.* 4.89, Amm. 21.6.2, *Inst. Iust.* 2.14.12, CIL VII 5784. For confusion between expressions denoting spatial location and motion, cf. Önnerfors (1955: 148 – 64).

[110] Cf. H-Sz 607.

[111] Instances such as *Ad.* 206 could be explained as causal; for Terence's avoidance of this construction cf. also Bennett (1910–14: I 90–2), H-Sz 607.

[112] For an exhaustive list of Plautine examples, cf. Bennett (1910–14: I 90–2).

v. 72 ***utrubi cenaturi estis, hicine an in triclinio?*** *Ceno* with a complement denoting place occurs also in Plautus, *Amph.* 732, *Capt.* 481, *Rud.* 1417, 1423, *Truc.* 359, 360 etc., Pompon. *atel.* 85. This construction does not appear in Terence, where *ceno* is either construed with a *cum quo* complement (*Eun.* 936) or is found in an absolute use (*Andr.* 89). As for *utrubi* introducing an indirect question, 'in which of two places?', see Plaut. *Stich.* 696, 750. This usage, absent from Terence, is an EL and archaising one (its distribution: Plautus, Cato, Ausonius, legal documents). At Cic. *Att.* 15.22 *utrubi* is simply a conjecture and has the meaning of 'on which side (of a conflict)?'.

v. 79 ***cum alio cantat*** *Cantare* = *canere*, in an absolute use as here, appears in Plautus as well, *Epid.* 316 *cantaret sibi*. In Terence the verb occurs in an absolute use at *Eun.* 442–3 *Pamphilam cantatum provocemus*. Elsewhere the verb in this sense is found in transitive usage with an accusative direct object, *Ad.* 905. In a figurative sense, *cano* occurs at *Heaut.* 260.

ex inc. v. 8 ***ea licet senile tractet retritum rutabulum?*** *Licet* is construed here with the subjunctive, as at Plaut. *Asin.* 718 *licet laudem Fortunam*, *Capt.* 303, *Merc.* 989, *Most.* 713, Caec. *com.* 47 *de via liceat legant*.[113] In Terence the construction appears once, at *Phorm.* 347 *postilla iam ut lubet ludas licet*, that is, in the last line of the scene preceding the one with the *advocati*, which, as Lefèvre (1978: 15–20) has convincingly demonstrated, is a Terentian innovation. At this point, the adoption by Terence of a linguistic feature common in the *palliata* but elsewhere avoided in his drama may also have a stylistic effect, in marking the transition from a scene found in the original to one he invents. Elsewhere in Terence *licet* is found in an absolute use, *Andr.* 805, or is construed with the neuter of a pronoun, *Eun.* 639, *per* + accusative syntagms, *Ad.* 108 (vs. *decet* K-L), the infinitive, *Hec.* 94, dative + infinitive syntagms, *Eun.* 35–6, or a.c.i. constructions, *Heaut.* 401.

Lexicon

Nouns and adjectives

v. 42 ***rivalis, salve*** *Rivalis* with the meaning of *aemulus* appears also at Plaut. *Bacch.* 1210, *Stich.* 434. In Terence this usage is restricted significantly to *Eunuchus*, vv. 268, 354, 1072.

v. 46 ***nimis homo formidulosus*** *Formidolosus* here has the meaning of *timidus, qui formidat*.[114] This is a meaning also found in Terence,

[113] For *licet* constructions in Plautus, cf. Hahn (1948: 316–27).

[114] Cf. also Gloss. φοβερός, δειλός, *timidus, pavidus, vel timens.*

significantly in *Eunuchus* only, v. 756 *num formidulosus obsecro es, mi homo?*, 757. Otherwise Terence uses synonymous expressions, e.g. *timidus* at *Hec.* 365–6 *nam modo intro me ut corripui timidus, alio suspicans morbo me visurum adfectam ac sensi esse uxorem.*[115] *Formidolosus* is found in Plautus as well, where the word is used in its active sense, *qui (quod) formidatur, terribilis*, Plaut. *Amph.* 1117 *nimis formidolosum facinus praedicas, Pseud.* 824.

v. 89 ***nec nimis erit morigera*** *Morigerus* in the sense of *morem gerens, obsequens* appears several times in Plautus as well, *Cist.* 84, 175, *Curc.* 169, *Epid.* 607, *Men.* 202, *Most.* 398, *Pseud.* 208. In Terence the word appears once at *Andr.* 294. The word, *hapax* in Terence, is found again in a scene where Terence deviates from his original by keeping Mysis on stage from the previous scene.[116]

v. 102 ***eius noctem nauco ducere*** In contrast to Terence, *naucum* occurs several times in Plautine drama for denoting a person or thing of small or no value, *Bacch.* 1102, *Truc.* 611, Enn. *com.* 428, Afran. *tog.* 431.

v. 131 (Rib.) ***butubatta*** Paulus Festus remarks (32) *buttubatta Naevius pro nugatoriis posuit, hoc est, nullius dignationis.* According to the testimony of GLK I 242. 10, the word was used in this sense by Plautus as well, *hoc Plautus pro nihilo et pro nugis posuit.*

ex inc. v. 1 ***res magnas manu . . . gessit*** *Manus* is used in the sense of *pugna militaris, vis, robur*, as in Plautus, *Truc.* 532 *<earum>patriam ego excidi manu.* In Terence the word does not occur with such a meaning. It is either used *proprie*, i.e. 'hand' (*Heaut.* 565 etc.), or in several *iuncturae, adeo manum = decipere* (*Heaut.* 818, Be. Fl.[2]. Ty), *ad manum* denoting direction (*Ad.* 576), *manibus pedibus = omni conatu* (*Andr.* 161, 676), *in manu (mihi/mea) est = in mea potestate est* (*Hec.* 493, 666), *prae manu do* = advance in someone's hand (*Ad.* 980). In some of the *iuncturae*, *manus* is often used as a legal term or in legal contexts (also *Andr.* 297 *in manum do* referring to a marriage, *Phorm.* 830 *emitto manu*, i.e. *manu mitti, Ad.* 194 *adsero manu* etc.).

ex inc. v. 18 ***et qui fuerit persibus*** Festus (453) remarks *sibus callidus vel acutus. Sibus* is also found once in Plautus, fr. 138 *nil deconciliare sibu's nisi qui persibus sapis.* In Terence, on the other hand, we find only synonymous words such as *callidus*.

ex inc. v. 19 ***appluda est hodie . . . nequior!*** *Nequam* in the sense of 'having no value', 'bad', 'useless' occurs also in Plautus, *Asin.* 178 *quasi piscis itidemst amator lenae: nequam est nisi recens.* In Terence *nequam* occurs with the meaning of 'morally worthless', 'depraved', 'scoundrel' (*Ad.* 528).[117]

[115] Cf. also Donat. ad loc. *pro timens.*
[116] Cf. Rambelli (1936: 130–60), Denzler (1968: 45–51).
[117] For this semantic categorisation, cf. *OLD* s.v. 1, 2.

Verbs

v. 50 ***animae pauxillulum in me habet*** *Habeo* is used here in the sense of *habito*, a usage which also occurs once more in v. 80 *ubi isti habent.* The verb occurs in this sense in Plautus as well, *Aul.* 5 *hic habet, Cas.* 749, *Trin.* 193, *Trin.* 390, *Truc.* 246. The verb has a similar usage in Afranius as well, *tog.* 136 *ubi hice Moschis . . . habet.* In Terence, on the other hand, we find only the common *habitare* in this sense, *Eun.* 107, 321, *Phorm.* 306, 934, *Hec.* 224, 589, *Ad.* 647, 654.

v. 61 ***tu nimis spisse atque tarde incedis*** *Incedo* is used here in the sense of *cedere, ambulare.* See also Andr. *com.* 3 *ornamento incedunt gnobilid ignobiles*, Plaut. *Amph.* 330, *Mil.* 872 *quam digne ornata incedit,* 1286, *Truc.* 463 etc., Caec. *com.* 266 *tristes incedunt*, 254. The verb also appears once in Terence at *Eun.* 918–19 *Parmenonem incedere video*, where it is equivalent to *accedere, venire, apparere.* At *Andr.* 730 it occurs in a figurative sense, construed with an *in* + accusative complement (EL and archaising usage, cf. *ThLL* VIII_1 857).

v. 75 ***datatim dat se et communem facit*** *Se dare* with erotic connotations, as here, appears also in Plautus, *Pseud.* 1277a, *idem amicae dabam me meae*, Trabea *com.* 5 *mihi se dedet*, Ter. *Eun.* 515–16 *ipsa accumbere mecum, mihi sese dare, sermonem quaerere*, 793. This is an unclassical usage. Elsewhere in Terence the verb has the sense of a simple *se praebere, praestare, exhibere, Hec.* 380, or, when construed with the dative, it has the meaning of *inserire alicui, se tradere alicui, Heaut.* 688, with no erotic flavour.

v. 81 ***patria peregre prodigunt?*** For *prodigere* in the sense of *perdere, dissipare, comedere*, 'waste', 'squander', Plaut. *Aul.* 380, Pompon. *atel.* 162.

ex inc. v. 2 ***cuius facta viva nunc vigent*** For *vigere* figuratively used for 'to thrive', 'flourish', see also Plaut. *Curc.* 299 *nam ita nunc mos viget.*

ex inc. v. 8 ***ea licet senile tractet retritum rutabulum?*** *Tracto* with the meaning of 'to subject to the action of hands', 'handle', occurs also in Plaut. *Trin.* 1005 *nisi qui illud (sc. tintinnabulum) tractat aut movet.* In Terence the verb occurs with the meaning 'to deal with a person', 'treat in a given matter' (*Heaut.* 101, 153, 366), 'to treat a subject or matter' (*Eun.* 924), 'to carry out,' 'practice', 'perform' (*Phorm.* 17).

ex inc. v. 26 ***linquis faveant atque adnutent, aut subserviant*** *Subservio* in the sense of 'to behave as a servant to' occurs also in Plautus, *Men.* 766–7 *quae viros supservire sibi postulant.* This is an EL and archaising usage (Plautus, Fronto, Apuleius). In Terence this unclassical formation does not appear. The verb is used in the transferred sense of 'to lend support to' (*Andr.* 735).

Adverbs

v. 1 ***Acontizomenos fabula est prime bona*** *Prime* has here the function of a reinforcing particle, with the sense *maxime, optime*. This function of the word is also found in Plautus, *Mil.* 794 *est prime cata.* In Terence, on the other hand, such an unclassical (EL and PC) reinforcing function of the word is not to be found. In his comedies we find instead synonymous reinforcing combinations, e.g. *maxume* syntagms, *Andr.* 835, *Heaut.* 393 etc.

vv. 37–8 ***nolo ego hanc adeo efflictim amare*** *Efflictim* is used here in the sense of *vehementer, impense*. This meaning of the adverb with reference to love (*de amore venerio*), absent from Terentian drama, appears in Plautus as well, *Amph.* 516–17 *numquam edepol quemquam mortalem credo ego uxorem suam sic ecflictim amare, Cas.* 49, Pompon. *atel.* 42, Laber. *mim.* 25. Terence again anticipates here later CL usage in avoiding this EL or archaising formation, which occurs later in Apuleius (*Apol.* 79, 100, *Met.* 1.8 etc.).

v. 42 ***attatae!*** This form of the interjection appears also in Plaut. *Cas.* 468, *Epid.* 457, *Merc.* 365. In Terence we find only the equivalent *attat* form, *Hec.* 449, *Eun.* 756, *Phorm.* 600.

v. 48 ***confestim*** *Confestim*, a synonym for *continuo, statim, sine mora*, appears in Plautus, *Merc.* 68 *rus rusum confestim exigi solitum a patre*.

v. 49 ***animae pauxillulum in me habet*** The double diminutive form *pauxillulum*[118] appears also at Plaut. *Poen.* 538, *Truc.* 940. In Terence it occurs at *Phorm.* 37, possibly with a stylistic effect as a colloquialism in the speech of the slave Davus. The form in the sense of *parvula quantitate*, eschewed by the purism of CL speech, occurs, apart from comedy, only in Hier. *epist.* 49.14.11[119] and other Late Latin Christian authors: *vita Hilar.* 25.9; Salv. *gub.* 1.15 (late fifth century). At Oros. *hist.* 4.12.13 there is also an alternative reading *paus-* for *paux-*.

ex inc. vv. 4–5 ***nunc primulum amasco*** The EL diminutive adverbial formation *primulum* occurs also in Plautus, *Men.* 916, fr. 82. It is attested also in Terence at *Ad.* 289, 898, in both instances in the mouth of old people (Canthara, Demea respectively), possibly as an intentional archaism.

ex inc. vv. 13–14 ***quid si taceat? Dum videat, tam sciat . . . quid scriptum sit*** *Tam* is used here in the sense of *tamen*, a usage common in Plautus, *Bacch.* 1193–4 *non tibi venit in mentem, amabo, si dum vivas tibi bene facias tam pol id quidem esse hau perlonginquom* ('my dear man, doesn't it occur to you that, supposing you do enjoy yourself all your life, this life is short after all'), *Merc.* 32ff., *Men.* 387. A similar usage

118 For double diminutive forms as a feature of colloquial speech, cf. Cooper (1895: 164–95 passim).

119 Var. ll. *pauxillum, paululum, pusillum.*

occurs also in Titinius, *tog.* 169 *bene cum facimus, tam male sapimus, ut quidem perhibent viri.* In Terence, at *Ad.* 278–9, Sy: *eamus; namque hic properat in Cyprum.* Sa: *ne tam quidem quam vis*, *tam* seems to be equivalent to *tantum* rather than to *tamen.*[120]

Style

ex inc. v. 30 a-c ***Cocus edit Neptunum Cererem et Venerem expertam Vulcanom Liberumque absorbuit pariter*** In this verse the names of gods are used as a metonymy for the things with which they are associated. In Plautus, such metonymic uses of the names of gods, especially that of *Liber*, are common enough (*Cas.* 640, *Cist.* 127 etc.). The only instance in Terence occurs in *Eunuchus*, v. 732 *sine Cerere et Libero friget Venus*, where *Liber* is used by metonymy as for *vinum* (otherwise the normal equivalent in Terence, *Hec.* 823, *Heaut.* 458 etc.) and *Ceres* for *panis.*

Individual iuncturae

Several word combinations point also to the linguistic and stylistic similarity between Plautine and Naevian drama. In particular:

nominal *iuncturae*: the *qui primus* formula (Naev. *com.* 18–19 *ut illum di perdant qui primum* . . . , Plaut. *Men.* 451, Aquil. *com.* 1); *libera lingua* (Naev. *com.* ex inc. 27, Plaut. *Cist.* 128, *Pers.* 280a); *deus propitius* (Naev. *com.* 68, Plaut. *Amph.* 1090, Ter. *Phorm.* 636 in a scene with four speakers[121]); *decuma pars* with reference to a sacrifice to the gods (Naev. *com.* 29, Plaut. *Bacch.* 666, *Stich.* 233); *amoris causa* (Naev. *com.* 95, Plaut. *Aul.* 750, *Cas.* 994, *Mil.* 1286, Turpil. *com.* 114, Ter. *Eun.* 878); *perna* and *callus* combinations (Naev. *com.* 104, Plaut. *Pseud.* 166), *admodum adulescentulus* (Naev. *com.* 28, Plaut. *Trin.* 366).

verbal *iuncturae*: *potiorem habeo* (Naev. *com.* 6, Plaut. *Stich.* 97); *laudes agere* (Naev. *com.* 34, Plaut. *Trin.* 821; in Terence only *laudo)*; *ludere datatim* (Naev. *com.* 75, Plaut. *Curc.* 296, Nov. *atel.* 22); *mutuum sumere* (Naev. *com.* 95, Plaut. *Amph.* 819).

adverbial *iuncturae*: *si* . . . *extemplo* combinations (Naev. *com.* 94–6, Plaut. *Amph.* 207. *Bacch.* 440–1, 710–11, *Capt.* 122, *Cist.* 96, *Mil.* 889–90, *Rud.* 815–16); *in proclivi* in the sense of 'on the down slope' (Naev. *com.* 26, Plaut. *Asin.* 710 vs. Ter. *Andr.* 701, where the syntagm has the meaning of 'requiring little effort', *facile*).

[120] Cf. H-Sz 495. [121] Cf. also Lowe (1983b: 431).

phrases: *quasi dedita opera* (Naev. *com.* 9, Plaut. *Cist.* 669–70, Ter. *Eun.* 841, for *dedita opera = consulto, de industria*, Afran. *com.* 373, Pompon. *atel.* 142), collocations of *pater, patria* (Naev. *com.* 91 *domos patris patriam ut colatis*, Plaut. *Capt.* 43, *Men.* 1083); *meus homo est* formula (Naev. *com.* 68 *deo meo propitio meus homo est*, Plaut. *Mil.* 334 *meus illic homo est, Pseud.* 381, 1124); combinations of *hercle* + an *opinor* parenthetic clause with the verb of the main clause following the *opinor* parenthesis (Naev. *com.* ex inc. 11. *mehercle, opino praefica est*, Plaut. *Rud.* 999, *Trin.* 869); *protinam se dare* (Naev. *com.* 36, Plaut. *Curc.* 363); *cave (ne) cadas* (Naev. *com.* 85, Plaut. *Most.* 324; see also *cave ne cadam, Pseud.* 1296).

alliterative combinations: alliterative collocations of *ludus* with words beginning with [l] (Naev. *com.* ex inc. 27 *libera lingua loquemur ludis Liberalibus*, Plaut. *Asin.* 13 *lepos ludusque, Bacch.* 129, *Capt.* 770, *Merc.* 846, Ter. *Eun.* 586–7 *quia consimilem luserat iam olim ille ludum*).

Conclusions

On the purely linguistic level, Naevius' language is much closer to that of Plautus and of the comic poets in his line (Caecilius, Turpilius etc.) than to that of the innovative Terence. In particular:

1. Several EL features found in Naevius, Plautus and Caecilius are avoided in Terentian drama. This is the case for example with the final *-d* after a final long *-e, med* in v. 10 etc. Such EL features, however, seem, up to a point, to be due simply to the historical development of Latin.
2. There are however several other features which require a specific choice on the part of a comic playwright; these features show that, in opposition to Terence, other comic dramatists, Caecilius, Turpilius, Plautus prefer the options made by Naevius and not those made by Terence. This is the case with (a) several colloquial options common in comic dramatists with the exception of Terence again, e.g. the colloquial use of temporal *quando* in v. 27 etc.; (b) several other linguistic options of Naevius, without any particular EL or archaising and/or colloquial character on the morphological or syntactical and lexical level (often of an unclassical character) are common in Plautus and/or in the comic writers in his line, but not in Terence, who chooses once more to stand apart, e.g. *prime* as a reinforcing particle with the meaning of *maxume* in v. 1, the use of *habere* in place of *habitare* in vv. 50 and 86, *tam* in the sense of *tamen* in *com.* ex inc. vv. 3–4 etc.; (c)

what is more, some stylistic options also point to a similarity between the drama of Naevius and that of Plautus, Caecilius, Turpilius etc., e.g. the redundant addition of diminutive suffixes to both noun and its modifying adjective, *viridulus adulescentulus* in *com.* ex inc. v. 7, the identification technique in *com.* ex inc. v. 11, etc.

Terence approximates to the Naevian linguistic tradition, as well as the Plautine, Caecilian and possibly Turpilian linguistic patterns, in his most traditional play, *Eunuchus.* In this play Terence prefers in certain instances the alternative option, found in Naevius and in other comic dramatists as well, and not the equivalent linguistic choice adopted by him in his other plays. This is the case for example with *formidulosus* in place of *timidus* in v. 46, the metonymic use of gods for foods in *com.* ex inc. v. 30 a–c etc.

The rest of the *palliata*

As for the remaining comic dramatists of the *palliata*, we may observe the following: the surviving lines from these plays are too scanty to allow any certain conclusions; from Livius Andronicus we possess only eight lines and half-lines, from Trabea six lines, from Atilius four lines and half-lines, from Juventius ten lines and half-lines, from Ennius eleven lines and half-lines, from Aquilius[122] ten lines and from Licinius Imbrex[123] and Luscius Lanuvinus only two lines.[124] In the few lines of these comic dramatists, especially those of Livius Andronicus, Ennius and Juventius, we still encounter, however, several linguistic peculiarities that, despite their frequency in Plautus and the authors in his linguistic line, are avoided again in Terence, with the exception once more of *Eunuchus*.

A remark on the text: for both Livius Andronicus and Ennius I use the most recent text, provided by Warmington (1967), in the Loeb Classical Library. Ribbeck's edition (1873) has also been taken into account. For the rest of the comic dramatists I have used only Ribbeck, since no more recent edition exists.

[122] For whether *Boeotia* should be ascribed to Aquilius or Plautus, cf. Wright (1974: 80–5).

[123] For Licinius Imbrex, cf. Diel (1926: 371).

[124] For Luscius Lanuvius, cf. Garton (1971: 17–37), Paratore (1959: 44–63).

Livius Andronicus[125]

Apart from the close affinity between the only extant fragment of Livius' *Gladiolus, pulices an cimices an pedes;?* and Plautus' *Curc.* 500 *ut muscae, culices, cimices pedesque pulicesque*,[126] I should add the following features.[127]

Lexicon

Nouns and adjectives

v. 3 ***ornamento***[128] ***incedunt gnobilid ignobiles*** According to Festus (182),[129] *nobilis* is used here in place of *notus*. This is quite a rare usage, which has, however, its parallels in Plautus, *Pseud.* 1111–12 *nec sermo convenit neque is [umquam] nobilis fui*,[130] the impersonal *nobile est* + a.c.i. construction in the sense of 'it is well known that' at *Trin.* 828–9 *nobilest apud homines pauperibus te parcere solitum. Nobilis* has in Terence only the regular meaning 'of a higher rank', *Heaut.* 227, 609, *Eun.* 204, 952, *Ad.* 15.[131] Similarly, *ignobilis* can be used in Plautus as a synonymous for *ignotus*, e.g. *Pseud.* 592. In Terence, on the other hand, *ignobilis* means only 'not of high rank', 'of no family', *Phorm.* 120 *ille indotatam virginem atque ignobilem*.[132] The verb *nobilito* is similarly used in the sense of 'to announce', 'to make something known', in Titinius, *tog.* 75 *magis quae famae obiectarent, ne eam malefactis nobilitarent* and once in Terence's *Eun.* 1021–2 *qui stultum adulescentulum nobilitas flagitiis.*

v. 5 ***vecorde et malefica vacerra*** *Maleficus* in the sense of *nefarius, sceleratus, improbus* as here[133] has its parallels in Plautus, *Bacch.* 279–80 *lembum conspicor longum, strigorem maleficum exornarier, Cas.* 783 *mores maleficos.* The word occurs also as a substantive with the same meaning in Plautine drama, *Trin.* 551.

[125] For the chronology of Livius Andronicus, cf. Mattingly (1957: 159–63), Marconi (1966: 125–213), Wright (1974: 15). Cf. also Warnecke (1925: 232–4).

[126] Cf. Wright (1974: 17).

[127] For this line, cf. also Fraenkel (1927: 357–70).

[128] For a discussion of *ornamentum*, cf. Wright (1974: 20–21).

[129] Cf. also Wright (1974: 21).

[130] Cf. also Arias Abellán (1991: 131), Woytek (1972: 254–6).

[131] For *notus*, on the other hand, cf. *Phorm.* 98.

[132] For *ignotus*, on the other hand, cf. *Phorm.* 751.

[133] Cf. *ThLL* VIII 176.

Adverbs

v. 4 ***adfatim edi*** This adverb, which has the sense of 'sufficiently,' 'enough,' 'amply' (*abunde, largiter, impense*), appears in Plautus as well, *Men.* 91, *Poen.* 867.

Style

v. 6 ***lepus tute es; et pulpamentum quaeris!***[134] This same line, which exhibits the so-called identification technique, common in Plautine drama, is also found in Terence, significantly in *Eunuchus* only, v. 426 *lepus tute' s, pulpamentum quaeris?*. A further instance of the identification technique occurs also in the only extant fragment of Licinius Imbrex, *nolo ego Neaeram te vocent, sed Nerienem, cum quidem Mavorti es in conubium data.*[135]

Ennius

For Ennius, I have already observed the use of the formulaic expression *nauci* denoting small value in v. 428 *illic est nugator nil, non nauci homo*, common in all comic dramatists with the exception of Terence again. One could further add:

Syntax

v. 384 ***cum desubito me orat mulier lacrimansque ad genua accidit*** This is one of the quite rare usages of the so-called *cum inversum* in EL. This usage is also found in Plautus, *Aul.* 520–1 *iam apsolutos censeas, quom incedunt, Men.* 1053–4 *tu clamabas . . . quom ego accurro.* In Terence it is found only once, significantly in the *Eunuchus*, v. 633–4 *longe iam abieram quom sensi.*

Lexicon

v. 430 ***an aliquid quod illi dono moraret?*** *Moro* in place of *moror* is also found in Naevius, *com.* 66, and reappears later in PC Latin.[136]

[134] As for whether the line should be attributed to Livius Andronicus, cf. Fraenkel (1931: 603), Wright (1974: 25–7, especially 25 n. 25). Hohl (1920: 306 n. 1) thinks that Terence wrote the line.

[135] Cf. Fraenkel (1960: 29–30), Wright (1974: 73–5).

[136] Cf. Itala *Gen.* 4.4, Rufin. *Clement.* 1.72, Stephan. 1 p. 37^{D}.

Juventius[137]

As for Iuventius, despite the fact that only five lines from his work have survived, we still find several linguistic options that, while having the sanction of Plautus, Titinius etc., are avoided by Terence.

I have already pointed out, in previous chapters, the use of the colloquial formulaic combination *flocci facere* in vv. 5–6 *pallium non facio flocci ut splendat*, common in all comic dramatists but restricted in Terentian drama, significantly, to *Eunuchus*. See also the unclassical adverbial formation *testatim* in *caput ei testatim diffregero* (v. 7), found also in Pomponius, *atel.* 178.[138] One should add the following:

Syntax

v. 1 ***quod potes, sile cela occulta tege tace mussa mane*** The construction of *celare* in the sense of *occultare* with a relative clause as its complement, and not its regular accusative complement, is a rare EL and PC syntagm which, however, has its parallels in Plautine drama, *Rud.* 1244–5 *ut quod ad me adlatum esse alienum sciam celem?*, *Bacch.* 403. As for *potare* in a transitive use as here, Plaut. *Men.* 90, 915, 950, *Rud.* 587, Caec. *com.* 155. In Terence the verb always occurs in intransitive use (*Ad.* 62).

Lexicon

Nouns and adjectives

v. 10 ***scrupipeda*** According to the *OLD* (s.v.), the word is a term of abuse applied to women, of uncertain form and sense, perhaps 'having ankles that stick out like sharp rocks'. This term of abuse is found once in Plautine drama, fr. 97 *scrattae, scruppedae, strittabillae, sordidae.*

Verbs

v. 1 ***sile cela occulta tege tace mussa mane*** *Mussare* for *murmurare* also occurs in Plautus, *Merc.* 49. More common is the frequentative *mussitare*, with the value of a simple *mussare*, also found in Plautus, *Mil.* 311, *Rud.* 1029, *Truc.* 723. In Terence the word appears only once, at *Ad.* 207 *accipiunda et mussitanda iniuria adulescentiumst*,

[137] For Iuventius, cf. Diel (1919: 1362). [138] Cf. Wright (1974: 77).

in a scene, however, where several other traditional linguistic features, common in the *palliata*, occur in concentration. From the point of view of style, the asyndetic accumulation of seven imperatives is a Plautine mannerism. Such long asyndetic lists are avoided in Terence, with the exception of *Eunuchus* again. As for *silere* in the sense of 'to make no sound', 'to be silent', see also *Poen.* 3 *sileteque et tacete atque animum advortite.* In Terence the verb is construed with a *de* complement in the sense 'to say nothing about', 'to omit mention of' (*Phorm.* 778).

v. 7 ***caput ei testatim diffregero*** *Diffringere* denoting to 'break up, apart', 'to shatter' also occurs in Plautus, *Asin.* 474, *Mil.* 156, 722, *Stich.* 191. Similarly Titin. *tog.* 33 *caput diffringam*, Nov. *atel.* 50 *digitos . . . diffregi meos.* In similar contexts Terence uses the synonymous verb *dim(m)inuo, Eun.* 803, in a threat similar to that found in Iuventius, *diminuam ego caput tuum hodie, Ad.* 571 *dimminuetur tibi quidem iam cerebrum.*

Iuncturae

v. 3 ***in unum locum*** A similar *iunctura* appears at Plaut. *Epid.* 527.

Trabea, Aquilius and Atilius

The evidence for these playwrights is too scanty for us to reach any conclusions concerning their language and style. The following data are adduced here nevertheless, for the sake of completeness.

Trabea[139]

Apart from the use of the verb *se dare* with erotic connotations in v. 5, common in Plautus and restricted in Terence to *Eunuchus*, in the case of Trabea I may also point out the following.

1. *delenire* in v. 1 *lena delenita argento* in the sense of *mitigare, mulcere, pellicere, sedare, placare.* This usage is common in Plautine drama, *Amph.* 844, *Asin.* 434, *Cist.* 517, *Stich.* 457. It also occurs once in Titinius, *tog.* 69 *dotibus deleniti.*
2. *iuncturae*: *Fores patere* (Trabea *com.* 3, Plaut. *Stich.* 309, Ter. *Eun.* 89, 282), *obviam venire* (*Trabea com.* 4, Plaut. *Merc.* 219, *Poen.* 1288, *Rud.* 206a, 308, Ter. *Eun.* 843).

[139] Cf. Kroll (1937: 1862).

The only linguistic feature common to Terence and Trabea but absent from Plautus is the use of *de improviso* for *ex improviso, improviso* in the sense of *subito, inopinato, repente*, Trabea *com.* 3, Ter. *Andr.* 360, 417, *Ad.* 407. *De improviso* appears for the first time in Trabea. Previously only *ex improviso, improviso* are found.

Aquilius[140]

Apart from the *qui primus* . . . formula in v. 1, found also in Plautus and Naevius but avoided in Terence, in the case of Aquilius I may also add the following.

Morphology

The passive form *estur* (v. 7) from *edo* is rare in CL (only in Ov. *Pont.* 1.1.69) and becomes more common in PC Latin (Celsus, Seneca, Pliny, Apuleius). This form is not attested in Terence. On the other hand, instances of passive forms of the verb appear in Plautus, *Mil.* 24, *Poen.* 835.

Lexicon

1. *comminuo* with the meaning of *rumpere, frangere* in v. 3 *qui mihi comminuit misero articulatim diem.* See also Plaut. *Bacch.* 1119, *Men.* 856, *Rud.* 1118.
2. *oppleo* in the sense of *magna copia instruo*, 'to endow or supply abundantly', 'cram with' in v. 8 *oppletum oppidumst solariis* is found in Plautus, *Aul.* 675. In Terence the verb is used in the sense of 'to overspread a surface', *Heaut.* 306 *lacrumis opplet os totum sibi.*
3. *iuncturae*: *Maior pars* + genitive partitive combinations (Aquil. *com.* 9, Plaut. *Poen.* 1285).

Atilius[141]

At v. 4 of Atilius *caedere* is found in an absolute use, without the instrumental ablative, as equivalent to *verberare, ferire, vulnerare.* See also Plaut. *Amph.* 160, *Cas.* 528, Ter. *Eun.* 783. Apart from *Eun.* 787, elsewhere in Terence the verb is construed with the ablative of means, *Andr.* 199, which is the common Ciceronian

[140] Cf. Wissowa (1895: 323).

[141] Cf. Marx (1896: 2076), Wright (1974: 70–3).

construction or it is used figuratively in the proverbial expression *dum sermones caedimus* (*Heaut.* 242), as equivalent to κόπτειν τὰ ῥήματα, *disserere*.

Final conclusion

The present study has shown that there exists a certain linguistic and stylistic unity within the Roman *palliata*, from which Terence regularly stands aside, anticipating later CL usage. As I have pointed out in chapter 7, Terence tends to assimilate common Plautine linguistic techniques mainly in *Eunuchus*, and occasionally in other plays, in a couple of scenes, where there is evidence that he deviates from his original. The present study has shown that Terence chooses to incorporate in such scenes, as well as in his *Eunuchus*, several other traditional linguistic peculiarities, elsewhere avoided in his comedies but commonly found in authors like Caecilius, Ennius, Naevius, Livius Andronicus and Turpilius, who demonstrably follow the linguistic trend of Plautus.

CHAPTER 9

TERENCE, PLAUTUS AND THE *TOGATA*

Afranius

Afranius flourished during the second half of the second century BC. Velleius Paterculus dates him in the time of Scipio Aemilianus, Laelius, M. Antonius and L. Crassus, 2.9.3 *clara etiam per idem aevi spatium (quo fuerunt Scipio Aemilianus, Laelius, M. Antonius, L. Crassus aliique oratores excellentes) fuere ingenia, in togatis Afranii, in tragoediis Pacuvii atque Acci*, and Cicero in *Brut.* 167[1] remarks that Afranius tried to imitate the orator C. Titius, who flourished in the last third of the second century BC.[2]

It is indeed true that in the extant lines of Afranius' work (we possess 43 titles and 300 fragments) we come across some well-known Terentian techniques, for example the use of the prologue for responding aggressively to negative critiques (e.g. the prologue of *Compitalia*).[3] From the point of view of language, however, it seems that Afranius opts to follow the traditional linguistic line of Naevius, Caecilius, Ennius, but above all Plautus, rather than that of the innovative Terence.

Bagnolini (1977) has already pointed out that the language of Afranius is closer to Plautus than to Terence; she does not, however, offer a comprehensive linguistic survey and is unable to show Terence's linguistic place in relation to both Plautus and Afranius. She restricts herself mainly to lexical options, failing to give a

[1] For reservations about the Ciceronian testimony, cf. Douglas (1966: 128), Daviault (1981: 28, 39).

[2] For internal evidence for the dating of Afranius, namely *Vopiscus* alluding to the repopulating campaign of C. Caecilius Metellus Macedonicus, censor in 131, as well as the allusion in v. 212 to the *Lex Coelia tabellaria* of 107, see Daviault (1981: 39); for the hostile relationship between Afranius and Lucilius, who must therefore have been a contemporary of Afranius, see Cichorius (1964: 190–202), Frassinetti (1953: 99–100), Krenkel (1970: II 591–3) vs. Christes (1971: 141–95).

[3] Cf. also Degl' Innocenti Pierini (1991: 242–6), Beare (1940: 47). For Afranius' place in the evolution of the *togata*, cf. Pociña (1975: 99–107).

full account of the range of linguistic features involved in such a comparative analysis, and, what is more, she does not classify her findings according to their specific EL–archaising, colloquial, or unclassical character etc., being thus unable to prove Terence's adherence to CL rules in contrast to all other comic dramatists. More importantly, she makes a crucial methodological mistake when discussing the occurrence of certain lexical items in these authors: the affinity between the language of Afranius and Plautus in comparison to that of Terence is not proved for example by the occurrence of the word *vestispica* (= woman responsible for clothing, wardrobe-woman) in the first two authors and by its being avoided in Terence; its absence there is simply due to the fact that thematically Terence did not need a word with this meaning.

The present section will show that:

1. Afranius' language is closer not only to that of Plautus but also to that of the comic playwrights in his line (Naevius, Ennius, Caecilius, Turpilius etc.).
2. Afranius continues the archaising linguistic tendency of Roman comedy as a genre, broken only by Terence. It is difficult indeed within EL to decide which features are used in a specific EL author simply because they were current, even though not very common, in the period in question, and which features are used as intentional archaisms. In any case, in Afranius' diction, as is also the case with Turpilius, we find several linguistic options that had already been completely replaced in the literary registers before Afranius' time, and which, furthermore, when found later in Latin literature, are used only in deliberately archaising authors (e.g. Gellius, Fronto etc.). In several instances the EL equivalent form used by Afranius has been ousted by its CL equivalent form not only in Terence, who regularly opts for CL alternative linguistic options, but even in Plautus.
3. Terence's language shows an affinity with the language of both Plautus and Afranius in *Eunuchus* and in those scenes in other plays (the Sannio scene in *Adelphoe* etc.) where Terence seems to deviate from his original.

Even though a relatively recent publication of the Afranian fragments exists, namely A. Daviault's, *Comoedia Togata* (Paris 1981), I follow mainly the edition by O. Ribbeck, *Scaenicae Romanorum Poesis Fragmenta* (Leipzig 1873), since the new one, as several critics have pointed out (Gratwick, Guardì), is insufficient from the point of both metre and textual criticism.

Morphology

Inflection

v. 364 ***effigia*** Several nouns commonly inflecting according to the fifth declension occasionally have double forms of the first declension. This is the case with *effigia* for *effigies*, an EL–archaising and PC formation, found also in Lucr. 4.46 al., Apul. *Soc.* 14. Such formations are completely avoided in Terence; cf., on the other hand, in Plautus, *effigia* at *Rud.* 420.

v. 396 ***sit necessum scire*** *Necessum* appears several times in Plautus, *Asin.* 895 *Cas.* 344, *Stich.* 219 etc. In Terentian drama we encounter either *necesse*, *Heaut.* 209, or the also EL form *necessus* at *Heaut.* 360, *Eun.* 998, preserved in both places by A etc. At *Phorm.* 296 *necessum* is the reading of C^1, P^1. The rest of the manuscript tradition gives *necesse*.

Derivation

v. 59 ***quam perspicace*** Cf. Non. 513 M *perspicace pro perspicaciter*. Adverbs in *-e* in place of *-ter* derived from third-declension adjectives are also found in Plautus and in Pomponius. Cf. the unclassical *fidele* for the CL *fideliter* at *Capt.* 439, *dapsile* for *dapsiliter* in Pompon. *atel.* 161, *memore* for *memoriter* in Pompon. *atel.* 109.

v. 68 ***indaudiat*** The old preposition *endo*, later spelt as *indo* and *indu* had dropped out of use before the time of Plautus. It remained in compounds like *indo-tueri* etc., most of which were in time ousted by their rival compounds with *in*, *intueri* etc., only a few surviving in CL, e.g. *indigeo*. *Indaudio* for *inaudio* is an EL form which appears frequently in Plautine drama, *Capt.* 30, *Mil.* 211, *Stich.* 77. The EL form has already been replaced in Terence by its CL equivalent *inaudio*, *Phorm.* 877. Afranius, once more, exhibits his archaising tendency in opting for the EL equivalent.

v. 85 ***seorsus*** *Seorsus* in place of *seorsum* appears also in Plautus, *Rud.* 1314. In Terence we find the equivalent form *seorsum*, more common than *seorsus* in Latin literature, *Ad.* 971.

v. 281 ***tentipellium*** Derivative compounds in *-ium* (*tentipellium*) are common in popular sources[4] as opposed to simple derivatives in *-ium*, which, although comparatively rare, are no more characteristic of a

[4] Cf. Cooper (1895: 302–5).

specific register of Latin than another. The classical authors seem in general to have avoided such derivative compound forms, although a few, such as *beneficium, municipium, sti(pi)pendium,* were in general use. Quintilian 1.6.28 remarks that *veriloquium ipse Cicero, qui finxit, reformidat,* and the *Appendix Probi* (GLK IV 198 32) recommends avoiding such formations, *terraemotus non terrimotium.* Unclassical formations of this kind are found in several comic writers, again with the exception of Terence. *Tentipellium* occurs also in Titin. *tog.* 171. In Plautus, *biclinium, cordolium, ferriterium, lumbifragium, multiloquium, stultiloquium.*

vv. 285–6 ***ita superbiter imperat*** *Superbiter* in place of *superbe* is an EL form which had already been replaced by its CL equivalent in both Plautus and Terence (Plaut. *Merc.* 998, Ter. *Phorm.* 915). Afranius shows his archaising tendency in opting for the distinct EL equivalent form, although it has already lost ground to its CL alternative option in the literary registers. *Superbiter* occurs elsewhere in Naev. *poet.* 45 (46).

v. 295 ***occulto*** Unclassical adverbial formations in *-o* (*occulto)* in place of their CL *-e* equivalents are common in Plautus. Terence regularly prefers the CL *-e* alternative, e.g. *occulte* at *Ad.* 328. Cf., on the other hand, *assiduo* in Plautus, *Capt.* 178, *Mil.* 50 (*adsidue* at Ter. *Heaut.* 39), *tempestivo* at Plaut. *Truc.* 61, *commodo* at Plaut. *Mil.* 644. Terence restricts himself to those forms regularly used later in CL, *raro, certo, vero,*[5] *sedulo.*

v. 346 ***partionis*** Verbal nouns in *-tio* seem to have acquired a colloquial flavour even within EL, being favoured by comedy in contrast to higher literary genres of the period, like tragedy and epic.[6] *Partio* is used here in place of the more common *partus*, a usage which also occurs in Plautus, *Truc.* 195. The word is found also in Var. *R.* 3.9.5 and reappears later in the archaising language of Gellius (3.16.9). Terence restricts himself to the CL *partus*, *Hec.* 396, *Andr.* 230 etc.

Conjugation

v. 177 ***olat*** *Olat* is a present subjunctive of the unclassical formation *olĕre* for the CL regular form *olēre*. Third-conjugation forms of the verb occur in Plautus, *Most.* 268, 278 and in Pompon. *atel.* 6. Terence employs the second-conjugation form, *Ad.* 117 *olet.*

v. 186 ***laverent*** The use of the third-conjugation form *lavere* is common in EL and PC authors, whereas in the CL prose register it is

[5] For *vero* and *vere*, cf. N-W II 631.

[6] For the colloquial character of such formations, cf. also Cooper (1895; 3–17), Wahrmann (1908: 80).

replaced by the equivalent first-conjugation form *lavare*. In CL such a third-conjugation form appears in poetry, where it is mainly used as an archaism.[7] Terence employs only the first-conjugation form, *Eun.* 595 etc. Third-conjugation forms, however, are found in Plautus, *Amph.* 1102, *Truc.* 902.

v. 192 ***execrabant*** The use of the active form *ex(s)ecrare* for the CL equivalent *ex(s)ecrari* also appears once in Titin. *tog.* 45. Deponent verbs are divided into two main categories. On the one hand, there are predicative verbs, i.e. those where there is an identification between the subject of the verb and the nominal or adjectival root of the verb, e.g. *dominor* = *dominus sum*. Such verbs can be derived from either nouns or adjectives. On the other hand, there are situative verbs, which on the contrary do not entail identification of the verb subject with the nominal root, e.g. *osculor* = *osculum sum*. These verbs are derived only from nouns.[8]

In the case of several situative verbs of the first conjugation, in all comic dramatists, with the exception of Terence, we encounter several unclassical (EL–archaising and PC) active verbs in place of their CL equivalent deponent formations, *contemplo* in Plaut. *Amph.* 441, Titin. *tog.* 92, *crimino* in Plaut. *Pseud.* 493, *infitio* in Plaut. *Cist.* 661, *miro* in Pompon. *atel.* 108, *moro* in Naev. *com.* 66, *mutuo* in Caec. *com.* 12, *omino* in Pompon. *atel.* 36, *osculo* in Titin. *tog.* 65, *expalpo* in Pompon. *atel.* 32, *perconto* in Nov. *atel.* 54, *perscruto* in Plaut. *Aul.* 657, *ruro* in Plaut. *Capt.* 84, *savio* in Pompon. *atel.* 84, Nov. *atel.* 81, *tumultuo* in Plaut. *Mil.* 172 etc., *venero* in Plaut. *Bacch.* 173.

Syntax

Clause syntax

vv. 10–11 ***quamquam non istis exercetur . . . delaborat*** *Quamquam* introducing an adversative clause, without a correlative particle in the main clause, is a common construction in Plautine drama, *Asin.* 710 *asta ut descendam nunciam in proclivi, quamquam nequam es*, *Asin.* 831, *Aul.* 359, *Bacch.* 1171a, *Cist.* 106 etc. Cf. also Caec. *com.* 21. The usage appears once in Terence, in the Sannio and Aeschinus scene in *Adelphoe*, *Ad.* 159. See also *Ad.* 205. Elsewhere in Terence, adversative clauses introduced by *quamquam* are regularly used in conjunction with a correlative particle in the main clauses (*tamen*, *verum tamen*, *at*, *tam*), *Eun.* 172–3.

[7] Cf. Williams (1968: 197).
[8] For such a linguistic distinction, cf. also Flobert (1975: 66).

v. 106 ***cum findat gelus***[9] In EL *quom* in all its meanings, temporal, causal and adversative, is regularly construed with the indicative. Most of the exceptions are the result of attraction, or are cases of the indefinite second singular. *Quom* with temporal meaning construed with a subjunctive which cannot be attributed either to attraction or to the indefinite second singular, as in the Afranian example, is occasionally found in Plautus, *Asin.* 395 *quom venisset, post non redit?*, *Merc.* 980. In Terence such a subjunctive with temporal *quom* is found once at *Eun.* 22 *magistratus quom ibi adesset occeptast agi.* In Afranius we encounter two more instances of this construction, vv. 151–2 and vv. 232–3.[10]

Verbal syntax

vv. 40–1 ***orbitatem tuae senectuti malam metui*** *Metuo* construed with both the accusative and the dative occurs in Plautus, *Asin.* 111 *nemo est quem iam dehinc metuam mihi.* In Terence *metuo* is found in an absolute use (*Eun.* 786) or it is construed with the accusative (*Eun.* 610), or *ut* or *ne* or *ne non* clauses (*Heaut.* 808). At *Andr.* 106 *ei metui a Chryside*, *ei* is an interjection.

vv. 47–8 ***qui conere noctu clanculum rus ire*** *Conor* in the sense of *tempto*, *incipio*, *audeo* (Gr. πειρῶμαι), construed with an infinitive complement, occurs also at Plaut. *Capt.* 62, *Trin.* 1150 etc. In Terence the verb is either found in an absolute use (*Heaut.* 240) or is construed with an accusative direct object (*Andr.* 197).

v. 107 ***comissatum protenis recta domum*** The use of the supine of *comissare* with verbs denoting motion or fetching is an unclassical (EL–archaising and PC) construction,[11] common in the comedy of Plautus, *Most.* 317 *nunc comissatum ibo ad Philolachetem*, *Pers.* 568, *Stich.* 775 etc. In Terence the construction appears at *Eun.* 442 *Phaedriam intro mittamus comissatum.*

v. 125 ***tamen fefelli*** The absolute use of *fallo* occurs also at Plaut. *Amph.* 392 etc. and at Ter. *Heaut.* 671, that is, in the monologue of Syrus, where Terence deviates from his original by adducing several romanisms in a Greek setting in the Plautine way, as well as by using in concentration several linguistic features common in Roman comedy but avoided elsewhere by him.[12]

[9] For a thematic similarity between this Afranian fragment from the *Epistula* (vv. 14–16) and the opening scene of Menander's *Misoumenos* and Plaut. *Amph.* 341ff., cf. Brown (1981: 25–6).

[10] For *quom* + subjunctive in EL, cf. also Petersen (1931: 386–404).

[11] Also in Livy, Apuleius, Donatus, Eugraphius.

[12] For the Plautine colour of the scene, cf. Lefèvre (1994: 137–8). One should also mention here the use of *bolus* in v. 673 in the sense of 'profit', common in Plautus (*Pers.* 658,

v. 129 ***abstinebis*** *Abstineo* as equivalent to the Greek ἀπέχομαι in an absolute use appears also in Plaut. *Aul.* 344–5 *quod te scio facile apstinere posse*, etc. In Terence the verb is either transitive with an accusative direct object (*Ad.* 781) or reflexive (*Hec.* 139). As for *auctor* = *suasor, impulsor* in ablative absolute constructions, Plaut. *Stich.* 603, Ter. *Eun.* 1013.

v. 194 ***illud memento, ne quid . . .*** *Memini* in the sense of *in memoriam sibi revocare / recordari*, construed with a final clause, appears also in Plautus, *Cas.* 823–4 *noctuque et diu ut viro subdola sis, quaeso, memento* etc. In Terence *memini* is construed with the accusative (*Andr.* 943), the genitive (*Heaut.* 1026), the infinitive either expressed or easily understood from the context (*Eun.* 340), a.c.i. syntagms (*Andr.* 429), or interrogative clauses (*Phorm.* 224).

v. 306 ***ne ego illos velitantis ausculto lubens*** *ausculto* with an accusative direct object occurs also at Plaut. *Aul.* 496 *ego hunc ausculto lubens* (here the common iunctura *lubens auscultare*), *Poen.* 841, *Pseud.* 523 etc. In Terence the verb appears in an absolute use (*Andr.* 664) or is construed with the dative (*Ad.* 935) or with a dependent clause (*Heaut.* 771). *Andr.* 536 is textually doubtful. *Pauca* is the reading of p[1], Prisc., Donat., Faircl., K-L; *pauca* is offered by C[1]P[1] and *paucis* is read in the rest of the manuscripts and the editors.

v. 356 ***cruciari tua te culpa*** *Cruciari* construed with the ablative denoting cause appears at Plaut. *Merc.* 247 *cura cruciabar miser*. In Terence the verb is used either absolutely (*Andr.* 851) or with an accusative object (*Heaut.* 1045) or a.c.i. syntagms (*Heaut.* 673). The ablative *omnibus . . . modis* at *Eun.* 384 denotes manner and not cause.

v. 403 ***aurito me parente natum*** The use of a bare ablative denoting origin with *natus* is a common syntagm in Plautine drama, *Merc.* 969, *Most.* 1141, *Pseud.* 356 etc. In Terence *natus* is regularly construed with prepositional syntagms, *ex* + ablative in place of a simple ablative, for denoting origin, *Heaut.* 1030 *ex me atque ex hoc natus es*, *Eun.* 460 etc.

v. 417 ***nostri miseritus tamen deus*** The personal use of *misereo* occurs also in Plaut. *Rud.* 197a *minus ne miserer*. In Terence the verb is normally used in impersonal constructions (*Phorm.* 99).

Moods

v. 264 ***di te mactassint malo*** Apart from formulaic affirmative perfect optatives of *facio, faxim, faxint* etc., all other instances of such optatives in Terence are followed by a particle, *Ad.* 507–8 *utinam hic sit modo defunctum*, *Heaut.* 617 etc. Affirmative perfect optatives without an

Poen. 101, *Truc.* 31, 724, 844), the figurative use of *retrahere* and *fugitivus* in v. 678, the EL a.c.i. construction with *crucior* in v. 673 *crucior bolum tantum mi ereptum tam desubito e faucibus* (Plaut. *Capt.* 600, *Mil.* 1321).

accompanying optative particle (*utinam*, *ut*), as in the Afranian example, are found in Plautus, *Asin.* 654 *di te servassint*, *Cas.* 324 etc.

Case syntax

v. 133 ***meretrix cum veste longa?*** *Cum* is used here in place of a simple ablative of description. A similar example appears in Plautus, *Stich.* 350 *illos itidemne esse censes quasi te cum veste unica?*. This use of *cum*, which has the sociative character of an instrumental ablative denoting quality (*ablativus qualitatis*),[13] appears in Terence at *Eun.* 906–7 *nolo me in via cum hac veste videat.*

Word order

v. 154 ***depellis mihi manum*** The construction of the sympathetic dative *mihi* with a transitive verb (*depello*) in a clause where the dative is placed before the noun of the sentence appears in Plautine drama as well, *Amph.* 183 *qui mihi advenienti os occillet*, *Men.* 842 etc. Cf. also Turpil. *com.* 147. In Terence, this word order appears once in the last act of *Heautontimoroumenos*, v. 1041 *mihi . . . adducere ante oculos*, and once more at *Eun.* 794 *quae mi ante oculos coram amatorem adduxti tuom.* Elsewhere in Terence the dative is postponed after the noun of the main clause, *Ad.* 244, *Heaut.* 330.

v. 354 ***igitur quiesce*** *Igitur* in first position in a syntagm occurs several times in Plautus, *Amph.* 301, 473, *Aul.* 817, *Capt.* 871 etc. In Terence *igitur* normally holds the second position (21 times, *Andr.* 154). It is also found in the third (*Andr.* 48), sixth (*Phorm.* 572–3) or fourth place (*Heaut.* 857).

Lexicon

Nouns and adjectives

v. 11 ***puera*** *Puera* for *puella* is an EL and archaising word (Livius Andronicus, Varro),[14] replaced by its equivalent CL *puella* from Plautus onwards. This is one of several archaisms avoided in both Plautus and Terence but occurring in the speech of Afranius.

v. 12 ***spiritum firmiter inflat*** *Spiritus* is used here in the sense of 'breath', as in Plaut. *Amph.* 233–4 *ex spiritu atque anhelitu nebula*

[13] For the ablative of quality in Terence, cf. Baloira Bértolo (1981–3: 203–20), Zebian (1965: 240–57).

[14] Cf. Pris. GLK II 231. 1 *'puera' dicebant antiquissimi*, Suet. *Cal.* 8.

constat. In Terence only *anima* is used in this sense, *Ad.* 324 *animam recipe*, *Phorm.* 868.

v. 61 ***sicca*** *Siccus* in the sense of *sobrius*, 'sober', 'dry', 'not drunk', occurs also in Plaut. *Curc.* 114–6 *Liber, tibi qui screanti, siccae, semi-somnae adfert potionem*, *Pers.* 822.

v. 67 ***mitem*** *Mitis* in the sense of *mollis* occurs in Plaut. *Mil.* 1424 *mitis sum equidem fustibus.* In Terence the adjective is used figuratively in the sense of *lenis*, *humanus*, *propitius*, *moderatus* (*Ad.* 276).

v. 70 ***diluculo.*** *Diluculum* in the sense of *prima lux diei* is also found in Plautus, *Amph.* 743 *egone aps te abii hinc hodie cum diluculo?*, 737. Apart from a few instances of this usage in Cicero (*S. Rosc.* 19, *Att.* 16.13.1), it is mainly an EL and PC expression. In Terence we find instead *cum primo luci(e)* at *Ad.* 841.

v. 116 ***proba*** *Proba* referring to a woman, with the meaning of *pudica*, occurs in Plaut. *Amph.* 678 *cives Thebani vero rumiferant probam*, *Rud.* 751 etc. In Terence the word appears in this sense once at *Ad.* 930 in a scene where Terence probably deviates from his original. Unlike in Terence, in the Menandrian original Micio did not resist the suggestion that he should marry Pamphila's mother (for Terence's deviation from his original here, cf. Donat. ad *Ad.* 938 *Terentius* εὑρετικῶς*)*.

v. 127 ***risu clandestino*** *Clandestinus* for *latens*, *occultus* appears in Plaut. *Cas.* 946 *clandestinae nuptiae*, *Amph.* 490, *Curc.* 49.

v. 132 **<*di te sospitem*> *servent tuis*** *Sospes* is used here with the meaning of *salvus*, *incolumis*, *sanus*. The word belongs mainly to the poetic register (it is not found at all in Cicero) and occurs with some frequency only in PC prose. The word appears several times in Plautus, *Asin.* 16–17 *unicum gnatum tuae superesse vitae sospitem et superstitem*, *Capt.* 873, *Cas.* 817 etc.

v. 156 ***formosa virgo*** In Republican drama, *formosus* occurs also in Plaut. *Merc.* 229 *formosam capram* and Titin. *tog.* 21, Afran. *tog.* 381.[15] The form occurs only once in Terence, at *Eun.* 730 *formonsior*, where, as in Titinius' fragment, we encounter the doublet form *formonsus*, uttered by a low character, the *ancilla* Pythias. This specific form seems to be vulgar in nature and is censured by ancient grammarians.[16]

v. 158 ***fortis*** According to *ThLL* VI_1 1152 *fortis* here is used in the sense of *formosus*, *pulcher* (also Non. 306 M *fortis* rursum *formosa)*. Cf. also Plaut. *Bacch.* 216–17 *Bacchis etiam fortis tibi visast? rogas? ni nanctus Venerem essem, hanc Iunonem dicerem*, *Mil.* 1106. In Terence the word occurs either as equivalent to *animosus*, *audax*, *non timidus*

[15] For the more popular flavour of the adjective in *-osus*, *formosus* as opposed to the less colloquial *pulcher*, cf. also Maltby (1976: 196), for *formosus = pulcher*, *speciosa forma praeditus*, cf. *ThLL* VI_1 1111.

[16] Cf. Ter. Scaur. GLK VII 21. 10 *Non mediocriter peccant etiam qui formoso in litteram assumunt*, *App. Probi* GLK IV 198. 9 *formosus non formunsus.*

(*Andr.* 702), or *honestus*, *bonus* (*Andr.* 445). *Fortis* in this Afranian fragment could, however, also have the meaning of *dives*. Such a meaning, absent from Terence again, appears in Plautine drama, *Trin.* 1133.

v. 239 ***clienta*** For *clienta* for *serva, famula, libertina*, cf. Plaut. *Mil.* 789, *Poen.* 1180.

v. 240 ***virile sexu*** *Virilis* in the sense of 'male offspring' occurs in Plaut. *Rud.* 107 *virile sexus numquam ullum habui*. In Terence it is used in the sense of 'characteristic or worthy of a true man', 'manly', 'masculine' (*Phorm.* 957).

vv. 367–8 ***hospitem cotidianum et lautum convivam domi*** *Lautus* is used here with the meaning of 'elegant', 'distinguished', 'well turned out', 'fine'. Cf. also Plaut. *Mil.* 787 *lautam vis an quae nondum sit lauta* ?, *Poen.* 1197. In Terence the word occurs only in its regular sense of *lavatus*, 'washed', 'clean', *Ad.* 425 *Phorm.* 339 or 'sumptuous', 'luxurious', *Heaut.* 798.

v. 375 ***cunctis copiis*** For *cunctus* for *totus*, cf. Plaut. *Amph.* 259, *Trin.* 544 etc.

Verbs

v. 2 ***dispertiantur*** *Dispertio* in the sense *of distribuere*, *dividere*, *separare* appears also in Plaut. *Aul.* 282 *ut dispertirem obsonium*, *Amph.* 220, *Aul.* 331, *Curc.* 189. In Terence, only the more common synonymous verbs are to be found, *distribuo* at *Ad.* 371,[17] or *divido* at *Andr.* 476.[18]

vv. 45–6 ***qui conciere cogites tantum mali*** *Conciere* in the sense of to 'stir up', 'to provoke', *aliquid excitando efficere*, *parare* occurs in Plaut. *Men.* 902, *suo qui regi tantum conciuit mali*,[19] *Amph.* 476 etc. *Conciere* occurs once in Terence, in the last act of *Heautontimoroumenos*, v. 970. Another instance at *Hec.* 313 is textually doubtful (*concluserit* in A). The verb occurs once more in Afran. *tog.* 112 *Tirrium autem maria Tyria conciet* in the sense of *excitare, movere*, *impellere,* a usage which also occurs in a similar context in Plautus, *Merc.* 877 *omnis fluctus conciet.*

v. 49 ***latites*** For *latito* in the sense of *latere*, λανθάνειν, cf. Plaut. *Trin.* 926–7 *quid ergo ille . . . mihi latitabat?.*

v. 50 ***patria partisset*** For *partio* for *dividere*, *distribuere,* cf. Plaut. *Asin.* 271, *Mil.* 707.

v. 83 ***deos ego omnis ut fortunassint precor*** Nonius remarks (109 M) *fortunare est prosperare, et omnibus bonis augere*. This use of the

[17] Donatus ad loc. *dispertitum per pulmentaria*.

[18] Cf. Donat. ad *Andr.* 475 *distributa*.

[19] Cf., on the other hand, a similar formula in Terence where *conciere* is replaced by *excitare*, at *Heaut.* 1013 *non vides quantum mali* ex ea re excites?, where *excitare* has the same sense of 'to stir up', 'to provoke'.

verb in formulaic wishes, as equivalent to *prosperum* or *felicem facere*, *provehere*, appears also in Plautus, *Trin.* 576 *di fortunabunt vostra consilia.* Terence opts for other, more common, wish formulas or prayer-formulaic expressions, e.g. *Ad.* 917–18 *di tibi, Demea, bene faciant.*

v. 94 ***remeare in ludum*** *Remeare* is used here in the sense of *revortor*. Cf. also Plaut. *Epid.* 662 *remeabo intro, ut adcurentur advenientes hospites*, *Asin.* 228.

v. 110 ***extundo*** According to Nonius (102 M), *extundere* here has the meaning of *extorquere*, *invenire*. This is an unclassical figurative usage[20] which appears in Plaut. *Most.* 220–1 *eundem animum oportet nunc mihi esse gratum, ut impetravi, atque olim, prius quam id extudi.*

vv. 118–19 ***qua contendi semita pervenire*** *Contendere* in the sense of *properare*, *proficisci* occurs in Plaut. *Cist.* 534 *qui recta platea cursum huc contendit suom?*.

v. 131 ***<vento per>culsam ratem*** *Percello* in the sense of *everto*, *percuto* appears in Plaut. *Epid.* 592 etc. The verb appears once in Terence at *Eun.* 379.

v. 135 ***consimili grassantur via*** *Grassari* is used here in place of *ambulare* (cf. Non. 316 M). The verb in this sense is avoided in CL by Cicero, Caesar, Vergil, but reappears in the literature with other Augustan poets (Ovid) and archaising authors. This use of the verb is common in many comic writers, with the exception of Terence, who, in a similar vein to the purists of CL, completely avoids the formation, Plaut. *Bacch.* 1136–8 *non vides, ut palantes solae, liberae grassentur?*, *Poen.* 514, *Rud.* 251, Titin. *tog.* 145, Nov. *atel.* 72, 74.

v. 152 ***mihi supponebas*** *Supponere* in the sense of 'to put in the place of another', 'substitute', appears in Plaut. *Cas.* 1018 *ei pro scorto supponetur hircus unctus nautea*, *Curc.* 256. In Terence the verb is used with the meaning of 'to introduce fraudulently into a situation', 'to introduce as somebody (something) that he (it) is not', *Eun.* 912.

v. 181 ***dimittit adsestricem*** *Dimittere* as equivalent to *a se mittere* appears also in Plaut. *Rud.* 1279 *dilectum dimisit* and in Ter. *Eun.* 814 *iam dimitto exercitum?*.

v. 202 ***potin' ut dicta facessas?*** According to Nonius (306 M), *facesso* is used in the sense of a simple *facere*. This use of the verb also appears once in Plautus, *Men.* 249, where a similar formulaic expression occurs: *dictum facessas*. In Terence the verb is used once, at *Phorm.* 635, in the sense of *hinc se faciat*, *abeat*.

v. 206 ***oboedibo tibi*** *Oboedio* here has the meaning of *obsequor*, *obtempero.* Cf. also Plaut. *Curc.* 555–6 *quid refert me fecisse regibus ut mi oboedirent*, *Merc.* 853, *Pers.* 273.

v. 237 ***sustine!*** For *sustinere* in the sense of 'to hold up', 'support', cf. also Plaut. *Asin.* 658 *nolo, ego te, qui erus sis, mihi onus istuc sustinere.*

[20] Also found in Valerius Maximus, Seneca, Suetonius, Apuleius.

In Terence the verb has the meaning of 'face or endure without giving way', 'stand up to', 'withstand', *Phorm.* 347.

vv. 246–7 ***occurrit nepos pausillus*** *Occurrere* is used here in the sense of a simple *currere*, *accurrere*, *advenire*, *adesse.* The verb appears several times with this sense in Plautine drama, *Merc.* 199–200 *ilico occucurri*, *Poen.* 43, *Pseud.* 1198. It also occurs once at *Eun.* 335.

v. 259 ***commercatis conquisite edulibus*** *Commercor* for *coemo* (mainly an EL and archaising word, Sall. *Iug.* 66.1, Amm.14.3.3) occurs at Plaut. *Capt.* 27 *coepit captivos commercari hic Aleos*, *Pers.* 749.

v. 264 ***di te mactassint malo*** *Mactare* in the sense of *malo afficere*, *auctare* appears in Plaut. *Aul.* 535 *dotatae mactant et malo et damno viros*, *Bacch.* 364, *Curc.* 537 etc., Nov. *atel.* 39, Pompon. *atel.* 137, where we also find an imprecation formula similar to the one in the Afranian line, *at te di omnes cum consilio . . . mactassint malo.* The word appears once in Terence, in the final scene of *Phormio*, v. 1028, where Terence deviates from his original.[21]

v. 273 ***aliquid sufferre Graece*** According to *OLD*, *suffero* here has the meaning of 'to place at a person's disposal', 'to offer'.[22] Cf. also Plaut. *Cas.* 950 *sufferamque ei meum tergum*, *Poen.* 855. In Terence the verb is used in the sense of 'to submit to', 'to endure', 'to suffer', *Andr.* 888, *Heaut.* 453.

v. 277 ***cursum cohibeam*** *Cohibeo* is used with the meaning of *retineo*, *impedio*, *prohibeo.* Cf. also Plaut. *Merc.* 64 *adeo arte cohibitum esse <se> a patre*, *Trin.* 1019. A similar usage appears also in Terence, in the last act of the *Heautontimoroumenos*, v. 919 *non tu te cohibes?*.

v. 283 ***gannire ad aurem*** *Gannire* in the sense of *murmurare*, *obstrepere*, *maledicere* appears also in Plaut. fr. 120 *Gannit odiosus omni totae familiae.* In Terence the verb appears at *Ad.* 556 *quid ille gannit?*, possibly as a colloquialism in the speech of the rustic Demea. For the colloquial character of the verb, see its distribution: comedy, Lucilius, Catullus, Apuleius. At Cassian. *c. Nest.* 3.6.6. the verb has the meaning of *garrire.*

v. 319 ***tamen animo ordire oportet minime paululo <rem> paululam*** *Ordior* is used here in the sense of *inchoare*, *incipere.* Cf. also Plaut. *Trin.* 1136 *hoc commodum orditur loqui.*

v. 350 ***quo casu cecidit spes*** *Cado* with the meaning of *desino esse*, *decresco*, *pereo* occurs in Plaut. *Poen.* 360 *omnia incassum cadunt.* In Terence the verb occurs either in its proper sense πίπτειν (*Ad.* 37) or with the meaning of *accidere, evenire* (*Ad.* 740).[23]

[21] Cf. Lowe (1983b: 431).
[22] Cf. Non. 397 M *sufferre significat dedere vel supponere.*
[23] For *cadere, accidere* denoting chance in Latin, cf. Shipp (1937: 209–12).

v. 357 ***quid de te et de illa . . . promerere*** *Promerere* is used in the sense 'to do somebody a good or bad turn', 'to acquire a claim to good (bad) treatment at someone's hands'. The verb exhibits a similar meaning in Plautus, *Capt.* 933 *proinde ut tu promeritu's de me*, *Men.* 1067. This usage appears once in Terence, in the farcical Sannio scene in *Ad.* 201. Elsewhere in Terence the verb has the meaning 'to deserve a good turn', *Phorm.* 516, *Ad.* 681.

v. 357 ***quam deamas*** *Deamare* is here equivalent to *vehementius amare.* Cf. also Plaut. *Epid.* 219 *cum illa quam tuos gnatus annos multos deamat, deperit*, *Poen.* 894. Terence uses instead several combinations of reinforcing or modifying adverbs with *amare* for denoting passionate love, *misere amare* at *Andr.* 520, *perdite amare* at *Heaut.* 97[24] etc., even though *de*-compounds with a reinforcing function are common enough in Terentian drama, *debacchor*, *defungor*, *demulceo*, *depeciscor*, *depecto*, *deverbero*. In Terence *deamo* occurs once, at *Heaut.* 825 *deamo te*, *Syre*. The verb here, however, is used in a different sense and does not refer to an amorous sentiment but expresses instead simple gratitude, thanks.

v. 374 ***concinno*** *Concinno* is used here as equivalent to *facere*, *efficere*. This mainly EL–archaising and PC usage of the verb appears several times in Plautus, *Truc.* 793 *livorem tute scapulis istoc concinnas tuis*, *Amph.* 529, *Capt.* 601, *Trin.* 684 etc.

v. 395 ***quae sit causa sciscere*** *Sciscere* is used here in the sense of 'to get to know', 'ascertain', *sciscitare*.[25] This is an EL usage, found in Plautus as well, *Bacch.* 302 *palam atque aperte, ut illi id factum sciscerent, Amph.* 1069. In Terence we find only the CL equivalent *sciscitari*, *Eun.* 548.

v. 419 ***mustriculam in dentes impingam tibi*** *Impingere* in the sense of *ferire*, *illidere*, *contrudere* appears in Plaut. *Bacch.* 800 *impinge pugnum*, *Rud.* 710. In Terence the verb has simply the meaning of *imponere*, *inferre*, *proponere*, *Phorm.* 439.

Adverbs and interjections

v. 51 ***diserte pactum*** *Diserte* is used here in the sense of *definite.* This is a rare usage, found only once in CL in Cicero's *Verr.* 3.126. Otherwise it occurs mainly in archaic or archaising authors (several instances in Livy, e.g. 21.19.3). This usage also appears in Plautus, *Amph.* 578 *satin hoc plane, satin diserte, ere. nunc videor tibi locutus esse.*

v. 81 ***secreto*** *secreto* in the sense of 'secretly', 'in private' appears several times in Plautus, *Amph.* 954 *solus secum secreto ille agat*,

[24] Cf., on the other hand, the unclassical formation *perditim* in Afran. *tog.* 353 *me illam amare perditim.*

[25] For *sciscere = sciscitare,* cf. Daviault (1981: 236), Sedgwick (1960: 129).

Aul. 133, *Bacch.* 1149, 1154. In Terence we find instead more common equivalent expressions, e.g. *clam* (= 'secretly', 'privately'), *Andr.* 444.

v. 82 ***repentino*** *repentino* in the sense of 'in an instant', 'at once' (also in Afran. *tog.* 327), is a colloquial usage,[26] found also in Plautus, *Pseud.* 39 *repentino occidi.* The formation appears once in CL, in Cic. *Quinct.* 14, an early speech, in which the orator employs several vulgarisms in both lexicon and syntax, later completely avoided by him.[27] At Caes. *Gal.* 2.33.2 we should read with β *repente.*[28] The form reappears later in archaising writers, Apul. *Mun.* 16. In Terence, we find more common equivalents, such as *repente*, *Heaut.* 23, *subito Eun.* 642.

v. 138 ***interibi loci*** *Interibi* for *interea / interim* appears several times in Plautine drama, *Asin.* 891, *Capt.* 951, *Mil.* 104, *Pers.* 165, *Poen.* 617 etc. This is an EL and archaising formation (its distribution: S. C. de Bacch., Gell., Apul.).

v. 220 ***cordate ac sanite*** *Cordate* in the sense of *prudenter*, *sapienter* is an EL usage, otherwise restricted in the whole of Latin literature to Plautine drama, *Mil.* 1088, *Poen.* 131.

v. 228 ***ea memoriter . . . confecta ut offendam*** *Memoriter* is used here as equivalent to *accurate*, *plane*, *recte.* Cf. also Plaut. *Amph.* 417 *res gestae memorat memoriter*, *Asin.* 584 *Capt.* 250, *Poen.* 562. The usage is found once in Terence, at *Eun.* 915 *cognoscitne? ac memoriter.* Otherwise the adverb occurs in Terence as equivalent to *ex / in memoria*, *Phorm.* 394.

vv. 351–2 ***impendio ex desiderio magis magisque maceror*** The reinforcing use of *impendio* in the sense of *multo*, *magnopere*, *valde*, *impense* with a comparative adverb is an EL construction, which survived later in the colloquial (Cic. *Att.* 10.4.9) and the archaising register (Gel. 11.8.4; Amm. 29.1.25). In Terence this construction appears only once, in *Eun.* 587 *inpendio magis animus gaudebat mihi.* Cf. also Plaut. *Aul.* 18–19 *atque ille vero minus minusque impendio curare.*

v. 369 ***cottidiano*** *Cot(t)idiano* is used here in place of *co(t)tidie.* Cf. also Plaut. *Capt.* 725. In Terence we find the more common form *cot(t)idie*, *Heaut.* 102 etc. Several adjectives of the second declension often form adverbs in *-o*, such as *cottidiano* here. Apart from common CL formations such as *cito*, *subito*, *immo*, *omnino*, *profecto*, unclassical adverbial formations in *-o* are avoided completely in Terence. Cf., on the other hand, in Plautus, *accubuo* at *Truc.* 422, *arbitrario* at *Poen.* 787, *horno* at *Most.* 159.

[26] Cf. H-Sz 42*.

[27] Cf. Löfstedt (1911; 13 note 2), H-Sz 42*.

[28] Cf. H-Sz 42*.

v. 376 ***excludat uxor tam confidenter virum?*** *Confidenter* is here equivalent to *audacter*. Cf. Plaut. *Capt.* 664 *ut confidenter mihi contra astitit*, *Mil.* 465, *Most.* 38. The adverb is used in this sense once in Terence, in the last act of *Heautontimoroumenos*, v. 1009 *in qua re nunc tam confidenter restas.*

v. 398 ***opera ni mirum mea*** For *nimirum* in the sense of *certe*, 'without doubt', 'certainly', cf. Plaut. *Aul.* 393. In Terence this usage is restricted to the *Eunuchus*, vv. 268, 508, 784.

Style

Figurative usages

v. 4 ***bona comest*** *Comedere* is used in a figurative sense for *dissipare*, *dilapidare*, *perdere.* Cf. also Plaut. *Curc.* 559–60 *argentum ut petam, ut ego potius comedim quam ille*, *Pseud.* 1107 etc., Titin. *tog.* 18, 141 Nov. *atel.* 1. The verb in Terence appears mainly in its literal sense, 'to eat', *Heaut.* 255 *quid comedent!*, *quid ebibent!*. It is used once in a figurative sense at *Eun.* 1086–7 *at ego . . . hunc comedendum vobis propino*, 'to be feasted upon', 'to be eaten out of house and home'.

vv. 16–17 ***pectus est laetitia onustum*** *Onustus* is used with the meaning of *oneratus*, *refertus*, *plenus*. This is an unclassical usage found in Plaut. *Stich.* 276 *onustum pectus porto laetitia lubentiaque*, *Epid.* 375, *Men.* 757.

v. 120 ***iactabit sese*** *Iactare* is used here with the meaning of *vehementer commovere*, *agitare*, *afflictare*, *vexare*. Cf. also Plaut. *Cist.* 206 *iactor, crucior, agitor*, *Trin.* 685.

Metatheatrical references

v. 7 ***Haut facul, ut ait Pacuvius, femina <una> invenietur bona*** Afranius here cites a line from Pacuvius.[29] Such a clear reference to a tragic script, avoided completely in Terence, appears on the other hand in Plautine drama, *Curc.* 591–2 *Antiquom poetam audivi scripsisse in tragoedia mulieres duas peiores esse quam unam.* Tragic lines, words, expressions, or syntactic formulas, appear also in Terence; there is no mention on the part of the playwright, however, of their tragic flavour, or any direct reference to the tragedy from which a particular line is drawn.

[29] Cf. also Zorzetti (1973: 71–5).

Terms of endearment

v. 311 *<o> **mel meum*** For this term of endearment, cf. Plaut. *Bacch.* 17–18 *cor meum, spes mea, mel meum, suavitudo, cibus, gaudium*, *Bacch.* 1197, *Curc.* 164.

Alliterative combinations

v. 38 ***lentus lente*** The alliterative combination of an adjective and an adverb of the same root is a common stylistic feature in Plautine drama, *optume optumam* at *Amph.* 278, *unice unum* at *Asin.* 208, *unice unicum* at *Bacch.* 407, *bella belle* at *Curc.* 521, *belle belliatula* at *Cas.* 854 etc. It seems to be a colloquial combination, also appearing in the *Epistles* of Cicero, *Att.* 3.23.5 *miserum misere*. Such an alliterative combination is never found in Terentian drama.

v. 295 ***curre cursim*** The alliterative combination of a simple verb and an adverb of the same root is a common stylistic feature of Plautine comedy, e.g. the similar *cursim curram* at *Pseud.* 358, *cupide cupis* at *Cas.* 267, *propere properas* at *Curc.* 535, *caveo cautius* at *Men.* 151, *misere miseret* at *Most.* 985, *memorat memoriter* at *Poen.* 562 etc. The last alliterative combination *memorat memoriter* occurs also in Afran. *tog.* 365 *memini memoriter* and in Pompon. *atel.* 109 *memore meministi.* This is an EL–archaising (Fro. Ver. 1.3.1 *desiderantius desideras*) and PC usage (Augustinus, Victorius Vitensis, *Vitae patrum* etc.). Terence avoids this unclassical construction.

v. 334 ***laudem . . . laborem*** *Paronomasia* with *laus* occurs also in Plaut. *Capt.* 770 *laudem, lucrum, ludum, iocum*, *Cist.* 201 *laudem et lauream*.

Individual iuncturae

Several individual word combinations or collocations point also to the linguistic and stylistic affinity of Afranius to Plautus rather than to Terence.

In particular:

nominal *iuncturae*: collocations of *cor/corpus* (Afran. *tog.* 77, Plaut. *Cist.* 551, *Mil.* 617), *virgo/mulier* (Afran. *tog.* 336–7, Plaut. *Pers.* 365), combinations of *sacer/malus* (Afran. *tog.* 185, Plaut. *Bacch.* 783–4), *bona femina* (Afran. *tog.* 7, Plaut. *Aul.* 135, *Cist.* 705), *fortuna bona* (Afran. *tog.* 429, Plaut. *Aul.* 100), *gnata parvula* (Afran. *tog.* 208, Plaut. *Poen.* 1104–5),[30] the EL–archaising

[30] This combination may have a colloquial flavour, as it is found in colloquial genres, i.e. comedy, Itala, CE.

and colloquial combination *verbis pauculis* (Afran. *tog*. 339, Plaut. *Epid*. 460).[31]

verbal *iuncturae*: *fortiter* = *animose* or *audacter* in verbal syntagms (Afran. *tog*. 227 *fortiter scicidistis*, Plaut. *Men*. 129 *pugnavi fortiter*, *com. pal. inc*. 57),[32] *cedo purpurissimum* (Afran. *tog*. 231, Plaut. *Most*. 261), *clamor oritur* (Afran. *tog*. 12 Plaut. *Aul*. 403, *Rud*. 614), *concelebrare diem* (Afran. *tog*. 103, Plaut. *Asin*. 311), *degere diem* (Afran. *tog*. 141, Plaut. *Most*. 534, Ter. *Ad*. 522, possibly as an archaism in the speech of Ctesipho when addressing the old slave Syrus), *nauci* + verb combinations (Afran. *tog*. 431 *nauci dare*, Plaut. *Bacch*. 1102, *Most*. 1042), *deus sinit* (Afran. *tog*. 359, Plaut. *Bacch*. 468, *Merc*. 323), *deos obsecrare* (Afran. *tog*. 170–1, Plaut. *Cist*. 664), *dictum facessere* (Afran. *tog*. 202, Plaut. *Men*. 249), *domi sedere* (Afran. *tog*. 210–11, Plaut. *Aul*. 73), *domum reducere* (Afran. *tog*. 350, Plaut. *Amph*. 207–8, *Bacch*. 1071), *dotem dicere* (Afran. *tog*. 160, Plaut. *Aul*. 256, Ter. *Heaut*. 937, 1048), *limen intrare* (Afran. *tog*. 5, Plaut. *Men*. 416), *locum invenire* (Afran. *tog*. 198, Plaut. *Merc*. 584), *tergo consuluere* (Afran. *tog*. 251, Plaut. *Asin*. 409), *mitto oratum* (Afran. *tog*. 303, Plaut. *Amph*. 20), *hinc ausculto* (Afran. *tog*. 265, Plaut. *Bacch*. 404, *Curc*. 279), *operam perire* (Afran. *tog*. 398, Plaut. *Trin*. 660), *finge fabricare* where *fabricare* = *astu fingere* (Afran. *tog*. 169, *Bacch*. 693).

adverbial *iuncturae*: *immo edepol* (Afran. *tog*. 103, Plaut. *Aul*. 262–fifteen times, see Lodge.s.v.), *in medium* where *medium* is substantivised (Afran. *tog*. 168, Plaut. *Amph*. 223, *Capt*. 649, Ter. *Eun*. 744), *postquam modo* (Afran. *tog*. 8, Plaut. *Truc*. 773), the unclassical syntagm *paulo prius* (Afran. *tog*. 75, Plaut. *Cist*. 546, *Men*. 681, 873a, *Pseud*. 896), *in dies* (Afran. *tog*. 351, Plaut. *Bacch*. 466, *Men*. 457 etc.).

phrases: *hodie* + adjectival complement + *dies* + *<est>* syntagms (Afran. *tog*. 163 *hodie ater dies est*, Plaut. *Pseud*. 775), *in quaestione esse* (Afran. *tog*. 280, Plaut. *Capt*. 253, *Cas*. 530, *Cist*. 593, *Pers*. 51, *Pseud*. 663).

There are also two further word collocations that Afranius has in common with Titinius, Caecilius, Pomponius: *lavere manum* (Afran. *tog*. 187, Titin. *tog*. 87–8, Pompon. *atel*. 11), EL *quam duriter* + verb combinations, where *duriter* = *severe*, *stricte*, *crudeliter* (Afran. *tog*. 251 *quam duriter nunc consulis tergo meo!*, Caec. *com*. 40).

[31] Also found in comedy, Fronto, Apuleius, Tertullian.

[32] In Terence *fortiter* is used as an *exclamatio approbantis*, *Ad*. 566

Conclusions

The present study has shown that Afranius stands much closer than Terence to the linguistic and stylistic tradition of Roman comedy as exemplified by authors such as Naevius, Caecilius Statius, Ennius, Turpilius, Plautus. Only a few linguistic options shared by Terence and Afranius but avoided in Plautus are to be found, the construction of *comparo* with an *ut* + subjunctive clause as its complement in v. 117, *Phorm.* 41–2, *deducere* for *contrahere*, *minuere* (Afran. *tog.* 340, Ter. *Eun.* 315), *illudere* in the sense of *ludibrio habere*, *insultare* (Afran. *tog.* 87, Ter. *Andr.* 758 etc.), the reflexive use of *praebeo* as equivalent to *ostendere*, *manifestum reddere*, *prodere* (Afran. *tog.* 316, Ter. *Ad.* 886), *defensor* in the sense of *is qui tuetur* (Afran. *tog.* 323, Ter. *Andr.* 813), the adjective *futtilis* with the meaning of 'unreliable', 'worthless' (Afran. *tog.* 35, Ter. *Andr.* 609), *scelerosus* for *scelestus, sceleratus* (Afran. *tog.* 66, Ter. *Eun.* 643), the following *iuncturae*: *caelum ruere* (Afran. *tog.* 9, Ter. *Heaut.* 719) *laudem invenire* (Afran. *tog.* 334, Ter. *Andr.* 66) *uxoria res* (Afran. *tog.* 86, Ter. *Andr.* 829).

In particular, evidence for the following has been adduced:

1. Several EL options which are common in Plautus but avoided in Terence are found in Afranius' fragments. This is the case, for example, with the form *indaudio* in place of the CL *ianaudio* in v. 69 etc. In several instances Afranius' archaising tendency is more evident through his use of linguistic elements of an EL or archaising character, although they had already been completely replaced by their CL equivalent, not only in Terence, who often opts for CL equivalent options anyway, but in Plautus as well, e.g. *superbiter* for *superbe* in v. 285, *puera* for *puella* in v. 11 etc.
2. Some colloquial options common in Plautus and other comic dramatists, but avoided again by Terence, are also to be found in Afranius' plays. This is the case for example with *repentino* for *repente* in v. 82.
3. Specific features on the morphological, syntactical and lexical level, with no particular colloquial and/or archaic flavour but mainly of an unclassical character, further demonstrate Afranius' adherence to the previous comic tradition, from which Terence distances himself. Cf. *extundere* for *extorquere* in v. 110 etc.
4. Certain other stylistic options, like the use of specific *iuncturae*, word groups, figurative usages etc., found in Plautus and the other comic dramatists but avoided in Terence, occur in Afranian drama, e.g. the

figurative use of *comedere* for *dissipare*, *dilapidare perdere* in v. 4, the alliterative combination of an adjective and an adverb of the same root, *lentus lente* in v. 38 etc.

Several linguistic and stylistic options common in the comic tradition and/or in Afranius are occasionally found in Terence as well. In these cases, however, these features are found in *Eunuchus*, or in other plays, in some specific scenes, where Terence deviates from his original. This is the case for example with *memoriter* as equivalent to *accurate*, *plane*, *recte* in v. 228 etc.

A few features that have the sanction of both Plautus and Afranius appear as *hapax* in Terentian drama and do not follow this distributional pattern (*Eunuchus*/Terentian scenes deviating from the original): *calleo* + accusative in the sense of *scire*, *callidum/peritum esse* (Afran. *tog.* 124, Plaut. *Most.* 279, Ter. *Ad.* 533), *exigo* for *expello* (Afran. *tog.* 167, Plaut. *Mil.* 1277, Ter. *Hec.* 242), the appositional syntagm *non modo . . . sed etiam* (Afran. *tog.* 25–8, Plaut. *Most.* 994–5, Ter. *Ad.* 386–7), *pertimeo* for *valde timeo* (Afran. *tog.* 270, Plaut. *Bacch.* 862, *Truc.* 773, Ter. *Phorm.* 601).

Titinius

According to the Byzantine historian Lydus (cf. *Mag.* 1.38), the dramatic activity of this playwright should be dated around 210 BC, namely at the beginning of the second Punic war, when Hannibal invaded Italy. This dating of the comic poet is further confirmed by the fact that in the enumeration of the comic poets by Varro which is probably in chronological order, Titinius is mentioned before Terence.[33]

Vereecke (1971) and Guardì (1981) have already observed that the language of Titinius is closer to that of Plautus than to that of Terence. As is the case with Bagnolini's work on Afranius, however, Vereecke's and Guardì's analysis cannot be considered

[33] For an allusion of the *Barbatus* to the *lex Oppia* of 215, cf. Przychocki (1922: 180–8). See also García Jurado (1997: 544); for other chronological hints, cf. Daviault (1981: 33–4); Vereecke (1968: 63–92), Guardì (1985: 18–19). Cf. also Martina (1978: 5–25, López López (1983: 20ff).

a comprehensive linguistic survey. Vereecke also makes the same crucial methodological mistake pointed out in the case of Bagnolini's work on Afranius: the affinity between the language of Titinius and Plautus is not proved, for example, by the occurrence of the word *cumatilis* (= green colour of the sea) in the first two authors and by its absence in Terence; Terence simply did not need, thematically, a word with this meaning. Only cases where a synonymous word occurs in Terence should have been taken into consideration. The subject therefore needs to be examined further.

The present section will establish that:

1. Titinius' language is closer not only to that of Plautus but also to that of the comic playwrights in his line (Naevius, Ennius, Caecilius, Turpilius, Afranius etc.).
2. Some of the features of Titinius' language which are avoided in Terence should simply be attributed to the historical development of the Latin language, while others are deliberately used as archaisms by Titinius and other comic dramatists, in contrast to Terence, who does not include such features in his archaising register.
3. Terence is closer to the language of both Titinius and Plautus mainly in *Eunuchus* and his more traditional scenes in his other plays, when, in an effort to distance himself from his original, he reworks his material in a more traditional way.

Morphology

Declension

v. 29 ***diu*** *Diu* is an unclassical (EL–archaising and PC) usage, also found in Plautus, *Cas.* 823. In CL the word occurs only in archaising authors like Sallust, *Hist.* 2.89; see also Tac. *Ann.* 15.12, Apul. *Met.* 9.28 etc.

v. 48 ***ibus*** *Ibus* is an EL–archaising form for *eis*[34] which also appears in Plautus, *Mil.* 74 and Pompon. *atel.* 104. Terence always opts for the regular CL form *eis*.

v. 104 ***me facit festinem*** Several adjectives of the second declension in *-us, -a, -um* have double forms following the third-declension. This seems also the case here with *festinem* in place of *festinum*.[35] Whereas

[34] For the feminine *eabus*, see Cat. *Agr.* 152.1 and Hem. *Hist.* 32.

[35] Cf. Non. 482 M; for an alternative opinion, namely *festinem* as a present subjunctive of *festino* in an *ut* clause, depending upon *facit* with *ut* not expressed, cf. Bennett (1910–14: I 226).

such equivalent third-declension forms appear quite frequently in Plautine drama, they are absent from Terence, *perpes* for CL *perpetuus* at *Amph.* 280, *gnaruris* for CL *gnarus* at *Most.* 100, *mansues* for CL *mansuetus* at Plaut. *Asin.* 145 etc. In Terence, on the other hand, we find only the CL equivalent formation *mansuetus, Andr.* 114. A possible exception to Terence's usual avoidance of unclassical doublet formations of the third declension occurs in *Eunuchus*, where the form *limes/is* may occur in place of *limus*, v. 601 *ego limis specto sic per flabellum clanculum.*[36]

v. 117 ***colos cumatilis*** *Colos* for *color* is an EL and archaising form,[37] which appears in Plautus, *Men.* 828, *Mil.* 1179. In Terence we find only *color*, the CL equivalent, *Andr.* 878.

v. 123 ***de aedi summa*** Several nouns of the third declension have retained alternative ablative forms in *-i* instead of *-e*, as is the case with *aedi* here in place of *aede*, a form which also appears in Plaut. *Poen.* 847. These EL–archaising and PC double formations in *-i* are common in many comic dramatists with the exception of Terence, *sorti* for *sorte* at Plaut. *Cas.* 428, *parti* for *parte* at Plaut. *Men.* 479, *lenti* for *lente* at Titin. *tog.* 175, *carni* for *carne* at Plaut. *Capt.* 914, *peni* for *pene* at Naev. *com.* 100. The only possible instance of unclassical double formation in *-i* appears in *Eunuchus, parti* for *parte* at *Eun.* 579. Cf., on the other hand, *parte* at *Heaut.* 57.

Derivation

v. 124 ***valentia*** Substantive derivatives in *-ntia* are common in the *sermo plebeius*, even though a large proportion of these words were in use in classical speech.[38] Whereas unclassical formations of this kind, like *valentia* here,[39] are common in Plautus, they are absent from Terence, in Plautus, *essentia, incogitantia, lubentia, stultiloquentia*. Cf. also Nov. *atel.* 38 *tolutiloquentia*.

v. 138 ***lotiolente*** Adjectives in *-lentus* are both archaic and vulgar.[40] Such unclassical formations, like *lotiolentus* here and *obstrudulentus* in v. 165, are common in Plautus: *bucculentus, corpulentus, frustulentus, macilentus, mustulentus, pisculentus*. Terence restricts himself to those that have the sanction of later CL speech (*truculentus*).

[36] In the verse under discussion, however, *limis* may be the ablative plural of *limus -a -um*, namely *limis oculis*, and not the nominative third-declension form. Cf. Donat. ad loc. *limis; si nominativus est singularis, transversus significat, si septimus pluralis, deest oculis*.

[37] Cf. Varro, Sallust, Livy, Pliny, Symmachus. [38] Cf. Cooper (1895: 32–5).

[39] Also found in Naevius, Titinius and PC Latin, Tertullian, Boethius.

[40] Cf. Cooper (1895: 132–3). For adjectives in *-lentus* in Plautus, cf. Stella (1982: 157–62), Ernout (1949).

v. 167 ***feminina*** Adjectives in *-inus* are very common in colloquial sources, especially adjectives derived from animal names. Unclassical (EL–archaising and PC) formations of this kind abound in Plautus, where they largely occur in proverbial expressions and metaphors, in the satirists and in rustic writers;[41] in Plautus *agninus*, *aquilinus*, *cantherinus*, *clurinus*, *colubrinus*, *formicinus, noctuinus, pantherinus*, *soricinus*. Cf. Pompon. *atel.* 177 *passerinus*. In Terence such an unclassical formation, *mustelinus*, appears only once at *Eun*. 689.

Syntax

Prepositional usage

v. 27 ***inter decem annos*** *Inter* in temporal function also appears in Plautus, *Truc.* 510 *inter tot dies*. In Terence, on the other hand, *inter* denotes locality, *Hec*. 93, or relation, *Andr.* 552. The only instance of a possible temporal usage of the preposition in Terence appears at *Eun*. 629–31 *Dum rus eo, coepi egomet mecum inter vias . . . cogitare.* Cf. RD s.v. *in via dum eo; inter saepe denotat temporis durationem* (cf. McGlynn I 296).

v. 52 ***extra consilium*** *Extra* is used here in the sense of *sine*, a usage which occurs in Plautus, *Poen*. 331–2 *tertia salve extra pretium*. In Terence *extra* denotes locality either literally or figuratively, *Phorm*. 876, *Heaut*. 298, or is used as an equivalent to *praeter, Phorm*. 98.

v. 60 ***advorsum illum res suas conqueritur*** *Adversus* here is used in the sense of *exadversus, ante, apud*, denoting spatial locality. Similarly in Plaut. *Amph*. 936 *ius iurandum verum te advorsum dedi, Asin*. 564, Afran. *tog*. 148. In Terence *advorsum* is used as a preposition with this sense once, at *Andr*. 265 *aliquid me advorsum hunc loqui*, in a scene (vv. 236–300) where Terence, as Rambelli (1936: 130–60) and Denzler (1968: 45–51) have shown, deviates from his original by keeping Mysis on stage from the previous scene. Elsewhere in Terence *contra* is used with the meaning of 'in the eyes or estimation of' (*Andr*. 42), *contra* (*Heaut*. 623), or it is used as an adverb with verbs denoting motion (*Ad*. 27).

v. 63 ***in foro*** *Apud* + accusative combinations are often used as equivalents to *in* + ablative syntagms for denoting spatial location (for *apud forum* = *in foro*, cf. H-Sz 224). Whereas in Terence we find only *apud forum* combinations denoting locality (*Andr*. 254, *Ad*. 154), *in foro* syntagms in place of equivalent *apud forum* ones, as in this Titinian line, appear several times in Plautus, *Amph*. 1012, *Capt*. 491, *Cist*. 775, *Curc*. 502, *Most*. 534 etc.

[41] Cf. Cooper (1895: 139–44).

Verbal and adverbial syntax

v. 41 ***hac domo abhorres*** *Abhorreo* construed with the simple ablative case, *hac domo*. In Terence the verb is construed with *ab* + ablative syntagms, *Hec*. 714, *Andr*. 829.

v. 56 ***has nocte suspicare crevi*** *Cerno* construed with an infinitive clause (EL usage) is also found in Plautus, *Cist*. 1 *te amavi mi amicam esse crevi*. In Terence the verb occurs either in absolute use, *Ad*. 439, or with a direct-object accusative, *Andr*. 135.

v. 65 ***osculavi privignae caput*** The verb in a transitive use as here occurs also in Plaut. *Asin*. 669, *Epid*. 583 etc., see also Turpil. *com*. 105. In Terence the verb occurs once in the last act of *Heautontimoroumenos* v. 900, in an absolute use, though, *mitto iam osculari atque amplexari*.

v. 155 ***fortasse <ei> votum fuisse*** The EL construction of *fortasse* with the infinitive occurs also in Plaut. *Asin*. 37, *Merc*. 782. Possibly it appears also at Ter. *Hec*. 313, where the line, however, is textually doubtful. The infinitive construction is the reading given by Donatus. On the other hand *concluserit* is found in A, *conciverit* in Σ, and *concivisset* in Iov.

vv. 182–3 ***quod rogas, neminem decet bonam*** *Decet* is used here in a personal construction, a syntagm often found in Plautine drama, Plaut. *Capt*. 208 *hau nos id deceat, Cist*. 19, *Men*. 131 etc., Titin. *tog*. 115. In Terence *decet* is used either absolutely, *Ad*. 108, or is construed in impersonal sequences with the accusative, *Andr*. 421, the dative, *Ad*. 491, infinitive or a.c.i. syntagms, *Eun*. 789, or, finally, with dative + infinitive constructions, *Hec*. 164.

Sentence syntax

v. 113 ***Paula mea, amabo, . . . addito 'praefiscini!'*** *Amabo* as a formulaic term, modifying a request in the imperative, is common in Plautus, *Aul*. 142, *Bacch*. 100, *Cist*. 110, *Curc*. 197, *Men*. 405, *Merc*. 503, *Most*. 166, *Pers*. 245, *Poen*. 240 etc. This mainly colloquial usage[42] occurs also in Naev. *com*. 85 *cave cadas amabo!*. In Terence the verb appears in this use in *Eunuchus*, vv. 130, 150, 534, 663, 838. At *Hec*. 398 all manuscripts give the reading *dicam abortum esse*, accepted by editors, with the exception of Fleckeisen, who unnecessarily emends to *dic amabo tuam esse*.

[42] Cf. Cicero in letters, e.g. *Att*. 16.2.2, Catul. 32.1, Mart. 8.76.1.

Lexicon

Nouns

v. 22 ***forma ferocem*** *Ferox* in the sense of *superbus, fretus, arrogans*, construed with the ablative of respect, appears also in Plautus, *Mil.* 1390 *formast ferox*, where we find the same alliterative combination. In Terence this use of *ferox* appears at *Eun.* 415 *eon es ferox quia habes imperium in beluas?*.

v. 150 ***omnium vitium . . . expertem*** *Expers* in the sense of *vacuus, liber* occurs also at Plaut. *Amph.* 170. In Terence, at *Heaut.* 652 *ne expers partis esset de nostris bonis*, the word is equivalent to *non particeps*, ἄμοιρος.

v. 168 ***arcam*** *Arca* for *cista* occurs also in Plaut. *Bacch.* 943, *Cas.* 664, Nov. *atel.* 109.

Verbs

v. 10 ***ferit quemquam hostem*** *Ferio* is used here with the meaning of *caedere*, as in Plaut. *Cist.* 641 *utrum hac me feriam an ab laeva latus?*. The verb occurs only once in Terence, at *Phorm.* 46–7 *Geta ferietur alio munere ubi era pepererit*. Here it is used in a figurative sense though, as equivalent to *punire*.

v. 18 ***qui rem disperdit et meam dotem comest*** *Disperdere* is used here in the sense of *funditus dissipare, absumere, divastare, dilapidare*. Cf. also Plaut. *Cas.* 248, where we find the same *iunctura*, *rem disperdere*, *Trin.* 334. In Terence we find the equivalent *dilapidare*, *Phorm.* 897 *priusquam dilapidat nostras triginta minas*. Donatus remarks ad loc. *dilapidet pecuniam: disperdat*.

v. 19 ***perbiteres*** *Perbito* is a rare EL verb, with the meaning of *pereo*. While it appears twice in Plautus, *Pseud.* 778 and *Rud.* 495, it is absent from Terence, who regularly opts for the CL semantic equivalent *pereo*.

v. 24 ***aspecta formam*** *Aspectare* in the sense of *aspicere, spectare* is also found in Plautus, *Amph.* 270 *caelum aspectat,* 1028. This use of the verb appears once in Terence, at *Eun.* 559 *quid me adspectas?*.

v. 45 ***aspellit domo*** The verb in the sense 'to drive away' appears also in Plautus, *Merc.* 115–16 *aspellito, detrude, deturba in viam, Amph.* 1000, *Capt.* 519.

vv. 49–50 ***clavis . . . abstrudi iubeo*** *Abstrudo* is used here in the sense of 'conceal from view', 'hide' *abdo, abscondo, celo, occulto*. The word appears in this sense several times within Plautine drama, *Aul.* 577, *Aul.* 617, *Curc.* 606, *Rud.* 1007 etc.

v. 58 ***aedibus facessat*** *Facessere* is used here in the sense of *recedere, discedere, abire*, as in Afran. *tog*. 203. It appears once in Terence, at *Phorm*. 635, in a part of the play where Terence once more deviates from his original.[43] Elsewhere in Terentian drama we encounter instead the synonymous *abire, discedere*.

v. 83 ***pernam totam diligit*** *Diligere* is used here in the unclassical sense of 'to cut', which is also found in Plautus, *Curc*. 424 *ubi machaera diligit*. In Terence *diligere* has its common CL meaning, *amo, faveo, studeo, cupio*, *Ad*. 873 etc.

v. 125 ***quoniam catapulta volat*** *Volare* in the sense of *celeriter currere* occurs also in Plaut. *Pers*. 199 *vola curriculo, Merc*. 486. In Terence this usage appears once, at *Hec*. 438 *quid cessas; vola*, in a scene where Terence once more deviates from his original in replacing a monologue with a dialogue (415–29).[44]

v. 128 ***verrite aedis, spargite*** For *spargere* in the sense of 'to sprinkle, spatter a surface', Plaut. *Pseud*. 164. In Terence the verb appears only in the transferred sense to 'variegate', 'fleck', 'dot with marking features', *Heaut*. 1062 *sparso ore*.

v. 130 ***qui illam derivet*** *Derivo* is used here in its literal meaning, i.e. *de aquarum ductu*, as in Plaut. *Truc*. 563 *quasi de fluvio qui aquam derivat sibi*. In Terence the verb is used figuratively at *Phorm*. 323 in the sense of 'to turn aside the wrath of an old man'. Once more a verb, the literal meaning of which is found in both Plautus and Titinius, appears in Terence in a figurative use only. This is the case with *ferveo* at Titin. *tog*. 125 *cocus magnum ahenum, quando fervit*, see also Plaut. *Pseud*. 840. In Ter. *Ad*. 534 *quom fervit maxume, tam placidum quam ovem reddo* (='when he is at his hottest'), it is used for the wrath of the old man Demea.

vv. 139–40 ***duo postica, quae loco mercede*** *Locare* is used here in the sense of *elocare*, as in Plaut. *Curc*. 464, *Most*. 535. In Terence the verb is used with reference to *matrimonium* (*Phorm*. 752).

vv. 171–2 ***tentipellium inducitur*** *Inducere* in the sense of *obducere, superducere*, περιτιθέναι occurs also in Plaut. *Most*. 827 *inducti pice*, Pompon. *atel*. 95. In Terence the verb occurs only in the formulaic combination *animum* or *in animum induco*. Elsewhere it has the meaning of *aliud adducere ad aliquid*, *Andr*. 399. At *Heaut*. 723 it possibly has the sense of *decipio*.

v. 181 ***domum se capessit*** *Se capessere* has here the meaning of a simple *abire*. This is an EL and colloquial *iunctura*, restricted in EL to comedy, Plaut. *Amph*. 262, *Asin*. 158, *Bacch*. 113 etc. It reappears later, possibly as an archaism, in Apuleius, *Met*. 1.22.

[43] Cf. Lowe (1983a: 431). [44] Cf. Lowe (1983a: 429).

Adverbs

v. 46 ***tandem ut moribus placeam viro*** *Tandem* is used here, according to Nonius (406 M), as equivalent to *tamen*, an EL usage which also occurs in Plautus, *Aul.* 371 *Volui animum tandem confirmare hodie meum.*[45] In Terence *tandem* is either equivalent to *denique, postremo, aliquando, Andr.* 586 or is used as an expletive in interrogative and/or exhortative clauses, *Andr.* 859.

v. 68 ***commode . . . exit*** *Commode* is used here in the rare sense of *eodem tempore*,[46] as in Plaut. *Rud.* 309 *quos perconter commode eccos video astare*. Terence employs instead *commodum*, the common CL equivalent, in the sense of *eodem tempore*, cf. *Eun.* 343.[47] *Commode* is used in Terence in its regular CL sense of *bene*, *Andr.* 475, *comiter, Heaut.* 152, *iucunde, Heaut.* 559 etc.

v. 127 ***munde facite . . . ut sita sint*** *Munde* here has the meaning of *lepide, laute, eleganter*. Cf. also Plaut. *Poen.* 1178, Pompon. *atel.* 54.

v. 151 ***disertim*** *Disertim* is an EL word,[48] semantically equivalent to *plane, palam*. Cf. also Plaut. *Stich.* 241.

Style

Terms of abuse or endearment

v. 71 ***scrattae muli<eris>*** This term of abuse is found in Plaut. fr. 97 *scrattae, scruppedae, strittabillae, sordidae*. The term seems to have been used for denoting the vices of a *meretrix*.[49]

v. 95 ***meae deliciae*** *Deliciae* is a common term of endearment in Plautus, never found in Terentian drama, Plaut. *Most.* 15, *Pers.* 204, *Poen.* 365, *Truc.* 921 etc.

vv. 148–9 ***pestis*** For *pestis* as a term of abuse cf. Plaut. *Pseud.* 204, Ter. *Ad.* 189, in the Sannio scene.

Figurative usages

v. 104 ***nunc hoc uror*** *Uro* is used here as equivalent to *torment*. This usage appears in Plaut. *Bacch.* 1091, *Pers.* 801, *Poen.* 770. In Terence such a figurative meaning of the verb is restricted to *Eunuchus*, vv. 274, 438.

45 Cf. H-Sz 497.

46 Found also in Plautus, Sisenna, Seneca. For the archaising character of the language of Sisenna, cf. Oakley (1997–8: I 145).

47 Cf. Donat. ad loc. *tantum quod vel ipso eodemque tempore*.

48 Cf. Andr. *poet.* 5(6), Lucil. 1156, Acc. *trag.* 350.

49 For its colloquial character, cf. Ernout and Meillet (1951: 1066–7).

v. 165 ***rus detrudetur*** *Detrudo* is used here with the meaning of *ad vilia servorum officia relegare*. Cf. also Plaut. *Poen.* 1152 *quos ego iam detrudam ad molas, Trin.* 551.

Collocations

v. 47 ***eu ecastor*** The interjection *eu* coupled with an oath, such as *ecastor* here, is a common combination in Plautine drama, *eu ecastor* at Plaut. *Mil.* 1062, 1066, *eu edepol* at Plaut. *Epid.* 72, *Men.* 160, *eu hercle* at *Plaut. Men.* 316, *Mil.* 394 etc. Such combinations of the interjection do not appear in Terence, who uses it for denoting joy or approbation in forms of address, *Eun.* 154 *eu noster, laudo, Phorm.* 869 *eu Geta!*.

Iuncturae

Several further word collocations or combinations also indicate a linguistic and stylistic affinity between Titinius and Plautus rather than Terence. In particular:

nominal *iuncturae*: *foetida anima* (Titin. *tog.* 23, Plaut. *Merc.* 574), *improbus homo* (Titin. *tog.* 166, Plaut. *Bacch.* 552, *Pers.* 762, *Truc.* 333), *longus sermo* (Titin. *tog.* 59, Plaut. *Men.* 760, *Trin.* 797), the asyndetic enumeration of food in v. 91 *farticula, cerebellum, lactes agninas*, Plaut. *Capt.* 850–1, *Pseud.* 814–15, Afran. *tog.* 142, 300, Naev. *com.* 104.

verbal *iuncturae*: *sermonem/sermones conferre* (Titin. *tog.* 78, Plaut. *Curc.* 290, *Poen.* 34), *domum se capessere* (Titin. *tog.* 181, Plaut. *Amph.* 262), *hostis fugare* (Titin. *tog.* 154, Plaut. *Pseud.* 1270), *auro privare* (Titin. *tog.* 2, Plaut. *Poen.* 774–5), *velo* + parts of the body collocations where *velo* = 'to cover for ritual or ceremonial purposes' (Titin. *tog.* 87, Plaut. *Amph.* 257), *verrere* + *spargere* combinations (Titin. *tog.* 128, Plaut. *Pseud.* 164), synonymous pairs of *contemplo* and *aspecto* (Titin. *tog.* 24, *Epid.* 622, *Most.* 172), the *quo te avortisti* formula (Titin *tog.* 94, Plaut. *Amph.* 899, *Truc.* 358), *parvi facio* (Titin *tog.* 98, Plaut. *Mil.* 1351, *Rud.* 697–8), *aedibus emigrare* (Titin. *tog.* 148–9, *Most.* 951), the *figura etymologica statuere statuam* (Titin. *tog.* 132, Plaut. *Asin.* 712, *Bacch.* 640, *Curc.* 139), [-m] alliterative combinations with the verb *multare*, v. 26 *multetur malo* (Naev. *com.* 34, Plaut. *Amph.* 852, *Merc.* 21, *Pseud.* 1228, etc.).

adverbial *iuncturae*: pleonastic combinations of the synonymous adverbs *repente* and *subito*, v. 79 *quid desubito tam repente ad me venisti?* (Plaut. *Mil.* 177).

phrases: *addo* + oratio recta + *quo* complements (Titin. *tog.* 113 *ad laudem addito 'praefiscini'*, Plaut. *Cas.* 518).

Conclusions

The present study has shown that Titinius stands closer to the traditional language as exemplified by writers such as Naevius, Ennius, Caecilius, Turpilius, Afranius, but mainly Plautus, than to the innovative Terence. The only similarities between Caecilius and Terence not to be found in Plautus are the use of *gestus* with the meaning of movement in v. 119 (see also *Phorm.* 890), *constituo* in the sense of *statuere, velle, placare, iudicare* construed with infinitive or a.c.i. syntagms (Titin. *tog.* 49, Ter. *Eun.* 205), the reflexive *se ostendere* with the meaning of 'to appear' (Titin. *tog.* 116, Ter. *Hec.* 626–7) whereas in Plautus it occurs in the sense of 'to reveal my true nature' (*Asin.* 862), and the following *iuncturae exporge frontem* in v. 178 (*Ad.* 839), *officium fungi* in v. 53 (see also *Heaut.* 66), *sibi vult* in the sense of 'to mean' in v. 103 (*Heaut.* 615). In particular:

1. Several EL features common in several comic dramatists, especially Plautus, but avoided by Terence, are found in Titinius' lines. (a) In several cases these features can be attributed simply to the historical development of Latin, as is the case for example with features that are avoided in authors after Titinius, with the exception of archaising authors as intentional archaisms, e.g. *tandem* for *tamen* in v. 46. (b) Alternatively, several features seem to have been used as intentional archaisms even by Plautus and other comic dramatists anterior to Titinius, as is shown for example by their restriction to the end of the line and/or half-line. This is the case for example with non-periphrastic forms of the verb *nolo* in v. 108.
2. Some colloquial options common in Plautus and other comic writers, but avoided in Terence, are also to be found in Titinius' plays. This is the case for example with the use of *se capessere* for *abire* in v. 181.
3. In the case of equivalent morphological, syntactical and lexical alternatives, Titinius opts for the one common in Plautus and the other comic dramatists and not for the Terentian equivalent. This is the case for example with unclassical doublet ablative forms in *-i* for *-e, aedi* in v. 123, the use of *diu* in v. 29 etc.
4. Certain other stylistic and lexical options, such as the use of specific word groups, figurative usages etc., common in Plautus and other

comic dramatists but avoided in Terence, are again to be found in Titinius, e.g. the formulaic combination *eu ecastor* in v. 47 etc.

Terence is closest to the language of both Plautus and Titinius mainly in *Eunuchus* and, in other plays, in those scenes where, distancing himself from his original, he reworks his material in a more traditional line. This is the case for example with *ferox* in the sense of *superbus, fretus, arrogans* in v. 22, *aspecto* in place of *aspicio, specto* in v. 24 etc.

Atta

According to St Jerome, Atta died in 77 BC (cf. Hier. *Chron.* ad Ol. 175.3 = 77 BC, *olympiade CLXXV, anno tertio, T. Quinctius Atta scriptor togatarum Romae moritur, sepultusque via Praenestina ad miliarium II*).[50]

The surviving lines from his plays are too scanty to allow any certain conclusions, being limited to 18 fragments and 25 lines. Even in these few lines, however, we still encounter several linguistic peculiarities that, despite their frequency in Plautus and the authors in his linguistic line, are avoided in Terence or used by him only for specific stylistic reasons, mainly in *Eunuchus*.

Morphology

Nouns

v. 25 ***vespera oriente*** The feminine *vespera* in place of the masculine *vesper* also appears in Plaut. *Curc.* 4 *prima vespera*. Here the form is used in an ablative construction, a syntagm avoided in CL and appearing only in EL–archaising (Livy, Tacitus, Fronto) and PC authors (Ammianus Marcellinus).[51] In Terence only the masculine form *vesper*, the more common equivalent in Latin literature, is found, the accusative *vesperum* at *Hec.* 442, the genitive *vesperi* at *Andr.* 768.

Verbs

v. 1 ***daturin estis aurum?*** The periphrastic conjugation *daturi estis* also appears in Plautus, *Most.* 62, 604, *Truc.* 4. In Terence we find only the regular non-periphrastic conjugation of the verb.

[50] Cf. Guardì (1985: 19–20).

[51] For the distribution of the form, cf. N-W I 855.

v. 2 ***pepugero*** There are several verbs in Latin, which, in forming their perfect tenses in analogy to Greek practice, reduplicate the first syllable by repeating the first consonant with an *-e* instead of the stem-vowel, e.g. *pepugi* in place of *pupugi* etc. Such perfect forms, like *pepugero* here and *memordisse* in v. 7 in place of *momordisse*, appear in Plautus, *Poen.* 1074 *memordit* etc.

Syntax

v. 10 ***cras est conmunis dies*** For the construction of *cras* with the indicative present, cf. also Plaut. *Most.* 654 *sat habeo si cras fero* etc. In Terence such a syntagm appears once, in *Eun.* 338–9 *cras est mihi iudicium.* Elsewhere in Terence, in cases of *cras* + indicative syntagms referring to the future, *cras* is construed with the future indicative, cf. *Ad.* 840–1, which is the most usual construction of *cras* in Latin literature.

Lexicon

vv. 5–6 ***occlusero fontem*** *Occludo* is here equivalent to *obserando claudere.* Cf. also Plaut. *Amph.* 1018 *aedis occluserunt*, *Aul.* 274, *Cist.* 649 etc. The usage appears in Terence only at *Eun.* 784 *de occludendis aedibus*. Elsewhere in Terentian drama the verb is used in a figurative sense, as equivalent to *secludo, intercludo, prohibeo*, *Andr.* 557.

v. 9 ***exornata sit*** *Exornare* is used here in the sense of a simple *ornare, decorare*. Such a usage appears several times in Plautus, *Cas.* 767–8 *candide vestitus, lautus exornatusque ambulat*, *Epid.* 226, *Poen.* 284 etc., but only once in Terence, at *Eun.* 683 *varia veste exornatus fui*. At *Heaut.* 950 *exornare* is used with the meaning of *foedare verberibus*.

v. 13 ***degularunt omnia*** *Degulare* in the sense of to ‘swallow down’, ‘devour’, *(de)vorare, comedere* is an EL verb which also appears in Afran. *tog.* 17 *iam dudum occuluisse, degulasse oportuit.*

Style

v. 15 ***in cera mucronique aremus osseo*** *Arare* is used here in a figurative sense in place of *scribere*. This usage appears also in Titin. *tog.* 179 *velim ego osse arare campum cereum.* It seems to be a colloquial usage, which reappears later in Martial, 4.86.11 *inversa pueris arande charta.*

CHAPTER 10

TERENCE, PLAUTUS AND THE *ATELLANA*

Comoedia atellana

The *fabula atellana* was developed by the Oscans in Campania and taken over by the Latins at an early stage (Livy 7.2 and Val. Max. 2.4). This form of comedy was particularly popular during the first century BC and took its literary form in the works of Pomponius Bononiensis – of his comedies seventy titles and almost two hundred lines have survived[1] – and Novius, Pomponius' contemporary *atellana* author – of his work forty-four titles and 118 lines survives. Novius' sense of humour had the approval of Cicero, who praises three of his jokes in *De or.* 2.

Velleius Paterculus (*Macr.* Sat. II. 12) claims that Pomponius was a contemporary of Rutilius Rufus, Claudius Quadrigarius and Valerius Antia. Therefore one should place his *floruit* between 150 and 70 BC.[2] Among his works one finds titles of *togata* plays (*Augur, Fullones*) and parodies of ancient myth (*Agamemnon suppositus, Armorum iudicia*). Most of the titles of his plays, however, show a real interest in the simple everyday life of Roman people and are full of the circular *atellana* figures (Bucco, Dossenus etc.). Novius started his dramatic activity a year after Pomponius.[3] His plays also have typical *atellana* figures (*Duo Dosseni, Bucco exsul* etc.), present the life of the Italian countryside (*Fullones, Decuma* etc.) and have typical Italian titles in *-aria* (*Gallinaria, Lignaria,*

[1] As to the problem whether Pomponius also wrote *praetextae, togatae* and satyr plays, cf. Wiseman (1988: 1–3). For Pomponious as a writer of the *atellana*, see also Jer. Chron. 150H (89 B.C., *L. Pomponius Bononiensis Atellanorum scriptor clarus habetur*), Gell. *NA* 10.24.5, 13.10.7, 16.6.7, Macr. *Sat.* I 4.22, VI 4.19, 9.4.

[2] For a later date (44 BC) based on Cic. *Fam.* 7.31, see Leo (1914: 169 n.2). For the life and the dramatic activity of Pomponius, cf. also Raffaelli (1987: 115–33), Traina (1992: 175–7), Citti (1994: 151–5), Brazzano (1999: 179–89), Georgala (1991: 269–75), Frassinetti (1953: 95–120).

[3] Cf. also Munk (1826: 43ff).

Tabellaria, Togularia).[4] He also wrote plays with a mythological argument, such as *Hercules coactor* and *Phoenissae*, and comedies satirising contemporary people and institutions (*Pappus praeteritus, Milites Pometinenses* etc.). One of the important features, however, of his work is his predilection for obscene wit.[5]

These are the two main representatives of the *literary atellana*. However, one line survives with the name of Aprissius,[6] and Macrobius claims that later the genre was revived by Mummius, under whose name three fragments have survived. *Atellana* plays, often used as *exodia* after tragedy performances, dealt mainly with the rustic life in the country or in the small provincial town, as it is evident from many of the titles (*Bubulcus, Vindemiatores, Pappus Agricola, Rusticus* etc.), were fond of farcical situations, especially cheating and trickery, and of obscenity, and had fixed characters (the *personae Oscae*), like Maccus, the fool, Bucco, the glutton or the braggart, Pappus, the silly old man, Dossenus, the cunning trickster, and Manducus, the constant eater (if not an alternative name for Dossenus).[7]

The present chapter offers the first line-by-line examination of the language and style of the *atellana*'s fragments (Pomponius and Novius; the evidence for Aprissius and Mummius is too scanty to allow us any conclusions). The result will be that

1. Both Pomponius' and Novius' language and style are close to the comic tradition (i.e. to the language of its main representatives, Plautus,[8] Caecilius etc.), in contrast to Terence's language and style, which stand apart.
2. Linguistic and stylistic usages common in Plautus, Pomponius and Novius but found *hapax* or rarely in Terentian drama are mainly found in the *Eunuchus*, where Terence deviates from his original, reworking his material in a more traditional way, as is shown by the accumulation of such traditional, mainly Plautine features, elsewhere avoided by him.

4 For *atellana* titles in *-aria*, cf. also Wölflin (1888: 308–9).
5 See also Marzullo (1973: 11ff.), Frassinetti (1953: 120–7), Kroll (1936: 1216).
6 For Aprissius, see Reiter (1925: 1435–9).
7 For the *atellana* figures, cf. also Hartman (1922: 225–38), Marx (1896b), Rossbach (1920: 331–5), Szilagyi (1941: passim).
8 For the influence of the *atellana* on Plautus, cf. also Beare (1930: 165–8).

Before we begin, a note on the text: I follow mainly the edition by O. Ribbeck, *Scaenicae Romanorum Poesis Fragmenta* (Leipzig 1873). P. F. Frassineti's edition, *Fabularum Atellanarum Fragmenta* (Turin 1955) and D. Romano, *Atellana Fabula* (Palermo 1953), have also been taken into account.

Pomponius Bononiensis

Morphology

Moods and tenses

v. 34 **vix nunc quod edim invenio** old optatives of the verb *edo* are often used in archaic or archaising texts in place of the normal CL subjunctive equivalents, as is *edim* here. Whereas archaic optatives of this kind are absent from the Terentian corpus, they occur in Plautus: as to *edim*, *Aul.* 430, *Poen.* 1284, *Trin.* 474, 475 (see also Caec. *com.* 16); *edis*, *Men.* 249, *Poen.* 867, *Trin.* 473; *edit*, Plaut. *Aul.* 672, *Capt.* 461, *Men.* 90, *Poen.* 9, *Vid.* 49 (see also Naev. *com.* 26); *edimus*, *Poen.* 537; *edint*, *Men.* 457. As to *editis*, see also Nov. *atel.* 6.

v. 107 ***non erat qui corpus tremulum famula tutaret toga*** the active *tuto* for the deponent CL *tutor* is also found in Plaut. *Merc.* 865 *vos, Lares viales, ut me bene tutetis*. The active form is also found in CIL 44456 and later in Hyg. *Fab.* 100.1. In Terence, on the other hand, only the CL deponent form occurs, *Hec.* 42, 735, *Phorm.* 466, 789, *Andr.* 288. The same also holds good for *frusto* in place of *frustor* in v. 79, also found in Plaut. *Bacch.* 548 *atque i se quom frustrant, frustrari alios stolidi existumant*. The active form is again the unclassical formation which Terence does not opt for.

v. 175 ***sed qui utrosque error vos agitat, expedibo*** Several of the verbs belonging to the fourth conjugation have in EL future by-forms in *-ibo* and not in *-iam*, as in CL. This is the case with *expedibo* here in place of *expediam*, also found in Plaut. *Truc.* 138 *ego expedibo*. The formation is restricted to EL authors[9] and is avoided in Terence, where only the CL form *expediam* occurs, *Andr.* 617 *at iam expediam*. The same also holds good for *aperibo*, found at Pompon. *atel.* 173 *aperibo; non possum pati*. This EL form appears also in Plaut. *Truc.* 763 *ego edepol <iam> tua probra aperibo omnia*. In Terence again only the CL form appears, *Ad.* 23 *senes qui primi venient i partem aperient*. Similarly, *reperibo* occurs in *atel.* 9 *cum nemo, qui a te recipiat, reperibitur*. For *reperibo*, Caec. *com.* 120 *reperibit* and Plaut. *Epid.* 151 *aliqua res*

[9] Its distribution: Ennius, Plautus, Pacuvius, Accius, Pomponius.

reperibitur. In Terence again only the CL future forms occur: *reperies* at *Hec.* 843, *reperiam* at *Phorm.* 235 and finally *reperient* at *Phorm.* 234.

Declension

v. 61 ***oro te, vaso, per lactes tuas*** *Vas*, although belonging to the third declension, has some by-forms following the second, as *vaso* here. Whereas unclassical second-declension forms are absent from Terence altogether (*vas* at *Heaut.* 141), they appear in Plautus, *Truc.* 53–4 *aut aliquod vasum argenteum aut vasum ahenum.*

Syntax

Verbal syntax

v. 34 ***quod edim invenio*** *Invenio* in the sense of *reperire, offendere* is construed here with a *quod* clause. Similarly at Plaut. *Bacch.* 219 *quod ames paratumst, quod des inventost opus*. Such a construction of the verb does not occur in the Terentian drama, where *invenio* is construed either with the accusative, *Andr.* 356, the a.c.i., *Andr.* 863 or an interrogative clause as its complement, *Eun.* 719.

v. 48 ***quin ergo, quando convenit, complectite?*** *Complector* is used here in the sense of *manus, lacertos circumevenire alicui* and is found in absolute use, as in Plautus, *Amph.* 290 *qui complexus cum Alcumena cubat amans, Asin.* 615, *Asin.* 640, 642, *Curc.* 188, *Men.* 1124, *Mil.* 1329, *Poen.* 1294, *Rud.* 1172, 1203, *Truc.* 370. In Terence the verb occurs only with an accusative as its direct object, *Andr.* 133 *mediam mulierem complectitur*.

v. 51 ***Mars, tibi facturum voveo, si umquam redierit, bidenti verre*** *Voveo* is construed here with the a.c.i., as in Plautus, *Curc.* 72 *me inferre Veneri vovi iaientaculum*. In Terence, on the other hand, the verb is construed with an *ut* clause, *Hec.* 434–5 *vovisse hunc . . . si salvos domum redisset . . . ut me ambulando rumperet.*

Nominal syntax

v. 74 ***simile est, quasi cum in caelo fulgit propter lunam lucifer*** The construction of *similis* with a *quasi* clause appears also in Plaut. *Cist.* 472 *similest ius iurandum amantum quasi ius confusicium*. In Terence, *similis* in the sense of 'similar', 'like', with comparison expressed through adverbs, as here, occurs only with *atque, Phorm.* 31 *ne simili utamur fortuna atque usi sumus*. Elsewhere it is found either in absolute use, *Hec.* 202, or construed with the genitive, *Heaut.* 1020, *Eun.* 313, etc.

Lexicon

Nouns and adjectives

v. 3 ***nec mortalis nec mortalium ullum in terra miseriust*** *In terra* or *in terris* is a common expression with the meaning of 'in the world', 'in existence', especially as an intensive phrase after superlatives. The singular form is common in EL, whereas CL usually substitutes singular with plural.[10] The EL singular expression occurs in Plaut. *Bacch.* 1170 *senex optume quantumst in terra, sine <me> hoc exorare aps te, Curc.* 141, *Mil.* 313. In Terence we find only genitive plural combinations (partitive genitive after local adverbs) in the sense of 'on earth', 'in the world', *Phorm.* 551. As for *terra* simply in the sense of 'earth', e.g. *Ad.* 790, *Eun.* 580 etc.

v. 9 ***tum prae se portant ascendibilem semitam*** *Semita* occurs here in the sense of 'a side path or track', 'alley', 'lane'. The word is used in this meaning also in Plaut. *Rud.* 212 *aut viam aut semitam monstret.* In Terence, on the other hand, we find only the synonymous *angiportum, Ad.* 576, 578, *Eun.* 845, *Phorm.* 891.

v. 89 ***nupsit posterius dotatae vetulae varicosae vafrae*** *Vetulus* is used here in the sense of 'somewhat advanced in years', 'elderly', *senex*, as in Pompon. *atel.* 132 and Plaut. *Epid.* 666–7 *Satine illic homo ludibrio nos vetulos decrepitos duos habet?, Most.* 275. In the case of *atel.* 132, what is more, the word is used as a substantive in a colloquial way, as in Priap. 68.27, Mart. 3.76.1, Juv. 13.55, Cic. *Fam.* 7.16.1.

v. 123 ***nam plus quaesti facerem*** *Questus* has here the meaning of 'wealth' or 'possessions', 'income'. This meaning also occurs in Plaut. *Asin.* 186 *ad suom quemque hominem quaestum esse aequomst callidum.* In Terence the substantive is used in the sense of 'acquisition' or 'pursuit of income', 'gainful occupation', *Hec.* 735, or of 'the production of profit', *Hec.* 50.

vv. 127–8 ***Rustici edunt libenter tristis atros intubos*** *Rusticus* has here the meaning of a countryman, peasant, rustic. Such a meaning appears twice in the Plautine corpus, *Capt.* 663 *nam semper occant prius quam sariunt rustici, Truc.* 263 *quae per ridiculum rustico suades stuprum.* In Terence the word is found once, at *Heaut.* 142–3 *nisi eos qui opere rustico faciundo facile sumptum exsercirent suom*, where, however, the word has the meaning 'of, or suited to, a farm or its cultivation'.

v. 144 ***cum tunderem labeas lubens*** *Labea* is used here as equivalent to *labrum.* The unclassical word, avoided in the Terentian drama, occurs in Plaut. *Stich.* 723a *tibicen, quando bibisti, refer ad labeas tibias*, Pompon. *atel.* 144, Titin. *tog.* 172.

[10] See Caes. *Gal.* 4.7.5, Cic. *Inv.* 1.5.2, *Att.* 4.18.2 (16.10).

v. 155 ***equites sperant spurcae*** *Spurcus* is used here in the sense of *obscenus, impurus, lutulentus*, with reference to sexual offences though. This is a colloquial usage also found in inscriptions, CIL 1. 2123. 9, the satire, Martial. 1.34.8 and the novel, Apul. *Met.* 8. 29. The use occurs also in Plautus, *Asin.* 807 *tot noctes reddat spurcas quot pure habuerit.*

Verbs

v. 5 ***ut, si quis dormitaret, expergisceret*** *Expergiscor* has here the meaning of *somno solvi, evigilare*. See also Plaut. *Amph.* 739 *sed, mulier, postquam experrecta es, Mil.* 218, *Poen.* 321. In Terence the verb is used in the sense of *animi mentis languore pulso evigilare, excitari, sollicitari, alacrem vegetum fieri, Ad.* 631 *cessatum usque adhuc est: iam porro, Aescine, expergiscere!.*

vv. 58–9 ***vocem reddam ego tenuem et tinnulam*** *Reddo* is used here in the sense of 'to give out', 'to produce', a meaning also found in Plaut. *Stich.* 768 *redd' cantionem veteri pro vino novam.* In Terence such a meaning of the verb does not occur, but *reddo* is used in the sense of 'to pay money due', 'discharge a debt', *Phorm.* 56, 'to return', *Hec.* 154, *Andr.* 333, 'to pay, render, exact a penalty', *Phorm.* 538, 'to grant a trial or other process', *Phorm.* 704, 'to make return of, produce, yield', *Phorm.* 680, 'to render, cause to turn out', *Heaut.* 330.

v. 68 ***numquid <nam> abscondidisti*** The verb in the sense of *occulere, occultare, recondere, abdere*, although avoided in Terence, appears also in Plaut. *Aul.* 63 *neu persentiscat aurum ubi est apsconditum.*

v. 110 ***non didici ariolari gratiis*** *Hariolari* here is used in the sense of *vaticinari*, as in Plaut. *Rud.* 377 *capillum promittam optumumst occipiamque hariolari.* This seems to be a colloquial use.[11] In CL it appears once in Cic. *Div.* 1.132. In Terence the verb is used in the sense of *suspicari, divinare, Ad.* 202, or *absurda loqui, Phorm.* 492.

v. 150 ***puls in buccam betet*** The verb *bito* (also *baeto, beto*) is found here with the meaning of *vadere, proficisci*. This is an EL and archaising use which also appears in Pacuv. *trag.* 227, 255, Varro *Men.* 553. As to Plautus, *Pseud.* 254 *licetne, opsecro, bitere an non licet?, Curc.* 141, *Merc.* 465, *Mil.* 997.

v. 171 ***in terram, ut cubat, nudam ad eum ut conquexi*** *Conquiniscere* is used here in the sense of *inclinare*. This is an EL and archaising use (also in Epit. *Alex.* 101) which occurs twice in the Plautine corpus, *Cist.* 657 *conquiniscam ad cistulam, Pseud.* 864 *si conquiniscet istic, conquiniscito.*

[11] Its distribution, Plautus, Pomponius, Apuleius, Arnobius, Vulgate.

v. 175 ***sed qui utrosque error vos agitat*** *Agitare* is here synonymous to *movere*, a usage also found in Plaut. *Asin.* 708 *nam iam calcari quadrupedo agitabo advorsum clivom.* In Terence the verb is equivalent either to *celebrare*, *Heaut.* 733, *Hec.* 93, or *excitare*, *Phorm.* 351 or *deliberare, considerare*, *Phorm.* 615.

Adverbs

v. 54 ***heus aptate, pueri, munde atque ampliter convinium!*** *Ampliter* is used here in the sense of 'in a liberal manner', 'generously', 'handsomely'. This is an EL and archaising use[12] found also in Plautus, *Cas.* 501 *argento parci nolo, opsonato ampliter, Merc.* 99. In Terence only the comparative form *amplius* occurs with the meaning of *magis, vehementius*, *Heaut.* 132, *longius, diutius*, *Ad.* 269, *porro, deinde, praeterea*, *Heaut.* 185, *Phorm.* 457.

Iuncturae

There are also several *iuncturae* that point to the relation of Pomponius to Plautus rather than Terence:

verbal combinations: *ominor* combinations in salutations where *ominor* has the meaning of *pro omine eloqui, intellegere, praesagire* (Pompon. *atel.* 35 *bene evertat! Ita fiat: et tibi bene sit, qui recte ominas*, Plaut. *Rud.* 337 *quid agis tu? aetatem hau malam male. Melius ominare*), *temetum* combinations where *temetum* is used in the sense of 'any intoxicating liquor', 'drink' (Pompon. *atel.* 59, Plaut. *Aul.* 355), *mane istic* (Pompon. *atel.* 133, Plaut. *Bacch.* 1052, *Pseud.* 1159, Ter. *Eun.* 909), *quidquid offero* (Pompon. *atel.* 58, Plaut. *Truc.* 429),

nominal combinations: *simitu* combinations where *simitu* is used with the meaning of 'at the same time', an EL and archaising usage (Lucilius 1011, Suetonius, fr. 176, Pompon. *atel.* 100, Plaut. *Merc.* 118, *Most.* 792, *Pseud.* 1012),

adverbial combinations: *tolutim* syntagms where *tolutim* has the meaning of 'at a trot', 'in the manner of a trotting horse' (Pompon. *atel.* 40, Nov. *atel.* 48, Plaut. *Asin.* 706, an EL and archaising usage, Lucil. 313, Var. *Men.* 559, Plin. *Nat.* 8.166, Fro. Aur. 1. p. 122 (23 N)).

[12] Also in Acc. *trag.* 282, Lucil. 443, Gel. 2.6.11.

Novius

Morphology

v. 8 ***primum quod dicebo*** There are several verbs of the third conjugation that have by-forms following the second. This is the case with *dicere* here, where one finds the future form *dicebo* (second conj.) instead of the common *dicam* (third conj.). In contrast to Terence, who avoids unclassical second-conjugation by-forms, such by-forms do occur in Plautus: *praecellet* at Plaut. *Pseud.* 680, *exsugebo* at Plaut. *Epid.* 188.

v. 16 ***artivit linguam in palatum*** There are several verbs of the first conjugation that have by-forms following the fourth, as is *artire* here (and in v. 41) for *artare*. Such by-forms, although absent from the Terentian corpus, do appear in Plautus, *fulguritum* at *Trin.* 539, the past participle of *fulgurire* in place of *fulgurare, impetritum* at Plaut. *Asin.* 259, the past participle of *impetrire* for *impetrare*. See also *tintinnire* at Afran. *tog.* 392 for *tintinnare*.

Syntax

v. 11 ***si ignotis inpertibis*** *Impertire* in the sense of *partem dare, communicare*, construed with the dative, as here, is an unclassical usage which seems to be favoured in colloquial sources (comedy, PC and Late Latin Christian authors).[13] In Plautus it occurs at *Vid.* 39 *quaesso ut m<ih>i impertias*. In Terence the verb is construed with the accusative of the person and the ablative of the thing (*accipientis persona per accusativum, res accepta per ablativum*), *Eun.* 271, *Ad.* 320.

Lexicon

Nouns and adjectives

v. 6 ***quod editis, nihil est; si vultis quod cacetis, copia est*** *Copia* is used here in the sense of *ambundantia, amplitudo, saturitas, satietas*, as in Plaut. *Asin.* 74–5 *nam me hodie oravit Argyrippus filius / uti sibi amanti facerem argenti copiam, Bacch.* 393, *Cas.* 499, *Curc.* 330, *Pers.* 415, *Pseud.* 736. In Terence the word has either the meaning of *facultas, potestas*, *Heaut.* 328, or *opes, divitiae, fortunae*, *Phorm.* 167, or, finally in the plural, *copiae*, with military connotations, *Heaut.* 669.

[13] Also in Apul. *Flor.* 9 p. 38 *magis . . . iudicio impertire quam commodo inservire*, Tert. *Apol.* 42.8, *Itala Rom.* 15.30, *Eph.* 4. 28, Pelag. *In I Cor.* 11. 21 p. 190. 20.

v. 38 ***o pestifera, portentifica, trux tolutiloquentia!*** *Trux* is used here in the sense of 'fierce', 'cruel', 'savage', as in Plaut. *Bacch.* 1148 *arietes truces non erimus.*

v. 49 ***limen superum*** *Limen* here has the meaning of 'one of the transverse beams in a doorframe'. For such a use, see Plaut. *Cas.* 815 *Sensim super attole limen pedes, Bacch.* 987, *Merc.* 830 (where we also find the *iunctura limen inferum*, as in v. 50, where *inferum* means *infra positum*). In Terence the word has simply the meaning of 'doorway', 'threshold', *Hec.* 378 *iam ut limen exirem, ad genua accidit.*

vv. 55–6 ***unde hoc tam repente iucundum indaudivi melum?*** *Iucundus* has here the meaning of *suavis, gratus*, also found in Plautus, *Poen.* 205–6, *I foras, Agorastocles, si vis videre ludos iucundissimus, Pseud.* 238. In Terence this adjective does not occur. See its synonyms: *gratus*, e.g. *Ad.* 251 and *suavis*, e.g. *Phorm.* 411.

vv. 67–8 ***vidit rostrum <in> tragoedia tantum Titi*** *Rostrum* is applied here to the part of the human face about the nose and the mouth. This is clearly a colloquial usage, as it appears from the distribution of the word in this sense, which is not included in Terence's colloquial register. See, however, Plaut. *Men.* 89 *apud mensam plenam homini rostrum deliges*. The substantive appears also in Lucil. 210, 1121, Petr. 75.10 and Var. *Men.* 259.

v. 70 ***supparum purum Melitensem linteum, <em> escam meram*** *Esca* is used here in the sense of *cibus*, as in Plaut. *Cas.* 221 *nam ubi amor condimentum inierit, quoivis placituram escam credo*, *Men.* 457, *Most.* 691, *Pseud.* 830. This is a mainly EL and PC usage (in CL, only Hor. *Sat.* 2.2.72, 2.8.5), avoided by Terence.

v. 76 ***prius in capulo quam in curuli sella*** *Capulum* is equivalent here to *feretrum, lectus mortuorum, sepulcrum.* For this use, avoided in Terence, see Plaut. *Asin.* 892 *perii misera, ut osculatur carnufex, capuli decus!*. It is an unclassical usage which appears in EL and archaising and colloquial authors.[14]

Verbs

v. 2 ***quia enim repuerascis*** The verb *repuerascere* is used in a transferred sense here, applied to grown men behaving like boys. The usage, which does not occur in Terence, appears in Plaut. *Merc.* 295–6 *senex quom extemplo est, iam nec sentit nec sapit, aiunt solere eum rusum repuerascere*. This is mainly an EL use which appears later in CL once, in Cic. *De Orat.* 2.22.

v. 4 ***quaeso ut in pectus tuum demittas*** *Demittere* has here the meaning of *deorsum mittere, deicere, deducere, deferre*. In contrast to Terence, who avoids the verb completely, Plautus uses it in the sense mentioned

[14] Its distribution: Lucilius, Varro, Lucretius, Apuleius, Tertullian.

above once, at *Rud.* 984 *ubi demisi ratem atque hamum, quidquid haesit extraho*. See also Afran. *tog.* 413.

v. 34 ***non multo post sonarium accepit*** *Accipio* is used here in the sense of '*manibus sumo*', a usage which also appears in Plaut. *Poen.* 1021–2 *certiorem te esse volt, ne quid clam furtim se accepisse censeas*. This is an unclassical use (EL and PC), which also appears in Ennius, *trag.* 355 and later in the Itala, the Vulgate and several Late Latin and Christian authors (Hieronymus, Ambrosius, Dracontius, Cassiodorus). Such an unclassical usage does not appear in Terence, where the verb has one of the following meanings, common in CL: δέχομαι, παραλαμβάνω, *Andr.* 298, *male vexare*, *Ad.* 166, *placere mihi*, *Andr.* 957, *suscipere*, *Hec.* 55, *intellegere, cognoscere*, *Eun.* 876, *audire*, *Hec.* 363, *pati*, *Ad.* 254.

v. 49 ***quod mei misero saepe confregit caput*** *Confringere* is used here in the sense of *frangere, rumpere*, as in Plaut. *Bacch.* 202 *scis tu ut confringi vas cito Samnium solet*, *Cist.* 503, *Mil.* 504, *Most.* 109, 453, *Rud.* 73. This is mainly an unclassical usage (in CL only Cic. *Flacc.* 73) which creeps up in literature again in Silver and PC Latin.

v. 59 ***calet pistillus*** *Caleo* is used here in the sense of *calidum esse, fervere*, as in Plaut. *Mil.* 835 *nam nimis calebat, amburebat gutturem*, *Bacch.* 105, *Rud.* 1326. In Terence one finds only the inchoative *calescere* at *Eun.* 85, where, however, it is used in a figurative sense, as equivalent to *excitari, commoveri, accede ad ignem hunc, iam coalesces plus*.

v. 69 ***quod res vis hunc privari pulchras quas uti solet*** *Privare* is used here in the sense of 'to cause to be parted from', 'deprive or rob of' as in Plaut. *Poen.* 775 *ut eo (sc. auro) me privent*. See also Caec. *com.* 156 *paelice ut meum privarem virum* and Afran. *tog.* 152 *me cum privares tui*. In Terence, on the other hand, the verb is used in the sense of 'to debar from the possession, use etc.', 'to prevent from having', Ter. *Phorm.* 517 *Pamphilamne hac urbe privari sines*?

vv. 77–8 ***id frunisci non queunt . . . . frunitus est*** *Fruniscor* is used here instead of *fruor*. It seems to be a colloquial formation, avoided by Terence but found in Plaut. *Rud.* 1012 *hinc tu nisei malum fruniscei nihil potes*. The verb appears in this sense also in Lucilius 554, in Paul. Fest p. 92 (about Cato), in Gell. 17.2.5 ff., in the Itala and in Inscriptions.[15]

vv. 84–5 ***filias <binas> habeo temulenta, sed eccas video incedere*** *Incedo* has here the meaning of *accedo, venio, advenio, appareo*. Such a use of the verb, without the indication of the destination of the movement, as here, appears also at Plaut. *Amph.* 119 *propterea ornatus in*

[15] For its distribution, cf. *ThLL* VI[1] 1422–3.

novom incessi modum, *Aul.* 473 *sed Megadorus meus adfinis eccum incedit a foro*, *Bacch.* 403, *Epid.* 102, *Stich.* 527. In Terence this use of the verb appears once, significantly in *Eunuchus*, vv. 918–19 *virum bonum eccum Parmenonem incedere video*.

v. 91 ***male cubandum est*** *Cubare* is used here in the sense of *dormire*, as in Plaut. *Amph.* 513 *prius abis quam lectus ubi cubuisti concaluit locus*, 735, 808, *Cas.* 482, 484, *Mil.* 470, 484, *Most.* 701, 707. See also Turpil. *com.* 118, Pompon. *atel.* 171. In Terence the verb appears at *Ad.* 851 and *Hec.* 138 in reference to *concumbentes*.

Adverbs

v. 15 ***ut pariter <eis> dispertiam*** *Pariter* is used here in the sense of '*ex aequo*', 'in equal quality, measure'. This use appears in Plautus, *Capt.* 329 *nunc hoc animum advorte, ut ea quae sentio pariter scias*, *Curc.* 48. In Terence, on the other hand, the adverb always has the meaning of 'in the same manner', 'alike', *Ad.* 957, *Heaut.* 132, *Phorm.* 786.

Iuncturae

There are also several *iuncturae* that bring Novius closer to Plautus than to Terence. In particular:

verbal *iuncturae*: combinations of the second plural imperative of *exire* with the second plural imperative of another verb, *agite, exite* (Nov. *atel.* 36, Plaut. *Mil.* 1338 *exite atque ecferte, Pseud.* 133), *venire ad ludos* (Nov. *atel.* 25, Plaut. *Cist.* 157), *mactare infortunio* (Nov. *atel.* 30, Plaut. *Bacch.* 364, 886, *Curc.* 537, *Poen.* 517, *Trin.* 993 and in the last scene of Terence's *Phormio*, v. 1028), *donis dare* (Nov. *atel.* 58, Plaut. *Amph.* 137, *Stich.* 656), *quid stas?* questions and forms of a reflexive use of *moveo* as an answer or a rhetorical question having the function of an answer (Nov. *atel.* 92 *quid stas? age, move te*, Plaut. *Trin.* 802 *quid nunc stas? quin tu hinc amoves et te moves?*)

nominal *iuncturae*: *cerussa* syntagms where *cerussa* is used in the sense of *medicamen faciei* (Nov. *atel.* 84, Plaut. *Most.* 258), *valgus* combinations where *valgus* has the meaning of 'having the legs converging at the knee and diverging from below the knock-kneed' (Nov. *atel.* 60, Plaut. fr. 116), *merus* combinations where *merus* means *integram et perfectam qualitatem alicuius rei* (Nov. *atel.* 70, Plaut. *Asin.* 155, *Bacch.* 50, *Capt.* 396, *Cist.* 314, *Curc.* 199, *Most.* 642, *Poen.* 268, *Poen.* 348, *Pseud.* 943, *Stich.* 748, *Trin.* 796 and Afran. *tog.* 30) and finally *mammia* combinations where *mammia* is used in the sense of *uber, papilla, in re amatoria* though (Nov. *atel.* 81, Plaut. *Pseud.* 1261).

Conclusions

The present chapter has shown that Pomponius and Novius are closer to the linguistic tradition of Plautus than to the innovative Terence. The only similarities between Pomponius and Novius, on the one hand, and Terence, on the other hand, not to be found in Plautus, are: *convivo* in the sense of *una cum aliis cenare, convivium facere, convivio adesse, comissari* (Pompon. *atel.* 85, Ter. *Heaut.* 206); *ringor* with the meaning of 'to show the teeth' (Pompon. *atel.* 124, Ter. *Phorm.* 341, a colloquial use also found in Hor. *Ep.* 2.2.128 and Petr. 75.6); *vecordia* in the sense of 'disordered state of the mind', 'frenzy' (Nov. *atel.* 40, Ter. *Andr.* 626); *consequi* in a figurative use, *de tempore*, as equivalent to *evenire, accidere* (Nov. *atel.* 35, Ter. *Heaut.* 209); *temulentus* in the sense of 'drunk' (Nov. *atel.* 35, Ter. *Andr.* 229). In particular:

1. Several EL features common in a number of comic dramatists, especially in Plautus, but avoided by Terence, are found in Pomponius and Novius. This is the case with future forms in *-ibo* in place of *-iam* for fourth-conjugation verbs (Pompon. *atel.* 9 and 173), *bito* in the sense of *vado, proficiscor* (Pompon. *atel.* 150), *capulum* for *feretrum* (Nov. *atel.* 76). All such EL features, although they appear in authors that are posterior to Terence, are not included in his archaising register.
2. Some colloquial options, common in Plautus and other comic writers, but avoided in Terence, are also to be found in Pomponius' and Novius' plays. This is the case, for example, with the use of *spurcus* for *obscenus, impurus* (Pompon. *atel.* 155), *hariolari* for *vaticinari* (Pompon. *atel.* 110), *rostrum* in the sense of 'mouth' (Nov. *atel.* 89) or *fruniscor* for *fruor* (Nov. *atel.* 77).
3. In the case of equivalent morphological, syntactical and lexical alternatives, Pomponius and Novius again opt for the one common in Plautus and not for the Terentian equivalent, which is often the one accepted in CL. This is the case, for example, with the following unclassical usages: second declension by-forms for third-declension nouns, *vaso* at Pompon. *atel.* 61; *impertire* in the sense of *partem dare, communicare* construed with the dative (Pompon.

atel. 11); *labea* for *labrum* (Pompon. *atel.* 144); *accipio* in the sense of *manibus sumo* (Nov. *atel.* 34).

Terence is closer to the language of Plautus, Novius and Pomponius mainly in the *Eunuchus*. This is the case for example with *maneo* + *istic* syntagms (Pompon. *atel.* 135), *incedo* in the sense of *accedo, venio, advenio* (Nov. *atel.* 84–5).

BIBLIOGRAPHY

Abbot, F. F. (1907) 'The use of language as a means of characterisation in Petronius', *CPh* 2: 43–50

Adams, J. N. (1972) 'The language of the later books of Tacitus' *Annals*', *CQ* 22: 350–73

(1973) 'The vocabulary of the speeches in Tacitus' historical works', *BICS* 20: 124–44

(1984) 'Female speech in Latin comedy', *Antichthon* 18: 43–77

Adams, J. N. and R. G. Mayer eds. (1999) *Aspects of the language of Latin poetry*, Oxford

Albrecht, M. von (1997) *A history of Roman literature*, Leiden

Allardice, J. T. (1929) *Syntax of Terence,* London

Altheim, F. (1932) 'Die Anfänge des Vulgärlateins', *Glotta* 20: 153–71

Anna, G. D' (1955) 'Contributo alla cronologia dei poeti latini arcaici, III: Quando esordí Gn. Nevio?', *RIL* 88: 301–10

Argenio, R. (1937) 'Il *Plocium* di Cecilio Stazio', *MC* 7: 359–68

Arnott, W. G. (1964) 'The confrontation of Sostratos and Gorgias', *Phoenix* 18: 110–23

(1970) '*Phormio parasitus*: a study in dramatic methods of characterisation', *G&R* 17: 32–57

(1972) 'Targets, techniques and traditions in Plautus' *Stichus*', *BICS* 19: 54–79

(1995) 'Menander's manipulation of language for the individualisation of character' in Martino, F. De and Sommerstein, A. H., eds., *Lo spettacolo delle voci* II, Bari, 147–64

Arias Abellán, M. del Carmen (1991) 'Die deverbalen Adjektive auf *-bilis* in den Werken des Plautus', *Glotta* 69: 124–36

Ashmore, S. G. (1897) 'A note on *faxo* with future indicative in Plautus', *TAPhA* 28: vii–viii

(1910) *The comedies of Terence,* New York

Austin, J. C. (1922) *The significant name in Terence*, Urbana

Austin, R. D. ed. (1964) *P. Vergili Maronis Aeneidos liber secundus*, Oxford

Axelson, B. (1945) *Unpoetische Wörter: ein Beitrag zur Kenntnis der lateinischen Dichtersprache*, Lund

Baerens, W. A. (1922) *Sprachlicher Kommentar zur vulgärlateinischen Appendix Probi*, Halle

Bailey, C. ed. (1949) *Titi Lucreti de rerum natura libri sex*, Oxford

Bain, D. (1984) 'Female speech in Menander', *Antichthon* 18: 24–42

Baloira Bértolo, M. A. (1981–3) 'La lengua de Terencio. Genitivo y ablativo de cualidad', *EClás*. 24: 203–20

Barchiesi, M. (1978) *La 'Tarentilla' rivisitata: studi su Nevio comico*, Pisa

Bardon, H. (1943–4) 'Le silence, moyen d' expression', *REL* 21–22: 102–20

(1952–6) *La littérature latine inconnue*, Paris

Barsby, J. ed. (1986) *Plautus: Bacchides*, Warminster

ed. (1999) *Terence: Eunuchus*, Cambridge

Baske, J. (1834) *De alliterationis usu Plautino particula prior*, Königsberg

Battisti, C. (1949) *Avviamento allo studio del latino volgare*, Bari

Beare, W. (1930) 'Plautus and the *Fabula Atellana*', *CR* 44: 165–68

(1940) 'The fabula togata', *Hermathena* 55: 35–55

(1977) *The Roman stage*, London

Bennett, C. E. (1910–14) *Syntax of Early Latin*, Boston

Bertschinger, J. (1921) 'Volkstümliche Elemente in der Sprache des Phaedrus', Diss., Bonn

Bigot, E. (1948) 'Sextus Turpilius', *RE* 7 A2²: 1428–30

Bini, M. (1981) 'Forme di asindeto in Terenzio', *GFF* 4: 115–22

Blänsdorf, J. (1996) 'Un trait original de la comédie de Plaute: le goût de la parodie', *CGITA* 9: 133–51

Bléry, H. (1965) *Syntaxe de la subordination dans Térence*, Rome

Bonfante, G. (1994) *La lingua parlata in Orazio*, Venosa

(1967) 'La lingua delle atellane e dei mimi' in Frassinetti, P. ed., *Atellanae Fabulae*, Rome, i–xxiv

Boscherini, S. (1999) 'Norma e parola nelle commedie di Cecilio Stazio', *SIFC* 27: 99–115

Bourciez, J. (1927) *Le sermo cotidianus dans les Satires d' Horace*, Paris

Boyce, B. (1991) *The language of the freedmen in Petronius' Cena Trimalchionis*, Leiden

Branden, A. V. den (1984) 'Le texte punique dans le *Poenulus* de Plaute', *B&O* 26: 159–80

Brakman, C. (1930) 'Ad Plinii *Nat. Hist.* Lib. xxvi-xxxvii', *Mnemosyne*: 58: 207–22

Brazzano, S. di (1999) 'Cacata charta', *MD* 43: 179–89

Brenk, F. E. (1987) '*Heteros tis eimi*: on the language of Menander's young lovers', *ICS* 12: 31–66

Brenous, J. (1895) *Etude sur les Hellénismes dans la syntaxe latine*, Paris

Brothers, A. J. ed. (1988) *Terence: the self-tormentor*, Warminster

Brotherton, B. E. M. (1921) *The vocabulary of intrigue in Roman comedy*, Chicago, Illinois

Brown, P. G. McC. (1981) 'Two notes on Menander's *Misoumenos*', *ZPE* 41 25–6

(1990) 'Plots and prostitutes in Greek New Comedy', *PLLS* 6: 241–66

Büchner, K. (1974) *Das Theater des Terenz*, Heidelberg

Calboli, G. (1991) 'Il *miles gloriosus* di Terenzio e l'infinito storico latino' in *Studi di filologia classica in onore di Giusto Monaco* II, Palermo, 599–632

(1997) *Über das Lateinische: vom Indogermanischen zu den romanischen Sprachen,* Tübingen

Callahan, J. (1964) 'The figurative use of *emungere*' in Henderson, C. ed., *Classical, mediaeval and Renaissance studies in honor of B. L Ullman* I, Rome, 67–78

Callebat, L. (1968) *Sermo cotidianus dans les Métamorphoses d' Apulée*, Caen

Canedo, J. (1935–36) 'Die lateinischen Inchoativa und ihr Verhältnis zur Komposition', *Glotta* 24: 257–66

Carney, T. F. ed. (1963) *P.Terenti Afri Hecyra*, Salisbury

(1964) 'The words *sodes* and *quaeso* in Terentian usage', *AClass* 7: 57–63

Cassio, A. C. (1979) 'Motivi di agone epirrematico in commedia nuova (Aristoph. *Nub*. 961 sgg., Plaut. *Bacch*, 420 sgg.)', *AION* (filol.) 1: 1–22

Christes, J. (1971) *Der frühe Lucilius, Rekonstruktion und Interpretation des XXIV Buches sowie von Teilen des XXX Buches*, Heidelberg

Cichorius, C. (1964) *Untersuchungen zu Lucilius*, Berlin

Citti, F. (1994) 'Una "mena" per cena, Pompon. "Atell." Fr. 80s. Ribb. 3', *MD* 33: 151–5.

Coleman, R. G. G. (1975) 'Greek influence on Latin syntax', *TPhS* 1975: 101–56

ed. (1977) *Vergil Eclogues*, Cambridge

(1987) 'Vulgar Latin and the diversity of Christian Latin' in Hermann, H. ed., *Latin vulgaire – latin tardif* I, Tübingen, 37–52

(1990) 'Dialectal variation in Republican Latin, with special reference to Praenestine', *Proceedings of the Cambridge Philological Society* 36: 1–25

(1999) 'Poetic diction, poetic discourse and the poetic register' in Adams and Mayer, eds., 21–93

Collart, J. (1978) 'Quelques remarques sur l' emploi de *gratia* chez les comiques' in Collart, J. ed. (1978) *Varron, grammaire antique et stylistique latine*, Paris, 293–7

ed. (1979) *Plaute: Curculio,* Paris

Conrad, F. (1930–32) 'Die Deminutiva im Altlatein, 1: Die Deminutiva bei Plautus', *Glotta* 19: 127–148 and 20: 74–84

Cooper, F. T. (1895) *Word Formation in the Roman Sermo Plebeius*, New York

Corbett, P. B. (1964) '"Vis comica" in Plautus and Terence: an inquiry into the figurative use by them of certain verbs', *Eranos* 62: 52–69

Cordier, A. (1939) *Etudes sur le vocabulaire épique dans l' Enéide*, Paris

Corno, D. del. (1975) 'Alcuni aspetti del linguaggio di Menandro', *SCO* 23: 13–48

Coulter, C. C. (1916) 'Compound adjectives in early Latin poetry', *TAPhA* 47: 153–72

Currie, H. M. (1983) 'Plautus' *Poenulus* 1174–1279 and a possible Semitic parallel', *LCM* 8: 85–6

Danese, R. (1985) 'Plauto, *Pseud.* 702–705a: la "costruzione stilistica" di un eroe perfetto', *MD* 14: 101–12

Daviault, A. (1981) *Comoedia Togata: fragments,* Paris

Degl' Innocenti Pierini, R. (1991) 'Un prologo polemico di Afranio, *Compitalia* 25–18 R[3]', *Prometheus* 17: 242–6

Denzler, B. (1968) *Der Monolog bei Terenz,* Zürich

De Saint-Denis, E. (1947) 'Syntaxe du latin parlé dans les *Res Rusticae* de Varron', *RPh* 21: 141–62

Dickey, E. (1996) *Greek forms of address: from Herodotus to Lucian,* Oxford

Diel, E. (1919) 'Iuventius', *RE* 10, 2: 1362

(1926) 'Licinius Imbrex', *RE* 13, 1: 371

Douglas, A. E. ed. (1966) *Cicero: Brutus,* Oxford

Dover, K. J. (1987) *Greek and the Greeks,* Oxford

Dressler, W. (1965) 'Die Funktion des hist. Infinitivs im lateinischen Verbalsystem', *Kratylos* 10: 191–6

Drexler, H. (1934) 'Die Komposition von Terenz' *Adelphen* und Plautus' *Rudens*', *Philologus* Suppl. 26.2: 1–40

Dziatzko, K. and Kauer, R. eds. (1903) *Ausgewählte Komödien des P. Terentius Afer, erklärt von K. Dz., II: Adelphoe, 2te Auflage, bearbeitet von R. K.,* Leipzig

Duckworth, G. E. (1952) *The nature of Roman comedy,* Princeton (repr. with bibliographical appendix by R. L. Hunter (1994) Bristol)

Durry, M. (1940) 'Le vocabulaire militaire dans le *Phormio*', *REL* 18: 57–64

Eckstein, F. (1921) 'Syntaktische Beiträge zu Plautus', *Philologus* 77: 142–73

Elmer, H. C. (1887) '*Que, et, atque* in the inscriptions of the Republic, in Terence, and in Cato', *AJPh* 8: 292–328

Engelbrecht, A. G. (1883) *Studia Terentiana,* Vienna

Enk, P. J. (1940) 'Observationes de sermonis cottidiani vestigiis apud Propertium obviis', *Mnemosyne* 8: 299–322

Ernout, A. (1931) 'Un example de répartition sémantique: les mots qui se rapportent à la maison', *REL* 9: 40–1

(1932) '*Domus, fores* et leurs substituts', *RPh* 6: 297–314

(1949) *Les adjectifs latins en -osus et en -lentus,* Paris

(1953) *Morphologie historique du latin,* Paris

Ernout, A. and Meillet, A. (1951) *Dictionnaire étymologique de la langue latine: histoire des mots,* Paris

Ernout, A. and Thomas, F. (1972) *Syntaxe latine,* Paris

Faider, P. (1908–9) 'Le poète comique Cecilius: sa vie et son oeuvre', *MB* 12: 269–341; 13: 5–35

Fantham, E. (1968) 'Terence, Diphilus and Menander: a reexamination of Terence's *Adelphoe* act II', *Philologus* 112: 196–216

(1972) *Comparative studies in Republican Latin imagery,* Toronto

ed. (1998) *Ovid Fasti Book IV,* Cambridge

Fassbender, C. (1909) *De Iulii Valeri sermone quaestiones selectae,* Münster

Fay, E. W. (1909) 'The Latin accusatives *med, ted*', *AJPh* 29: 301–10

Fay, H. C. ed. (1983) *Plautus Rudens*, Bristol

Feneron, J. S. (1974) 'Some elements of Menander's style', *BICS* 21: 81–95

Flury, P. (1968) *Liebe und Liebessprache bei Menander, Plautus und Terenz*, Heidelberg

Flobert, P. (1975) *Les verbes déponents latins des origines à Charlemagne*, Paris

Focardi, G. (1972) 'Linguaggio forense nei prologhi terenziani', *SIFC* 44: 55–88

Fordyce, C. J. ed. (1977) *P. Vergili Maronis Aeneidos Libri VII-VIII with a commentary*, Oxford

Foster, W. E. (1912) 'Studies in archaism in Gellius', Diss., Columbia

Frank, T. (1927) 'Naevius and free speech', *AJPh* 48: 105–10

(1930) *Life and literature in the Roman Republic*, Cambridge

Fraenkel, E. (1927) 'Die Vorgeschichte des Versus quadratus', *Hermes* 62: 357–70

(1928) *Iktus und Akzent im lateinischen Sprechvers*, Berlin

(1931) 'Livius Andronicus', *RE* Suppl. 5: 598–607

(1935) 'Naevius', *RE* Suppl. 6: 622–40

(1960) *Elementi Plautini in Plauto*, Florence (translation with addenda of *Plautinisches im Plautus*, Berlin 1922)

Frassinetti, P. (1953) *Fabula Atellana: saggio sul teatro popolare latino*, Genova

ed. (1955) *Fabularum Atellanarum Fragmenta*, Turin

Fridh, Å. (1950) *Etudes critiques et syntaxiques sur les Variae de Cassiodore*, Göteborg

Gagnér, A. (1920) *De hercle mehercle ceterisque id genus particulis priscae poesis latinae scenicae*, Greifswald

Gaide, F. (1988) *Les substantifs masculins latins en . . . (i)o, . . . (i)onis*, Louvain and Paris

Gamberale, L. (1967) 'L' inizio proverbiale di Menandro fr. 333 K-Th', *RFIC* 95: 162–4

García Jurado, F. (1997) 'Commentario a Titin. com.1 (Ribb.): *inauratae atque inlautae mulieris*', *Latomus* 56: 544–50

García Jurado, F. and López Gregoris, R. (1995) 'Las metáforas de la vida cotidiana en el lenguaje plautino come procedimiento de caraterización de los personajes', *SIFC* 13: 233–45

Garton, C. (1971) 'The *Thesaurus*: a comedy of Luscius Lanuvius', *AJPh* 92: 17–37.

Georgala, Priovolou, S. (1991) 'Il "pedante" nel mimo, nell' atellana e nel teatro comico greco', *Dioniso* 61: 269–75

Gérard, V. (1897) 'Le latin vulgaire et le langage familier dans les satires de Perse', *MB* 1: 81–103

Gestri, L. (1940) 'Studi Plautini II: Il monologo di Nicobulo in *Bacch.* V. 1 (=1087–1103)', *SIFC* 17: 237–60

Gilleland, M. E. (1979) 'Linguistic differentiation of character type and sex in the comedies of Plautus and Terence', Diss., Virginia, Charlottesville

(1980) 'Female speech in Greek and Latin', *AJPh* 101: 180–3
Gilula, D. (1980) 'The concept of the *bona meretrix*: a study of Terence's courtesans', RFIC 108: 142–65
Gomme, A. W. and Sandbach, F. H. (1973) *Menander: a commentary,* Oxford
Grandgent, C. H. (1908) *An introduction to vulgar Latin*, Boston
Gratwick, A. S. (1971) 'Hanno's Punic speech in the *Poenulus* of Plautus', *Hermes* 99: 25–45
ed. (1987) *Terence: The Brothers,* Warminster
ed. (1993) *Plautus: Menaechmi*, Cambridge
Green, R. P. H. (1991) *The works of Ausonius*, Oxford
Grimal, P. (1953) *Le siècle des Scipions,* Paris
Gruen, E. S. (1993) *Culture and national identity in republican Rome,* London
Guardì, T. (1974) *Cecilio Stazio: I frammenti*, Palermo
(1981) 'Note sulla lingua di Titinio', *Pan* 7: 145–65
(1985) *Titinio e Atta, Fabula Togata; I frammenti*, Palermo
Haadsma, R. A. and Nuchelmans, J. (1963) *Précis de latin vulgaire*, Groningen
Haffter, H. (1934) *Untersuchungen zur altlateinischen Dichtersprache,* Berlin
(1953) 'Terenz und seine künstlerische Eigenart', *MH* 10: 1–20, 73–102
Hahn, E. A. (1948) '*ilicet, scilicet, videlicet*', *TAPhA* 79: 308–37
Harsh, P. W. (1940) 'The position of archaic forms in the verse of Plautus', *CPh* 35: 126–42
Hartman, I. I. (1922) 'De atellana fabula', *Mnemosyne* 50: 225–38
(1923) 'Ad Titinium', *Mnemosyne* 51: 179
Happ, H. (1967) 'Die lateinische Umgangssprache und die Kunstsprache des Plautus', *Glotta* 45: 60–104
Haverling, G. (2000) *On sco-verbs, prefixes and semantic functions*, Göteborg
Heap, A. M. (1992) 'Word order in Menander', *LCM* 17: 56–8
Heraeus, W. (1937) *Kleine Schriften*, Heidelberg
Herman, J. (1967) *Le Latin vulgaire*, Paris
Heusch, H. (1954) *Das Archaische in der Sprache Catulls*, Bonn
Hodgman, A. W. (1901)'On variations of gender in Plautus', *TAPhA* 32: lxxxiii–lxxxv
(1902) 'Noun declension in Plautus', *CR* 16: 294–305
Hoffmann, Z. (1980–81) 'Gebetsparodien in Plautus' Komödien', *Helikon* 20–21: 207–18
Hofmann, J. B. (1951) *Lateinische Umgangssprache*, Heidelberg
Hofmann, J. B. and Szantyr, A. (1965) *Lateinische Syntax und Stilistik*, Munich
Hofmann, W. (1992) 'Zur Funktion der Fremdsprachen bei Plautus' in Müller, C. W. ed., *Zum Umgang mit fremden Sprachen in der griechisch-römischen Antike: Kolloquium der Fachrichtungen Klassische Philologie der Universitäten Leipzig und Saarbrücken am 21. und 22. November 1989 in Saabrücken*, Stuttgart, 143–58
Hohl, E. (1920) 'Über den Ursprung der *Historia Augusta*', *Hermes* 55: 296–310

Holford Strevens, L. (1988) *Aulus Gellius,* London

Hough, J. N. (1940) 'Miscellanea Plautina: vulgarity, extra-dramatic speeches, Roman allusions', *TAPhA* 71: 186–98

(1947) 'Terence's use of Greek words', *CW* 41: 18–21

Hunter, R. L. (1985) *The New Comedy of Greece and Rome,* Cambridge

Jocelyn, H. D. ed. (1967) *The tragedies of Ennius: the fragments edited with an introduction and commentary,* Cambridge

(1969) 'The poet Gn. Naevius, P. Cornelius Scipio and Q. Caecilius Metellus', *Antichthon* 3: 32–47

(1972) 'Ennius as a dramatic poet', *Fondation Hardt* 17: 39–88

(1993) 'Sprache, Schriftlichkeit und Characterisierung in der römischen Komödie (Plautus, *Pseudolus* 41–73, 998–1014)' in Vogt-Spira, G. ed., *Beiträge zur mündlichen Kultur der Römer*, Tübingen, 125–39

Johnston, E. (1905) 'Gemination in Terence', *TAPhA* 36: 44

Jones, K. S. (1987) *Synonymy and semantic classification*, New York

Katsouris, A. G. (1975) *Linguistic and stylistic characterisation: tragedy and Menander,* Ioannina

Knapp, C. (1917) 'References to painting in Plautus and Terence', *CPh* 12: 143–57

Krahmalkov, C. R. (1988) 'Observations on the Punic monologue of Hanno in the *Poenulus*', *Orientalia* 57: 55–66

Krenkel, W. ed. (1970) *Lucilius Satiren*, Leiden

Krieter Spiro, M. (1997) *Sklaven, Köche und Hetären: das Dienstpersonal bei Menander: Stellung, Rolle, Komik und Sprache,* Stuttgart

Kroll, W. (1910–12) 'Der lateinische Relativsatz', *Glotta* 3: 1–18

(1931) 'Der Tod des Naevius', *Hermes* 66: 469–72

(1936) 'Novius', *RE* 17, 1: 1216.

(1937) 'Trabea', *RE* 6, 2^2: 1862

Kühner, R. and Stegmann, C. (1966) *Ausführliche Grammatik der lateinischen Sprache*, Part II, Hanover

Laidlaw, W. A. (1938) *The prosody of Terence,* London

Langen, P. (1886) *Plautinische Studien,* Berlin

Lee, G. M. (1965) 'Caecilius, 136–7', *Latomus* 24: 954

Lefèvre, E. (1978) *Der Phormio des Terenz und der Epidikazomenos des Apollodor von Karystos*, Munich

(1994) *Terenz und Menanders Heautontimoroumenos*, Munich

Lejay, P. (1966) *Oeuvres d' Horace. Satires*, Hildesheim

Lentano, M. (1993) '*Parce ac duriter*: Catone, Plauto e una formula felice', *Maia* 45: 11–16

Leo, F. (1913) *Geschichte der römischen Literatur*, Berlin

(1914) 'Römische Poesie in der sullanischen Zeit', *Hermes* 49: 161–94

(1966) *Plautinische Forschungen: zur Kritik und Geschichte der Komödie*, Darmstadt

Leumann, M. (1945) 'Der lateinische Genetiv Achilli', *MH* 2: 237–58

(1947) 'Die lateinische Dichtersprache', *MH* 4: 116–39
(1977) *Lateinische Laut- und Formenlehre*, Munich
Lilja, S. (1965) *Terms of abuse in Roman comedy,* Helsinki
Lindholm, E. (1931) *Stilistiche Studien zur Erweiterung der Satzglieder im Lateinischen*, Lund
Lindsay, W. M. ed. (1900), *The Captivi of Plautus*, London
(1922) *Early Latin verse,* Oxford
Lloyd-Jones, H. (1973) 'Terentian technique in the *Adephi* and the *Eunuchus*', *CQ* 23: 279–84
Lyons, J. (1996) *Linguistic semantics: an introduction*, Cambridge
Lodge, G. (1924–33) *Lexicon Plautinum,* Stuttgart
Löfstedt, B. (1982) 'Die vulgärlateinische Sprachforschung in diesem Jahrhundert. Rückschau und Ausblick', *Aevum* 56: 200–4
Löfstedt, E. (1911) *Philologischer Kommentar zur Peregrinato Aetheriae: Untersuchungen zur Geschichte der lateinischen Sprache*, Uppsala
(1912) 'Plautinischer Sprachgebrauch und Verwandtes', *Glotta* 3: 171–91
(1956) *Syntactica: Studien und Beiträge zur historischen Syntax des Lateins,* Lund
Lopez Lopez, A. (1983) *Fabularum togatarum fragmenta*, Salamanca
Lowe, J. C. B. (1983a) 'The *Eunuchus*: Terence and Menander', *CQ* 33: 428–44
(1983b) 'Terentian originality in the *Phormio* and *Hecyra*', *Hermes* 111: 431–52
Ludwig, W. (1968) 'The originality of Terence and his Greek models', *GRBS* 9: 169–82
MacCary, W. T. and Willcock, M. M. eds. (1976) *Plautus: Casina,* Cambridge
McGlynn, P. (1963–7) *Lexicon Terentianum*, London and Glasgow
Maltby, R. (1976) 'A comparative study of the language of Plautus and Terence', Diss., Cambridge
(1979) 'Linguistic characterisation of old men in Terence', *CPh* 74: 136–47
(1983) 'The last act of Terence's *Heautontimoroumenos*', *PLLS* 4: 27–41
(1985) 'The distribution of Greek loan-words in Terence', *CQ* 35: 110–23
Maniet, A. (1966) '"Frapper à la porte" en latin préclassique: notes morphosemantiques sur *pello* et ses dérivés', *Latomus* 25: 28–36
Mankin, D. ed. (1995) *Horace Epodes,* Cambridge
Marache, R. (1957) *Mots nouveaux et mots archaïques chez Fronton et Aulu-Gelle,* Paris
Marconi, G. (1966) 'La cronologia di Livio Andronico', *Atti Accad. dei Lincei* 363 MAL VIII, 12, 2 125–213
Marmorale, E. V. (1950) *Naevius poeta,* Florence
Marouzeau, J. (1926) 'Plaute et la première "crise du latin"', *REL* 4: 99–103
ed. (1947) *Térence I: Andrienne, Eunuque,* Paris
Marti, H. (1963) 'Terenz 1909–1959', *Lustrum* 8: 5–101
Martin, R. H. ed. (1959) *Terence: Phormio*, London
ed. (1976) *Terence: Adelphoe*, Cambridge

(1995) 'A not-so-minor character in Terence's *Eunuchus*', *CPh* 90: 139–51
Martina, M. (1978) 'Sulla cronologia di Titinio', *QFC* 1: 5–25
Marx, F. (1896) 'Atilius', *RE* 2, 2: 2076
(1909) 'Atellanae Fabulae'', *RE* 2, 2:1914–21
(1909) 'Die Beziehung des Altlateins zum Spätlatein', *Neue Jahrbücher für das Klassische Altertum*: 434–48
ed. (1959) *Plautus Rudens: Text und Kommentar*, Amsterdam
Mates, B. (1950) 'Synonymity', *UCPPh* 25: 201–26
Marzullo, A. (1973) *Dalla satira al teatro popolare latino*, Rome
Mattingly, H. B. (1957) 'The date of Livius Andronicus', *CQ* 7: 159–63
(1960) 'Naevius and the Metelli', *Historia* 9: 414–39
Maurach, G. (1983) *Enchiridion poeticum: hilfsbuch zur lateinischen Dichtersprache*, Darmstadt
(1995) *Lateinische Dichtersprache*, Darmstadt
Mayer, R. G. ed. (1994) *Horace Epistles Book I*, Cambridge
(1999) 'Grecism' in Adams and Mayer, eds., 157–82
Meister, K. (1909) 'Altes Vulgärlatein', *IF* 26: 69–90
Minarini, A. (1983) 'Note sul diminutivo terenziano', *Paideia* 38: 161–73
Miniconi, P. J. (1958) 'Les termes d' injure dans le théâtre comique', *REL* 36: 159–75
Mohrmann, C. (1932) *Die altchristliche Sondersprache in den Sermones des hl. Augustin*, Nijmegen
Müller, A. (1913) 'Die Schimpfwörter in der römischen Komödie', *Philologus* 72: 492–502
Müller, H. F. and Taylor, P. (1932) *A chrestomathy of Vulgar Latin*, Boston
Müller, R. (1997) *Sprechen und Sprache: dialoglinguistische Studien zu Terenz*, Heidelberg
Munk, E. (1826) *De Pomponio Bononiensi Atellanarum poeta*, Glagovia
Nelson, H. L. Q. (1951) 'Le rapport entre le latin littéraire, la langue de conversation et la langue vulgaire au temps de Pétrone' in *Actes du premier congrès international des études classiques*, Paris, 220–9
Neue, F. and Wagener, C. (1892–1905) *Formenlehre der lateinischen Sprache*, Leipzig
Neumann, E. (1925) *De cottidiani sermonis apud Propertium proprietatibus*, Königsberg
Nicolson, F. W. (1893) 'The use of *hercle (mehercle), edepol (pol)* and *ecastor (mecastor)* by Plautus and Terence', *HSCPh* 4: 99–103
Nougaret, L. (1945) 'La langue militaire chez Térence', *REL* 23: 70–4
Norden, E. (1898) *Die antike Kunstprosa* II, Leipzig
Nuñez, S. (1995) 'Materiales para una sociología de la lengua latina: Terencio y los modificadores de imperativo', *FlorIlib* 6: 347–66
Oakley, S. P. (1997–98) *A commentary on Livy Books VI–X*, Oxford
Oksala, P. (1953) *Die griechischen Lehnwörter in den Prosaschriften Ciceros*, Helsinki

Oniga, R. (1994) 'L' allitterazione in Plauto e Terenzio: un esperimento di analisi quantitativa', *Lexis* 12: 117–34

Önnerfors, A. (1955) 'Zur Vermischung der Ausdrücke für Ortsruhe und Bewegung im Lateinischen', *Eranos* 53: 148–64

Opelt, I. (1965) *Die lateinischen Schimpfwörter und verwandte sprachliche Erscheinungen: eine Typologie*, Heidelberg

Oppermann, H. (1939) 'Caecilius und die Entwicklung der römischen Komödie', *F&F* 15: 196–7

Palmer, L. R. (1954) *The Latin language,* London

Papadimitriou, M. (1982) 'Παρέλκον', *Dodone* 11: 427–47

(1994) '"Ε λλειψις κι "Αποσιώπησις' στο υπόμνημα του Αίλιου Δονάτου', *Dodone* 23: 77–113

(1998) Στοιχεία της ομιλούμενης Λατινικής στον Τερέντιο και η χρήση τους στη διαφοροποίηση του λόγου των χαρακτήρων του, Ioannina

Paratore, E. (1959) 'Studi sulla palliata, ad Ter. *Eun.* 7–13', *RCCM* 1: 44–63

Pasquazi Bagnolini, A. (1977) *Note sulla lingua di Afranio,* Florence

Perruzzi, E. (1976) 'Prenestino conea e lat. ciconia', *QIFL* 4: 45–51

Petersen, W. (1931) 'The evidence of early Latin on the subjunctive in *cum*-clauses', *CPh* 26: 386–404

Petersmann, H. (1977) 'Petrons urbane Prosa: Untersuchungen zu Sprache und Text', *Sitzungsberichte der Österreichischen Akademie der Wissenschaften*, Philos.-Hist. Klasse 323

(1995) 'Zur mündlichen Characterisierung des Fremden in der Komödie des Plautus' in Benz, L., Stärk, E. and Vogt-Spira, G. eds., *Plautus und die Tradition des Steigreifspiels*. Festgabe für E. Lefèvre zum 60. Geburtstag, Tübingen, 123–36

(1996–7) 'Die Nachahmung des *sermo rusticus* auf der Bühne des Plautus und Terenz', *AAntHung* 37 (3–4): 199–211

(1999) 'The language of the Early Roman satire: its function and characteristics' in Adams and Mayer, eds., 289–310

Piccaluga, G. (1991) '*At ego aiio id fieri in Graecia et Carthagini / Et hic . . .* (Plaut. *Cas.* 71 sg.): il linguaggio 'religioso' in Plauto', *RSA* 21: 9–22

Ploen, H. (1882) *De copiae verborum differentiis inter varia poesis Romanae antiquioris genera intercedentibus*, Strasbourg

Pociña, A. (1975) 'Lucio Afranio y la evolución de la fabula togata', *Habis* 6: 99–107

(1980) 'El comediografo Cecilio Estacio', *Sodalitas* 1: 209–31

(1981–3) 'El comediografo Cecilio Estacio', *EstClás* 25: 63–78

Povsic, B. S. (1987) 'Locutiones cotidianae quae in T. Macci Plauti comoediis leguntur', *VL* 105: 30–6, 106: 27–31

Prescott, H. W. (1920) 'Inorganic rôles in Roman comedy', *CPh* 15: 245–81

(1942) 'Exit monologues in Roman comedy', *CPh* 37: 1–21

Przychocki, G. (1922) 'De Titinii aetate' in *Charisteria Casimiro de Morawsky septuagenario oblata ab amicis, collegis, discipulis*, Cracow, 180–8

Pulgram, E. (1950) 'Spoken and written Latin', *Language* 26: 458–66
Radice, B. (1976) *Terence: The Comedies*, London
Radke, G. (1951) 'Terenz und die Mythologie', *Gymnasium* 58: 73–5
Raffaelli, R. (1987) 'Pomponio e l' atellana (spunti di analisi stilistiche e tematiche)' in *Cispadana e leteratura antica. Atti del convegno di studi tenuto ad Imola nel maggio 1986*, Bologna
Ramage, E. S. (1973) *Urbanitas: ancient sophistication and refinement*, Cincinnati
Rambelli, G. (1936) 'Studi terenziani: due scene dell' *Andria*', *SIFC* 13: 130–60
Reich, V. (1933) 'Sprachliche Characteristik bei Terenz (Studien zum Kommentar des Donat)', *WS* 51: 72–94
Reiter, S. (1925) 'Der Atellanendichter Aprissius', *Philol. Woch.* 45: 1435–9
Ribbeck, O. ed. (1898) *Scaenicae Romanorum poesis fragmenta*, vol. II Comicorum Fragmenta, Leipzig
Riedweg, C. (1993) 'Menander in Rom – Beobachtungen zu Caecilius Statius *Plocium* fr. I (136–53 Guardì)', in Slater, N. W. and Zimmermann, B. eds., *Drama* 2: 133–59
Riemann, O. (1885) *Etudes sur la langue et la grammaire de Tite Live*, Paris
Rieth, O. (1964) *Die Kunst Menanders in den 'Adelphen' des Terenz*, Hildesheim
Risch, E. (1984) *Gerundivum und Gerundium. Gebrauch im klassischen und älteren Latein. Entstehung und Vorgeschichte*, Berlin
Risicato, A. (1966) *Lingua parlata e lingua d' arte in Ennio*, Messina and Florence
Ritschl, F. (1965) *Parerga zu Plautus und Terenz*, Amsterdam
Robson, D. O. (1938) 'The nationality of the poet Caecilius Statius', *AJPh* 59: 301–8
Rohlfs, G. (1956) *Sermo vulgaris Latinus: vulgärlateinisches Lesebuch*, Tübingen
Romano, D. ed. (1953) *Atellana fabulla*, Palermo
Rossbach, O. (1920) 'Atellanen des L. Pomponius und des Novius', *Woch. für klass. Philol.* 33–4: 331–5
Rosén, H. B. (1970) '*Uterum dolet* und Verwandtes', *Folia Linguistica* 4: 135–47
Rosén, H. (1981) *Studies in the syntax of the verbal noun in early Latin*, Munich
(1999) *Latine loqui: trends and directions in the crystallisation of classical Latin*, Munich
Rowell, H. T. (1949) 'The Campanian origin of Cn. Naevius and its literary attestation', *MAAR* 19: 15–34
Ruckdeschel, F. (1911) *Archaismen und Vulgarismen in der Sprache des Horaz*, Munich
Rychlewska, L. ed. (1971) *Turpilii comici fragmenta*, Leipzig
Sabbadini, S. (1935) *Poeti latini: Nevio*, Udine
Salat, P. (1967) 'L'adjectif *miser*, ses synonymes et ses antonymes chez Plaute et chez Térence', *REL* 45: 252–75
Sandbach, F. H. (1970) 'Menander's manipulation of language for dramatic purposes', *Fondation Hardt* 26: 113–36
Sandys, J. E. (1885) *M. Tulli Ciceronis ad M. Brutum Orator*, Cambridge

Schmeck, H. (1955) *Aufgaben und Methoden der modernen vulgärlateinischen Forschung,* Heidelberg

Sblendorio-Cugusi, M. T. (1991) *I sostantivi latini in -tudo,* Bologna

Schuster, M. (1931) 'Zum archaistischen Element im Stile Frontos', *WS* 49: 153–7

Sedgwick, W. B. ed. (1960) *Plautus: Amphitruo*, Manchester

Sideri Tolia, A. (1988) 'The compound adjectives in Naevius, Ennius, Plautus, Terentius and Cicero', *Parousia* 6: 205–21

Shackleton Bailey, D. R. (1953) '*Num* in direct questions: a rule restated', *CQ* 3: 120–5

Sheets G. A. (1983) 'Plautus and Early Roman tragedy', *ICS* 8: 195–209

Shipp, G. P. (1937) '"Chance" in the Latin vocabulary (*evenire, cadere, accidere, contingere*)', *CR* 51: 209–12

ed. (1960) *P. Terenti Afri Andria*, Melbourne

Skutsch, F. (1892) *Plautinisches und Romanisches*, Leipzig

(1897a) 'Caecilius Statius', *RE* 3, 1: 1189–92

(1897b) 'Dossenus', *RE* 5, 2: 1609–10

Skutsch, O. (1951) 'Naevius', *CR* 1: 174–7

ed. (1985) *The Annals of Q. Ennius,* Oxford

Sloman, A. ed. (1936) *P. Terenti Adelphi*, Oxford

Smith, K. W. (1890) *Archaisms of Terence mentioned in the Commentary of Donatus,* Baltimore

Soles, M. (1954) 'Studies in the colloquial language in the poems of Catullus', Diss., Michigan

Sommer, F. (1914) *Handbuch der lateinischen Laut- und Formenlehre*, Heidelberg

Spencer, F. B. T. (1906) *Adnominatio in the plays of Plautus*, Rome

Stefenelli, A. (1962) *Die Volkssprache im Werk des Petron im Hinblick auf die romanischen Sprachen*, Vienna

Stein, J. P. (1971) 'Compound word coinages in the plays of Plautus', *Latomus* 30: 598–606

Steinthal, J. (1918) *De interpolationibus Plautinis,* Berlin

Stella, V. (1982) 'Note semantiche sugli aggettivi in *-lentus* presenti in Plauto', *SRIC* 5: 157–62

Stinner, A. (1879) *De eo quo Cicero in epistulis usus est sermone*, Oppeln

Stockert, W. (1982) 'Zur sprachlichen Characterisierung der Personen in Plautus' *Aulularia', Gymnasium* 89: 4–14

Sturtevant, E. H. (1925) 'Concerning the influence of Greek on vulgar Latin', *TAPhA* 56: 5–25

Svennung, J. (1935) *Untersuchungen zu Palladius und zur lateinischen Fach- und Volkssprache*, Uppsala

Szilagyi, G. I. (1941), *Atellana. Studi sull'arte scenica antica*, Budapest

Sznajder, L. (1996) 'Construction paratactique et *sermo cotidianus* dans la langue de Plaute' in Dangel, J. and Moussy, C. eds., *Les structures de l'oralité en latin: colloque du centre Alfred Ernout, Université de Paris IV, 2, 3, et 4 Juin 1994*, Paris, 167–90

Tarrant, R. J. ed. (1976) *Seneca: Agamemnon,* Cambridge
Thierfelder, A. (1939) 'Plautus und römische Tragödie', *Hermes* 74: 155–66
Thesleff, H. (1960) *Yes and no in Plautus and Terence,* Helsingfors
Thomsen, H. (1930) *Pleonasmus bei Plautus und Terentius* I *Ausgewälte zeitliche (und verwandte) Begriffe,* Uppsala
Traina, A. (1957–8) 'Sul' "*vertere*" di Cecilio Stazio', *AIV* 116: 385–93
(1969) *Comoedia: antologia della palliata,* Padua
(1992) '"Ed è subito pera": il pranzo del parassita (Pomponio, fr. 80 s. Ribb.[3], 76 s. Frass.)', *MD* 28: 175–7
Tromaras, L. (1985) '*Ibi inerat pictura haec* (Terent. *Eun.* 584–589)', *Hellenika* 36: 268–77
ed. (1994) *P. Terentius Afer: Eunuchus*, Hildesheim (revised German version of Greek edition, Thessaloniki, 1991)
Tschernjaew, P. (1900) *Terentiana,* Kasan
Tuchhaendler, N. (1876) *De vocabulis Graecis in linguam Latinam translatis,* Berlin
Väänänen, V. (1959) *Le latin vulgaire des inscriptions pompéiennes,* Berlin
(1967) *Introduction au latin vulgaire,* Paris
Vaccaro, G. (1951) 'Introduzione allo studio della lingua dell' uso in Catullo', *GIF* 4: 33–42
Valmaggi, L. (1891) *L' arcaismo in Tacito, studio grammaticale lessicografico,* Turin
Vereecke, E. (1968) 'Titinius, témoin de son époque', *RecPhL.* 2: 63–92
(1971) 'Titinius, Plaute et les origines de la fabula togata', *AC* 40: 156–85
Vossler, K. (1954) *Einführung ins Vulgärlatein,* Munich
Wahrmann, P. (1908) 'Vulgärlateinisches bei Terenz', *WS* 30: 75–103
Warmington, E. H. ed. and tr. (1935–40) *Remains of Old Latin,* London
Warnecke, B. (1925) 'Zum Leben des Livius Andronicus', *RhM* 74: 232–4
Watt, W. S. (1963) '*Heus*', *Glotta* 41: 138–43
Waters, W. E. (1902) 'The uses of the preposition *cum* in Plautus', *TAPhA* 33: lxxv–lxxvii
Webster, T. B. L. (1970) *Studies in later Greek comedy,* Manchester
(1974) *An introduction to Menander*, Manchester
Williams, G. (1968) *Tradition and originality in Roman poetry*, Oxford
Wiseman, T. P. (1988), 'Satyrs in Rome? The background to Horace's *Ars Poetica*', *JRS* 78: 1–13
Wissowa, G. (1895) 'Aquilius', *RE* 2, 1: 323
Wölflin, E. (1876) 'Bemerkungen über das Vulgärlatein', *Philologus* 34: 137–65
(1878) 'Atellanen und Mimentitel', *RhM* 43: 308–9
Woytek, E. (1972) 'Bemerkungen zur plautinischen Verwendung einiger Adjektiva auf *-bilis* statt eines Participium Perfecti passivi', *RhM* 115: 249–60
Wright, J. (1972) 'Naevius, *Tarentilla* fr. I (72–74 R[3])', *RhM* 115: 239–42
(1974) *Dancing in chains: the stylistic unity of the comoedia palliata,* Rome
ed. (1981) *Plautus: Curculio Introduction and notes,* Ann Arbor

Zagagi, N. (1980) *Tradition and originality in Plautus,* Göttingen
(1994) *The comedy of Menander: Convention, variation & originality*, London
Zebian, G. (1965) 'The relative use of the ablatives of quality and respect in Latin literature', *AJPh* 86: 240–57
Zetzel, J. E. G. ed. (1995) *Cicero De Re Publica selections*, Cambridge
Zini, S. (1938) *Il linguaggio dei personaggi nelle commedie di Menandro*, Florence
Zorzetti, N. (1973) 'Una citazione di Pacuvio in Afranio', *QTTA* 3: 71–5

INDEX LOCORUM

INDEX NOMINUM ET RERUM